ENCYCLOPEDIA OF
THE SPANISH-AMERICAN & PHILIPPINE-AMERICAN WARS

Jerry Keenan

D0162633

A B C ☰ C L I O

SANTA BARBARA, CALIFORNIA   DENVER, COLORADO   OXFORD, ENGLAND

SOMERSET CO. LIBRARY
BRIDGEWATER, N.J. 08807

All illustrations are taken from the Library of Congress unless stated otherwise.

Copyright © 2001 by Jerry Keenan

All rights reserved. No part of this publication may be reproduced, stored in a retrieval system, or transmitted, in any form or by any means, electronic, mechanical, photocopying, recording, or otherwise, except for the inclusion of brief quotations in a review, without prior permission in writing from the publishers.

Library of Congress Cataloging-in-Publication Data

Keenan, Jerry.
    Encyclopedia of the Spanish-American and Philippine-American wars / Jerry Keenan.
        p. cm.
Includes bibliographical references (p.   ) and index.
    ISBN 1-57607-093-X (hardcover : acid-free paper); 1-57607-568-0 (e-book)
1. Spanish-American War, 1898—Encyclopedias.
2. Philippines—History—Philippine American War,
1899–1902—Encyclopedias.   I. ABC-CLIO Information Services.   II. Title.
    E715.K27 2001
973.8'9'03—dc21

                                                    2001004421

06   05   04   03   02   01   10   9   8   7   6   5   4   3   2   1

This book is also available on the World Wide Web as an e-book.
Visit abc-clio.com for details.

ABC-CLIO, Inc.
130 Cremona Drive, P.O. Box 1911
Santa Barbara, California 93116-1911
This book is printed on acid-free paper.

Manufactured in the United States of America

ENCYCLOPEDIA OF

THE SPANISH-AMERICAN & PHILIPPINE-AMERICAN WARS

In loving memory of my sister,
Mary Margaret Keenan Otto,
a gallant Irish lady

" 'Tisn't life that matters! 'Tis the courage you bring to it."
—Sir Hugh Walpole

CONTENTS

ENCYCLOPEDIA OF
THE SPANISH-AMERICAN
AND PHILIPPINE-AMERICAN WARS

PREFACE

This book is intended to serve as a general reference work to provide students and other interested readers with basic information about the Spanish-American and Philippine-American Wars. It is designed to be a starting point where the reader will find essential information: names, dates, and summaries of the significant events related to those wars.

I make no pretense of having plowed new furrows or presenting fresh research here. But I hope, nevertheless, that readers will find this a helpful and easy-to-use tool. The "References and Further Readings" at the end of each entry, together with the extensive bibliography at the back of the book, will direct readers to a wide range of both general and specialized studies with which to pursue further research and a more complete understanding of a crucial period in U.S. history. The arrangement of entries is alphabetical, but it is suggested that readers first review the Chronology at the front of the volume to acquire a preliminary grasp of the subject matter.

The topic of this book is war, and the focus is mainly military. Recognizing, however, that no war can be truly detached from the politics of which it is inescapably an extension, I have also included the essential political background that is necessary to arrive at a broad understanding of what these conflicts were all about.

As with my earlier *Encyclopedia of the American Indian Wars,* the biggest challenge in creating this work involved selection—what to include and how much to say about any given topic. My initial criterion was to select those subjects that simply could not be omitted. One could not, for example, write about the Spanish-American War without reference to Theodore Roosevelt, William McKinley, the Battle of Manila Bay, or San Juan Hill. Beyond these obvious choices, however, the selection process was less clear. Ultimately, I decided to choose subjects that, in my opinion, were important because of their military or political significance. Admittedly, this was a purely subjective process. With the goal of keeping the material accessible and therefore not overly detailed or lengthy, I tried to provide as much information as seemed appropriate given the topic's relative importance.

It is impossible to produce a work of nonfiction in a vacuum, and I am indebted to many individuals for the help they offered along the way. I wish to thank the librarians at the University of Colorado's Norlin Library, especially those in the Inter-Library Loan Department who so faithfully serve scholars and researchers. And a special thanks goes to Anna Ferris of Norlin Library for providing the English translation to Spanish titles. I am also grateful to the staff of ABC-CLIO and particularly my editor, Alicia Merritt, who believed in the project and supported it throughout its sometimes bumpy development. And as always, my wife, Carol, has been a tower of support—thank you, *mon ami* and *mon amour*. To one and all, I offer my heartfelt appreciation. For any errors of commission or omission, I, of course, remain solely responsible.

Jerry Keenan

INTRODUCTION

It has been said that wars belong to the generations that fight them, as of course they do, but in a broader sense, all wars belong to all generations, though they may be largely forgotten beyond their own time. This observation seems particularly true of the U.S. war with Spain, perhaps because in the years since the *Maine* disaster, San Juan Hill, and Manila Bay were the subjects of front-page stories, that war has somehow escaped the kind of attention that aids in preserving memories of historical events for future generations. Although a substantial body of literature about the conflict exists, as the bibliography in this book attests, the Spanish-American War has yet to find a Ken Burns or a Margaret Mitchell to enshrine it in the public consciousness.

Most Americans of course know that the United States has been involved in a number of wars throughout its history, and many can identify some of those conflicts and perhaps even articulate a little of what they were all about. But I suspect that more than a few would express surprise to learn that their nation fought a second war with Great Britain, that (even more astonishing) it fought a war with Spain, and that hard on the heels of that conflict came a three-year war with the Filipinos that gave Americans their first bitter taste of counterinsurgency warfare in an Asian jungle setting. It would not be America's last such experience.

The conflict with Spain was the briefest officially declared war in U.S. history, lasting less than four months in 1898. Yet as a result of those thirteen weeks of combat, the United States was transformed from a young giant of the Western Hemisphere to an international force, and the balance of power in the Pacific—indeed, the world—was changed forever.

One should not, however, overlook the fact that the war with Spain was not just America's war. Cubans and Filipinos were very much a part of that conflict; it was their war, too, even if the United States preferred not to recognize them as official partners. Thus, the Spanish-American War should more properly be known as the Spanish-Cuban-Filipino-American War, although that designation is, to be sure, a trifle awkward. For the sake of simplicity only, I have generally used the traditional term for the conflict—*the Spanish-American War*—in the pages that follow, but it is important to at least acknowledge here the role played by Cuba and the Philippines in the fight against Spain.

As a result of the war with Spain, the United States became something the founding fathers had never anticipated: a colonial power. Suddenly, the nation was faced with the enormous responsibility of administering the Philippines, a sprawling archipelago of islands that most turn-of-the-century Americans, including the president of the United States himself, were hard-pressed to locate on a map. It was a mantle Americans assumed somewhat uncomfortably, with considerable uncertainty and a good amount of heated debate. There was, after all, no provision in the Constitution for administering a colony, and no one was quite sure exactly how to go about it. But U.S. leaders plunged ahead—*muddled* might be a better word—with the nearly impossible goal of walking a line between ruler and kindly uncle. Surprisingly, perhaps, they earned decent grades on the latter score because, despite the often brutal and vicious nature of the Philippine-American War, much good emerged from that experience for the Filipino people, including improvements in their educational system, medical assistance, and general social reform. In short, there was, happily, far more depth to the Philippine experience than the implications inherent in the "Civilize 'em with a Krag" slogan. Much good was done by the army in the Philippines.

How the Spanish-American and Philippine-American Wars came about is a question of considerable complexity. Spain's failure to end the Cuban Revolution, begun in 1895, became a growing concern for William McKinley, who was elected to the U.S. presidency in November 1896. During the year following his inauguration in March 1897, diplomatic negotiations and behind-the-scenes entreaties failed to bring about a satisfactory resolution to the Cuban problem. The destruction of the U.S. battleship *Maine* in Havana harbor on the night of 15 February 1898, coupled with public outrage over the perceived mistreatment of Cubans by the Spanish, heightened tensions between Spain and the United States, ultimately leading to a declaration of war in April of that year.

Although U.S. strategists regarded the navy as the main offensive weapon of the war, land forces were not ignored by any means. The regular army was doubled, and more than 200,000 volunteers were taken into the federal service. Plans called for a landing in Cuba, initially with Havana as the objective, but that scenario was later changed as a result of the movements of Adm. Pascual Cervera y Topete's Spanish fleet.

Even as the situation in the Caribbean was taking shape, Commodore George Dewey's Asiatic Squadron scored a stunning victory over the Spanish fleet in Manila Bay, Philippine Islands, on 1 May, expanding the parameters of the Spanish-American War and setting the stage for the later Philippine-American War.

Meanwhile, on 19 May, Admiral Cervera's Spanish Squadron reached the harbor of Santiago de Cuba unobserved, but it was soon discovered and blockaded. With the Spanish fleet in the Caribbean neutralized, the focus of U.S. strategy now shifted from Havana to Santiago. On 14 June 1898, the U.S. Fifth Corps sailed from Tampa, Florida, landing at Daiquirí and Siboney in Cuba. Ten days later, the advance of Gen. William R. Shafter's command, under Maj. Gen. Joseph "Fighting Joe" Wheeler of Civil War fame, attacked the Spanish at Las Guásimas in the second land action of the campaign (Guantánamo was the first). On 1 July, U.S. forces secured the high ground outside Santiago known as San Juan Heights, accepting the surrender of the city ten days later. On 3 July, Cervera's squadron was destroyed by the waiting U.S. naval fleet when it attempted to sortie.

On 25 July, a strong U.S. expeditionary force commanded by Lt. Gen. Nelson A. Miles landed on the island of Puerto Rico. Over the next three weeks, four columns of troops under Generals Theodore Schwan, George Garretson, James Wilson, and John Brooke moved out from Guánica, Ponce, and Arroyo to clear the island of Spanish troops, their ultimate objective being San Juan. The campaign was brief, however, because on 12 August, the United States and Spain signed a protocol of peace that temporarily ended the war.

While the war in Cuba and the Caribbean was being waged, the U.S. Eighth Corps, under the command of Maj. Gen. Wesley Merritt, reached the Philippines in three segments between 30 June and 25 July 1898. On 13 August, Merritt's troops, led by Brig. Gen. Francis Greene and Brig. Gen. Arthur MacArthur and supported by Admiral

Dewey's naval squadron, captured the city of Manila, albeit twenty-four hours after the signing of the Protocol of Peace between the United States and Spain—a fact that did not become known in the Philippines until later.

With the war temporarily ended, President McKinley appointed a peace commission, which met with Spanish commissioners in Paris beginning on 1 October 1898. Throughout the fall, negotiations were pursued, and on 10 December, the Treaty of Paris was signed, although it was not ratified by the U.S. Congress until 11 April 1899.

Under the provisions of the treaty, Spain agreed to relinquish its ownership of Cuba and to cede Puerto Rico, the island of Guam, and the entire Philippine Archipelago to the United States. The annexation of the Philippines had been the most difficult issue for the commissioners to resolve; the United States finally agreed to pay Spain $20 million for the islands.

The Spanish-American War resulted in just under 2,000 U.S. combat casualties, and 2,500 American troops died from camp diseases and tropical fevers. Spanish combat losses amounted to about 1,500; how many Spanish soldiers succumbed to disease is unknown. Despite its brevity, the conflict cost the United States approximately $250 million to $300 million.

If the war with Spain was short-lived and produced three glorious victories for U.S. arms, the quest for victory in the Philippine-American War was to prove far more elusive for the United States. In the wake of deteriorating relations between Emilio Aguinaldo's Filipino Nationalists and U.S. forces, war between the two sides erupted on 4 February 1899, only two days before the U.S. Senate approved the Treaty of Paris. (Congress would not formally proclaim the treaty for two more months.)

The Philippine-American War can be divided into two phases: conventional and guerrilla. The conventional phase lasted about a year, by which time superior U.S. weaponry and better-trained U.S. soldiers compelled Aguinaldo to shift from conventional to guerrilla warfare. The second phase of combat was far costlier for the United States and much more difficult to contain, much like the war in Vietnam would be decades later. From the U.S. perspective, the Philippine and Vietnam experiences differed in significant ways, but there were distinct similarities as well. For example, just as in Vietnam, the guerrilla (or unconventional) style of warfare carried on in the Philippines made it virtually impossible for U.S. troops to distinguish friend from foe. In that fluid, shifting kind of war, guerrilla forces employed slash-and-run tactics and then melted away into the surrounding countryside. And as with the Vietnam conflict, both sides in the Philippine war committed atrocities against the prisoners they held. The Philippine-American War was not, however, waged throughout the entire archipelago. Indeed, in many locales, one scarcely knew that a war of any sort was being fought elsewhere in the region.

Early on, President McKinley believed that the United States had an obligation to deal with the Filipinos in a kindly and paternalistic manner, thereby introducing them to American culture. Accordingly, U.S. military representatives in the archipelago were directed to implement the policy that McKinley called "benevolent assimilation," and in carying out this policy, U.S. troops did much to improve daily life for the Filipinos. But the soldiers found it increasingly difficult to express benevolence toward the island residents in the face of atrocities committed by Filipino guerrillas against U.S. troops. The American soldiers soon learned to respond with their own brand of atrocities.

In March 1901, Aguinaldo was captured by the colorful and controversial Col. Frederick Funston and a party of Filipino scouts. The episode, during which the colonel was disguised as a prisoner in order to gain access to Aguinaldo's camp, made Funston the U.S. hero of the Philippine-American War.

One of the weaknesses of the Filipino republican movement was its divisiveness. Although Aguinaldo was perhaps the most recognized Filipino figure in the independence movement, he by no means exercised central control throughout the archipelago. In many cases, local *jefes* (chiefs) ran operations to suit themselves, and the capture of Aguinaldo only splintered the movement further.

By 1902, most of the Filipino insurgent leaders had grown weary of the fight. Aguinaldo had been captured, and other key leaders had died during the three years of conflict. As a consequence, the resistance movement slowly withered, and Theodore Roosevelt, who had become president in 1901 after McKinley was assassinated, declared the "insurrection" ended on 4 July 1902. However, in the southern portion of the Philippines—in northern Mindanao and the Sulu and Jolo Archipelagoes—the Muslims (or Moros) fiercely resisted the U.S. presence, even as they had resisted the Spanish, until well after the official end of the Philippine-American War.

The acquisition of the Philippines was the first and only adventure in colonialism for the United States, and it officially ended when the Commonwealth of the Philippines was established in 1934. Full independence for the archipelago was finally proclaimed in 1946.

CHRONOLOGY

1868   **10 October:** Ten Years' War begins in Cuba against Spain

1878   **10 February:** Ten Years' War ends with the Pact of Zanjón

1895   **24 February:** *Grito de Baíre* (cry of Baíre, a Cuban village) ushers in Second Cuban Revolution

1896   **10 February:** Valeriano Weyler y Nicolau appointed governor-general of Cuba; he initiates *reconcentrado* policy

Summer: The Katipunan, a militant revolutionary society in the Philippines, launches revolt against Spanish rule

November: William McKinley is elected president of the United States

1897   **5 March:** President McKinley appoints Russell Alger as secretary of war and John D. Long as secretary of the navy

22 March: Emilio Aguinaldo becomes de facto leader of Filipino revolution

6 April: President McKinley appoints Theodore Roosevelt assistant secretary of the navy

8 August: Spanish prime minister Antonio Cánovas del Castillo is assassinated; he is succeeded by Práxedes Sagasta

30 October: Adm. Pascual Cervera y Topete assumes command of Spanish naval squadron at Cádiz

31 October: Weyler is replaced as governor-general of Cuba by Ramón Blanco y Erenas; Prime Minister Sagasta attempts to resolve Cuban crisis with a softer policy

14 December: Aguinaldo signs Pact of Biyak-na-Bató, ending the revolution; he agrees to go into exile in Hong Kong in exchange for financial considerations

1898 **January:** Rioting in Havana by Spanish hard-liners raises concerns for safety of U.S. citizens and property in Cuba

3 January: Commodore George Dewey assumes command of U.S. Navy's Asiatic Squadron in Hong Kong

25 January: U.S. battleship *Maine* arrives in Havana harbor, supposedly to resume goodwill visits abandoned during President Grover Cleveland's administration (concerns for U.S. citizens and property in area are underlying reasons)

9 February: *New York Journal* publishes de Lôme letter, severely criticizing President McKinley

15 February: The *Maine* blows up in Havana harbor, killing 268 seamen

25 February: As acting secretary of the navy for one day, Theodore Roosevelt issues orders to Commodore Dewey to keep his ships fueled and to steam to Philippines and engage Spanish fleet in the event of war with Spain

9 March: Congress passes Fifty Million Dollar Bill to prepare U.S. military for war

19 March: U.S. battleship *Oregon* departs San Francisco and begins historic voyage around Cape Horn to join North Atlantic fleet

21 March: Naval board of inquiry determines the *Maine* was destroyed by underwater explosion caused by person or persons unknown

1 April: Archbishop John Ireland of Minneapolis meets with President McKinley, offering the Vatican's efforts to mediate differences between Spain and the United States

7 April: Admiral Cervera is ordered to move his naval squadron from Cádiz to the Cape Verde Islands

11 April: President McKinley asks Congress for authorization to use military force to intervene in Cuban crisis if diplomatic efforts fail

19 April: Congress authorizes military intervention in Cuba and passes Teller Amendment, declaring the United States has no permanent design on Cuba and will intervene in island's affairs only long enough to ensure that Cuba is freed of Spanish rule

21 April: President McKinley orders navy to blockade north coast of Cuba

23 April: Spain declares war on the United States; President McKinley issues first call for volunteers

25 April: President McKinley asks Congress to declare war on Spain; Congress complies but sets date at 21 April to make Cuban blockade a legitimate act of war; Theodore Roosevelt resigns post in navy department to help organize First U.S. Volunteer Cavalry Regiment

26 April: Congress authorizes an increase in size of the regular army

27 April: Three U.S. Navy ships exchange fire with Spanish batteries at Matanzas in first official engagement of Spanish-American War

29 April: Admiral Cervera's fleet departs the Cape Verde Islands, headed for San Juan, Puerto Rico; Gen. William R. Shafter is ordered to Tampa, Florida, with instructions to prepare for invasion of Cuba

May–June: U.S. troops assemble in Tampa and other locations to prepare for invasion of Cuba

1 May: U.S. Navy's Asiatic Squadron, under Commodore Dewey, scores stunning victory over Spanish fleet in Manila Bay

11 May: U.S. Navy ships exchange fire with Spanish batteries at Cienfuegos and Cárdenas, Cuba; detachments from the *Marblehead* and the *Nashville* cut two of three submarine cables

12 May: Adm. William T. Sampson's squadron bombards San Juan, Puerto Rico

19 May: Having chosen to avoid San Juan, Admiral Cervera takes his fleet into Santiago de Cuba harbor; Aguinaldo returns to the Philippines after exile in Hong Kong

25 May: President McKinley issues second call for volunteers

26 May: Admiral Cervera's fleet is bottled up in Santiago harbor by Commodore Winfield Scott Schley's Flying Squadron

14 June: U.S. Fifth Corps sails from Tampa for Cuba

16 June: Adm. Manuel de la Cámara departs Cádiz with naval squadron to reinforce Spanish command in the Philippines

22–24 June: U.S. Fifth Corps lands in Cuba at Daiquirí and Siboney

24 June: Battle of Las Guásimas is fought in Cuba

30 June: First contingent of the U.S. Eighth Corps, under Brig. Gen. Thomas Anderson, arrives in Manila, Philippine Islands

1 July: Battles of El Caney and Santiago Heights, including charge of Rough Riders up Kettle and San Juan Hills, are fought in Cuba

3 July: Spanish fleet is destroyed by U.S. Navy forces under Admiral Sampson in Battle of Santiago

7 July: En route to the Philippines, Admiral Cámara is ordered to return to Spain

17 July: Spanish surrender city of Santiago and outlying posts; second contingent of U.S. Eighth Corps, commanded by Brig. Gen. Francis Greene, arrives in Manila

25 July: U.S. troops under Maj. Gen. Nelson Miles invade Puerto Rico; third and last contingent of Philippine Expeditionary Force, under Brig. Gen. Arthur MacArthur and accompanied by Eighth Corps commander Maj. Gen. Wesley Merritt, reaches Manila

4 August: Senior commanders in U.S. Fifth Corps sign and send "Round Robin" letter to General Shafter, urging immediate withdrawal of corps from Cuba due to devastating effect of tropical fevers

12 August: United States and Spain sign Protocol of Peace, temporarily ending Spanish-American War

13 August: First elements of U.S. Fifth Corps reach Camp Wikoff at Montauk Point, New York, from Cuba; U.S. forces under General Merritt attack and capture Manila, unaware that Protocol of Peace has been signed

25 August: General Merritt is relieved of command of U.S. Eighth Corps at his own request

29 August: General Merritt is replaced by Maj. Gen. Elwell S. Otis

1 October: U.S. and Spanish peace commissioners hold first meeting in Paris

10 December: U.S. and Spanish commissioners sign Treaty of Paris, officially ending Spanish-American War; United States acquires Puerto Rico, Guam, and the Philippines (paying Spain $20 million for the Philippines)

1899   **4–23 February:** Philippine-American War begins when patrol of First Nebraska Volunteers exchanges fire with Filipino Nationalists near Santa Mesa, on outskirts of Manila (fighting during this period is sometimes referred to as Second Battle of Manila)

6 February: U.S. Congress ratifies Treaty of Paris

11 February: U.S. troops capture Iloilo City to begin campaign in the Visayas in the central Philippines

2 March: Congress passes Army Act, authorizing president to enlist U.S. volunteers (as opposed to state volunteers) for service specifically in the Philippines

31 March: U.S. troops capture Malolos, newly designated capital of the Philippine Republic

20 June: Admiral Dewey—who had been promoted as a result of his victory in Manila Bay—is replaced as commander of Asiatic Squadron by Rear Adm. John C. Watson

1 August: Alger resigns as secretary of war and is replaced by Elihu Root

19 August: U.S. Navy blockades Philippine ports to stem flow of supplies to insurgent forces

20 August: Brig. Gen. John C. Bates enters into treaty with Moro tribes of the southern Philippines

13 November: Aguinaldo declares guerrilla war against the United States

2 December: Battle of Tirad Pass, the "Filipino Thermopylae," is fought; in this battle, Gen. Gregorio del Pilar's rearguard action allows Aguinaldo to escape; Pilar dies along with 51 of his 60 men

1900   **January:** Philippine-American War shifts from conventional to guerrilla combat, in keeping with Aguinaldo's 13 November 1899 proclamation

Spring: Relief expedition to China during Boxer Rebellion siphons off some U.S. ground and naval forces from the Philippines

5 May: Gen. Arthur MacArthur replaces General Otis as military governor of the Philippines

November: President McKinley is reelected, with Theodore Roosevelt as vice president

1901   **23 March:** Aguinaldo is captured by Col. Frederick Funston, together with four officers and detachment of Macabebe scouts

3 June: Second Philippine Commission, headed by William Howard Taft, arrives in the Philippines

4 July: General MacArthur turns over civil governorship of the Philippines to Taft and military responsibilities to Maj. Gen. Adna R. Chaffee

6 September: President McKinley is shot

14 September: President McKinley dies from complications of gunshot wound; his vice president, Theodore Roosevelt, becomes president

28 September: Forty-eight soldiers are killed in Balangiga Massacre on island of Samar in the Philippines

1902   **May:** Col. Frank Baldwin attacks Moro forts at Bayan and Bindayan, Mindanao

4 July: President Roosevelt proclaims end to Philippine Insurrection

September: Capt. John J. Pershing destroys Moro forts at Guaun and Bayabao, Lake Lanao region, Mindanao

1903   **7 April:** Captain Pershing destroys Moro fort at Bacolod, Lake Lanao region, Mindanao

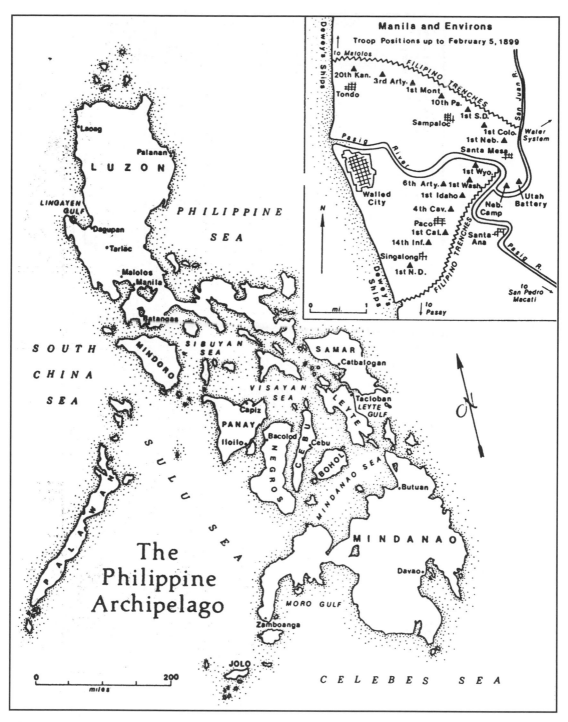

The Philippine Archipelago during the Philippine-American War
Source: *Stuart C. Miller,* Benevolent Assimilation: The American Conquest of the Philippines, 1899–1903 *(New Haven, CT: Yale University Press, 1983), p. 45. Copyright Yale University Press.*

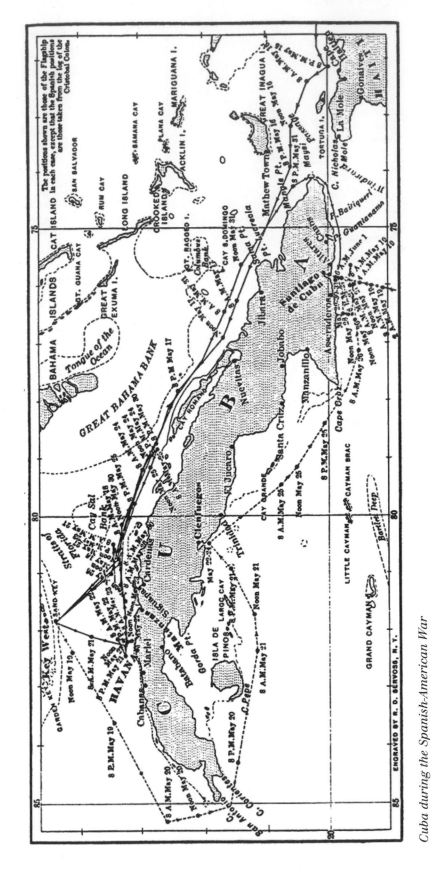

Cuba during the Spanish-American War
Source: *W.A.M. Goode, With Sampson Through the War (New York: Doubleday & McClure Co., 1899), p. 80*

Adams, Charles Francis, Jr. (1835–1915)

Charles Francis Adams Jr. was a principal figure in the Anti-Imperialist movement of the 1890s, which adamantly opposed the U.S. acquisition of the Philippines after the Spanish-American War. A member of the distinguished Adams family of Massachusetts, Adams Jr. was born in Boston, the son of Charles Francis Adams (1807–1886) and the grandson of John Quincy Adams (1767–1848).

A lawyer, historian, author, and authority on railroading, Adams served in the Civil War in the First and Fifth Massachusetts Volunteer Cavalry Regiments, rising to the rank of brevet brigadier general of volunteers by the war's end. Adams later became chairman of the Massachusetts Board of Railroad Commissioners and for a time served as president of the Union Pacific Railroad. He authored several books, including *Railroads: Their Origin and Problems* and a biography of Richard Henry Dana.

After the reelection of William McKinley in 1900, which the Anti-Imperialists had opposed, Adams became disillusioned by the lack of unity among the Anti-Imperialists and characterized them as "the most impracticable set of cranks probably to be found on the face of the earth." For all practical purposes, the Anti-Imperialist movement ended with McKinley's reelection.

See also Anti-Imperialist League.
References and Further Readings
Healy, David. *US Expansionism: The Imperialist Urge in the 1890s.* Milwaukee: University of Wisconsin Press, 1970.

Agoncillo, Don Felipe (1859–1941)

An attorney from Taal, Batangas Province, in the Philippines, Don Felipe Agoncillo was appointed agent or contact person for the Filipino insurgent movement in 1897. He was charged with seeking assistance from the United States in overthrowing Spanish rule.

From his Hong Kong office, Agoncillo approached U.S. Consul General Rounseville Wildman early in 1898, proposing that the insurgents cooperate with and support the United States in the event of a war with Spain. The quid pro quo was that the United States would provide arms and ammunition, to be paid for once the new Filipino government was in place. The United States rejected the offer, however, judging that complications might arise from any involvement with the insurgents.

Later that year, as the United States and Spain were preparing to enter into peace protocol negotiations, Agoncillo journeyed to Washington, where he was granted an interview with President William McKinley. Speaking through an interpreter, he described the cruel treatment of his people by the Spanish and requested representation on the peace commission then forming in Paris. The president listened patiently throughout a long afternoon, in what one historian described as a "desolate dialogue," and finally rejected Agoncillo's request on the grounds that his inability to speak English would prove a detriment to the proceedings. In point of fact, the real reason the request was rejected was that McKinley did not wish to compromise the U.S. position with regard to the future of the Philippine Archipelago by including a Filipino national on the peace committee. Indeed, both the United States and Spain avoided Agoncillo. Nevertheless, he filed an unofficial memo with the State Department on behalf of Filipino independence. He then went to Paris on his own to appeal his case to the peace commissioners but failed to even get a hearing. His efforts were unsuccessful because the United States had no intention of supporting Philippine independence at that point.

See also Aguinaldo y Famy, Emilio; Filipino Revolutionary Movement; Protocol of Peace; Treaty of Paris.

References and Further Readings
Brands, H. W. *Bound to Empire: The United States and the Philippines.* New York: Oxford University Press, 1992.
Morgan, H. Wayne, ed. *Making Peach with Spain: The Diary of Whitlaw Reid, September–December 1989.* Austin: University of Texas Press, 1965.
Trask, David F. *The War with Spain in 1898.* Lincoln: University of Nebraska Press, 1996.
Wolff, Leon. *Little Brown Brother: America's Forgotten Bid for Empire Which Cost 250,000 Lives.* New York: Kraus Reprint, 1970.

Aguadores River (Cuba), Demonstration at

Fort Aguadores, a Spanish strong point in Cuba on the Aguadores River east of San Juan Heights, was the site of significant action during the Spanish-American War. In the summer of 1898, the fort was held by fewer than 300 defenders. The United States believed that an effort against this position would divert the Spanish away from the main U.S. attack against San Juan Heights. On 1 July 1898, a 2,500-man brigade of Michigan troops under the command of Brig. Gen. Henry M. Duffield moved on the fort. The effort was brief and had little effect on the main U.S. movement.

See also San Juan Hill, Charge up; Santiago, Campaign and Siege of.
References and Further Readings
Feuer, A. B. *The Santiago Campaign of 1898.* Westport, CT: Praeger Publishers, 1993.
Trask, David F. *The War with Spain in 1898.* Lincoln: University of Nebraska Press, 1996.

Aguinaldo y Famy, Emilio (1869–1964)

Of Chinese and Filipino Tagalog ancestry and by 1897 the acknowledged military leader of the Filipino rebellion against Spanish rule, Emilio Aguinaldo y Famy was born in Cavite Province on the island of Luzon in 1869. By the end of the nineteenth century, Spain's once powerful colonial empire was crumbling. In both Cuba and the Philippines, revolutions were under way, preceding the Spanish-American War.

Aguinaldo was first attracted to the Filipino revolutionary movement in 1896 while serving as the mayor of Kawit. The movement, known as the Katipunan (Most Honorable Society of the Sons of the Country), had been cofounded by Andrés Bonifacio. Although the revolutionary movement's principal figure was Bonifacio, there were many lesser local leaders who sought to strengthen their own positions, often to the detriment of the larger organization.

Emilio Aguinaldo, ca. 1898. Although Alguinaldo was generally recognized as the leader of the Filipino fight for independence, his sphere of influence was essentially limited to the island of Luzon.

The departure of Emilio Aguinaldo and Filipino chieftains from Calumpit for voluntary exile in Hong Kong, in accordance with the terms of the Pact of Biyak-na-Bató.

A charismatic individual, Aguinaldo quickly attracted a strong following, and his great victory over the Spanish at the Battle of Imis River propelled him to the forefront of the revolutionary movement. By late March 1897, growing dissatisfaction with the movement's success, due partly to jealousies within the Katipunan society as well as a fresh Spanish resolve to crush the rebellion, led to the creation of a new revolutionary party, of which Aguinaldo was elected president.

As a result of Aguinaldo's election, Bonifacio became a minority figure, and in subsequent weeks, it was alleged by Aguinaldo's followers that Bonifacio planned a coup against the new leadership. Based on this allegation, Bonifacio was arrested, charged with treason, and executed, probably on Aguinaldo's orders (although this has never been proven). With Bonifacio dead, Aguinaldo stood alone as the primary figure of the Filipino revolutionary movement.

Unwilling to face what seemed certain to become a protracted guerrilla war, the Spanish offered Aguinaldo attractive surrender terms, which he accepted. The surrender agreement, signed in December 1897, was known as the Pact of Biyak-na-Bató.

As a part of the surrender agreement, Aguinaldo was allowed to go into exile in Hong Kong with a small group of followers. Spain also agreed to pay the Filipino leader $500,000 in return for his neutrality. As it turned out, both sides were less than serious in their intent to comply. Spain proved delinquent in its payment, and Aguinaldo prepared to return to the Philippines, something he had probably planned to do anyway.

As the United States and Spain edged closer to war, Aguinaldo and his junta opened communication with U.S. officials who, Aguinaldo claimed, encouraged his return to the Philippines. Following Dewey's victory at Manila Bay, Aguinaldo did return to the islands to play a role in the revolution that was again under way. On 12 June 1898, Aguinaldo proclaimed an independent Philippine Republic.

On 25 July 1898, Gen. Wesley Merritt arrived in the Philippines to take command of the American Expeditionary Force. Since U.S. objectives would be better served if the insurgents were excluded from any peace talks with the Spanish, Merritt was under orders not to cooperate with the revolutionary forces.

Relations between Aguinaldo and the U.S. military had been tenuous from the beginning and steadily deteriorated during the summer of 1898. A tense situation was exacerbated when the Filipino Republican Army was prevented from entering Manila by U.S. soldiers after the city's surrender by the Spanish garrison.

Although the fighting between Spain and the United States ended with the signing of the Protocol of Peace on 12 August 1898, Aguinaldo continued to maintain a strong military presence in Manila and its environs. The tension between Americans and Filipinos worsened, and on the night of 4 February 1899, fighting erupted and quickly turned into full-scale war.

With the outbreak of the Philippine-American War (or Philippine Insurrection, as it is sometimes still referred to), Aguinaldo at first attempted to fight the United States on conventional terms. However, superior U.S. weaponry and training eventually prevailed, forcing Aguinaldo to resort to guerrilla warfare.

Although Aguinaldo is generally regarded as the leader of the Filipinos, there was considerable divisiveness within the overall revolutionary movement, as local leaders sought to further their own ambitious designs.

If Aguinaldo possessed charismatic qualities, his military and political leadership left much to be desired. His decision to fight the United States on conventional terms, for example, was a serious error in judgment because his army, lacking weapons and disciplined training, was ill prepared to wage conventional war. Aguinaldo prosecuted a war he could not win based on the belief that Philippine independence would be realized if William Jennings Bryan defeated William McKinley in the 1900 election. He reasoned that Bryan, being opposed to U.S. involvement in the Philippines, would be more inclined to grant independence and order a prompt withdrawal of U.S. forces from the islands. However, since Bryan's chances of victory were slim, this, too, proved a flawed strategy.

In March 1901, Aguinaldo was captured by forces under the command of Col. Frederick Funston and taken to Manila. Perhaps in the belief that further resistance against the United States was futile or perhaps simply realizing that his own influence had deteriorated too much to warrant a continuation of the struggle, Aguinaldo signed an oath of allegiance to the United States and encouraged his followers to do the same.

Despite signing the oath, Aguinaldo felt no strong sense of attachment to the United States. During World War II, he tried unsuccessfully to have the Japanese appoint him president, a move they wisely avoided. He did live to see the Philippines granted full independence from the United States in 1946. He died in 1964 at age 95.

See also Bonifacio, Andrés; Funston, Frederick; Manila, Second Battle of; McKinley, William, Jr.; Merritt, Wesley; Otis, Elwell Stephen.

References and Further Readings

Agoncillo, Tedoro A. *Malolos: The Crisis of the Republic.* Quezon City: University of the Philippines Press, 1960.

Alberts, Don E. *Brandy Station to Manila Bay: A Biography of General Wesley Merritt.* Austin, TX: Presidial Press, 1980.

Gates, John Morgan. *Schoolbooks and Krags: The United States Army in the Philippines, 1898–1902.* Contributions in Military History no. 3. Westport, CT: Greenwood Press, 1973.

Linn, Brian McAllister. *The U.S. Army and Counterinsurgency in the Philippine War, 1899–1902.* Chapel Hill: University of North Carolina Press, 1989.

———. *The Philippine War, 1899–1902.* Lawrence: University Press of Kansas, 2000.

Wolff, Leon. *Little Brown Brother: America's Forgotten Bid for Empire Which Cost 250,000 Lives.* New York: Kraus Reprint, 1970.

Alejandrino (Alexandrino), José (1871–1951)

A Filipino revolutionary, José Alejandrino served as a general officer under Emilio Aguinaldo, first in the war against Spain and later against the U.S. Army during the so-called insurrection.

An official member of the revolutionary party, Alejandrino accompanied Aguinaldo to Hong Kong in late 1897 when the latter was exiled from the Philippines in accordance with the terms of the Pact of Biyak-na-Bató. Later, Alejandrino joined Aguinaldo on the journey to Manila Bay with Commodore George Dewey's Asiatic Squadron.

Like Aguinaldo, Alejandrino saw independence, not reform, as the Filipino goal. When the movement for independence needed help in 1898, Alejandrino told Austrian Ferdinand Blumentritt that the movement was willing to take advantage of what the United States had to offer, not the least of which were arms and ammunition.

In the fight against the United States, which followed the end of Spanish rule in the Philippine Archipelago, Alejandrino headed operations in central Luzon. In June 1900, he discussed an amnesty with Gen. Arthur MacArthur (father of Douglas MacArthur). But his influence waned after the turn of the century, and early in 1901, he was replaced by Aguinaldo's cousin, Baldomero Aguinaldo.

In 1949, Alejandrino's account of the fight for Philippine independence was published under the title *The Price of Freedom*.

See also Aguinaldo y Famy, Emilio; Katipunan.

References and Further Readings

Alejandrino, José M. *The Price of Freedom.* Manila: Reprint Solar Publishing, 1987.

Linn, Brian McAllister. *The U.S. Army and Counterinsurgency in the Philippine War, 1899–1902.* Chapel Hill: University of North Carolina Press, 1989.

———. *The Philippine War, 1899–1902.* Lawrence: University Press of Kansas, 2000.

Wolff, Leon. *Little Brown Brother: America's Forgotten Bid for Empire Which Cost 250,000 Lives.* New York: Kraus Reprint, 1970.

Alfonso XII (1857–1885)

Alfonso XII was the son of Isabella II and Francisco de Aziz of Spain. In November 1874, he assumed the throne on the abdication of his mother. Though only 17, he promoted the concept of a constitutional monarchy, receiving the support of some Moderates and Liberal Unionists. In late December of that year, aided by these backers and a group of disgruntled military leaders, Alfonso was proclaimed king of Spain, thereby ending the short-lived Spanish republic. He was one in a long line of Spanish monarchs by this name.

Alfonso is generally regarded as having been a popular king, credited with restoring order and suppressing the troublesome opposition of the Carlists. In 1879, he married María Cristina, daughter of Archduke Charles Ferdinand of Austria. The union produced a son, Alfonso XIII, who was born in 1885, the year his father died at the age of 28. Alfonso XIII, just 13 years old in 1898, was king of Spain at the time of the Spanish-American War. However, María Cristina functioned as queen regent until Alfonso came of age.

See also Alfonso XIII; María Cristina, Queen Regent of Spain.
References and Further Readings
Ferrara, Orestes. *The Last Spanish War: Revelations in Diplomacy.* Translated from the Spanish by William E. Shea. New York: Paisley Press, 1937.
Musicant, Ivan. *Empire by Default: The Spanish-American War and the Dawn of the American Century.* New York: Henry Holt and Company, 1998.

Alfonso XIII (1885–1941)

Alfonso XIII was the last of the Spanish rulers of that name. His father (Alfonso XII) died shortly after his birth. Only 13 when war broke out with the United States, Alfonso was too young to discharge the responsibilities of his crown. Thus, the task of governing Spain devolved on his mother, María Cristina, who ruled as queen regent. Alfonso later assumed the throne, though social unrest in Spain led to his exile in 1931.

See also Alfonso XII; María Cristina, Queen Regent of Spain.
References and Further Readings
Chadwick, Rear Adm. French Ensor. *Relations of the United States and Spain: The Spanish American War.* 2 vols. New York: Charles Scribner's Sons, 1911 (reprinted in 1968).
Trask, David F. *The War with Spain in 1898.* Lincoln: University of Nebraska Press, 1996.

Alger, Russell Alexander (1836–1907)

Russell Alexander Alger served as President William McKinley's secretary of war from March 1897 to August 1899. As such, he was pivotal in the U.S. war with Spain. Born in Medina County, Ohio, on 27 February 1836, he was orphaned at age 11 but managed to support himself and two younger brothers through various jobs, including farm labor. He also acquired enough education to teach school. Alger, who may have been a distant relative of Horatio Alger, went on to study law and was admitted to the Ohio bar at age 21. In 1860, he moved to Michigan.

During the Civil War, Alger was appointed captain in the Second Michigan Cavalry, eventually rising to the rank of colonel in the Fifth Michigan Cavalry in Gen. George Custer's brigade. A very capable field commander, Alger served with distinction in the eastern theater, including the battles of Gettysburg and the Wilderness. He left the army in 1864 after contracting typhoid fever. He had, by that time, attained the rank of brevet major general of volunteers.

After the war, Alger founded the Michigan chapter of the Grand Army of the Republic (GAR) and served as the state's governor from 1885 to 1887. During the 1896 presidential campaign, Alger organized Civil War veterans in support of William McKinley, who subsequently named him secretary of war.

As secretary of war, Alger was regarded as the most militant member of McKinley's cabinet and an outspoken promoter of war with Spain. Nevertheless, he came to be viewed as an inept civilian head of the army. He would perhaps have been a more able administrator in quieter times, but in the frantic days of the late 1890s, he lacked the aggressive posture that many, including Theodore Roosevelt, felt was needed. Alger seemed to be out of step with the military and was constantly at odds with the army's senior officers, particularly General of the Army Nelson A. Miles.

Nonetheless, Alger responded to the call to arms with a certain dedication and sincerity. The passage of the so-called Fifty Million Dollar Bill in March 1898 was intended to put the United States on a war footing. With the amount apportioned to the army (about $19 million), Alger directed various administrative bureaus (Quartermaster, Ordnance, and so forth) to increase their inventories. However, it soon became clear that the army's infrastructure was unprepared to handle a massive buildup. The problems that arose from this condition were perceived to be the fault of the secretary of war. The miscues and bungling resulted in the creation of the term *Algerism,* which became synonymous with incompetent officialdom. To his credit, however, Alger, together with the army's adjutant general, Henry C. Corbin, did much to streamline the movement of supplies and equipment from the army's various bureaus to the expeditionary forces.

Eventually, the real director of the nation's military affairs came to be the president, partly because McKinley tended to involve himself in army matters, having once been a soldier, and partly because Alger was unable to function as an effective secretary of war. His constant squabbling with Miles and other senior officers diverted energies away from the prosecution of the war and thus forced McKinley to involve himself more actively than he might otherwise have done.

After Cuba was secured, Alger thought U.S. troops should remain on the island, despite outbreaks of yellow fever, malaria, and typhoid, which had laid low many in Gen. William Shafter's Fifth Corps. As these diseases spread, the press criticized Alger, who finally ordered the troops back to the United States. Unfortunately, upon reaching

Montauk Point, New York, which had been designated as the separation point, the troops found that there were no facilities to accommodate them.

Within the year, McKinley became convinced that a new secretary of war was needed and requested Alger's resignation. However, the secretary refused to step down and instead asked for and received a formal hearing. The Dodge Commission, the body that heard his case, found that Alger had done his best to deal with problems that were largely beyond his control. Following a bitter meeting with McKinley, Alger resigned in July 1899 and was replaced by Elihu Root.

The criticism of his conduct as secretary of war did little to harm Alger's reputation in the United States. He remained a political power in Michigan and was named to finish the term of U.S. senator James McMillan, who died in 1902. Alger held this position until his own death on 24 January 1907.

See also Army, U.S.; Corbin, Henry Clark; McKinley, William, Jr.; Miles, Nelson Appleton; War Department, U.S.

References and Further Readings

Alger, Russell A. *The Spanish-American War.* New York: Harper & Brothers, 1901.

Cosmas, Graham. *An Army for Empire: The United States Army in the Spanish-American War.* College Station: Texas A&M University Press, 1998.

Leech, Margaret. *In the Days of McKinley.* New York: Harper & Brothers, 1959.

Allen, Charles H. (1848–1934)

Born in Lowell, Massachusetts, Charles Allen was an experienced banker, manufacturer, state senator, and U.S. representative. When Theodore Roosevelt resigned his post as assistant secretary of the navy to join the Rough Riders at the outbreak of the Spanish-American War, Allen filled the vacancy.

A solid, devoted secretary, Allen worked tirelessly in this capacity until 1900. He then resigned to accept an appointment as the first civil governor of Puerto Rico, a position he held until 1902.

See also Long, John Davis; Navy, U.S.; Roosevelt, Theodore.

References and Further Readings

Leech, Margaret. *In the Days of McKinley.* New York: Harper & Brothers, 1959.

Trask, David F. *The War with Spain in 1898.* Lincoln: University of Nebraska Press, 1996.

Allen, Henry Tureman (1859–1930)

A Kentuckian, Maj. Henry T. Allen combatted Filipino guerrillas on the islands of Samar and Leyete, in what historian Brian Linn called the "most controversial campaign of the Philippine War." Leading a battalion of the Forty-third U.S. Volunteers, Allen believed that Filipinos should be treated humanely, although he recognized that guerrilla warfare would exact a heavy toll.

See also Atrocities; Benevolent Assimilation; Pacification Program; Samar Campaigns.

References and Further Readings

Bradford, James C., ed. *Crucible of Empire: The Spanish-American War and Its Aftermath.* Annapolis, MD: Naval Institute Press, 1993.

Gates, John Morgan. *Schoolbooks and Krags: The United States Army in the Philippines, 1898–1902.* Contributions in Military History no. 3. Westport, CT: Greenwood Press, 1973.

Linn, Brian McAllister. *The U.S. Army and Counterinsurgency in the Philippine War, 1899–1902.* Chapel Hill: University of North Carolina Press, 1989.

Wolff, Leon. *Little Brown Brother: America's Forgotten Bid for Empire Which Cost 250,000 Lives.* New York: Kraus Reprint, 1970.

Allianca Incident

In March 1895, a Spanish gunboat fired on the *Allianca,* a U.S. merchant ship en route to New York from Panama, as it passed near the Cuban coast. The *Allianca* outran the Spanish ship and quickly moved beyond range, reaching its destination without damage. Ironically, although U.S.-registered vessels were quite active in filibustering activities, the *Allianca* was carrying a benign cargo. The *Allianca* incident, which occurred shortly after the start of the Cuban Revolution (1895), underscored the deteriorating relations between Spain and the United States. The *Competitor* incident, which occurred a year later, further heightened tensions between the two nations.

See also *Competitor* Incident; Filibuster.

References and Further Readings

Chadwick, Rear Adm. French Ensor. *Relations of the United States and Spain: The Spanish American War.* 2 vols. New York: Charles Scribner's Sons, 1911 (reprinted in 1968).

Wisan, Joseph Ezra. *The Cuban Crisis as Reflected in the New York Press (1895–1898).* New York: Columbia University Press, 1934.

Almodóvar del Río, Duque de (Juan Manuel Sánchez y Gutiérrez de Castro) (1859–1906)

Late in 1897, following the assassination of Antonio Cánovas del Castillo, Práxedes Mateo Sagasta, head of the Spanish Liberal Party, assumed power in Spain. In May 1898, Sagasta named Duque de Almodóvar del Río to replace Pío Gullón as Spain's foreign minister. It would be his job to represent Spanish interests abroad during the recently declared war with the United States.

Almodóvar's task, difficult to begin with, was immediately made more challenging when Adm. Pascual Cervera's naval squadron arrived at the port of Santiago de Cuba. Cervera's vessels were soon bottled up in a harbor from which there was no escape without confronting a superior U.S. naval squadron.

In July, recognizing the futility of further resistance, Almodóvar launched a peace initiative, requesting that the French government authorize Jules Cambon, its ambassador to the United States, to present Spain's offer of Cuban independence in exchange for peace. However, the proposal was sidetracked for a week when the French government was unable to act on the request due to the absence and illness of personnel. In the meantime, Puerto Rico was invaded by the United States, and U.S. forces arrived in the Philippines.

Almodóvar's effort was followed by Queen Regent María Cristina's request-for-peace letter to President McKinley, which was received in Washington on 26 July 1898. During the next two weeks, the McKinley administration discussed terms for peace, while Almodóvar concerned himself with the fall of Manila: The loss seemed imminent and could profoundly affect any peace negotiations should it occur before an agreement was reached. The Peace Protocol with Spain was signed on 12 August 1898, and one day later, Manila surrendered. Almodóvar argued that the city was not captured territory since the fall occurred after the protocol was signed. The United States countered that hostilities cease only when commanders in the field are notified, not when a document is signed.

During the Peace Protocol negotiations, which were conducted in Paris and continued until the end of 1898, Almodóvar, acting in accordance with Spanish strategy, was instructed to delay the proceedings for as long as possible. Perceiving that U.S. goals included acquisition of the entire Philippine Archipelago, Spanish leaders hoped that a sufficient delay might enhance Spain's bargaining position. President McKinley, however, would not be swayed from his demands, and on 25 November 1898, Almodóvar directed that the treaty be accepted and signed under protest.

See also McKinley, William, Jr.; Protocol of Peace; Sagasta, Práxedes Mateo.

References and Further Readings

Leech, Margaret. *In the Days of McKinley.* New York: Harper & Brothers, 1959.

Musicant, Ivan. *Empire by Default: The Spanish-American War and the Dawn of the American Century.* New York: Henry Holt and Company, 1998.

Anderson, Thomas McArthur (1836–1917)

Born in Ohio, Thomas McArthur Anderson enlisted in the Union army in 1861 as a private and ended the war as a captain. He remained in the army after the Civil War, rising to the rank of colonel. Shortly after war with Spain broke out, Anderson was promoted to brigadier general of volunteers and appointed to command the first wave of the Philippine Expeditionary Force—officially, the Eighth Army Corps. After securing the island of Guam without any fighting, Anderson's command arrived in the Philippines on 1 June 1898 and immediately moved against Manila.

By late July, reinforcements had arrived, and Gen. Wesley Merritt, overall commander of the Philippine Expeditionary Force, was on the scene. Preparations for taking Manila got under way. During the ensuing battle for the capital city of the Philippines, Anderson commanded the Second Division in Gen. Francis Greene's Second Brigade, which advanced on Manila along General Merritt's left flank while Gen. Arthur MacArthur's First Brigade moved on the right.

Following the fall of Manila on 13 August 1898, Anderson was promoted to major general of volunteers and remained in the Philippines until 1899, at which time he returned to the United States and retired in 1900.

See also Aguinaldo y Famy, Emilio; Manila, First Battle of; Philippine Expeditionary Force.

References and Further Readings

Alberts, Don E. *Brandy Station to Manila Bay: A Biography of General Wesley Merritt.* Austin, TX: Presidial Press, 1980.

Cosmas, Graham. *An Army for Empire: The United States Army in the Spanish-American War.* College Station: Texas A&M University Press, 1998.

Gates, John Morgan. *Schoolbooks and Krags: The United States Army in the Philippines, 1898–1902.* Contributions in Military History no. 3. Westport, CT: Greenwood Press, 1973.

Wolff, Leon. *Little Brown Brother: America's Forgotten Bid for Empire Which Cost 250,000 Lives.* New York: Kraus Reprint, 1970.

Anti-Imperialist League

A national organization, the Anti-Imperialist League was formed in June 1898 and represented a powerful voice against expansionism during its brief existence. The organization began as a series of smaller Anti-Imperialist leagues in the East and spread westward during 1899. At one time, the league was thought to number about 30,000 individuals, including some of the most prominent and influential men in the country, such as labor leader Samuel Gompers; Samuel Clemens (Mark Twain); Carl Schurz; E. L. Godkin, editor of *The Nation*; Samuel Bowles, editor of the *Springfield (Massachusetts) Republican*; Charles Francis Adams; attorney Moorfield Storey; and Andrew Carnegie, whose vast fortune helped fund the league's activities.

The Anti-Imperialist League was diametrically opposed to U.S. annexation of Hawaii and the Philippines, arguing that the U.S. Constitution did not allow for the acquisition and governing of foreign colonies. The league also viewed blacks and Filipinos as inferior races and not deserving of being enfranchised as U.S. citizens.

During the long debate over the annexation of Hawaii, Gompers took the position that Hawaiian annexation would result in an influx of cheap Asian labor. Despite Gompers's opposition, President William McKinley received strong support from the labor community over the annexation issues.

Not surprisingly, the league was vehemently opposed to ratification of the Treaty of Paris, signed in December 1898, which ceded Puerto Rico, Guam, and the Philippines to the United States. The league also campaigned against President McKinley's reelection but failed in that effort as well. McKinley's reelection and congressional ratification of the Paris Treaty effectively ended the league's existence.

See also Imperialism/Expansionism; Treaty of Paris.

References and Further Readings
Beisner, Robert L. *Twelve against Empire: The Anti-Imperialists, 1898–1900.* New York: McGraw-Hill, 1968.
Brands, H. W. *Bound to Empire: The United States and the Philippines.* New York: Oxford University Press, 1992.
Gould, Lewis L. *The Spanish-American War and President McKinley.* Lawrence: University of Kansas Press, 1982.
Healy, David. *US Expansionism: The Imperialist Urge in the 1890s.* Milwaukee: University of Wisconsin Press, 1970.
Leech, Margaret. *In the Days of McKinley.* New York: Harper & Brothers, 1959.
Tompkins, E. Berkeley. *Anti-Imperialism in the United States: The Great Debate, 1890–1920.* Philadelphia: University of Pennsylvania Press, 1970.

Antilles

The Antilles is an archipelago better known as the West Indies. Although seldom referred to today as the Antilles, that name does appear occasionally in the literature of the Spanish-American War; thus, it is useful to understand exactly what the area encompasses.

The Antilles is composed of four island groups:

- The Bahamas
- The Greater Antilles: Cuba, Jamaica, Hispaniola, and Puerto Rico
- The Lesser Antilles: Leeward and Windward Islands, Barbados, Trinidad, and Tobago
- The Dutch West Indies (Netherland Antilles): Aruba, Curaçao, and Bonaire

Together, the islands of the Antilles Archipelago form a chain that separates the Atlantic from the Caribbean. During the war with Spain, only the islands of Cuba and Puerto Rico figured prominently.

See also Cuban Revolution.
References and Further Readings
Foner, Philip S. *The Spanish-Cuban-American War.* 2 vols. New York: Monthly Review Press, 1972.
Thomas, Hugh. *Cuba: The Pursuit of Freedom.* New York: Harper & Row, 1971.

Armistice: United States and Spain

See **Protocol of Peace**

Army, Filipino Nationalist

Although insurgent groups had long operated against Spanish rule, the constitution of the new Philippine Republic, formally proclaimed by Emilio Aguinaldo in June 1898, gave the Filipino Nationalist Army an official status.

Aguinaldo sought to create a military establishment modeled after the prevailing European style. His troops, however, were poorly armed and poorly disciplined. Although the new army could muster perhaps 50,000 men, fewer than half that number were armed with modern rifles. The standard weapon for most Filipino soldiers was a broad-bladed knife known as a bolo. Thus, lacking solid training and modern weaponry, the Filipino Army was no match for the U.S. military in a conflict waged according to conventional standards. After the Philippine conflict shifted to guerrilla-style warfare, however,

Aguinaldo's forces proved far more effective in combating the Americans.

See also Aguinaldo y Famy, Emilio; Bates, John Coalter; Bell, James Franklin; Funston, Frederick; MacArthur, Arthur.

References and Further Readings

Gates, John Morgan. *Schoolbooks and Krags: The United States Army in the Philippines, 1898–1902.* Contributions in Military History no. 3. Westport, CT: Greenwood Press, 1973.

Linn, Brian McAllister. *The U.S. Army and Counterinsurgency in the Philippine War, 1899–1902.* Chapel Hill: University of North Carolina Press, 1989.

Wolff, Leon. *Little Brown Brother: America's Forgotten Bid for Empire Which Cost 250,000 Lives.* New York: Kraus Reprint, 1970.

Army, Spanish (Ejército de España)

Like the armies of other European nations, the Spanish Army was composed mainly of conscripted peasants and young men from urban areas. At the onset of the Cuban Revolution in 1895, Spain had mobilized 100,000 men. By 1898, its army numbered close to half a million, of which nearly 200,000 were in Cuba, 50,000 in the Philippines, and another 5,000 in Puerto Rico.

As a military force, the Spanish Army was well armed and disciplined. Its major deficits were deficient leadership and poor marksmanship. The ratio of officers to enlisted men was far higher than it should have been, and too few of the officers were capable leaders. In the field, for example, the army's leaders lacked the skills to effectively deploy their troops in combat situations.

Although armed with the Mauser rifle, which fired bullets propelled by smokeless powder (U.S. weapons still used black-powder cartridges that revealed their positions as a result of the smoke created by the powder), the Spanish soldier was a poor marksman, thereby negating any advantage he might have enjoyed as a result of his superior weaponry.

Typically, the Spanish soldier was attired in a light-colored tropical uniform and canvas shoes. He carried about 150 rounds of ammunition, plus a blanket, eating utensils, and rations. The Spanish Army had the highest death rate from disease of any major European army as a result of its service in the Tropics.

Notwithstanding the preceding deficiencies, the Spanish Army proved a tough foe. Most of the units deployed in Cuba were made up of veteran troops who acquitted themselves well in action

The last of the Spanish Army in Havana, Cuba, under the palace colonnade, 1898.

against the Americans. They also had the advantage of being acclimatized to Cuba, unlike their U.S. counterparts.

During the Spanish-American War, most land action between Spain and the United States was concentrated in Cuba; thus, Spanish troops in the Philippines and Puerto Rico played a comparatively insignificant role in the clash between the two nations.

See also Army, U.S.; Cuban Campaign; Cuban Revolution; El Caney, Battle of; Manila, First Battle of; San Juan Hill, Charge up; Santiago, Campaign and Siege of.

References and Further Readings

Linn, Brian McAllister. *The U.S. Army and Counterinsurgency in the Philippine War, 1899–1902.* Chapel Hill: University of North Carolina Press, 1989.

Musicant, Ivan. *Empire by Default: The Spanish-American War and the Dawn of the American Century.* New York: Henry Holt and Company, 1998.

Nofi, Albert A. *The Spanish-American War, 1898.* Conshohocken, PA: Combined Books, 1998.

Army, U.S.

In 1897, one year before the war with Spain broke out, the U.S. Army numbered about 28,700 officers and men. It was a cadre of veterans, for the most part well trained and equal to the demands that had been placed upon them in the three decades since the Civil War. However, the army's role during that period—that is, as a subjugator of recalcitrant Native American tribes and as strikebreaker (e.g., in the 1894 Pullman strike)—suggests that it operated more like a national police force than as an army per se.

As established by Congress, the regular army was authorized 25 regiments of infantry, 10 of cavalry, and 5 of artillery (increased to 7 for war service). Of these, 2 regiments each of infantry and cavalry were composed of black soldiers and white officers. In the event of war, the state militia (or National Guard, as it had come to be known by the 1890s) would augment this cadre of regulars. The army had honed its small-unit performance to a fine edge, but it was not prepared for a major undertaking. Not since the Civil War had the army been asked to operate on a large scale. Seldom were campaigns conducted with any unit larger than regimental size, and even that was infrequent. On occasion, as during the Sioux War of 1876, a field commander might have more than one regiment at his disposal, but for the most part, the Indian wars of the West were waged by patrol-, company-, or battalion-size units.

Save for a handful of very senior commanders, no officers on active duty had any experience handling large bodies of troops. Continual cost-cutting by Congress barely allowed the army to maintain its authorized strength. Promotions were slow, and competition for the few vacancies that did occur was stiff and often cutthroat. Thus, given the budgetary restraints under which the army was forced to operate, the condition in which it found itself was much like that at the onset of the Civil War thirty-six years earlier.

Although a joint army-navy planning board had been formulating strategy for a war with Spain since 1895, the army was ill prepared to meet the demands of the approaching twentieth century even on the highest administrative level. There was neither a chief of staff nor a general staff, as those concepts are understood today.

In 1821, then Secretary of War John C. Calhoun created the post of general of the army. The assignment went to the army's senior major general and was originally intended to be all that the title implied. In practice, however, the position never received the congressional authorization needed to make it an all-encompassing post. As a consequence, the commanding general exercised authority only over the army's so-called line or field units, that is, infantry, cavalry, and artillery. He had no control over any of the army's ten administrative bureaus: the Adjutant General, Inspector General, Quartermaster, Judge Advocate General, Subsistence, Ordnance, Corps of Engineers, Medical Department, Signal Bureau, and Paymaster. Each bureau was an entity unto itself and virtually autonomous. Each bureau chief was appointed by the president and reported directly to the secretary of war. Of the ten bureaus, the Adjutant General was the most influential.

But if the army had its shortcomings, it also had visionaries, some of whom were responsible for creating the Military Service Institution of the United States, whose purpose was to encourage the study and discussion of military history and science. There had also been considerable progress in the development of ordnance and weaponry. Breech-loading weapons had largely replaced the Civil War–vintage muzzle-loading artillery. Likewise, the old 1873 single-shot Springfield breechloader, the standard infantry and cavalry shoulder arm of the Indian wars period, had given way to the new

.30-caliber Krag-Jörgensen five-shot bolt-action rifle. Both the Krag and the newer artillery field pieces fired smokeless-powder bullets and shells, in contrast to the old weapons that used slower-burning black powder that produced much smoke when ignited, thereby identifying the location of the shooter. Unfortunately, many who served in the expanded army during the Spanish-American War were supplied with the old Springfields because there were not enough Krags to go around.

As the 1890s drew to a close, the U.S. Army stood as an organization that was forward-looking in some ways but needing change and overhaul in others. Thus, if there were encouraging signs that some progress was evident, the onset of the Spanish-American War quickly revealed that the U.S. military system was not prepared to meet the challenge that was thrust upon it in the spring of 1898. In the excitement and rush of events that followed the declaration of war against Spain, the various bureaus quickly found themselves overwhelmed by the logistical demands of supplying and equipping a large army.

In terms of mobilizing an army, perhaps the federal government's thorniest problem was dealing with the politically powerful National Guard, which opposed the idea of serving under regular army authority. Eventually, representatives of the guard agreed to a covenant with the War Department whereby the latter would accept guard units that volunteered intact. In this way, guardsmen could serve with friends and neighbors and also under their own officers, rather than submit to the authority of some regular army commander.

The president initially planned to call up 60,000 guardsmen, but almost immediately, he increased that figure to 125,000, which actually exceeded the total number of available guard troops. His reasoning in doing so may have been to avoid President Abraham Lincoln's mistake in being too conservative in his first call for volunteers. Furthermore, by calling up the entire body of guardsmen, both the federal government and the states would be protected from adverse criticism by any guard unit that was not activated.

Congress also authorized President McKinley to enlist special units such as engineers, signalmen, and cavalrymen, not enough of whom would otherwise be available to fill the needs of an expanded army. One such unit was the First U.S. Volunteer Cavalry, known as the Rough Riders.

At its peak strength during the war with Spain, the U.S. Army numbered more than 270,000 men, organized into 7 army corps, of which only 3 were involved in the fighting. The First Corps served in Puerto Rico, the Fifth in Cuba, and the Eighth in the Philippines. For administrative reasons, the Sixth Corps was never actually organized as such.

See also Alger, Russell Alexander; Fifty Million Dollar Bill; McKinley, William, Jr.; Miles, Nelson Appleton.

References and Further Readings

Alger, Russell A. *The Spanish-American War.* New York: Harper & Brothers, 1901.

Cosmas, Graham. *An Army for Empire: The United States Army in the Spanish-American War.* College Station: Texas A&M University Press, 1998.

DeMontravel, Peter R. *A Hero to His Fighting Men: Nelson A. Miles, 1839–1925.* Kent, OH: Kent State University Press, 1998.

Nofi, Albert A. *The Spanish-American War, 1898.* Conshohocken, PA: Combined Books, 1998.

Artists and Illustrators

The Spanish-American War not only attracted journalists such as Richard Harding Davis and Stephen Crane, it also attracted a bevy of artists and illustrators who recorded wartime scenes in Cuba and the Philippines for the nation's newspapers and periodicals. Virtually every publication in the country supplemented its stories with the sketches and paintings of Frederic Remington, Howard Chandler Christy, Charles Johnson Post, and a host of others. Despite its brevity— only three months—the war with Spain produced a considerable body of art to complement the written narratives.

See also Christy, Howard Chandler; Post, Charles Johnson; Remington, Frederic Sackrider; Zogbaum, Rufus Fairchild.

References and Further Readings

Goldstein, Donald M., and Katherine V. Dillon, with J. Michael Wenger and Robert J. Cressman. *The Spanish-American War: The Story and Photographs, Centennial Edition.* Washington, DC: Brasseys, 1998.

Harrington, Peter, and Frederic A. Sharf. *"A Splendid Little War": The Spanish-American War, 1898—The Artists' Perspective.* London: Greenhill Books, 1998.

Asiatic Squadron, U.S. Navy

As a means of protecting U.S. interests in the Far East and to establish a presence in that part of the world, the U.S. Navy stationed a small strike force known as the Asiatic Squadron at Hong Kong.

When war with Spain began to appear likely, U.S. naval strategists favored a swift strike against Manila by the Asiatic Squadron.

In January 1898, Commodore (later Rear Adm.) George Dewey was assigned to command the Asiatic Squadron, due largely to the urging of then Assistant Secretary of the Navy Theodore Roosevelt. At that time, the squadron consisted of the protected cruisers *Olympia* and *Boston,* with the former becoming Dewey's flagship. The squadron also had one gunboat (the *Petrel*) and the *Monocacy,* an old paddle wheeler of Civil War vintage. Between January and May 1898, the squadron was reinforced by another gunboat (the *Concord*), two more protected cruisers (the *Baltimore* and *Raleigh*), a revenue cutter (the *McCulloch*), and two support vessels.

It was this force, minus the *Monocacy* and the two support vessels, that Dewey took to the Philippines to defeat the Spanish Squadron under Adm. Patricio Montojo in the Battle of Manila Bay on 1 May 1898.

See also Dewey, George; Manila Bay, Battle of.

References and Further Readings

Nofi, Albert A. *The Spanish-American War, 1898.* Conshohocken, PA: Combined Books, 1998.

Trask, David F. *The War with Spain in 1898.* Lincoln: University of Nebraska Press, 1996.

Astor, John Jacob (1864–1912)

Great-grandson of a fur magnate, John Jacob Astor, third of that name, was an 1888 Harvard graduate. One of the wealthiest men in the United States, Astor embraced the Spanish-American War with a patriotic fervor. He loaned his private yacht, the *Nourmahal,* to the navy and financed a battery of artillery for service in the Philippines. Astor himself was commissioned a lieutenant colonel and saw action in Cuba as a member of Gen. William Shafter's staff. He was promoted to full colonel at the end of the war.

In addition to his business interests, Astor was something of a Renaissance man, being an inventor and an author of science fiction. He lost his life on the *Titanic* in April 1912.

See also Navy, U.S.; Shafter, William Rufus.

References and Further Readings

O'Toole, G. J. A. *The Spanish War: An American Epic, 1898.* New York: W. W. Norton, 1984.

Atrocities

During the Spanish-American War, atrocities and brutal treatment were widespread throughout Cuba and the Philippines. All parties involved in the conflict were guilty—the Americans, the Spanish, and the revolutionary forces in each country. It is also true, however, that reports of such incidents were exaggerated by the sensationalist newspapers of the day, whose coverage of the war came to be embodied by the phrase *yellow journalism.*

Perhaps the best-known example of brutal treatment was that inflicted on Cuban civilians by Governor-General Valeriano Weyler. His strategy in dealing with the revolutionaries was to isolate civilians from the rebels by confining the civilians to concentration camps. Thus, anyone found outside the perimeter of these camps, known as *reconcentrados,* was considered a rebel and dealt with accordingly. Conditions within the camps were wretched, and reports of inhumane treatment inflamed public opinion against the Spanish.

Other reports from Cuba told of the execution of both prisoners of war and civilians. In May 1897, a *New York Herald* reporter, Sylvester Scovel, wrote that Cuba was a "country of horrors." By November, Scovel's columns were stating that he could document more than 200 cases of Spanish brutality.

In the Philippines, there were numerous charges about U.S. troops indiscriminately killing civilians in their pursuit of Filipino guerrillas. But the situation was not one-sided. U.S. troops were often lured into traps by Filipinos who addressed them as "amigos"; then, using their deadly bolos, the insurgents killed and mutilated the soldiers unfortunate enough to fall prey to the ruse. The U.S. soldiers developed their own response, the best known of which was the so-called water cure. After forcing several gallons of water down the throat of a prisoner, bloating the man horribly, one of his captors would kneel on the prisoner's stomach until he revealed the sought-after information.

An especially ugly by-product of the war was that the Filipino guerrillas often turned their wrath on their own countrymen who had cooperated with the earlier Spanish colonial masters. Cruelty begat cruelty.

Although the slogan "civilize 'em with a Krag" reflected a feeling that the only way to deal with the guerrillas was with a weapon (the .30-caliber Krag-Jörgensen rifle was then the infantry standard issue), there was more to the picture. Historian John Gates has observed that to view the Philippine conflict purely from the standpoint of atrocities is to ignore the many "humane efforts undertaken by individual American soldiers."

See also "Civilize 'em with a Krag"; Pacification Program; *Reconcentrado* System; Weyler y Nicolau, Valeriano "Butcher."
References and Further Readings
Brown, Charles H. *The Correspondents' War: Journalists in the Spanish-American War.* New York: Charles Scribner's Sons, 1967.
Gates, John Morgan. *Schoolbooks and Krags: The United States Army in the Philippines, 1898–1902.* Contributions in Military History no. 3. Westport, CT: Greenwood Press, 1973.
Wolff, Leon. *Little Brown Brother: America's Forgotten Bid for Empire Which Cost 250,000 Lives.* New York: Kraus Reprint, 1970.

Augustín Dávila, Don Basilio (1840–1910)

Don Basilio Augustín Dávila was appointed governor-general of the Philippines in April 1898, just days before the war with the United States broke out. Accordingly, he had little opportunity to prepare an effective strategy for defending the archipelago, though he did not let that deter him from doing what he could.

The Spanish had allowed the defense of the Philippines, especially that of Manila, to languish. With the approach of war, there was little time to correct the situation. Nevertheless, working with the limited resources at his disposal, Augustín moved to strengthen the military forces by adding sympathetic Filipinos to the ranks of the Spanish Army. Additionally, he instituted martial law in Manila, with courts empowered to issue death sentences for those suspected of treason.

Augustín insisted that any defensive scheme for the Philippines must include Manila. As a consequence, Adm. Patricio Montojo was compelled to concentrate his naval squadron in Manila Bay, rather than dispersing it in strategic locations throughout the archipelago, which would have avoided his disastrous encounter with Commodore George Dewey.

Following Dewey's smashing victory of 1 May 1898, Augustín dispersed the Spanish garrison to deal with Filipino revolutionaries. However, he lacked the manpower to successfully maintain his defensive perimeter outside Manila, known as the Zapote Line, and the Spanish were ultimately forced to withdraw. Augustín's was an impossible assignment, for he operated without reinforcements and supplies, neither of which was forthcoming in time to seriously challenge the Americans.

See also Dewey, George; Manila Bay, Battle of; Montojo y Pasarón, Patricio.

References and Further Readings

Chadwick, Rear Adm. French Ensor. *Relations of the United States and Spain: The Spanish American War.* 2 vols. New York: Charles Scribner's Sons, 1911 (reprinted in 1968).

Musicant, Ivan. *Empire by Default: The Spanish-American War and the Dawn of the American Century.* New York: Henry Holt and Company, 1998.

Nofi, Albert A. *The Spanish-American War, 1898.* Conshohocken, PA: Combined Books, 1998.

Trask, David F. *The War with Spain in 1898.* Lincoln: University of Nebraska Press, 1996.

Auñón y Villalón, Ramón (1844–1925)

Ramón Auñón y Villalón was appointed Spanish minister of marine on 18 May 1898, replacing Segismundo Bermejo y Merelo. Against the wishes of Adm. Pascual Cervera, who commanded the Spanish naval squadron at Santiago de Cuba, Auñón supported Ramón Blanco (governor-general of Cuba) and ordered Cervera's squadron to sortie from Santiago harbor. Cervera reluctantly sallied forth into the waiting guns of the U.S. ships, and his squadron was subsequently demolished in the battle on 3 July 1898. In Auñón's view, the rationale to abandon the protection of Santiago harbor was a matter of honor: better to go down fighting than to be forced to scuttle the ships and surrender.

See also Blanco y Erenas, Ramón; Cámara y Libermoore, Manuel de la; Cervera y Topete, Pascual; Santiago de Cuba, Naval Battle of.

References and Further Readings

Chadwick, Rear Adm. French Ensor. *Relations of the United States and Spain: The Spanish American War.* 2 vols. New York: Charles Scribner's Sons, 1911 (reprinted in 1968).

Trask, David F. *The War with Spain in 1898.* Lincoln: University of Nebraska Press, 1996.

Auxiliary Squadron, U.S. Navy

During the Spanish-American War, the U.S. Navy was organized into 5 operational squadrons. One, the auxiliary squadron or force, was popularly known as the "Mosquito Squadron." Consisting of 8 single-turret monitors, 7 yachts, and 1 tugboat, the squadron was headquartered in New York harbor and charged with guarding the eastern U.S. seaboard. The squadron was manned primarily by naval militia under the command of Rear Adm. Henry Erben. The squadron did not participate in any naval actions of the war.

See also Militia, Naval; Naval Strategy, U.S.

References and Further Readings

Feuer, A. B. *The Spanish-American War at Sea.* Westport, CT: Greenwood Press, 1995.

Trask, David F. *The War with Spain in 1898.* Lincoln: University of Nebraska Press, 1996.

Balangiga Massacre (Philippines)
(28 September 1901)

On 28 September 1901, the residents of Balangiga on the island of Samar in the central Philippine Archipelago launched a surprise attack on Company C of the Ninth U.S. Infantry. The massacre at Balangiga was one of the most unfortunate incidents of the Philippine-American War.

The Ninth Infantry, part of the military occupation of the island, had recently been assigned to garrison Balangiga. The army's treatment of the local inhabitants was harsh: Many residents were forced to live in extremely crowded conditions, and others had to work without pay. On top of this, there were incidents of rape and looting by the soldiers. Yet the troops apparently had no inkling that the townspeople, aided and encouraged by still-active guerrillas, were planning a retributive strike. Army intelligence had learned of a possible attack—but not in time to alert Company C.

The Filipinos carefully planned their attack. During the preceding day, many Filipino men from outside the village entered the town disguised as women, carrying bolos concealed in their clothing. The men of Company C were up early on Sunday, 28 September, anticipating a mail delivery. In addition, they had recently learned of the assassination of President William McKinley. Perhaps preoccupied with this news, the men were not as alert as they might have been. While at breakfast and with their weapons not at hand, the men were suddenly attacked by some 400 Filipinos brandishing bolos, axes, and other weapons. A few soldiers were able to reach their own weapons and beat back the attackers, allowing 36 survivors from the company to escape by boat, leaving 48 dead comrades behind in the village.

After the massacre, Gen. Jacob Smith ordered harsh reprisals against the Filipinos. He sent a marine detachment, under the command of Maj. Littleton W. T. Waller, into the area with orders to take no prisoners. In eleven days, Waller and his men killed 39 people and destroyed much property. (Waller was later tried for murder but acquitted.) Although Maj. Gen. Adna R. Chaffce, military commander in the Philippines, was outraged by the incident at Balangiga and directed his subordinates to take stern measures, Smith exceeded his prerogatives and was subsequently court-martialed and retired from the service.

Meanwhile, a detachment of the Ninth Infantry returned to Balangiga the day after the massacre to retrieve equipment and bury their dead comrades. After completing their grim task, the troops burned the village and departed. Shortly thereafter, 2 companies of the Eleventh Infantry arrived to take station in the area, remaining there until October when they were replaced by a marine detachment.

When the Eleventh Infantry returned to the United States in 1908, they took with them two large bronze bells and an old cannon from Balangiga. The regiment was subsequently assigned to Fort D. A. Russell (now Warren Air Force Base) near Cheyenne, Wyoming, where the bells and cannon remain. The Philippine government would like the trophies returned, but their future is still to be decided by the president and Congress.

See also Benevolent Assimilation; Chaffee, Adna Romanza; Smith, Jacob Hurd.

References and Further Readings
Adams, Gerald M. *The Bells of Balangiga.* Cheyenne, WY: Lagumo Corp., 1998.
Gates, John Morgan. *Schoolbooks and Krags: The United States Army in the Philippines, 1898–1902.* Contributions in Military History no. 3. Westport, CT: Greenwood Press, 1973.
Linn, Brian McAllister. *The U.S. Army and Counterinsurgency in the Philippine War, 1899–1902.* Chapel Hill: University of North Carolina Press, 1989.

Baldwin, Frank Dwight (1842–1923)

Frank Dwight Baldwin serves as a good example of the career army officer who found it difficult to be both firm and tactful in dealing with the Moros of Mindanao. Born near Manchester, Michigan, in 1842, Baldwin was commissioned a second lieutenant in the Nineteenth Michigan Infantry in 1861. He served with distinction throughout the Civil War and later during the Indian wars. He was twice awarded the Medal of Honor—for his conduct at the Battle of Peachtree Creek, Georgia, during the Civil War and for his actions in the fight at McClellan's Creek, Texas, during the Red River War.

By 1890, he had attained the rank of captain. He was promoted to major and almost immediately to lieutenant colonel after war with Spain broke out. In 1899, he was sent to the Philippines and assigned to command the Fourth Infantry. Following a successful campaign on the island of Cavite in which his regiment played a key role in the capture of Emilio Aguinaldo, Baldwin was promoted to full colonel and returned to the United States. However, he was immediately ordered back to the Philippines as commander of the Twenty-seventh Infantry on the island of Mindanao, where he had to deal with the troublesome Moros.

Baldwin's fair but tough approach in dealing with the Moros was an outgrowth of his experience with the Indians. In May 1902, he successfully attacked and destroyed a Moro stronghold at Bayang. Baldwin's aggressive approach made him a difficult subordinate for Brig. Gen. George Davis, his department commander, and Maj. Gen. Adna R. Chaffee, recently appointed overall military commander of the Philippines. Actually, Baldwin and Chaffee had disliked each other since their days on the frontier, which may well have contributed to their strained relations on Mindanao.

Promoted to brigadier general, Baldwin returned to the United States, where he commanded the army's Department of Colorado until his retirement in 1906.

See also Chaffee, Adna Romanza; Lake Lanao Campaigns; Moros.
References and Further Readings
Hutton, Paul Andrew, ed. *Soldiers West: Biographies from the Military Frontier.* Lincoln: University of Nebraska Press, 1987.
Steinbach, Robert H. *A Long March: The Lives of Frank and Alice Baldwin.* Austin: University of Texas Press, 1989.

Baler, Siege of (Philippines) (1 July 1898–2 June 1899)

During the summer of 1898, Spanish governor-general Don Basilio Augustín of the Philippines, with some 26,000 Spanish troops at his disposal, was prepared to conduct an effective defense of the archipelago for which he was responsible. Augustín initially hoped to win the support of the Filipinos, thereby creating a unified front against the Americans. When this strategy failed because the populace, tired of Spanish control, did not respond to his efforts, he prepared to defend the islands with his own Spanish troops.

Of Augustín's 26,000-man army, only 9,000 were concentrated in the Manila area, the rest being dispersed so as to respond to any uprising by the native population. The strategy proved ill conceived because many of his outlying units either surrendered to the insurgents or were captured.

A notable exception to that pattern provided Spain with at least one proud moment in a war that otherwise wrote the finis to its status as an international power. Filipino insurgents first attacked a detachment of 47 men at Baler on the island of Luzon on 1 July 1898. After the detachment's commanding officer, Capt. Enrique de las Morenas, was killed, command devolved to Lt. Saturnino Cerezo, who continued to defend his position against the Filipino insurgents until long after Spain had surrendered and the war with the United States had ended. In the spring of 1899, a detachment of U.S. Marines marched to the relief of Baler but was ambushed en route; many soldiers were taken prisoner. Meanwhile, the Baler defenders hung on until 2 June 1899, when they finally surrendered, ending a defense that had lasted 337 days.

See also Augustín Dávila, Don Basilio; Luzon Campaigns.

References and Further Readings

Martín Cerezo, Saturnino. *El sitio de Baler (notas y recuerdos).* Guadalajara: n.p., 1904. Translated by F. L. Dodds as *Under the Red and Gold: Being Notes and Recollections of the Siege of Baler.* Kansas City, MO: Franklin Hudson Publishing, 1909.

Trask, David F. *The War with Spain in 1898.* Lincoln: University of Nebraska Press, 1996.

Balloons (U.S. Signal Corps)

Balloons were first used by the Union army during the Civil War to provide high observation platforms from which to track enemy movements. During the Spanish-American War, the U.S. Signal Corps had a 27-man balloon detachment serving in Cuba under the command of Lt. Col. Joseph E. Maxfield.

The effectiveness of balloons during the Civil War proved limited, largely because the balloons were unstable. However, some progress had been made in balloon development since the Civil War. Although Maxfield's balloon, the *Santiago*, was old, it was serviceable and capable of reaching an altitude of 14,000 feet.

On 30 June 1898, Maxfield's detachment made three successful flights, reporting that the Spanish fleet was in the harbor of Santiago de Cuba. The balloonists also reported on conditions along the route of Gen. William Shafter's Fifth Corps as it moved toward El Caney and San Juan Heights. The balloon was finally forced down by enemy fire on its third flight. Not until World War I would the U.S. military again employ balloons.

See also El Caney, Battle of; San Juan Hill, Charge up.
References and Further Readings
Beede, Benjamin R., ed. *The War of 1898 and U.S. Interventions,*
1898–1934. New York: Garland Publishing, 1994.
Chadwick, Rear Adm. French Ensor. *Relations of the United States*
and Spain: The Spanish American War. 2 vols. New York: Charles
Scribner's Sons, 1911 (reprinted in 1968).
Dierks, Jack Cameron. *A Leap to Arms: The Cuban Campaign of*
1898. Philadelphia: J. B. Lippincott, 1970.
Jackson, Donald Dale. *The Aeronauts* (The Epic of Flight Series).
Alexandria, VA: Time Life Books, 1980.
Parkinson, Russell J. "United States Signal Corps Balloons,
1871–1902." *Military Affairs,* winter, 1960–1961.

Bandholtz, Harry Hill (1864–1925)

Born in Michigan, Harry Hill Bandholtz graduated from West Point
in 1890. In the years following graduation, he served at various army
posts and as an instructor at Michigan Agricultural College. He was
a 35-year-old infantry captain when the United States declared war
against Spain in 1898. Later, he would become the only American
elected to the governorship of a Philippine province.

After serving in Cuba, Bandholtz was transferred to the
Philippines, where his outgoing personality and natural diplomatic
skills stood him in excellent stead. Working closely with locals, he
established town councils and successfully persuaded Filipino leaders to accept U.S. rule. Bandholtz was named governor of Tayabas
Province in 1902 but resigned a year later to accept an appointment
to the newly created Philippine Constabulary, of which he was
named head in 1907. During his tenure in the Philippines, Bandholtz
was active in politics and served as personal adviser to future president Manuel Quezon.

Bandholtz returned to the United States in 1913, served in
France during World War I, and retired in 1923.

See also Philippine Constabulary.
References and Further Readings
Coats, George Yarrington. "The Philippine Constabulary:
1901–1917." Ph.D. diss., Ohio State University, 1968.
Karnow, Stanley. *In Our Image: America's Empire in the Philippines.*
New York: Random House, 1989.

Barton, Clara (Clarissa) Harlowe (1821–1912)

Clara Harlowe Barton was born in Oxford, Massachusetts. A former
schoolteacher, she first attracted attention for her humanitarian work

during the Civil War when she nursed wounded soldiers in army camps and also searched for those missing in action. That work proved to be the beginning of a lifelong involvement with humanitarian causes, which led her to found the American Red Cross in 1881 (the International Red Cross having been created in 1864). At the time of the Spanish-American War, Barton frequently found herself at odds with the army, which was reluctant to allow nonmilitary personnel to enter Cuba. Despite that obstacle, she and her associates attended to the needs of many ill and wounded soldiers there, as well as Cuban victims of the hated Spanish *reconcentrado* policy.

Barton's authoritarian manner and refusal to delegate authority eventually led to her loss of power within the Red Cross. By the time of the Spanish-American War, an aging Clara Barton often came into conflict with those now in control of the organization she had created.

In 1900, President William McKinley, long a staunch admirer of Barton's, supported a Senate resolution recognizing her work. In addition to her humanitarian efforts, Clara Barton also authored several books, including *The Red Cross in Peace and War.*

See also Diseases; Medical Department, U.S. Army.

References and Further Readings

Leech, Margaret. *In the Days of McKinley.* New York: Harper & Brothers, 1959.

Pryor, Elizabeth Brown. *Clara Barton, Professional Angel.* Philadelphia: University of Pennsylvania Press, 1987.

Bates, John Coalter (1842–1919)

John Coalter Bates was born in Missouri to a staunch Union family. His father, Edward Bates, served as Lincoln's attorney general from 1861 to 1864. Young John Coalter joined the volunteers in 1861 at age 18. Commissioned a second lieutenant in the Eleventh Infantry, he was attached to the Army of the Potomac. Bates remained in the army after hostilities ended, participating in campaigns against Indians on the western frontier. By 1892, he had risen to the rank of colonel. When war with Spain broke out, he was promoted to brigadier general of volunteers. His Spanish-American War service was particularly notable for the treaty he entered into with the Moros of Mindanao in the Philippines.

During the initial stage of the Cuban Campaign, he led the Independent Brigade of the Third Division and was briefly in command of the base at Siboney before being assigned to Henry Lawton's Second Division prior to the Battle of El Caney. Promoted to major general, he commanded the Third Division throughout the remainder of the Cuban Campaign.

After the fighting ended in Cuba, he returned to the United States before being sent back to Cuba, where he served briefly as commander of U.S. forces in the Santa Clara District. From Cuba, he was transferred to the Philippines in the spring of 1899. His rank of major general of volunteers having expired, he arrived in the Philippines a brigadier general but would regain his status as a two-star general of volunteers by the end of the year.

In July 1899, he was directed by Gen. Elwell S. Otis to work out a treaty with the troublesome Moros on the island of Mindanao. Bates was eminently successful, striking a bargain with the Moros whereby they agreed to accept U.S. rule in exchange for being allowed to keep their old customs. The Bates Treaty, as it came to be known, remained in effect for five years.

Late in 1899, Bates was placed in command of the Department of the South on the island of Luzon, where he initiated several campaigns against the revolutionary army of Emilio Aguinaldo. Bates had little use for the government's humanitarian approach as a way to deal with the Filipino insurrectionists. As a consequence, he was perhaps not as effective a department commander as he might otherwise have been.

In 1902, he was promoted to major general in the regular army. Four years later, he was named chief of staff and promoted to lieutenant general.

> **See also** Bates Treaty; Benevolent Assimilation; Cuban Campaign; El Caney, Battle of; Luzon Campaigns; Moros.
>
> **References and Further Readings**
>
> Gates, John Morgan. *Schoolbooks and Krags: The United States Army in the Philippines, 1898–1902*. Contributions in Military History no. 3. Westport, CT: Greenwood Press, 1973.
>
> Linn, Brian McAllister. *The U.S. Army and Counterinsurgency in the Philippine War, 1899–1902*. Chapel Hill: University of North Carolina Press, 1989.
>
> Sexton, Capt. William Thaddeus. *Soldiers in the Sun: An Adventure in Imperialism*. Harrisburg, PA: Military Service Publishing Company, 1939 (reprinted by Books for Libraries Press, Freeport, NY, 1971).
>
> Wolff, Leon. *Little Brown Brother: America's Forgotten Bid for Empire Which Cost 250,000 Lives*. New York: Kraus Reprint, 1970.

Bates Treaty (Philippines) (1899)

On 20 August 1899, Brig. Gen. John C. Bates, U.S. Volunteers, concluded an important agreement with the Moros of Mindanao and the

Sulu Archipelago. For their part, the participating Moro bands agreed to recognize U.S. sovereignty, fly the American flag, and cooperate with the United States in suppressing piracy. Additionally, the Moros agreed to free their slaves and ban the use of firearms. The United States, in turn, recognized the power of the Moro sultan and agreed to protect and defend the Sulu Archipelago from foreign attack.

The treaty worked effectively for five years. Eventually, growing discontent among a number of the Moro bands led to deteriorating conditions that compelled the United States to finally resort to military force. As a consequence, a number of bloody and harsh clashes, including those at Bud Bagsak and Bud Daju, occurred.

See also Bates, John Coalter; Bud Bagsak, Battle of; Bud Daju, Battle of; Pershing, John Joseph; Wood, Leonard.

References and Further Readings

Linn, Brian McAllister. *The U.S. Army and Counterinsurgency in the Philippine War, 1899–1902.* Chapel Hill: University of North Carolina Press, 1989.

———. *Guardians of Empire: The U.S. Army and the Pacific, 1902–1940.* Chapel Hill: University of North Carolina Press, 1997.

Wolff, Leon. *Little Brown Brother: America's Forgotten Bid for Empire Which Cost 250,000 Lives.* New York: Kraus Reprint, 1970.

Battlefield Medicine

See **Medical Department, U.S. Army**

Bayang (Moro Province, Philippines), Battle of (2 May 1902)

The Battle of Bayang marked the first clash between the United States and the Moro tribesmen of southern Mindanao and the Sulu Archipelago. Although the United States actively sought peace, many (though not all) of the Moro bands waged a jihad, or holy war, against all outsiders. This conflict would continue at varying levels of intensity until 1913.

As U.S. forces moved into the interior of Mindanao early in 1902, the Moros clashed with Col. Frank D. Baldwin's troops who were attempting to build a road to Lake Lanao. In addition, they raided army livestock and generally created a disturbance in the area, harassing non-Moro villages. Some soldiers were later found hacked to death by the deadly Moro knives known as bolos.

Gen. Adna R. Chaffee, U.S. military commander in the Philippines, informed Moro leaders—called *datus* or *dattos*—that they would be held responsible for such acts of violence and had to surrender all guilty parties to U.S. authorities. When the *datus* arrogantly refused to comply with Chaffee's ultimatum, Colonel Baldwin, who believed in using a hard-line approach with the Moros, was finally authorized to advance.

Leading a strong column of some 1,800 men, Baldwin began his movement from Malabang to Lake Lanao in mid-April. When the Moro leaders rejected a final ultimatum to surrender, Baldwin attacked the Moro fort (*cotta*) at Pandapatan. Constructed of rock and earth and surrounded by a 10-foot-deep moat, it was one of the most formidable strong points in the area, defended by some 600 tribesmen, most of whom were from Bayang.

On the afternoon of 2 May 1902, Baldwin's artillery began shelling the *cotta,* with destructive results. Following this punishing fire and an assault by the infantry, the Moros finally surrendered. Baldwin's losses amounted to 10 killed and some 40 wounded; the Moros suffered an estimated 300 to 400 casualties.

General Chaffee believed the campaign had been successful in that it destroyed the power of the Moros in that region. The newly convened Philippine Commission, however, was more critical, suggesting that the army had forced the confrontation.

See also Baldwin, Frank Dwight; Chaffee, Adna Romanza; Moros; Pershing, John Joseph.

References and Further Readings

Scott, Hugh Lenox. *Some Memories of a Soldier.* New York: Century Company, 1928.

Steinbach, Robert H. *A Long March: The Lives of Frank and Alice Baldwin.* Austin: University of Texas Press, 1989.

Beef Scandal

Next to the destruction of the battleship *Maine* and the Spanish-American War itself, no other topic at the end of the nineteenth century captured the headlines of U.S. newspapers and aroused the American public as thoroughly as the so-called beef scandal.

At the time of the Spanish-American War, army rations included both refrigerated beef and roast beef packed in tins (sometimes referred to as canned roast beef). Selected by Commissary General Charles P. Eagan, the tinned beef was expected to provide troops with a hearty, nutritious ration. The rations would, however, prove to be a nightmare.

The refrigerated beef was fairly popular, but the tinned beef was universally loathed. Col. Theodore Roosevelt, who commanded the

Rough Riders, thought it "nauseating." If not actually harmful to ingest, its appearance and putrid taste made it the most unappetizing bill of fare ever set before U.S. soldiers. The tinned beef was supposed to be cooked before it was eaten, but field conditions frequently prevented the troops from doing that. Consequently, the meat was often consumed cold, despite its hideous odor. In addition, the oppressive, moist heat of Cuba and the Philippines resulted in a high rate of spoilage. There was another problem as well, albeit not widespread, for some tins were found to contain dead maggots, pieces of rope, and other foreign bodies, which of course added to the meat's unsavory reputation. Tinned beef was not new, having been available to the army during the Indian wars on the western frontier; however, it was not widely distributed until the Spanish-American War.

Refrigerated beef was not without its critics either, foremost of whom was William Daley, a volunteer surgeon on Gen. Nelson Miles's staff. During an inspection tour of various camps in the summer of 1898, Daley sampled the meat and believed he tasted boric acid and certain other chemicals used to preserve the beef, which eventually gave rise to the unappetizing sobriquet "embalmed beef."

Daley reported his findings to Miles, who had also received disturbing reports about the safety of the tinned beef, but took no immediate action. By late fall, Miles decided that there was sufficient evidence to bring charges against the War Department and specifically Secretary of War Russell Alger, with whom he had been feuding for some time.

In testimony before the Dodge Commission (headed by Gen. Grenville M. Dodge), which investigated the conduct of the war, Miles leveled harsh charges against the War Department, indirectly accusing Commissary General Eagan of failing to provide U.S. soldiers with nourishing food. Livid at accusations that he believed impugned his motives, Eagan retaliated with a vengeance that ultimately resulted in official charges of insubordination and for which he was subsequently dismissed from the army.

Not surprisingly, reports about "embalmed beef" soon attracted journalists, whose stories brought the matter to the nation's attention. The issue rapidly developed into a scandal, fueled by charges and countercharges made by those involved.

Although the Dodge Commission found no evidence of criminal negligence or corruption, it did conclude that it was a poor decision to issue tinned beef for use in the Tropics and under conditions that often prevented troops from cooking it. Undaunted, Miles persisted in his allegations. In response, President William McKinley formed an army board to investigate the matter further. However, as the "beef court" looked into the matter, Miles began to retract or dilute his earlier accusations. By the time the committee completed its work at the end of April 1899, it concluded that there was no substance to the charge that the refrigerated beef had been laced with preservatives. Miles, however, did not emerge unscathed and was sharply criticized for failing to report his findings immediately.

See also Alger, Russell Alexander; Eagan, Charles Patrick; Miles, Nelson Appleton.

References and Further Readings

Cosmas, Graham. *An Army for Empire: The United States Army in the Spanish-American War.* College Station: Texas A&M University Press, 1998.

Musicant, Ivan. *Empire by Default: The Spanish-American War and the Dawn of the American Century.* New York: Henry Holt and Company, 1998.

Bell, James Franklin (1856–1919)

An innovative officer who developed controversial methods of dealing with guerrilla warfare, James Franklin Bell was born in Kentucky. He entered West Point in 1874, graduating thirty-eighth in his class four years later. Assigned to the Ninth Cavalry upon graduation, he transferred to the late Lt. Col. George Custer's famous Seventh Cavalry Regiment in August. He spent the next several years participating in various Indian campaigns in the West. When war with Spain broke out, he held the rank of captain and was stationed at Fort Apache, Arizona Territory.

Bell promptly requested an assignment in Cuba but was sent instead to the Philippines, where he put his Indian-fighting experience to good use against the Filipino guerrillas. Promoted to colonel of the Thirty-sixth Volunteer Infantry in July 1899, he was awarded the Medal of Honor for gallantry in action near Porac, Luzon. Made brigadier general of volunteers in February 1901, he led his newly formed Third Separate Brigade on a tough but effective campaign through the southern provinces of Luzon. Bell's campaign remains controversial to this day, with some historians severely criticizing him for his harsh measures against the Filipinos and others praising him for the efficacy of his measures against the guerrillas.

As a result of his experience in the Indian wars and in the Philippines, Bell developed a theory for waging counterinsurgency warfare. (Interestingly, many of the problems and concerns he addressed would resurface decades later in Vietnam.) Promoted to brigadier general in the regular army in 1901, Bell was appointed army chief of staff by President Theodore Roosevelt in 1906.

See also Luzon Campaigns.

References and Further Readings

Gates, John Morgan. *Schoolbooks and Krags: The United States Army in the Philippines, 1898–1902.* Contributions in Military History no. 3. Westport, CT: Greenwood Press, 1973.

Linn, Brian McAllister. *The U.S. Army and Counterinsurgency in the Philippine War, 1899–1902.* Chapel Hill: University of North Carolina Press, 1989.

Sexton, Capt. William Thaddeus. *Soldiers in the Sun: An Adventure in Imperialism.* Harrisburg, PA: Military Service Publishing Company, 1939 (reprinted by Books for Libraries Press, Freeport, NY, 1971).

Wolff, Leon. *Little Brown Brother: America's Forgotten Bid for Empire Which Cost 250,000 Lives.* New York: Kraus Reprint, 1970.

Benevolent Assimilation

As a result of the Treaty of Paris, signed 10 December 1898, the United States gained control of the Philippine Islands. Faced with the problems inherent in governing his nation's first colonial possession, President William McKinley, acting out of a sense of noblesse oblige, directed that U.S. policy toward the Filipinos be protective and respectful of rights and property. It was McKinley's desire that U.S. forces in the Philippines earn the respect of the Filipinos, introduce them to American beliefs and standards, and acculturate them in a kindly, paternal manner. The phrase he coined to define this U.S. mission was "benevolent assimilation."

However, during the period between the end of the Spanish-American War and the signing of the Treaty of Paris, the relationship between U.S. troops and the Filipino people was often strained. Many soldiers treated the Filipinos with disrespect, and many Filipinos were angry at the presence of U.S. troops in the archipelago. As a consequence, each side frequently used inflammatory language toward the other and tensions steadily mounted. Eventually, relationships deteriorated to the point that, on 4 February 1899, an accident between a U.S. picket and a Filipino patrol resulted in the start of the Philippine-American War.

See also Aguinaldo y Famy, Emilio; Manila, Second Battle of; McKinley, William, Jr.

References and Further Readings

Karnow, Stanley. *In Our Image: America's Empire in the Philippines.* New York: Random House, 1989.

Leech, Margaret. *In the Days of McKinley.* New York: Harper & Brothers, 1959.

Linn, Brian McAllister. *The U.S. Army and Counterinsurgency in the Philippine War, 1899–1902.* Chapel Hill: University of North Carolina Press, 1989.

———. *Guardians of Empire: The U.S. Army and the Pacific, 1902–1940.* Chapel Hill: University of North Carolina Press, 1997.

Benjamin, Anna Northend (1874–1902)

Born in Massachusetts, Anna Northend Benjamin was one of only two official women correspondents during the Spanish-American War, the other being Kathleen Blake Watkins. Both women reported on the condition of the army in Tampa, Florida, while the troops prepared for the invasion of Cuba. Despite considerable resistance from army officers and male reporters, Benjamin wrote informative stories on army life in Tampa, including such topics as rations, camp conditions, and soldier behavior. Her stories sometimes described the activities of the Cuban rebels, with details that were often absent from the stories of her male counterparts.

Like her colleague Watkins, Benjamin was refused permission to accompany the Fifth Corps to Cuba, but she bribed the captain of a collier to provide her with passage to the island, where she reported on Cuba and the war for *Leslie's Magazine.* After the fighting in Cuba ended, she went on to cover action in the Philippines and the Boxer Rebellion for the *New York Tribune* and the *San Francisco Chronicle.* Her promising career was cut short by her death from a brain tumor at age 27.

See also Journalism; Watkins, Kathleen Blake.

References and Further Readings

Benjamin, Anna Northend. "The Darker Side of War." *Leslie's Magazine,* August 4, 1898.

———. "A Woman's Visit to Santiago." *Leslie's Magazine,* August 25, 1898.

Brown, Charles H. *The Correspondents' War: Journalists in the Spanish-American War.* New York: Charles Scribner's Sons, 1967.

Milton, Joyce. *The Yellow Kids: Foreign Correspondents in the Heyday of Yellow Journalism.* New York: Harper & Row, 1989.

Bennett, James Gordon, Jr. (1841–1918)

The son of James Gordon Bennett (1795–1872), founder of the *New York Herald,* James Gordon Bennett Jr. served as a naval officer during the Civil War. In 1867, he took over management of the newspaper from his father, and he was at its helm throughout the Spanish-American War. Under his stewardship, the paper continued to be known for its journalistic excellence. Along with Joseph Pulitzer and William Randolph Hearst, Bennett was one of the colorful, flamboyant newspapermen of the Gilded Age. It was he who sent Henry Stanley into Africa to find David Livingstone, and he also dispatched one Januarius MacGahan to search for the Northwest Passage. A controversial figure himself, Bennett's heavy drinking and outlandish public behavior often created as much sensation as the stories he published in his paper. Horsewhipped by his fiancée's brother for breaking off his engagement, he also fought a duel. In 1877, he moved to France and ran the *Herald* from his office in Paris.

In the years immediately preceding the Spanish-American War, Bennett's *Herald* took a somewhat softer stance toward Spain than the other leading U.S. papers, leading some to charge that Bennett was sympathetic to Spain because of his financial interests. Indeed, in July 1898, William Randolph Hearst attacked his competitor on those grounds in his own paper, the *New York Journal.* The criticism did little to squelch the controversial Bennett. In 1899, Bennett and his paper were highly critical of Secretary of War Russell Alger for his incompetent management of the War Department during the Spanish-American War.

See also Alger, Russell Alexander; Hearst, William Randolph; Journalism.

References and Further Readings

Brown, Charles H. *The Correspondents' War: Journalists in the Spanish-American War.* New York: Charles Scribner's Sons, 1967.

Seitz, Don C. *The James Gordon Bennetts.* Indianapolis, IN: Bobbs-Merrill Company, 1928.

Bigelow, Poultney (1855–1954)

Poultney Bigelow was a newspaper reporter during the Spanish-American War, known for his outspoken criticism of the U.S. government. Born in New York, he earned degrees at both Yale and Columbia. His father, John Bigelow, a former diplomat, was co-owner (with William Cullen Bryant) and managing editor of the *New York Evening Post,* so it is perhaps not surprising that Poultney, too, chose a career in journalism. After completing his education, he traveled widely. He wrote several books on foreign countries and in 1885 founded *Outing,* a publication devoted to outdoor sports. In 1892, he was expelled from Russia for his outspoken political writings.

During the Spanish-American War, Bigelow worked as a reporter for *Harper's Weekly* and the *Times* (London). He captured the attention of the country in a 28 May 1898 story in *Harper's* in which he reported on command snafus in the American Expeditionary Force then assembling at Tampa, Florida, for the invasion of Cuba. His sharp criticism of the government for its failure to provide U.S. troops with sanitary camp conditions, proper food, and tropical uniforms resulted in his being branded unpatriotic and cost him his credentials to accompany Gen. William Shafter's Fifth Corps to Cuba.

Interestingly, Bigelow's scathing remarks were publicly challenged by one of his colleagues, Richard Harding Davis. The disagreement between the two reporters became one of the controversies of the day. Despite his public statements, Davis was privately in accord with Bigelow's views but felt that if he and others reinforced those reports, the outcry from across the nation would prove too damaging and disruptive. As a consequence, Bigelow's stories probably failed to provoke any real corrective measures.

See also Camps, Staging Areas, and Embarkation Points, U.S. Army; Davis, Richard Harding; Journalism.

References and Further Readings

Brown, Charles H. *The Correspondents' War: Journalists in the Spanish-American War.* New York: Charles Scribner's Sons, 1967.

Biyak-na-Bató (Philippines), Pact of (14–15 December 1897)

The Pact of Biyak-na-Bató was an agreement between Emilio Aguinaldo, the de facto head of the Filipino revolutionary movement, and the Spanish authorities in the Philippines. Unsuccessful in his efforts to throw off the Spanish yoke by fighting a conventional war, Aguinaldo withdrew his army into the mountains during the summer of 1897 and from there waged guerrilla warfare against the Spanish. Although this proved a more successful strategy, it was not enough to overcome Spain's superior resources, and Aguinaldo was finally compelled to surrender at Biyak, some 60 miles north of Manila.

On 14 and 15 December 1897, Aguinaldo agreed to a Spanish proposal whereby he and some 30 of his closest followers would accept exile to Hong Kong in exchange for payment of 800,000 Mexican pesos. Payment was to be made in three installments, of which only two were actually made. Aguinaldo, who had no intention of giving up the struggle for Philippine independence, banked the two-thirds that was paid in anticipation of a renewed uprising in the future.

See also Aguinaldo y Famy, Emilio.
References and Further Readings
Linn, Brian McAllister. *The U.S. Army and Counterinsurgency in the Philippine War, 1899–1902.* Chapel Hill: University of North Carolina Press, 1989.
Wolff, Leon. *Little Brown Brother: America's Forgotten Bid for Empire Which Cost 250,000 Lives.* New York: Kraus Reprint, 1970.

Black American Soldiers

Nearly 200,000 African Americans served in the Union army during the Civil War, and between 1865 and 1898, blacks maintained a presence in the nation's shrunken peacetime army. When war broke out with Spain, there were four all-black regiments in the army: the Ninth and Tenth Cavalry Regiments and the Twenty-fourth and Twenty-fifth Infantry Regiments. During the Indian wars, black soldiers generally performed as well as their white counterparts and were called "buffalo soldiers" because their black hair reminded Indians of buffalo.

In 1898, in addition to the 4 regiments of black regulars, Congress also created 10 regiments of "immunes," 4 of which were composed of African Americans. The men of these units were so named because it was believed that as a result of having lived in the South, they were immune to tropical diseases such as malaria and yellow fever. In 1898, there was only one black West Point graduate in the army. Generally, black regiments were officered by whites, although in the "immunes" units, black noncommissioned officers (NCOs) often served as company officers with higher billets continuing to be filled by white officers.

Despite a fine record of military service, blacks were noticeably scarce in President William McKinley's initial call for volunteers. However, due to protests from black leaders and others, the president made an effort to increase their participation. Perhaps because of the oppression and racism in their own backyard, blacks felt a certain empathy toward Cubans and, like most others in the United States, felt that injustices perpetrated by the Spanish regime had to cease. During the Spanish-American War (as in the Civil War), blacks were further motivated by the belief that honorable military service would hasten the arrival of equality and dignity. Accordingly, they wanted to be a part of what many Americans looked upon as a crusade to free Cubans from the yoke of tyranny.

Eventually, more than 13,000 blacks were in the military during the Spanish-American War. Of these, however, only the four regiments of regular troops and one regiment of volunteers saw action in Cuba, where they distinguished themselves in hard fighting at the "Hornet's Nest" at El Caney and at Las Guásimas during the Santiago Campaign. In the mad scramble up San Juan Hill, blacks fought side by side with whites, leaving no question as to their fighting ability.

The Ninth U.S. Cavalry, the famous regiment of black American soldiers, 1898.

Within the black community, there was opposition to the use of black troops in the Philippines against a racially similar people. There was opposition as well on the part of some U.S. military commanders. Eventually, however, both the Twenty-fourth and Twenty-fifth Infantry Regiments were sent to the Philippines to replace volunteer units.

Unfortunately, the contributions blacks made in Cuba and the Philippines did not advance their cause nearly to the extent hoped for.

See also Army, U.S.; El Caney, Battle of; Las Guásimas, Battle of; San Juan Hill, Charge up.

References and Further Readings

Cashin, Herschel V. *Under Fire with the Tenth U.S. Cavalry.* Niwot: University Press of Colorado, 1993.

Cosmas, Graham. *An Army for Empire: The United States Army in the Spanish-American War.* College Station: Texas A&M University Press, 1998.

Fletcher, Marvin. "The Black Volunteers in the Spanish-American War." *Military Affairs,* vol. 38, no. 2, April 1974.

Gatewood, Willard B., Jr. *Black Americans and the White Man's Burden: 1898–1903.* Urbana: University of Illinois Press, 1975.

Scott, Edward Van Zile. *The Unwept: Black American Soldiers and the Spanish-American War.* Montgomery, AL: Black Belt Press, 1996.

Black, Wilsone (1837–1909)

A British army veteran of the Crimea, South Africa, and Jamaica, Maj. Gen. Sir Wilsone Black was acting governor of the British Crown Colony of Hong Kong in 1898. In this capacity, he was obligated to notify Commodore George Dewey on 23 April 1898 that a state of war existed between the United States and Spain. As a result, the U.S. Navy's Asiatic Squadron, commanded by Dewey, was required to leave Hong Kong. Though sympathetic to the U.S. position, Black was compelled to issue his directive in order to comply with the international laws of neutrality.

See also Asiatic Squadron, U.S. Navy; Dewey, George.

References and Further Readings

Chadwick, Rear Adm. French Ensor. *Relations of the United States and Spain: The Spanish American War.* 2 vols. New York: Charles Scribner's Sons, 1911 (reprinted in 1968).

Trask, David F. *The War with Spain in 1898.* Lincoln: University of Nebraska Press, 1996.

Blanco y Erenas, Ramón (1833–1906)

Born in San Sebastian, Spain, Ramón Blanco y Erenas served in Cuba during the Cuban War of Independence (1868–1877). Later, he was governor of the Philippine island of Mindanao and governor-general of Cuba from 1879 to 1881 and again from 1897 to 1898, at which time he replaced the notorious Gen. Valeriano "Butcher" Weyler.

A moderate, Blanco sought to deal with the problems in Cuba by forging a coalition of Cubans and Spanish troops with which to defeat the Americans. However, the relationship between Spain and the Cuban people had by that time deteriorated too far for such a strategy to be an effective deterrent to U.S. intervention.

When Adm. Pascual Cervera's Spanish fleet was placed under Blanco's command, Blanco ordered it to sortie from Santiago harbor, feeling that it was better to lose the fleet in battle than to be placed in a position of having to scuttle the vessels, a decision for which he has been criticized.

See also Cervera y Topete, Pascual; Cuban Revolution; Santiago de Cuba, Naval Battle of; Weyler y Nicolau, Valeriano "Butcher."

References and Further Readings

Musicant, Ivan. *Empire by Default: The Spanish-American War and the Dawn of the American Century.* New York: Henry Holt and Company, 1998.

O'Toole, G. J. A. *The Spanish War: An American Epic, 1898.* New York: W. W. Norton, 1984.

Trask, David F. *The War with Spain in 1898.* Lincoln: University of Nebraska Press, 1996.

Ramón Blanco y Erenas, governor-general of Cuba during the Spanish-American War.

Bliss, Tasker Howard (1853–1930)

Born in Lewisburg, Pennsylvania, the son of a Baptist preacher, Tasker Howard Bliss was an energetic and able army officer who drew on his experiences in the Spanish-American War to help create the modern general staff system. Bliss graduated from West Point in 1875. A scholar, he was proficient in the classics and history. He served as an instructor at West Point and later taught military science at the U.S. Naval Academy.

Bliss enjoyed a long and fruitful military career. Although only a junior officer, he was appointed military attaché to Stewart L. Woodford when the latter was named U.S. minister to Spain in 1897. While stationed in Madrid, Bliss compiled useful intelligence data about Spain's military capability. Later, during the war with Spain, he served as chief of staff for Gen. James H. Wilson's First Division in the Puerto Rican Campaign.

Named brigadier general in 1901, he served as adviser to Secretary of War Elihu Root. In 1903, he was appointed first commandant of the new army war college.

See also Puerto Rican Campaign; Root, Elihu; Wilson, James Harrison; Woodford, Stewart Lyndon.

References and Further Readings

Jessup, Philip C. *Elihu Root.* 2 vols. New York: Dodd, Mead & Company, 1938.

Palmer, Frederick. *Bliss, Peacemaker: The Life and Letters of Tasker Howard Bliss.* New York: Dodd, Mead, 1934.

Wilson, James Harrison. *Under the Old Flag: Recollections of Military Operations in the War for the Union, the Spanish War, the Boxer Rebellion, etc.* 2 vols. New York: D. Appleton & Company, 1912.

Blockade

See **Naval Blockade of Cuba**

Boca Grande, Philippines

See **Manila Bay, Battle of**

Bonifacio, Andrés (1863–1897)

A Filipino Nationalist hero in the fight against Spain, Andrés Bonifacio was born into a middle-class family in Tondo, Manila. Following the early deaths of his parents, Bonifacio left school to help support his younger siblings. Despite an abbreviated education, he apparently learned to read and did so widely, being especially drawn to works on the French Revolution, which inspired Bonifacio and others who sought freedom and independence for their own peoples.

When José Rizal began to promulgate his message of Filipino independence, Bonifacio allied himself with the revolutionary movement. However, after Rizal's capture, Bonifacio decided to form a new movement, believing that Spain would never grant the Philippines its freedom unless compelled to do so. This resulted in the creation of a group known as the Katipunan, a secret organization whose goal was to overthrow the Spanish government by armed revolt. The new movement drew a wide following from the working class but did not fare as well in attracting the more affluent Filipinos, who had little to gain.

By 1896, internal dissatisfaction over the progress made by the Katipunan led to the creation of a new movement, with Emilio Aguinaldo elected president. As a result of this election, the dynamics of the movement changed. Charged with treason by Aguinaldo's followers, who alleged that he planned to move against the new regime, Bonifacio was subsequently executed, probably on Aguinaldo's orders (although this has never been proven).

See also Aguinaldo y Famy, Emilio; Katipunan.

References and Further Readings

Bain, David Haward. *Sitting in Darkness: Americans in the Philippines.* Boston: Houghton Mifflin, 1984.

Linn, Brian McAllister. *The U.S. Army and Counterinsurgency in the Philippine War, 1899–1902.* Chapel Hill: University of North Carolina Press, 1989.

Olson, James S., ed. *Historical Dictionary of the Spanish Empire, 1492–1975.* New York: Greenwood Press, 1992.

Wolff, Leon. *Little Brown Brother: America's Forgotten Bid for Empire Which Cost 250,000 Lives.* New York: Kraus Reprint, 1970.

Boxer Rebellion (Uprising) (1899–1901)

Although unrelated to the war with Spain, the Boxer Rebellion is nevertheless important because it occurred at a time when the United States was already involved in the Philippine-American War. Thus, it marked the second U.S. Involvement in the Far East at the turn of the twentieth century. U.S. interests in China as a trade market—interests shared with other nations of the Western world—drew heavy criticism from many of those who opposed U.S. involvement in the Philippines. In addition, troops needed for duty in the Philippines were sent to the China relief expedition.

A complex and important movement in Chinese history, the Boxer Rebellion was born out of a long-standing resentment toward foreign presence in China. The movement, properly known as the Society of Righteous Harmonious Fists, originated in the north of China and spread throughout the rest of the country. With much social unrest in China, the Boxers, as the movement's adherents came to be known, found ready acceptance. A division within China's royal dynasty further aided the growth of the movement.

In June 1900, after the Japanese legation's chancellor and the German minister were murdered by an angry mob, Boxers laid siege to the foreign embassies in the city of Peking (Beijing). In response, a multinational relief column, 2,000 strong, was turned back by the Boxers. On 4 August, a second, heavily reinforced column marched from Tientsin (Tianjin) in relief of the embassies, defeating Chinese forces in two battles on 4 and 5 August. Gen. Adna R. Chaffee, who had commanded the Third Brigade, Second Division of the Fifth Corps in Cuba, led the U.S. column. Chaffee's second in command was Gen. James H. Wilson, who had been in the Puerto Rican Campaign and later served as a military governor in Cuba.

Arriving at Peking, segments of the relief column were assigned to attack the various gates to the walled city. By dark on 14 August, the city had been breached and the besieged embassies rescued. The following day, elements of the relief expedition also rescued some 4,000 Chinese Christians and Catholic clergy from Beidang Cathedral. The Christians had also been under siege and were defended by only a small detachment of French and Italians, who had somehow managed to repulse the assaults of 2,000 Boxers.

Poorly organized and led, the uprising was doomed to failure, and in 1901, a treaty protocol was signed with Boxer representatives, effectively ending the trouble. As a result of the Boxer Rebellion, China was severely penalized by being compelled to pay an indemnity of more than $700 million.

See also Chaffee, Adna Romanza; Wilson, James Harrison.

References and Further Readings

Kolb, Robert K. "Marching through Hell in China." *VFW Magazine,* vol. 87, no. 9, May 2000.

Wilson, James Harrison. *Under the Old Flag: Recollections of Military Operations in the War for the Union, the Spanish War, the Boxer Rebellion, etc.* 2 vols. New York: D. Appleton & Company, 1912.

Bradford, Royal Bird (1844–1914)

During negotiations that led to the Treaty of Paris (31 December 1898), the U.S. ultimatum demanded that Spain accept $20 million for the Philippines, guarantee religious freedom for the inhabitants of the Caroline Islands, and grant the right to annex Kusaie Island in the Caroline Archipelago. As chief of the navy's Bureau of Equipment and naval attaché to the Paris Peace Commission, Comdr. Royal Bird Bradford recognized the island's strategic value as a coaling station and made the peace commissioners aware of that fact. Indeed, Bradford, an avowed expansionist, believed the United States should take possession of all Spanish territory.

Bradford also recognized Germany's designs in the Pacific and, although some favored a partitioning of the Philippines, he was firmly opposed to that idea and set forth a persuasive argument against partitioning that influenced President McKinley's position on the issue. Although the Treaty of Paris eventually resulted in the acquisition of the Philippines by the United States, the matter of the Carolines was absent from the agreement. The islands were later purchased by Germany, and following World War I, they were mandated to Japan.

See also McKinley, William, Jr.; Treaty of Paris; von Bülow, Prince Bernhard.

References and Further Readings

Leech, Margaret. *In the Days of McKinley.* New York: Harper & Brothers, 1959.

Morgan, H. Wayne, ed. *Making Peace with Spain: The Diary of Whitelaw Reid—September–December, 1898.* Austin: University of Texas Press, 1965.

Musicant, Ivan. *Empire by Default: The Spanish-American War and the Dawn of the American Century.* New York: Henry Holt and Company, 1998.

Trask, David F. *The War with Spain in 1898.* Lincoln: University of Nebraska Press, 1996.

Breckinridge, Joseph Cabell (1842–1920)

Born in Baltimore, Maryland, Joseph Cabell Breckinridge served in the Civil War, first as an officer of volunteers and later transferring to the artillery branch in the regulars. By 1898, he had reached the rank of major general of volunteers. He was an ally of General of the Army Nelson Miles, whom he supported during the notorious "beef scandal."

During the war with Spain, he was sent to Cuba to serve as inspector general. Following the Santiago Campaign, he returned to the United States and was placed in charge of Camp Thomas, Chickamauga, Georgia, the first stop for volunteers returning from the fighting in Cuba. Conditions at the camp were in disarray—morale was bad, discipline was virtually nonexistent, and unsanitary conditions prevailed throughout the camp. Breckinridge ordered that the camp be cleaned up. He also organized activities for the troops to keep them occupied until they were released from active duty.

Breckinridge was promoted to major general in the regular army in April 1903 and retired the following day.

See also Beef Scandal; Miles, Nelson Appleton.

References and Further Readings

Chadwick, Rear Adm. French Ensor. *Relations of the United States and Spain: The Spanish American War.* 2 vols. New York: Charles Scribner's Sons, 1911 (reprinted in 1968).

Cosmas, Graham. *An Army for Empire: The United States Army in the Spanish-American War.* College Station: Texas A&M University Press, 1998.

Brooke, John Rutter (1838–1926)

Born in Montgomery County, Pennsylvania, John Rutter Brooke was commissioned in the volunteers during the Civil War and by 1865 had been promoted to brigadier general of volunteers. Brooke remained in the regular army after the war, being appointed lieutenant colonel in 1866. In 1888, he was promoted to brigadier general and in 1897 to major general. He later served as the first military governor of Cuba.

Following the declaration of war with Spain, Brooke was named to command the First Corps at Camp Thomas, Chickamauga, Georgia, before being assigned to the Department of the Gulf. Later, he was a senior commander under Gen. Nelson Miles during the Puerto Rican Campaign and led a column of 5,000 men in an advance on Aibonito. After the war, he served as the first governor of Puerto Rico. On 1 January 1899, following the signing of the Peace Protocol between the United States and Spain, Brooke accepted the formal surrender of Spanish forces in Cuba.

Appointed military governor of Cuba, Brooke was faced with bringing order to a country that had suffered privation from years of war, a challenge he met with reasonable success. After restoring order, he distributed food and reestablished civil government. He also began work on Cuba's road system, harbors, and public buildings and negotiated the surrender of the Cuban Revolutionary Army. Nevertheless, Brooke came to be viewed as something less than an able administrator. Among other things, critics charged that he relied too heavily on his Cuban advisers and lacked a firm hand. In December 1899, Brooke was replaced by the younger and more aggressive (and controversial) Brig. Gen. Leonard Wood, who would serve as one of four military governors of Cuba.

Following his service in Cuba, Brooke returned to the States, where he commanded the army's Department of the East.

See also Cuba; Miles, Nelson Appleton; Puerto Rican Campaign; Wilson, James Harrison.

References and Further Readings

Leech, Margaret. *In the Days of McKinley.* New York: Harper & Brothers, 1959.

Pohanka, Brian C. *Nelson A. Miles: A Documentary Biography of His U.S. Military Career, 1861–1903.* Glendale, CA: Arthur H. Clark Company, 1985.

Trask, David F. *The War with Spain in 1898.* Lincoln: University of Nebraska Press, 1996.

Bryan, William Jennings (1860–1925)

One of the grand figures in U.S. history, William Jennings Bryan was a speaker of rare and powerful eloquence in an era when oratory was still highly regarded. Not surprisingly, he was quite active regarding the U.S. wars in Cuba and the Philippines. Bryan was born in Salem, Illinois. He graduated from Illinois College in 1881 and went on to study at the Union College of Law in Chicago. After practicing law in Jacksonville, Illinois, he moved to Lincoln, Nebraska, where his oratorical gift soon earned him the sobriquet "Boy Orator of the Plains." He was also known as the "Great Commoner" because he often allied himself with the working man.

Bryan was elected to Congress in 1891 but failed in his bid to reach the Senate in 1894. He was an ardent supporter of Free Silver, a political movement that advocated the unlimited coinage of silver as a means of relieving the debt burden of many, especially in the western states. In 1896, Bryan ran for president on the Democratic ticket, delivering his famous "Cross of Gold" speech in which he declared that mankind should not be crucified on a cross of gold. Despite the power of his oratory and his considerable appeal to many voters, he lost the election to William McKinley.

When the war with Spain broke out, Bryan requested and was given a commission as colonel of the Third Nebraska Infantry, a regiment he was largely responsible for developing. The regiment, however, remained in the States and saw no action in Cuba or the Philippines. Whether the decision to keep the unit at home was part of McKinley's strategy to prevent a powerful political opponent from enhancing his reputation by winning glory on the field of battle is purely a subject of conjecture. The Third Nebraska was not the only regiment to remain at home.

When the war ended, Bryan returned to his more familiar role as a political activist and leader of the national Democratic Party. A strong Anti-Imperialist, he was initially adamantly opposed to the subjugation of the Philippines. He later altered his views and supported McKinley's position to acquire the archipelago, with the proviso that the Filipinos be given the assurance of independence in the future.

In 1900, Bryan sought the presidential office a second time but lost again to McKinley. A third try also proved unsuccessful when he lost to William Howard Taft in 1908. A strong religious fundamentalist, Bryan was one of the prosecuting attorneys in the famous *Scopes* trial of 1925.

See also Anti-Imperialist League; McKinley, William, Jr.; Spanish-American War, U.S. Public Reaction to.

References and Further Readings

Anderson, David D. *William Jennings Bryan.* Boston: Twayne Publishers, 1981.

Leech, Margaret. *In the Days of McKinley.* New York: Harper & Brothers, 1959.

Trask, David F. *The War with Spain in 1898.* Lincoln: University of Nebraska Press, 1996.

Bud Bagsak (Philippines), Battle of (13–15 January 1913)

The Battle of Bud Bagsak in 1913 marked the effective end of Moro resistance to the U.S. presence in the Philippines. The Philippine-American War (Insurrection) had officially ended in 1902 with the surrender of Emilio Aguinaldo's insurgent forces. However, fighting continued in various parts of the Philippine Archipelago for the next decade, particularly with the Moros on the island of Mindanao and in the Sulu Archipelago, which was the bailiwick of the sultan of Jolo, the spiritual leader of all Philippine Moros.

Despite efforts to control the Moros without resorting to force of arms, certain particularly recalcitrant Moro bands (some did prove cooperative) persisted in harassing friendly villagers and U.S. troops. Additionally, their refusal to comply with U.S. disarmament directives eventually resulted in a campaign against them.

In January 1913, Capt. John J. Pershing, the provincial governor, led a mixed force of Philippine constabulary and Philippine scouts against a Moro contingent led by chiefs (*datus*) Naquib Amil, Jami, and Sahipa. Two battles followed, resulting in the capture of two Moro forts (*cottas*). The Moros then withdrew to a high peak known as Bud Bugsak, forcing a large number of noncombatants to accompany them.

Concerned for the safety of the noncombatants, Pershing opened negotiations with the Moros, who subsequently agreed to let the noncombatants return to their homes. The remaining Moro warriors, numbering between 300 and 400, advised Pershing they would not surrender or relinquish their weapons.

On 11 June 1913, Pershing ordered his units to attack. Five days of hard, bloody fighting followed. On 15 June, Pershing's artillery opened fire on the Moro stronghold, driving the defenders out. Brandishing krises and bolos, the Moros assaulted Pershing's troops, suffering horrendous casualties in the process. Some *datus* and a few followers managed to escape, but most of the Moros died in a vain effort to overrun the troops. Pershing's command sustained 27 casualties.

The battle provoked much controversy. Pershing was criticized for what many claimed was a massacre, despite the fact that there was ample evidence to support his conduct of the affair. Bud Bagsak largely ended Moro resistance.

See also Bud Daju, Battle of; Moros; Pershing, John Joseph.
References and Further Readings
Linn, Brian McAllister. *Guardians of Empire: The U.S. Army and the Pacific, 1902–1940.* Chapel Hill: University of North Carolina Press, 1997.
Smythe, Donald. "Pershing and the Mount Bagsak Campaign of 1913." *Philippine Studies,* no. 12, 1964.
———. *Guerrilla Warrior: The Early Life of John J. Pershing.* New York: Charles Scribner's Sons, 1973.
Vandiver, Frank E. *Black Jack: The Life and Times of John J. Pershing.* 2 vols. College Station: Texas A&M University Press, 1977.

Bud Daju (Philippines), Battle of (5–7 March 1904)

The Battle of Bud Daju in 1904 stands out as one of the bloodiest clashes in the U.S. war against the Moro tribesmen of the Philippines. The Moros were concentrated in parts of Mindanao and the Sulu Archipelago, a region that U.S. authorities designated as Moro Province.

In August 1903, Brig. Gen. Leonard Wood had been appointed to command Moro Province. Unlike his predecessors, who believed that only the Moro bands that were troublesome should be punished, Wood took the position that all Moros needed a firm hand. His large November 1903 expedition around Lake Lanao, unwisely conducted during the monsoon season, proved an utter failure and revealed his lack of understanding of both the region and its inhabitants.

The Moros on the island of Jolo in the Sulu Archipelago avoided paying taxes imposed by the U.S. colonial authorities and took refuge on a high volcanic peak known as Bud Daju. Determined to chastise the Moros, Wood sent some 800 troops, augmented by the Philippine Constabulary, to break up the Moro concentration on Bud Daju.

On 3 March 1904, Col. Joseph Duncan, commanding the troops, reached the town of Jolo at the foot of Bud Daju. Above him, the Moros were on the summit, positioned behind their rock forts called *cottas.* Dividing his command into four columns, Duncan launched an attack against the Moro stronghold. Supported by artillery, the troops ascended the mountain, halting for the night halfway to the summit. That night, the troops listened to Moro chants and the pounding of drums. Occasionally, Moro snipers fired on the troops when a target presented itself.

In the morning, the advance resumed, again under cover of artillery fire that was ineffectually answered by the Moro's own antiquated cannons. On 7 March, the final assault on the summit culminated in a bloody, daylong battle that saw Moro defenders cut down by machine-gun fire. Hundreds were killed. Duncan's losses amounted to 21 killed and 73 wounded.

In the battle's wake, Wood was severely criticized for his harsh policy toward the Moros, just as John Pershing would be a decade later. Critics claimed the fight was a massacre, with women and children killed; defenders pointed out that some Moro women were dressed as warriors and that others used children as shields. Wood's policy, however, was fully supported by President Theodore Roosevelt and Secretary of War William Howard Taft, among others. The criticism did little to derail Wood's military career, as soon thereafter he was placed in overall command of the Philippine Division.

See also Bliss, Tasker Howard; Moros; Pershing, John Joseph; Wood, Leonard.

References and Further Readings

Bacevich, A. J. *Diplomat in Khaki: Major General Frank Ross McCoy and American Foreign Policy, 1898–1949.* Lawrence: University Press of Kansas, 1989.

Linn, Brian McAllister. *The U.S. Army and Counterinsurgency in the Philippine War, 1899–1902.* Chapel Hill: University of North Carolina Press, 1989.

———. *Guardians of Empire: The U.S. Army and the Pacific, 1902–1940.* Chapel Hill: University of North Carolina Press, 1997.

Smythe, Donald. *Guerrilla Warrior: The Early Life of John J. Pershing.* New York: Charles Scribner's Sons, 1973.

Vandiver, Frank E. *Black Jack: The Life and Times of John J. Pershing.* 2 vols. College Station: Texas A&M University Press, 1977.

Bullard, Robert E. Lee (1861–1947)

One of a handful of army officers who made a significant contribution to the pacification of the Moros of Mindanao and Sulu, Robert E. Lee Bullard was born in Alabama the year the Civil War began. He first followed a career as an educator and then entered the U.S. Military Academy in 1877. After graduating from West Point in 1881, Bullard served in the Southwest during the Apache Campaigns. In May 1898, he was promoted to major in the Alabama Volunteer Infantry, and he became a colonel in August. Transferred to the Philippines in 1899, he commanded the Thirty-ninth U.S. Volunteers, which soon became known as "Bullard's Indians" because he employed Apache-style tactics in combating the Filipino guerrillas.

In 1902, Bullard was sent to negotiate a peace arrangement with the Lanao Moros in southern Mindanao. Successful in this endeavor, he then employed Moro laborers to construct a road at Lake Lanao, making it the only road around this large body of water. He completed this difficult task in 10 months. Perhaps even more significant, Bullard gained the confidence and respect of many Moros, not only because he treated them as individuals but also because he expressed a serious interest in their language and customs. Previously, most Moros had known Americans only as adversaries. This confidence placed Bullard in good stead when a cholera epidemic struck the Lanao area and he was able to persuade the Moros that the Americans were not responsible.

Appointed head of the Lanao District in 1903 by General Wood, Bullard reluctantly led and participated in several expeditions against bands of Moros who steadfastly refused to accept the U.S. presence in the area. Poor health compelled Bullard to resign his post and return to the United States in 1904.

During World War I, Bullard served in France, and he eventually rose to the rank of lieutenant general before retiring from the army in 1925.

See also Moros; Pershing, John Joseph; Wood, Leonard.

References and Further Readings

Gates, John Morgan. *Schoolbooks and Krags: The United States Army in the Philippines, 1898–1902.* Contributions in Military History no. 3. Westport, CT: Greenwood Press, 1973.

Linn, Brian McAllister. *Guardians of Empire: The U.S. Army and the Pacific, 1902–1940.* Chapel Hill: University of North Carolina Press, 1997.

Wolff, Leon. *Little Brown Brother: America's Forgotten Bid for Empire Which Cost 250,000 Lives.* New York: Kraus Reprint, 1970.

Bundy, Omar (1861–1940)

Born in Newcastle, Indiana, Omar Bundy graduated from West Point in 1883. During his early army career, he saw action against the

Apaches in the Southwest. By the start of the Spanish-American War, he had been promoted to captain in the Sixth Infantry. Bundy distinguished himself at El Caney and in the siege of Santiago, for which he received the brevet rank of major.

In 1899, Bundy was sent to the Philippines, where he remained until 1902, serving both in the field and on staff assignments. Following a three-year tour of duty in the United States, he returned to the Philippines to see action against the troublesome Moros. In the Battle of Bud Daju, he led one of four attacking columns composed of the Sixth Infantry, Fourth Cavalry, and a contingent of friendly Moro scouts.

Bundy returned to the United States in 1907. During World War I, he served in France, and he was promoted to major general in 1921. He returned to the Philippines to command the Philippine Division from 1921 to 1924.

See also Bud Daju, Battle of; El Caney, Battle of; Moros; Santiago, Campaign and Siege of.

References and Further Readings

Linn, Brian McAllister. *Guardians of Empire: The U.S. Army and the Pacific, 1902–1940.* Chapel Hill: University of North Carolina Press, 1997.

Smythe, Donald. *Guerrilla Warrior: The Early Life of John J. Pershing.* New York: Charles Scribner's Sons, 1973.

Cadarso, Luis (1844–1898)

A gallant Spanish naval officer, Luis Cadarso was captain of the *Reina Cristina,* one of the ships in the Spanish Squadron in the Philippines. When his ship was torn apart by fire from Commodore George Dewey's squadron during the Battle of Manila Bay, Cadarso died while trying to save members of his crew.

See also Manila Bay, Battle of.

References and Further Readings

Dewey, George. *Autobiography of George Dewey, Admiral of the Navy.* Annapolis, MD: Naval Institute Press, 1987.

Nofi, Albert A. *The Spanish-American War, 1898.* Conshohocken, PA: Combined Books, 1998.

Russell, Henry B. *The Story of Two Wars.* Hartford, CT: Hartford Publishing Company, 1899.

Cailles, Juan (ca. 1868–?)

Juan Cailles was one of Filipino Nationalist leader Emilio Aguinaldo's most loyal and devoted commanders. Part French and part Hindustani, he was seemingly a born adventurer; slim and handsome, Cailles was described by historian Leon Wolff as "a Hollywood Star born decades too soon."

During the U.S.-Filipino investiture of Manila in the summer of 1898, Cailles, then a lieutenant colonel, served as second in command to Gen. Mariano Noriel. Although opposed to the growing U.S. presence in the Philippines, Cailles's loyalty to Aguinaldo caused him to accede to Washington's strategy for capturing Manila and wresting control of the archipelago from Spain.

With the defeat of Spain and the departure of the hated Spanish troops, Cailles, who had been promoted to general, remained a champion of Filipino independence. Like those of his chief, Aguinaldo, Cailles's efforts were now directed toward defeating the interlopers from the United States. He vigorously opposed the spread of the new

Filipino Federal Party, created in late 1900 with the objective of pacifying the Philippines.

Following the capture of Aguinaldo in March 1901, Cailles and other Nationalist leaders, perceiving that further struggle was futile, eventually surrendered.

See also Aguinaldo y Famy, Emilio; Luzon Campaigns; Manila Bay, Battle of.

References and Further Readings

Gates, John Morgan. *Schoolbooks and Krags: The United States Army in the Philippines, 1898–1902.* Contributions in Military History no. 3. Westport, CT: Greenwood Press, 1973.

Linn, Brian McAllister. *The Philippine War, 1899–1902.* Lawrence: University Press of Kansas, 2000.

Wolff, Leon. *Little Brown Brother: America's Forgotten Bid for Empire Which Cost 250,000 Lives.* New York: Kraus Reprint, 1970.

Cámara y Libermoore (Livermore), Manuel de la (1836–1920)

A veteran Spanish naval officer, Manuel de la Cámara y Libermoore had served as head of the Spanish naval commission and the naval general staff at Havana. He was later assigned to command the Spanish home fleet based at Cádiz. He was serving in this capacity at the outset of the Spanish-American War.

Following Commodore George Dewey's victory at Manila Bay on 1 May 1898, the Spanish minister of marine, Ramón Auñón y Villalón, ordered Cámara and a fleet of 11 vessels, including 2 transports carrying some 4,000 troops, to sail for the Philippines.

Cámara's destination was the island of Mindanao, some 700 miles south of Manila. Auñon's instructions were intentionally vague, allowing Cámara wide discretion in determining a course of action. Depending on the situation in the archipelago upon his arrival, Cámara could choose to operate either in the Mindanao region or around Manila. He was expected to exercise caution, however, in exposing his fleet to unnecessary damage by the U.S. squadron.

On 16 June 1898, Cámara sailed from Cádiz, anticipating a mid-August arrival in the Philippines. The war situation, however, soon changed the picture for both Spain and Cámara. Following the great U.S. victory over Admiral Cervera's Spanish fleet outside Santiago de Cuba on 3 July 1898, Minister Auñón called Cámara back to Spain to defend the homeland against an expected U.S. attack on its coastal cities.

See also Auñón y Villalón, Ramón; Naval Strategy, Spanish; Spain.

References and Further Readings

Chadwick, Rear Adm. French Ensor. *Relations of the United States and Spain: The Spanish American War.* 2 vols. New York: Charles Scribner's Sons, 1911 (reprinted in 1968).

Trask, David F. *The War with Spain in 1898.* Lincoln: University of Nebraska Press, 1996.

Cambon, Jules Martin (1845–1935)

The French ambassador to Washington during the Spanish-American War, Jules Martin Cambon played a key role in the treaty negotiations between Spain and the United States. After the fall of Santiago de Cuba, he was asked to mediate Spain's negotiations with the United States. Although a skilled diplomat, Cambon would find that his assignment was not easy. His responsibility was to protect the Spanish position, which grew weaker as the negotiations—primarily over the disposition of the Philippines—dragged on. The negotiations culminated in the Treaty of Paris, signed in December 1898. Despite his difficult assignment, Cambon served Spain's interests well and honorably.

Cambon was later the French ambassador to Madrid (1902–1907) and Berlin (1907–1914).

See also Protocol of Peace; Treaty of Paris.

References and Further Readings

Leech, Margaret. *In the Days of McKinley.* New York: Harper & Brothers, 1959.

Morgan, H. Wayne. *America's Road to Empire: The War with Spain and Overseas Expansion.* New York: John Wiley & Sons, 1965.

"Camp Fever"

See **Diseases**

Camps, Staging Areas, and Embarkation Points, U.S. Army

Mobilization of the U.S. Army during the Spanish-American War created a need for many new training camps and assembly points. Although the size of the regular army was increased substantially, volunteers comprised the largest segment of the incoming troops. These volunteer regiments first gathered where they were mustered in to federal service (later, there were also mustering-out camps). Once a unit had been mustered in, it moved on to training/staging (preparation) camps and embarkation points.

At the outset of hostilities with Spain, the War Department designated several points along the Gulf of Mexico and the Atlantic coast as staging areas and ports of embarkation. Tampa, Florida, Mobile, Alabama, New Orleans, Louisiana, Charleston, South Carolina, Savannah, Georgia, and Newport News, Virginia, were among the original sites selected for concentrating Caribbean expeditionary forces. In addition, San Antonio, Texas, became the assembly and training site for the famous Rough Riders volunteer cavalry regiment, which later moved to Tampa to join Gen. William Shafter's Fifth Corps.

Tampa was by far the most active camp. From there, the Fifth Corps, composed primarily of regular army units, assembled and departed for Cuba. Lakeland, Florida, was also used for a short time as a staging area to help relieve crowding at Tampa. Troops bound for Puerto Rico later sailed from Newport News, Virginia, Charleston, South Carolina, and Jacksonville, Florida. Philippine units mobilized at the Presidio in San Francisco.

It soon became apparent that the appointed staging areas were simply unable to handle the huge influx of volunteers together with an expanded regular army. The War Department, acting upon the recommendation of General of the Army Nelson A. Miles, created Camp Thomas, Georgia, and Camp Alger, Virginia. Miles believed that to handle the huge volume of men, it was first necessary to assemble the volunteer regiments in the new camps, where they could undergo training and be organized into brigades and divisions before being sent to staging areas for eventual transport to the war zone.

In general, the camps did not provide a clean and healthful environment. It soon became clear that the army's medical and supply systems could not meet the needs of a greatly expanded army. As the war progressed, deteriorating conditions necessitated a transfer to new locations, where some improvements were made.

The following list provides a broad survey of sites used during the Spanish-American War and its immediate aftermath.

Camp Alger, Virginia: Created in early May 1898 and located just south of Washington, DC, the camp was named for then Secretary of War Russell A. Alger. The camp became home to the army's Second Corps and by August contained some 25,000 troops. There, as at other sites, health and sanitary conditions were awful; disease was prevalent. To make matters worse, the troops were poorly trained and equipped. Because of camp conditions and other problems in the army's system, Alger's name came to be synonymous with bureaucratic scandals and bungling. Eventually, troops were

transferred to the newly established Camp George Gordon Meade, where conditions were markedly improved.

Camp Columbia, Cuba: Camp Columbia was erected near Havana to house U.S. Army regular troops who served as an occupational force in Cuba.

Camp Cuba Libre, Florida: Camp Cuba Libre was created near Jacksonville, Florida, to accommodate the overflow of troops assembling at Tampa. Gen. Fitzhugh Lee, of Civil War fame, organized the Seventh Corps there. Although conditions were bad at Camp Cuba Libre, they were better than those at Camps Alger and Thomas, thanks to Lee's efforts to keep the camp well-drained and serviced with proper plumbing.

U.S. soldiers at Port Tampa, Florida, embarkation area, 1898.

Camp George Dewey, Philippines: Camp George Dewey, located approximately 3 miles from Manila, was named for Commodore Dewey, the hero of Manila Bay. It was created in July 1898 by Brig. Gen. Thomas Anderson, who needed a closer base of operations from which to launch his attack on Manila.

Camp George Gordon Meade: Located near Middletown, Pennsylvania, Camp George Gordon Meade was created in August 1898 and named for Civil War hero General Meade. Camp Meade was selected as an alternate site, with new buildings and improved sanitary systems.

Camp George H. Thomas: Located at Chickamauga, Georgia, on the site of the famous Civil War battle and named for General Thomas, the Union hero and "Rock of Chickamauga," Camp Thomas was the largest of the army's new camps. By early summer 1898, it housed nearly 60,000 troops of the First, Third, and Sixth Corps (although the Sixth Corps was never actually created).

A shortage of staff officers to oversee and enforce camp discipline, together with a glaring lack of equipment with which to create proper latrines and a fresh water supply, soon led to polluted and unsanitary conditions. In addition, no effort was made to properly dispose of garbage. An outbreak of typhoid fever soon affected more men than the hospital could handle.

Eventually, the army addressed the problems at Camp Thomas and at other sites as well. Conditions improved after Gen. John Breckinridge took command of the site and installed a system of reforms. Despite this belated effort, health problems at the camp were so severe that a War Department investigation was held. As at Camp Alger, troops were transferred to more healthful locales. The First Corps moved first to Lexington, Kentucky, and later to Knoxville, Tennessee, while the Third Corps transferred to Anniston, Alabama.

Camp Wikoff: Located on Montauk Point, some 125 miles from New York City, Camp Wikoff was named in honor of Col. Charles Wikoff, who died in the fighting on San Juan Heights, Cuba.

The camp was created in August 1898 to serve as a rehabilitation and quarantine center for troops returning from Cuba, many of whom were ill with malaria and typhoid fever. In addition, several thousand cavalrymen and their horses, left behind in Florida when the Fifth Corps sailed for Cuba, were shipped to Camp Wikoff.

Initially, conditions at the camp were insufficient to care for ill and combat-weary soldiers. However, through tireless efforts by members of the War Department, conditions slowly improved.

Charleston, South Carolina: Charleston served as the port of embarkation for the elements of the Puerto Rican Expeditionary Force.

Fernandina, Florida: During the late summer of 1898, the Fourth Corps was transferred from Tampa to Fernandina in north Florida, then finally to Huntsville, Alabama.

Jacksonville, Florida: The city of Jacksonville served as a port of embarkation for elements of the Puerto Rican Expeditionary Force and the Seventh Corps that later occupied Havana.

Mobile, Alabama, and New Orleans, Louisiana: Although initially designated as points of concentration, neither Mobile nor New Orleans played a significant role in the army's mobilization plans.

Newport News, Virginia: Newport News served as port of embarkation for elements of the Puerto Rican Expeditionary Force.

San Francisco, California (the Presidio): The Presidio served as a point of assembly and embarkation for the (Eighth Corps) Philippine Expeditionary Force and the Hawaiian Occupation Force.

Savannah, Georgia: Like Mobile and New Orleans, Savannah did not play a significant role in the army's mobilization plans.

Tampa, Florida: Tampa was established as a point of concentration and embarkation for both the Fourth Corps and the Fifth Corps. Elements of the former later served as an occupation force in Puerto Rico and Cuba. The Fifth Corps carried out the Cuban land campaign.

Some units were also quartered for a time at Camp Shipp, Alabama, and Camp Conrad, Georgia.

See also Alger, Russell Alexander; Army, U.S.; Cuban Campaign; Diseases; Philippine Expeditionary Force; Puerto Rican Campaign; Rough Riders.

References and Further Readings

Cosmas, Graham. *An Army for Empire: The United States Army in the Spanish-American War.* College Station: Texas A&M University Press, 1998.

Hard, Curtis V. *Banners in the Air: The Eighth Ohio Volunteers and the Spanish-American War.* Edited by Robert H. Ferrell. Kent, OH: Kent State University Press, 1988.

Greguras, Fred. "Spanish-American War Camps, 1898–99 Period." *Journal of America's Military Past,* vol. 26, no. 3, winter 2000.

Leech, Margaret. *In the Days of McKinley.* New York: Harper & Brothers, 1959.

Nofi, Albert A. *The Spanish-American War, 1898.* Conshohocken, PA: Combined Books, 1998.

Walker, Dale L. *The Boys of '98: Theodore Roosevelt and the Rough Riders.* New York: Forge Books, 1998.

Canary Islands

The Canary Islands are a group of seven islands in the Atlantic Ocean, west of Morocco and southwest of Spain. Ideally situated to serve as a base for attacking Spain, any defensive strategy for the Iberian Peninsula had to take these islands into account. The United States also recognized the value of the Canaries. Although the islands did not play an active role in the war, Spain could ill afford to ignore their potential as a base for its opponents.

See also Naval Strategy, Spanish; Naval Strategy, U.S.

References and Further Readings

Chadwick, Rear Adm. French Ensor. *Relations of the United States and Spain: The Spanish American War.* 2 vols. New York: Charles Scribner's Sons, 1911 (reprinted in 1968).

Feuer, A. B. *The Spanish-American War at Sea.* Westport, CT: Greenwood Press, 1995.

Trask, David F. *The War with Spain in 1898.* Lincoln: University of Nebraska Press, 1996.

Cannon, Joseph Gurney (1836–1926)

Born in North Carolina, Joseph Gurney Cannon entered politics at an early age, serving as an Illinois congressman for more than four decades. Called "Uncle Joe" by his associates, he was chairman of the powerful House Appropriations Committee during the Spanish-American War. In reference to President William McKinley's continuous efforts to stay abreast of public opinion as a means of gauging the people's reaction to the Cuban crisis and the Spanish-American War, Cannon once remarked that McKinley was so close to the ground that "his ear is full of grasshoppers."

The events of early 1898 pointed the United States increasingly toward war with Spain. In the wake of the famous letter defaming McKinley that was authored by the Spanish ambassador to the United States, Enrique Dupuy de Lôme, and the destruction of the battleship *Maine,* President McKinley urged Cannon and his colleagues to provide the financial resources needed to prosecute a war with Spain. Cannon subsequently introduced legislation that eventually became the famed "Fifty Million Dollar" bill.

See also Dupuy de Lôme, Enrique; Fifty Million Dollar Bill; McKinley, William, Jr.

References and Further Readings

Gould, Lewis L. *The Spanish-American War and President McKinley.* Lawrence: University of Kansas Press, 1982.

Leech, Margaret. *In the Days of McKinley.* New York: Harper & Brothers, 1959.

Cánovas del Castillo, Antonio (1828–1897)

A scholarly man of great prestige in Spain and a strong monarchist, Antonio Cánovas del Castillo was twice head of the Spanish government (1874–1881 and 1883–1885). Although he was instrumental in putting down the Cuban Revolution of 1878, he came to believe in Cuban autonomy, seeing it as the only real solution to a thorny problem. His assassination by Miguel Angiolillo in 1897 paved the way for Práxedes Mateo Sagasta—the man who headed the Spanish government during the Spanish-American War—to become prime minister.

> **See also** Cuban Revolution; Sagasta, Práxedes Mateo.
> **References and Further Readings**
> Ferrara, Orestes. *The Last Spanish War: Revelations in Diplomacy.* Translated from the Spanish by William E. Shea. New York: Paisley Press, 1937.
> Leech, Margaret. *In the Days of McKinley.* New York: Harper & Brothers, 1959.
> Musicant, Ivan. *Empire by Default: The Spanish-American War and the Dawn of the American Century.* New York: Henry Holt and Company, 1998.

Cape Tunas (Cuba)

Cape Tunas is a port city on Cuba's southern coast, some 70 miles east of Cienfuegos. Originally, Cape Tunas was slated to be the landing site for Gen. William Shafter's Fifth Corps. Plans were changed, however, when it was learned that the Spanish naval squadron had departed from the Cape Verde Islands, bound for Cuba or perhaps the East Coast of the United States. Given this uncertainty, the Cape Tunas plan was aborted.

> **See also** Cervera y Topete, Pascual; Shafter, William Rufus.
> **References and Further Readings**
> Cosmas, Graham. *An Army for Empire: The United States Army in the Spanish-American War.* College Station: Texas A&M University Press, 1998.
> Trask, David F. *The War with Spain in 1898.* Lincoln: University of Nebraska Press, 1996.

Cape Verde Islands

A 1,560-square-mile archipelago consisting of 10 islands and located 300 miles west of Senegal, Africa, the Cape Verde Islands belonged to Portugal in 1898. Strategically located, the islands served as a point of departure for Spanish admiral Pascual Cervera's fleet during the Spanish-American War. Just as Commodore George

Dewey's Asiatic Squadron was forced to leave Hong Kong because of British neutrality, so, too, was Cervera forced to leave the Cape Verde Islands when Portugal declared its neutrality on 29 April 1898.

Some historians have argued that the Spanish cause would have been better served had Cervera remained at sea, thereby posing a threat to both the eastern U.S. seaboard and a U.S. invasion of Cuba. Instead, he slipped into Santiago harbor, where he soon found his fleet trapped and subsequently destroyed when it attempted to break out.

> **See also** Cervera y Topete, Pascual; Santiago de Cuba, Naval Battle of.
> **References and Further Readings**
> Chadwick, Rear Adm. French Ensor. *Relations of the United States and Spain: The Spanish American War.* 2 vols. New York: Charles Scribner's Sons, 1911 (reprinted in 1968).
> Trask, David F. *The War with Spain in 1898.* Lincoln: University of Nebraska Press, 1996.

Capitulation Agreement, Santiago de Cuba (16 July 1898)

By 14 July 1898, the Spanish garrison at Santiago appeared ready to surrender. Gen. William R. Shafter, commanding the U.S. Fifth Corps in Cuba, was advised by Gen. José Toral, military governor of Santiago (he had assumed personal command after Gen. Arsenio Linares was wounded) that his garrison was ready to capitulate. He had received the blessing of Capt. Gen. Ramón Blanco, governor-general of Cuba, but still needed permission from Madrid. In the meantime, Toral suggested they begin to work out the details of the surrender.

The subsequent agreement allowed Spain to surrender with full military honors. Spanish officers would be permitted to keep their side arms, and the rank-and-file troops would be permitted to keep their personal possessions. For their part, the Spanish agreed to surrender the garrisons at Santiago, Guantánamo, and several other locations; to aid in clearing Santiago harbor of mines, as well as other navigational obstructions; and to provide an inventory of their military resources. The United States agreed to absorb the expense of returning Spanish troops to Spain.

The agreement seems to have been drafted in a climate of misunderstanding. Toral claimed he needed Madrid's permission, but U.S. officials viewed the agreed-upon terms as binding. When it became clear that Toral wanted Madrid's permission before signing, there was concern that Spain was simply stalling; the agree-

ment was threatening to dissolve. Eventually, Toral and the Spanish signatories—Gen. Federico Escario, Lt. Col. Ventura Fontán, and Robert Mason, English consul in Santiago—agreed to sign regardless of the repercussions from home.

U.S. troops cheer at learning of Santiago's fall, 1898.

U.S. signers included Gen. Joseph Wheeler, Gen. Henry Ware Lawton, and General Shafter's personal representative, Lt. John D. Miley. In an interservice rebuff, the U.S. Navy was not invited to participate in the surrender negotiations or sign the capitulation agreement. Adm. William T. Sampson was sent a copy of the terms for his information but justifiably felt slighted. General Shafter subsequently apologized.

See also Sampson, William Thomas; Santiago, Campaign and Siege of; Shafter, William Rufus; Toral y Veláquez, José.

References and Further Readings

Chadwick, Rear Adm. French Ensor. *Relations of the United States and Spain: The Spanish American War.* 2 vols. New York: Charles Scribner's Sons, 1911 (reprinted in 1968).

Musicant, Ivan. *Empire by Default: The Spanish-American War and the Dawn of the American Century.* New York: Henry Holt and Company, 1998.

Watterson, Henry. *History of the Spanish-American War, Embracing a Complete Review of Our Relations with Spain.* Hartford, CT: American Publishing, 1898.

Cárdenas (Cuba)

Cárdenas is a port city on Cuba's north coast, east of Havana. The harbor at Cárdenas lacked sufficient depth for all but fishing vessels and therefore could not accommodate blockade runners. Nevertheless, the city was included in Adm. William Sampson's plans to prevent supplies and reinforcements from reaching the Spanish. The city's close proximity to Florida enabled ships with low fuel capacities, of which Sampson had a number, to quickly and easily return for refueling.

Cárdenas was also the scene of naval clashes in April and May 1898. On 8 May 1898, the torpedo boat *Winslow,* while enticing a Spanish gunboat out to do battle in deeper water, suffered heavy damage when fired on by a Spanish battery not known to be in the area. Unable to move under its own power, the *Winslow* had to be towed out of harm's way.

See also Naval Blockade of Cuba.
References and Further Readings
Bernadou, Lt. J. B. "The 'Winslow' at Cardenas (May 11, 1898)." *Century Magazine,* March 1899.
Chadwick, Rear Adm. French Ensor. *Relations of the United States and Spain: The Spanish American War.* 2 vols. New York: Charles Scribner's Sons, 1911 (reprinted in 1968).
Trask, David F. *The War with Spain in 1898.* Lincoln: University of Nebraska Press, 1996.

Carnegie, Andrew (1835–1919)

A leading American industrialist of the nineteenth and early twentieth centuries, Andrew Carnegie was born in Scotland. After serving in the transportation section of the U.S. War Department during the Civil War, Carnegie became an eminently successful industrialist and a noted philanthropist. Along with Mark Twain, Samuel Gompers, and other key figures of the day, Carnegie was adamantly opposed to the annexation of the Philippines and a staunch supporter of the Anti-Imperialist League.

See also Anti-Imperialist League; Philippine Islands, Acquisition of, by the United States.
References and Further Readings
Karnow, Stanley. *In Our Image: America's Empire in the Philippines.* New York: Random House, 1989.
Leech, Margaret. *In the Days of McKinley.* New York: Harper & Brothers, 1959.

Casualties

The Spanish-American War was the briefest war in U.S. history, and combat casualties were correspondingly low. Army casualties amounted to 281 killed and 1,577 wounded; navy losses totaled 16 killed and 68 wounded. However, 2,500 died from various diseases

Field hospital on the night after the charge up San Juan Hill (watercolor by William Glackens, 1898).

(more than eight times the number killed in combat), including typhoid, malaria, and yellow fever. Of the deaths from disease, many occurred in camps in the United States, such as Camp Thomas, in Chickamauga, Georgia, where typhoid, for example, ran rampant.

Spanish losses are more difficult to determine. Army casualties reportedly numbered around 200 killed and 400 wounded, and naval losses amounted to 500 to 600 killed and 300 to 400 wounded. The higher naval losses may be attributed to the disastrous naval defeats inflicted on the Spanish at Manila Bay and Santiago de Cuba.

The number of Cuban and Filipino casualties cannot be estimated.

See also Cuban Campaign; Diseases; El Caney, Battle of; Guantánamo, Battle of; Las Guásimas, Battle of; Luzon Campaigns; Manila Bay, Battle of; Manila, First Battle of; Manila, Second Battle of; Puerto Rican Campaign; Samar Campaigns; Santiago, Campaign and Seige of; Santiago de Cuba, Naval Battle of; Visayan Campaigns.

References and Further Readings

Cosmas, Graham. *An Army for Empire: The United States Army in the Spanish-American War.* College Station: Texas A&M University Press, 1998.

Musicant, Ivan. *Empire by Default: The Spanish-American War and the Dawn of the American Century.* New York: Henry Holt and Company, 1998.

Cavite (Philippine Islands)

A province and walled city on an inlet approximately 10 miles from Manila proper, Cavite had been fortified by the Spanish who located their naval arsenal there. Indeed, Cavite was the focal point of Spanish naval operations in the area. Adm. Patricio Montojo defended Manila at Cavite, rather than at Corregidor. The consensus of his ship captains was that the deeper waters around Corregidor would result in significantly more casualties if any ships had to be abandoned.

During the Battle of Manila Bay, the U.S. gunboat *Petrel* fired on Spanish defenses at Cavite, inducing what was perceived to be a surrender. The Spanish, however, regarded the move as only a temporary cease-fire. Finally, after a U.S. demand for surrender of the city, the Spanish withdrew, and Cavite was occupied by a U.S. naval and marine landing party.

See also Manila Bay, Battle of; Montojo y Pasarón, Patricio.

References and Further Readings

Fiske, Lt. B. A., U.S.N. "Why We Won at Manila." *Century Magazine,* November 1898.

Spector, Ronald. *Admiral of the New Empire: The Life and Career of George Dewey.* Greenville: University of South Carolina Press, 1988.

Trask, David F. *The War with Spain in 1898.* Lincoln: University of Nebraska Press, 1996.

Censorship

To avoid disseminating information that might compromise its position, the United States censored news stories emanating from Florida during the first two months of the Spanish-American War. On 25 April 1898, the Navy Department took control of the cable line that ran from Santiago de Cuba east to Haiti and then north to New York. Another submarine cable ran from Havana to Key West, Florida. President William McKinley directed the U.S. Army Signal Corps to install a censor in each of New York's six cable offices.

News stories that mentioned the movement of troops or naval vessels were censored. Cable messages to the West Indies or Spanish possessions were forbidden because they might jeopardize U.S. operations by revealing either plans or knowledge of enemy movements and suspected intentions.

At Tampa, Florida, where the Fifth Corps was assembling, Gen. William Shafter had news stories censored after the much publicized *Gussie* affair in May 1898. The *Gussie* was an ancient side-wheel steamboat that the U.S. Army used to try to run arms and munitions to Cuban rebels. The effort failed but received wide press coverage and proved an embarrassment to the army. As a result, no further stories were allowed out of Tampa without the censor's approval.

Not surprisingly, the press was indignant over the censorship, although the restriction was not as severe as some journalists claimed. Only stories that might affect U.S. military operations were censored. Other stories—for example, those about the naval blockade of Cuba—were not censored. After Shafter's Fifth Corps landed in Cuba, continued censorship was no longer needed.

See also Dorst, Joseph Haddox; Journalism.

References and Further Readings

Brown, Charles H. *The Correspondents' War: Journalists in the Spanish-American War.* New York: Charles Scribner's Sons, 1967.

Cervera y Topete, Pascual (1839–1909)

A highly respected Spanish naval officer who eventually rose to command the Spanish fleet in the Caribbean, Pascual Cervera y Topete was born in Medina-Sidonia in the south of Spain. He was educated

The destruction of Admiral Cervera's Spanish fleet off Santiago de Cuba, 1898 (lithograph).

at the Spanish naval academy in San Fernando from 1848 to 1851 and later served in Morocco, the Philippines, and Cuba.

In 1892, he was named minister of marine in the Sagasta administration and was appointed to command the Spanish fleet in 1897. His friend Segismundo Bermejo y Merelo replaced him as minister of marine.

In developing a strategy for war with the United States, which seemed increasingly likely, Bermejo wanted the Spanish fleet to blockade the eastern seaboard of the United States, despite the fleet's lack of resources to undertake such an assignment. He also believed that Spain would be supported by other European powers in a war with the United States. Cervera, for his part, was not at all sanguine about Spain's chances in such a war and sought to persuade Bermejo to adopt a more conservative strategy.

Despite his position on the issue, Cervera was ordered to sail from Cádiz to the Cape Verde Islands on 7 April 1898; the Spanish fleet was located there when war with the United States was declared that month. However, owing to the Cape Verde Islands' neutral stance in the war, Cervera was compelled to depart on 29 April.

Ordered to proceed to Puerto Rico, he first divided the fleet, leaving a portion to protect the Spanish coast and the Canary

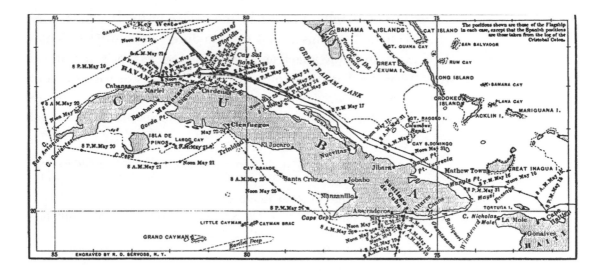

Islands. He then headed toward the Caribbean with the rest of the fleet. When news of Cervera's movement became known, the U.S. Atlantic fleet quickly went in search of its new enemy.

On 12 May, Cervera learned that the U.S. fleet was at San Juan, Puerto Rico, and that the Cuban blockade now barred him from Havana. In need of coal for his fuel bunkers but unable to obtain it from Cuba, he acquired a small amount of coal at Curaçao in the Netherland Antilles. His fleet was then able to slip into the harbor of Santiago de Cuba, which had not been covered by the blockade.

In the meantime, Bermejo, in view of Commodore George Dewey's stunning victory at Manila Bay, authorized Cervera to return to Spain. However, faced with insufficient coal for a return journey, Cervera had little choice but to remain where he was for the time being. The matter proved to be academic because Bermejo was replaced as minister of marine by Ramón Auñón Villalón, who countermanded Bermejo's last order and directed the fleet to remain in Santiago harbor. Villalón was concerned that the fleet's departure would destroy the will to fight of the Spanish soldiers in Cuba.

Cervera's presence in the harbor at Santiago de Cuba was soon discovered by the U.S. Navy, which wasted little time blockading the harbor entrance and bottling up the Spanish fleet. As the Cuban Campaign pressed on, Cervera became increasingly concerned for the safety of his ships. If the Americans were able to place heavy guns on the heights around the harbor, havoc would be wrought on his fleet. In view of this, Cervera sought and finally received authorization to leave the harbor and, it was hoped, escape from the U.S. ships waiting just beyond.

On 3 July 1898, the Spanish fleet sortied from Santiago harbor

U.S. naval operations against the Spanish fleet in the West Indies, 1898.
Source: *W. A. M. Goode,* With Sampson Through the War *(New York: Doubleday & McClure Co., 1899), p. 80.*

and was subsequently attacked and destroyed by the U.S. fleet under Adm. William T. Sampson and Commodore Winfield Scott Schley. Cervera survived the attack and, after a period as a prisoner of war, was returned to Spain in September. In Spain, he was tried by a military court but cleared of any wrongdoing. He was promoted to vice admiral in 1901 and named chief of staff of the Spanish Navy the following year.

See also Auñón Villalón, Ramón; Navy, Spanish; Santiago de Cuba, Naval Battle of.

References and Further Readings

Cervera y Topete, Pascual. *The Spanish-American War.* Washington, DC: U.S. Government Printing Office, 1899.

Trask, David F. *The War with Spain in 1898.* Lincoln: University of Nebraska Press, 1996.

Céspedes, Carlos Manuel de (1819–1874)

Born in Bayamo, Cuba, Carlos Manuel de Céspedes was educated in Spain and later became an important figure in the Cuban revolutionary movement. In 1868, Céspedes led the initial revolt that set off the conflict known as the Ten Years' War. That conflict presaged the rebellion of 1895, which eventually led to the Spanish-American War.

See also Ten Years' War.

References and Further Readings

Quesada, Gonzalo de. *The War in Cuba: Being a Full Account of Her Great Struggle for Freedom.* Washington, DC: Liberty Publishing, 1896.

Chadwick, French Ensor (1844–1919)

Born in Morgantown, Virginia (now West Virginia), French Ensor Chadwick was recognized as an intellectual and a historian. He graduated from the U.S. Naval Academy in 1861 and after serving in the Civil War had extensive sea duty. He also made a careful study of European naval systems and prepared a paper on the subject that was considered a model of its kind. Because of his linguistic skills—he spoke French and Spanish fluently—Chadwick was appointed naval attaché in London. During the war with Spain, he commanded the battleship *New York* and later wrote a two-volume history of the war.

In 1898, Chadwick was named head of the naval Bureau of Equipment in Washington, where he worked closely with Assistant Secretary of the Navy Theodore Roosevelt, who came to value his expertise.

Following the loss of the battleship *Maine,* Chadwick was named to the board of inquiry that was charged with investigating the disaster. During the war with Spain, he was named chief of staff to Adm. William Sampson, who commanded the U.S. Navy's North Atlantic Squadron. He was thus intimately acquainted with naval movements and strategy, and his book on the Spanish-American War, published in 1911, is still highly regarded by historians of the period.

Chadwick was appointed president of the Naval War College in 1900 and later commanded the South Atlantic Squadron. He was promoted to rear admiral in 1906.

See also *Maine,* Inquiries into the Sinking of; Navy, U.S.; North Atlantic Squadron, U.S. Navy; Sampson, William Thomas.

References and Further Readings

Chadwick, Rear Adm. French Ensor. *Relations of the United States and Spain: The Spanish American War:* 2 vols. New York: Charles Scribner's Sons, 1911 (reprinted in 1968).

Coletta, Paolo E. *French Ensor Chadwick, Scholarly Warrior.* Lanham, MD: University Press of America, 1980.

Trask, David F. *The War with Spain in 1898.* Lincoln: University of Nebraska Press, 1996.

Chaffee, Adna Romanza (1842–1914)

Adna Romanza Chaffee, a distinguished commander who saw service in both Cuba and the Philippines, was born in Orwell, Ohio, in 1842. He enlisted in the army at the start of the Civil War and quickly rose to the rank of sergeant. In 1863, he received a commission in the cavalry. His service throughout the Civil War was notable. Evidently, he found a soldier's life to his liking because he remained in the army after the war and saw considerable service in the western Indian wars.

Chaffee was promoted to brigadier general of volunteers in May 1898 and major general in July of the same year. During the Cuban Campaign, he commanded a brigade in Gen. William R. Shafter's Fifth Corps and saw action at El Caney.

After the war, Chaffee served as chief of staff to the military governor of Cuba. In 1900, he commanded the U.S. relief expedition to China during the Boxer Rebellion. Promoted to lieutenant general in 1901, he was appointed military governor of the Philippines, where he inherited the difficult task of dealing with the troublesome

Gen. Adna Romanza Chaffee. A veteran of the Civil War and the Indian wars, he also served in Cuba and the Philippines and commanded the U.S. relief expedition to China during the Boxer Rebellion. During his career, he rose from private to lieutenant general.

Moros. He was named commander of the Department of the East in 1902 and army chief of staff in 1904. He retired in 1906.

An able soldier, Chaffee was also something of a martinet. He was the only chief of staff to enlist in the army and hold all ranks from private to lieutenant general. His major failing, especially as a senior commander, was his inability to work well with other branches of the military. For example, he was often at odds with the U.S. Marine detachment in the Philippines and in China during the Boxer Rebellion.

See also Baldwin, Frank Dwight; Boxer Rebellion; El Caney, Battle of; Moros; Pershing, John Joseph.

References and Further Readings

Cosmas, Graham. *An Army for Empire: The United States Army in the Spanish-American War.* College Station: Texas A&M University Press, 1998.

Linn, Brian McAllister. *Guardians of Empire: The U.S. Army and the Pacific, 1902–1940.* Chapel Hill: University of North Carolina Press, 1997.

Steinbach, Robert H. *A Long March: The Lives of Frank and Alice Baldwin.* Austin: University of Texas Press, 1989.

Chandler, William Eaton (1835–1917)

A lawyer and politician, William Eaton Chandler was born in Concord, New Hampshire. His political career was long and varied and included the distinction of holding office under three presidents: Abraham Lincoln, Andrew Johnson, and Chester A. Arthur. He first served as assistant secretary of the treasury (1865–1867) and later as secretary of the navy (1882–1885). As secretary of the navy, Chandler initiated the steel warship program, paving the way for the powerful, modern navy that was key to defeating the Spanish during the Spanish-American War.

From 1887 to 1901, he served as U.S. senator from New Hampshire. Chandler recommended Commodore John Howell to fill the command vacancy in the navy's Asiatic Squadron, while Theodore Roosevelt, then serving as assistant secretary of the navy, lobbied for Commodore George Dewey, who subsequently received the appointment.

Along with Henry Cabot Lodge, Joseph Benson Foraker, and Cushman Davis, Chandler was one of the Senate's war hawks, advocating military intervention in Cuba.

See also Dewey, George; Navy, U.S.; Roosevelt, Theodore.

References and Further Readings

Coletta, Paolo E. *A Survey of U.S. Naval Affairs, 1865–1917.* Lanham, MD: University Press of America, 1987.

Leech, Margaret. *In the Days of McKinley.* New York: Harper & Brothers, 1959.

Morgan, H. Wayne. *America's Road to Empire: The War with Spain and Overseas Expansion.* New York: John Wiley & Sons, 1965.

Chichester, Edward (1849–1906)

Edward Chichester commanded the British Squadron in the Philippines during the Spanish-American War. With 4 gunboats and 1 armored cruiser, Chichester's squadron was the strongest international force in the area, which included military contingents from Germany, Japan, and France. Since Britain was sympathetic to the U.S. position vis-à-vis Spain and the Philippines, Chichester's presence provided a nervous Adm. George Dewey with a welcome measure of reassurance. In the event of trouble, the British Squadron could be counted on for support, since it was in Britain's interest to keep the archipelago out of the hands of the other foreign powers hovering around the area, especially Germany.

See also Dewey, George; Manila Bay, Battle of; Spanish-American War, International Reaction to.

References and Further Readings

Bailey, Thomas A. "Dewey and the Germans at Manila Bay." *American Historical Review,* 45, October 1939.

Spector, Ronald. *Admiral of the New Empire: The Life and Career of George Dewey.* Greenville: University of South Carolina Press, 1988.

Trask, David F. *The War with Spain in 1898.* Lincoln: University of Nebraska Press, 1996.

China

See **Boxer Rebellion**

Christy, Howard Chandler (1873–1952)

An illustrator and portrait artist, Howard Chandler Christy was born in Ohio. He was working in New York as an illustrator when the war with Spain broke out. He accompanied the Second U.S. Regulars to Cuba on assignment for *Leslie's Magazine.* He witnessed the action at Las Guásimas and San Juan Heights, including the part played by the Rough Riders. His illustrations depicting the war in Cuba, which appeared in *Harper's Magazine, Scribner's Magazine,* and *Leslie's*

Magazine among others, brought the drama of war home to U.S. readers in a particularly vivid way.

After the war, Christy worked on the staff of several well-known periodicals and illustrated numerous books. As a prominent portrait artist, his subjects included Warren G. Harding, President and Mrs. Calvin Coolidge, Benito Mussolini, and Amelia Earhart.

> **See also** Artists and Illustrators; Las Guásimas, Battle of; San Juan Hill, Charge up.
>
> **References and Further Readings**
>
> Harrington, Peter, and Frederic A. Sharf. *"A Splendid Little War":
> The Spanish-American War, 1898—The Artists' Perspective.* London:
> Greenhill Books, 1998.
>
> King, William N. *The Story of the Spanish-American War and the
> Revolt in the Philippines.* New York: P. F. Collier, 1898.

Cienfuegos (Cuba), Cutting the Cable at (May 1898)

Located about 140 miles southeast of Havana on Cuba's southern coast, Cienfuegos possessed a fine harbor, as well as rail connections with Havana. Because of its excellent location, it figured in the navy's strategy for conducting a war with Spain.

The U.S. Navy's plan originally involved a blockade of Cuba and the seizure of Cienfuegos. Although the blockade was successful, the plan to capture Cienfuegos never became a reality. Nevertheless, the area was the scene of some brisk action early in the war. On 29 April 1898, 48 hours after the blockade of Cuba, the navies of

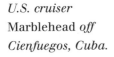

U.S. cruiser Marblehead *off Cienfuegos, Cuba.*

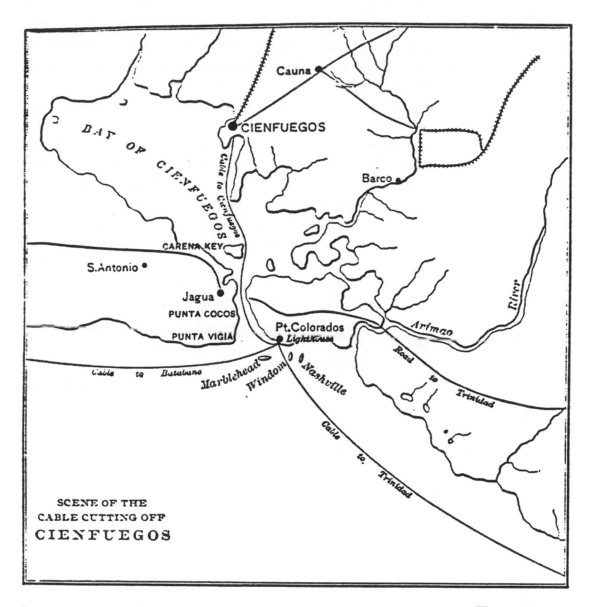

SCENE OF THE
CABLE CUTTING OFF
CIENFUEGOS

the two warring countries exchanged fire in a brief engagement near Cienfuegos.

Despite the overall effectiveness of the naval blockade, the Spanish Army was able to communicate with authorities in Madrid using the three underwater telegraph lines that connected Cuba with Madrid, via the West Indies. To complete its isolation of Spanish forces in Cuba, the U.S. Navy was directed to cut the underwater cables at Cienfuegos.

On 11 May 1898, the Fourth Division of the blockade force, under Comdr. B. H. McCalla, received instructions to sever the cables at Cienfuegos. McCalla's force was composed of the crusier *Marblehead,* the gunboat *Nashville,* the converted yacht *Eagle,* the revenue cutter *Windom,* and the collier *Saturn.*

The attack on the Spanish cables at Cienfuegos, Cuba, by the U.S. Navy.
Source: *Edgar Stanton Maclay,* A History of the United States Navy from 1775 to 1902 *(New York: D. Appleton and Company, 1902), III, p. 121.*

The boats approached Cienfuegos harbor via a 3-mile-long channel. A lighthouse was situated some 25 yards from the shore, but the cable house was only 20 or 30 feet from the water's edge. A line of rifle pits, hidden by tall grass and bushes, lay between the two.

Actual command of the cable-cutting expedition was assigned to Lt. Cameron McRae Winslow, with Lt. E. A. Anderson second in command. The expedition was composed of 16 men, including Winslow and Anderson as well as a blacksmith and a carpenter's mate. Half of the men were armed with rifles, half with revolvers.

The expedition was mounted in two launches from the *Marblehead* and *Nashville* and towed toward shore by steam cutters from the two mother vessels. Under strong covering fire from the *Marblehead* and *Nashville,* Winslow's men closed to within 100 feet of the shore, where the water was clear enough to reveal the cable.

Using grapnels (small anchorlike devices with one or more hooks), the men grabbed one cable and, with great effort, hauled it aboard the launch. The blacksmith then severed the line and removed a section from the cable. The operation was conducted in the face of heavy rifle fire from the trenches, despite supporting fire from the *Marblehead* and *Nashville* as well as that from Winslow's force.

The expedition eventually cut two of the cable lines, but the third remained intact and allowed Spanish forces to maintain contact with Madrid, via Jamaica, throughout the war.

Winslow's losses amounted to 2 killed and 7 wounded.

See also Communications; Naval Blockade of Cuba; Navy, U.S.
References and Further Readings
Feuer, A. B. *The Spanish-American War at Sea.* Westport, CT: Greenwood Press, 1995.
Trask, David F. *The War with Spain in 1898.* Lincoln: University of Nebraska Press, 1996.
Winslow, Cameron McRae. "Cable-cutting at Cienfuegos." *Century Magazine,* March 1899.

Cisneros, Evangelina (ca. 1880–?)

Of the many stories depicting the plight of Cubans under Spanish rule, perhaps none inflamed American public opinion against Spain as much as that of Evangelina Cisneros.

Seventeen-year-old Evangelina Cisneros was a beautiful young woman and the daughter of Cuban president Salvador Cisneros Betancourt, who had been banished to the Isle of Pines for his role in the Ten Years' War. Evangelina accompanied her father and reportedly was subjected to much mistreatment while on the isle. Later, she was sent to the nefarious Casa de Recojidas prison in Havana as punishment for her part in the attempted assassination of the military commandant at the Isle of Pines. It is more likely, however, that she was being punished for rejecting the commandant's advances.

Her situation was discovered by a pair of William Randolph Hearst's enterprising reporters, who sent a report to the paper's New York office. Sensing a grand story, Hearst campaigned to free Evangelina, calling on the women of the United States to cry out for her freedom. Roused by the indignant treatment of the young Cuban, more than 15,000 women signed a petition calling on the queen regent of Spain to intercede on Evangelina's behalf. Varina Howell Davis, wife of former Confederate president Jefferson Davis, also wrote personally to the queen and to Julia Ward Howe, composer of "Battle Hymn of the Republic," which had stirred an earlier generation, to compose a protest in support of the movement to free Evangelina.

Despite this outcry, Evangelina remained imprisoned. The governor-general of Cuba, the notorious Valeriano "Butcher" Weyler, declared that justice should be served and that she should stand trial for her part in the assassination attempt. However, in October 1897, Evangelina, aided by a young *New York Journal* reporter and two compatriots, escaped, providing a thrilling and happy finish to a fearful story.

The young reporter, Karl Decker, and two Cuban patriots sawed through the iron bars of the window in Evangelina's cell. Then, using a ladder to span the distance between the prison roof and the buildings on the other side of the street, they completed the escape. Evangelina was disguised as a young sailor, and she and her cohorts made their way to the waterfront, where they boarded a steamer for the United States.

Decker's story preceded their arrival, and when the ship finally docked, Evangelina was met by a throng of spectators who had come to see this Cuban heroine. Later, Evangelina was received by President William McKinley.

The following May, after the United States and Spain had declared war, Evangelina, in a fitting conclusion to her saga, married Carlos Carbonelle, a Cuban dentist and one of the three men who had helped her escape from the hated Casa de Recojidas.

See also Cuban Revolution; Hearst, William Randolph; Journalism.

References and Further Readings

Brown, Charles H. *The Correspondents' War: Journalists in the Spanish-American War.* New York: Charles Scribner's Sons, 1967.

Cisneros, Evangelina, and Karl Decker. *The Story of Evangelina Cisneros*. Richmond, VA: n.p., 1897.

Milton, Joyce. *The Yellow Kids: Foreign Correspondents in the Heyday of Yellow Journalism*. New York: Harper & Row, 1989.

Russell, Henry B. *The Story of Two Wars*. Hartford, CT: Hartford Publishing Company, 1899.

"Civilize 'em with a Krag"

"Civilize 'em with a Krag" is a line from an old army song that originated during the Philippine-American War. The phrase expressed the frustration and anger experienced by U.S. soldiers as they waged a costly guerrilla war with Emilio Aguinaldo's Filipino Nationalists and bandits known as *ladrones*. The "Krag" referred to the new Krag-Jörgensen rifle issued to regular army units during the Spanish-American War and the Philippine-American War.

> Damn, damn, damn, the Filipinos!
> Cut-throat khakiac *ladrones*!
> Underneath the starry flag,
> Civilize them with a Krag,
> And return us to our beloved home

See also Army, U.S.

References and Further Readings

Cosmas, Graham. *An Army for Empire: The United States Army in the Spanish-American War*. College Station: Texas A&M University Press, 1998.

Gates, John Morgan. *Schoolbooks and Krags: The United States Army in the Philippines, 1898–1902*. Contributions in Military History no. 3. Westport, CT: Greenwood Press, 1973.

Karnow, Stanley. *In Our Image: America's Empire in the Philippines*. New York: Random House, 1989.

Clark, Charles Edgar (1843–1922)

Born in Vermont, Charles Edgar Clark was captain of the battleship *Oregon* on its historic voyage around Cape Horn to join the U.S. fleet during the Spanish-American War. Departing from San Francisco on 12 March 1898, the *Oregon* completed its voyage in a record-setting 74 days, arriving in Florida on 24 May.

A bold sea captain, Clark had hoped to intercept the Spanish cruisers and draw them on in pursuit and then use his superior speed and weaponry to destroy them. However, Adm. Pascual Cervera's Spanish fleet had already reached the harbor at Santiago de Cuba undetected.

See also Cervera y Topete, Pascual; Navy, U.S.
References and Further Readings
Alden, John D. *The American Steel Navy.* Annapolis, MD: Naval
Institute Press, 1972.
Hagan, Kenneth J. *This People's Navy: The Making of American Sea
Power.* New York: Free Press, 1991.

Clayton-Bulwer Treaty (19 April 1850)

The Clayton-Bulwer Treaty stipulated that the United States and Great Britain exercise joint control over an east-west waterway (canal) through Nicaragua. Although the treaty had no direct bearing on the Spanish-American War, it is worth noting that the extraordinary voyage of the *Oregon* around Cape Horn to join the North Atlantic fleet underscored the need for an isthmian canal.

The (John Middleton) Clayton–(Sir Henry) Bulwer agreement was supplanted in 1901 by the (John) Hay–(Sir Julian) Pauncefote Treaty, which granted the United States exclusive right of ownership, maintenance, and control of the waterway that subsequently became the Panama Canal.

See also *Oregon.*
References and Further Readings
McCullough, David. *The Path between the Seas.* New York: Simon
and Schuster, 1977.
Miller, Nathan. *Theodore Roosevelt: A Life.* New York: William
Morrow, 1992.

Cleveland, (Stephen) Grover (1837–1908)

Born in New Jersey, Democrat Grover Cleveland served twice as president of the United States—from 1885 to 1889 and again from 1893 to 1897. His second term in office immediately preceded the Spanish-American War.

Although Cleveland sympathized with the plight of the Cubans, he maintained a neutral policy, despite mounting public support for U.S. involvement. Congress, too, was active, passing numerous resolutions in support of the Cuban cause, but Cleveland remained firm in his policy of neutrality.

As pressure and tensions mounted, the Cleveland administration presented a plan of pacification that, it was hoped, would temper public opinion against Spain. The proposal called for the United States to act as a mediator in bringing about Cuban autonomy. Spain, however, viewed the proposal as nothing more than an attempt by the Cleveland administration to mollify U.S. citizens. Having to deal with the voice of its own people, who were decidedly anti-American, Spain rejected the plan.

Cleveland ended his presidency still holding to a position of neutrality, though recognizing that military action might be necessary if the Cuban issue was not resolved. This situation was inherited by William McKinley when he took office in March 1897.

See also Cuban Junta; Cuban Revolution.

References and Further Readings

Leech, Margaret. *In the Days of McKinley.* New York: Harper & Brothers, 1959.

Welch, Richard E., Jr. *The Presidencies of Grover Cleveland.* Lawrence: University Press of Kansas, 1988.

Coaling Stations

By the time of the Spanish-American War, most of the world's naval vessels, including those of the United States and Spain, were powered by steam produced in coal-fired boilers. Although steam power was a faster and far more consistent method of propulsion, it was not without its drawbacks. Ships consumed coal at a prodigious rate, and on extended voyages especially, the need to replenish the coal supply was obviously of critical importance. Moreover, hard anthracite coal burned better than soft coal and hence was more desirable, though often not available.

Supply ships, known as colliers or coal lighters, could refuel a vessel at sea, but it was a hard, dirty job that involved transferring bags or baskets of coal. Once on board, the coal was dumped into the ship's coal bunkers via chutes located on deck. In port, the coal might be loaded by cranes or by hand.

As the world's navies converted to steam power, coaling stations—that is, ports where ships could refuel—became of great importance, particularly in the vast reaches of the Pacific. The island of Guam, for example, was ideally located in the Pacific to provide a good coaling stop for vessels en route to the Philippines. Thus, it became an important acquisition for the United States during the Spanish-American War.

See also Navy, U.S.; Treaty of Paris.

References and Further Readings

Coletta, Paolo E. *A Survey of U.S. Naval Affairs, 1865–1917.* Lanham, MD: University Press of America, 1987.

Dierks, Jack Cameron. *A Leap to Arms: The Cuban Campaign of 1898.* Philadelphia: J. B. Lippincott, 1970.

Hagan, Kenneth J. *This People's Navy: The Making of American Sea Power.* New York: Free Press, 1991.

Tomlinson, Rodney G. *A Rocky Mountain Sailor in Teddy Roosevelt's Navy: The Letters of Petty Officer Charles Fowler from the Asiatic Station, 1905–1910.* Boulder, CO: Westview Press, 1998.

Coastal Defenses, U.S.

During the latter part of the nineteenth century, military theorists perceived that the greatest threat to the United States was an enemy attack on one of its major harbors or seaboard cities, causing much destruction (as Great Britain had inflicted on Washington and Baltimore during the War of 1812). Accordingly, emphasis was placed on developing a strong coastal defense system.

As a consequence, Alfred Thayer Mahan (author of the provocative *Influence of Sea Power upon History*) and others argued for the creation of new, modern coastal defense fortifications to replace those of Civil War vintage and older. These new forts would be built of concrete instead of masonry and equipped with modern breech-loading weapons of a caliber heavy enough to effectively ward off armored enemy battleships.

Earlier, Congress had created various boards to study the matter and make recommendations. One, the Endicott Board, headed by then Secretary of War William C. Endicott, concluded in 1887 that no less than $127 million would be required to create an adequate coastal defense system. Although the recommendation was considered totally unrealistic, Congress did provide enough funding to begin the project, which was nowhere near completion in 1898.

Passage of the Fifty Million Dollar Bill, to help finance the war with Spain, provided additional funding. Some $19 million was allocated to the War Department and $29 million to the Navy Department. Of the total assigned to the army, $15 million was for use in the coastal defense system, since the army would be charged with operating and maintaining that system.

Fortunately, the United States did not have to deal with an attack on its coastline by Spanish naval forces. After the Spanish-American War, improvements in coastal defense fortifications continued until the advent of World War II.

See also Fifty Million Dollar Bill; Mahan, Alfred Thayer.

References and Further Readings

Cosmas, Graham. *An Army for Empire: The United States Army in the Spanish-American War.* College Station: Texas A&M University Press, 1998.

Hagan, Kenneth J. *This People's Navy: The Making of American Sea Power.* New York: Free Press, 1991.

Weigley, Russell F. *History of the United States Army.* New York: Macmillan Publishing, 1967.

Coast Guard, U.S.

See **Revenue Cutter Service, U.S.**

Colonial Policies, U.S.

Although the United States had acquired Johnston Atoll in the Pacific in 1858, the country did not become a full-fledged colonial power until the end of the Spanish-American War. As a result of the Treaty of Paris, consummated in December 1898 and ratified by Congress the following year, the United States suddenly found itself in possession of much new and widely separated territory, including the Philippine Archipelago as well as Midway and Wake Islands in the Pacific. Additionally, it also controlled Puerto Rico in the Caribbean.

Unlike England and France, which had been governing colonies for centuries, the United States had no colonial policy in 1898 and no infrastructure for implementing such a policy. Although it was President William McKinley's intent to eventually create a bureau of colonial affairs, the administration of these new territories was initially assigned to the War Department's newly created Bureau of Insular Affairs.

In August 1899, McKinley named Elihu Root to replace outgoing Secretary of War Russell Alger. The choice seemed odd, since Root had no military background and no understanding of the army and its ways. Nevertheless, it was McKinley's belief that Root, a thoroughgoing lawyer, would be the right individual to oversee the governance of these new possessions.

At that time, the challenges that confronted Root were immense. The United States still had not dealt fully with the problems and concerns relating to the future states of Oklahoma, Arizona, New Mexico, and especially Alaska. Now, Root was being asked to formulate a governing policy that embraced Puerto Rico and the far-off Philippines as well. Finally, the annexation of Hawaii, rejected by the Cleveland administration in 1893, also became a reality in 1898, thereby adding to the burden of superintending these new territorial possessions.

The Spanish-American War compelled the United States to create a colonial policy almost overnight. Looming large in this issue was whether the Constitution permitted the United States to exercise sovereign control over a foreign territory such as the Philippines. However, while arguments pro and con continued, U.S. rule in the islands became de facto law. The legality of the issue remained unresolved until 1902, when the Supreme Court ruled that a territory might be subject to U.S. control without having been made a part of the United States. Until the Supreme Court ruling, Root was faced with the challenge of dealing with the many issues of colonial administration that crossed his desk while preventing any legal snare for the McKinley administration.

In addition to its new territorial possessions, the United States also established a protectorate over the new Republic of Cuba to help restore social, economic, and political integrity to the island. By 1902, Cuba was judged sufficiently recovered for the United States to relinquish its protectorate role.

There was little opposition to U.S. rule in Puerto Rico, where the native peoples seemed to welcome the departure of the Spanish. A military government controlled the island's affairs until the formation of a civilian government in 1901.

The Philippines proved to be the most difficult possession to administer because of the opposition to the U.S. presence in the archipelago. There, McKinley's approach was to establish a policy known as "benevolent assimilation." McKinley's vision called for U.S. military forces in the islands to earn the respect of the Filipino people by demonstrating regard for personal and property rights while at the same time asserting authority. Though an admirable approach, it proved unrealistic and nearly impossible to implement due to inflexible attitudes on both sides.

See also Benevolent Assimilation; Insular Affairs, Bureau of; McKinley, William, Jr.; Root, Elihu.

References and Further Readings

Jessup, Philip C. *Elihu Root.* 2 vols. New York: Dodd, Mead & Company, 1938.
Leech, Margaret. *In the Days of McKinley.* New York: Harper & Brothers, 1959.

Colwel, John Charles (1856–?)

A U.S. Army officer and spy who worked out of London, John Charles Colwel was generally regarded as the mastermind behind the U.S. intelligence system during the Spanish-American War. Colwel, together with his equally effective counterpart, Navy lieutenant William Sims, provided President William McKinley's office with valuable and timely information, such as the movement of Adm. Manuel Cámara's Spanish fleet toward the Philippines. Colwel's carefully placed contacts also fed Spanish authorities with false and misleading information. During the war, Colwel's intelligence network cost the United States approximately $27 million, money that would appear to have been well spent.

See also Sims, William Sowden.
References and Further Readings
O'Toole, G. J. A. *The Spanish War: An American Epic, 1898.* New York: W. W. Norton, 1984.

Committee on the Philippines

Not to be confused with the Philippine Commission, the Committee on the Philippines was an inquiring body convened by the U.S. Senate to examine affairs in the Philippine Archipelago.

The 13-member committee, chaired by Sen. Henry Cabot Lodge of Massachusetts, included Sen. William Allison of Iowa, Sen. Eugene Hale of Maine, Sen. Redfield Proctor of Vermont, Sen. Albert Beveridge of Ohio, and Sen. Julius Caesar Burrows of Michigan. The committee convened on 31 January 1902 and, for the next four months, heard testimony relative to the war and the government's management of the archipelago thereafter. The wide-ranging testimony came from civil officials, military leaders, enlisted personnel, and prominent Filipino officials. The committee adjourned at the end of May 1902.

See also Lodge, Henry Cabot; Philippine Commission; Taft, William Howard.
References and Further Readings
Garraty, John A. *Henry Cabot Lodge: A Biography.* New York: Alfred A. Knopf, 1953.
U.S. Senate Committee on the Philippines. *Affairs in the Philippine Islands: Hearings before the Committee on the Philippines.* 3 vols. Washington, DC: U.S. Government Printing Office, 1902.

Communications

Communications technology had made significant advances over the thirty-three years between the end of the Civil War in 1865 and the beginning of the Spanish-American War in 1898. As the turn of the century approached, telegraphy remained the primary means of fast national communication, but other new developments were rapidly changing the way Americans lived and carried on their daily business.

The most meaningful of these advances, certainly in terms of international relations, was the completion of the Atlantic cable in 1865. After it was completed, the United States had virtually instant communication with Great Britain and major cities in other European nations, as well as parts of the West Indies. However, no trans-Pacific cable existed in 1898 (it would not become a reality until 1903). As a consequence, news of Asian matters reached the United States via Europe. A submarine cable linked the Philippines with Hong Kong, but it was severed after the Battle of Manila, though it is not clear whether the Spanish or Commodore George Dewey was responsible. As a result, the Philippines were isolated until 22 August 1898, ten days after the Protocol of Peace was signed.

The telephone, which became a reality in 1876, had been improved significantly by 1898. No less than 15 lines connected the White House with the Senate and the House of Representatives. President William McKinley was especially fond of the telephone, finding it a convenient method of communication. The president also used an early version of the dictating machine.

During the war with Spain, a room in the southeast corner of the White House that had formerly served as a clerical office was converted to a "war room," where updated maps and reports were kept.

The White House war room, where President William McKinley directed the Spanish-American War. The room contained 15 telephone lines and 26 telegraph lines.

From there, President McKinley was able to better follow the progress of the war, especially in terms of geography. For the first time, a U.S. chief executive was making decisions regarding the prosecution of a two-ocean war. Because of their close proximity to the United States, the West Indies represented reasonably familiar territory, but the vast Pacific and the Philippines were less well known. Thus, understanding the geography of these areas was extremely important.

In the field and at sea, communications continued to rely on the more traditional methods. Army commanders, for example, still used couriers to carry dispatches. Additionally, the U.S. Army Signal Corps had a balloon detachment that saw limited service in Cuba. Small, fast gunboats served as the naval version of the army courier to deliver messages to ships. Not until the further development of wireless telegraphy (first introduced in 1891) and the radio (in the 1920s) would communications between ships and field commanders change significantly.

See also Balloons; McKinley, William, Jr.

References and Further Readings

Chadwick, Rear Adm. French Ensor. *Relations of the United States and Spain: The Spanish American War.* 2 vols. New York: Charles Scribner's Sons, 1911 (reprinted in 1968).

Cosmas, Graham. *An Army for Empire: The United States Army in the Spanish-American War.* College Station: Texas A&M University Press, 1998.

Gould, Lewis L. *The Spanish-American War and President McKinley.* Lawrence: University of Kansas Press, 1982.

Leech, Margaret. *In the Days of McKinley.* New York: Harper & Brothers, 1959.

Standage, Tom. *The Victorian Internet.* New York: Walker & Company, 1998.

Competitor Incident

The schooner *Competitor,* used to carry supplies to Cuban revolutionaries, landed at Punta Berracos near Havana on 25 April 1896 with a load of arms and ammunition. Subsequently captured by the Spanish, it was the only filibustering vessel seized by Spain during the Cuban Revolution. Like the *Virginius* affair of 1873 and the *Allianca* incident of 1895, the *Competitor* incident drew international attention and was yet another illustration of the steadily worsening relations between Spain and the United States.

The *Competitor*'s crewmen—one citizen from the United States and one from Great Britain together with three Cubans—were taken to Havana, where four of them were sentenced to death. The U.S. consul general argued, unsuccessfully, that the crew should be tried in court for violation of neutrality laws. The execution verdict would have been carried out if U.S. Secretary of State Richard Olney had not protested vigorously. After considerable political maneuvering and dialogue, the prisoners were released six months later.

The original death sentence was vigorously supported in Spain; in the United States, the press was outraged and the men were cheered as heroes for their support of the Cuban cause.

See also *Allianca* Incident; Filibuster; *Virginius* Affair.

References and Further Readings

Chadwick, Rear Adm. French Ensor. *Relations of the United States and Spain: The Spanish American War.* 2 vols. New York: Charles Scribner's Sons, 1911 (reprinted in 1968).

Musicant, Ivan. *Empire by Default: The Spanish-American War and the Dawn of the American Century.* New York: Henry Holt and Company, 1998.

Wisan, Joseph Ezra. *The Cuban Crisis as Reflected in the New York Press (1895–1898).* New York: Columbia University Press, 1934.

Converse, George Albert (1844–1909)

Comdr. George Albert Converse of the U.S. Navy commanded the cruiser *Montgomery,* which was berthed in Havana harbor when the *Maine* was destroyed. Because of his recognized expertise with explosives, particularly of the underwater variety, he was called as an expert witness in the *Maine* inquiry.

Converse testified that he believed that there had been two explosions, one of which had been external, suggesting that a mine had destroyed the ship. Converse's testimony was a key factor in the court's decision, which ultimately concluded that the *Maine* had been destroyed by a mine placed by a person or persons unknown.

See also *Maine,* Inquiries into the Sinking of.

References and Further Readings

Blow, Michael. *A Ship to Remember: The* Maine *and the Spanish-American War.* New York: William Morrow, 1992.

Rickover, H. G. *How the Battleship* Maine *Was Destroyed.* Washington, DC: Department of the Navy, 1976.

Samuels, Peggy, and Harold Samuels. *Remembering the* Maine. Washington, DC: Smithsonian Institution Press, 1995.

Weems, John Edward. *The Fate of the* Maine. New York: Henry Holt and Company, 1958.

Cook, Francis Augustus (1843–1916)

Francis Augustus Cook was the commander of the U.S. armored cruiser *Brooklyn* throughout the Spanish-American War. Born in Massachusetts, the son of an army officer, Francis Augustus Cook graduated from the U.S. Naval Academy in 1863 and had extensive service in the Civil War.

In 1896, Cook assumed command of the *Brooklyn* and held the post until 1899. During the Battle of Santiago Bay, the *Brooklyn* nearly collided with the battleship *Texas* while pursuing the Spanish fleet as it sortied out of Santiago harbor. The near collision became somewhat controversial. Although Cook came under criticism, he was not officially censured for what happened.

See also Santiago de Cuba, Naval Battle of.

References and Further Readings

Chadwick, Rear Adm. French Ensor. *Relations of the United States and Spain: The Spanish American War.* 2 vols. New York: Charles Scribner's Sons, 1911 (reprinted in 1968).

Dierks, Jack Cameron. *A Leap to Arms: The Cuban Campaign of 1898.* Philadelphia: J. B. Lippincott, 1970.

Sampson, Rear Adm. William T. "The Atlantic Fleet in the Spanish War." *Century Magazine,* April 1899.

Trask, David F. *The War with Spain in 1898.* Lincoln: University of Nebraska Press, 1996.

Corbin, Henry Clark (1842–1909)

During the Spanish-American War, President William McKinley relied on the advice of Gen. Henry Clark Corbin, adjutant general of the army, when it came to military matters. Born in Ohio, Corbin was studying law when the Civil War broke out. He joined the Ohio Volunteers and was soon named commander of the Fourteenth U.S. Colored Infantry. By the end of the war, he had risen to the rank of brigadier general of volunteers. After serving on the western frontier during the Indian wars, he was appointed to the adjutant general's office and eventually named adjutant general of the army.

Efficient and thorough, Corbin was also a diplomatic and politically astute officer, possessing the ideal temperament and skills for the job of adjutant general. During the Spanish-American War, as the feud between General of the Army Nelson Miles and Secretary of War Russell Alger corrupted the relationship between those two men, President McKinley increasingly turned to his adjutant general for council. As the president's confidante in military matters, Corbin became perhaps the most influential army officer of his day.

At the time of his death in 1909, Corbin had risen to the rank of lieutenant general and authored *Legislative History of the General Staff of the Army of the U.S.*

See also Alger, Russell Alexander; Army, U.S.; McKinley, William, Jr.; Miles, Nelson Appleton.

References and Further Readings

Cosmas, Graham. *An Army for Empire: The United States Army in the Spanish-American War.* College Station: Texas A&M University Press, 1998.

Leech, Margaret. *In the Days of McKinley.* New York: Harper & Brothers, 1959.

Correa, Miguel (1830–1900)

A Spanish Army veteran of nearly fifty years, Miguel Correa was named minister of war by Práxedes Mateo Sagasta in 1898, just before the outbreak of war with the United States.

Correa's views on Spain's naval strategy were at odds with those of most others in the Spanish government. He believed Spain's navy was inferior to the U.S. fleet and felt caution should be exercised before risking any major confrontation with the latter. In Correa's opinion, the Spanish fleet would be beaten and perhaps destroyed, thereby resulting in a serious blow to Spanish morale.

Correa also urged, in the strongest possible terms, that Gen. Arsenio Linares, who was commanding Spanish forces in Cuba, stand firm despite what appeared to be an untenable position at Santiago. Similarly, he argued for taking a strong stance in Puerto Rico, believing that to do so would strengthen Spain's bargaining position in future negotiations with the United States.

See also Naval Strategy, Spanish; Navy, Spanish.

References and Further Readings

Chadwick, Rear Adm. French Ensor. *Relations of the United States and Spain: The Spanish American War.* 2 vols. New York: Charles Scribner's Sons, 1911 (reprinted in 1968).

Trask, David F. *The War with Spain in 1898.* Lincoln: University of Nebraska Press, 1996.

Corregidor Island (Philippines)

Corregidor is a 2-square-mile island situated in a potentially strategic position at the entrance to Manila Bay. Corregidor's location creates a two-channel approach to Manila Bay. North of the island is

Boca Chica Passage, and to the south lies the larger Boca Grande Passage.

Although the island itself was a natural fortress—a large rocky mass with numerous deep caves that made it impervious to gunfire—it was underutilized by the Spanish. Because of its strategic location, Corregidor could have presented a real threat to Commodore George Dewey's Asiatic Squadron when it arrived on 1 May 1898. However, Adm. Patricio Montojo, commander of the Spanish fleet, was dissuaded from using the island as the keystone of his defense by his fleet captains, who argued that the deep waters surrounding the island would result in heavy casualties if any of the ships had to be evacuated. As a consequence, Corregidor had only one battery of 6-inch guns with which to defend the approach to Manila Bay.

After the Spanish-American War, the United States strengthened Corregidor's defenses, taking advantage of its natural fortress characteristics. During World War II, events on Corregidor became the stuff of legend when U.S. forces there held out against Japanese bombardment for five months before finally surrendering.

See also Manila Bay, Battle of.

References and Further Readings

Beede, Benjamin R., ed. *The War of 1898 and U.S. Interventions, 1898–1934.* New York: Garland Publishing, 1994.

O'Toole, G. J. A. *The Spanish War: An American Epic, 1898.* New York: W. W. Norton, 1984.

Trask, David F. *The War with Spain in 1898.* Lincoln: University of Nebraska Press, 1996.

Cortelyou, George Bruce (1862–1940)

Born in New York, George Bruce Cortelyou spent time in the educational system and as a journalist before beginning a career as stenographer and private secretary to the two presidents most directly involved in events preceding and during the war with Spain—Grover Cleveland and William McKinley.

An extraordinarily able individual, Cortelyou was devoted to President McKinley and worked tirelessly to ease the president's burden during the stressful weeks before and during the war with Spain. Since William McKinley left little in the way of personal correspondence from which historians might better understand and assess his decisions, Cortelyou's diaries, kept during his years in the White House, provide an intimate view of the president.

See also McKinley, William, Jr.

References and Further Readings
Leech, Margaret. *In the Days of McKinley.* New York: Harper &
    Brothers, 1959.

Cottas

Cottas were forts erected by the Moros of the southern Philippine
island of Mindanao and the Sulu Archipelago. They were usually
strong earthwork positions but were sometimes constructed of
stones. Generally, they stood 12 to 15 feet high and were surrounded
by deep ditches, often with deadly traps composed of sharpened
bamboo shafts. Some of the hardest fighting in the Philippines
occurred when U.S. troops had to storm the Moro *cottas.*

See also Baldwin, Frank Dwight; Bayang, Battle of; Bud Daju, Battle
of; Moros; Pershing, John Joseph.

References and Further Readings
Smythe, Donald. "Pershing and the Mount Bagsak Campaign of
    1913." *Philippine Studies,* no. 12, 1964.
———. *Guerrilla Warrior: The Early Life of John J. Pershing.* New
    York: Charles Scribner's Sons, 1973.
Steinbach, Robert H. *A Long March: The Lives of Frank and Alice
    Baldwin.* Austin: University of Texas Press, 1989.

Crane, Stephen (1871–1900)

The author of the well-known *Red Badge of Courage,* Stephen Crane
was a veteran war correspondent at the time of the Spanish-
American War. In addition to reporting on the Greco-Turkish War of
1897, he covered the war in Cuba throughout the summer of 1898.
Born in New Jersey, the son of a Methodist minister, Crane attended
several eastern colleges but was only a mediocre student. After completing his education, he decided to pursue a career as a newspaper
journalist and writer. The publication of *The Red Badge of Courage*
in 1895 propelled him to the forefront of contemporary U.S. writers
when he was just 24 years of age.

Crane's reporting, however, frequently got him in trouble. In
1896, he found himself in disfavor with the New York Police
Department for his critical coverage of it. His stories angered no less
a personage than Theodore Roosevelt, New York's police commissioner at the time.

With the tensions in Cuba growing more strained, the Bacheller
news syndicate assigned Crane to Cuba as a special correspondent.
In Jacksonville, Florida, he signed on as a seaman on one of the

War correspondent Stephen Crane, author of the classic Red Badge of Courage, *provided extensive coverage of the Cuban Campaign.*

filibuster ships that regularly ran guns and ammunition to the Cuban revolutionaries. When the vessel ran aground, Crane and three others, including the captain, took to a small boat and, after a trying day at sea, made it back to Florida.

Recovering from this experience, Crane became a correspondent for William Randolph Hearst's *New York Journal.* In 1897, he was assigned to cover the war between Turkey and Greece.

With the outbreak of the Spanish-American War, Crane returned to the United States and tried to enlist in the navy but failed the physical examination. He next joined Joseph Pulitzer's *New York World* and sailed to Cuba aboard Adm. William Sampson's flagship, the *New York.*

In the early days of the war, the location of the Spanish fleet was uppermost in the minds of U.S. military authorities. In May 1898, Crane was aboard a special dispatch ship set up by Pulitzer's *World,* hoping to be on hand when the Spanish fleet was discovered, but it proved a fruitless endeavor.

In June, Crane landed with the marine detachment that captured Guantánamo. A few days later, he participated in yet another landing, this time with Gen. William Shafter's Fifth Corps at Daiquirí. Later, he accompanied the advance toward Santiago and witnessed the Battle of San Juan Hill. Crane later incurred the disfavor of Joseph Pulitzer when he filed the report of his wounded colleague, Edward Marshall, at Siboney. This event seems to have set the stage for Crane's later dismissal, the basis for which was a piece he ostensibly wrote charging that there was panic on the part of some officers at San Juan Hill. Although it was later determined that he could not possibly have written the story, Pulitzer fired him anyway. Rehired by W. R. Hearst, Crane then covered the Puerto Rican Campaign.

Crane left the United States for Europe late in 1898, but his health was deteriorating. He died of tuberculosis in Germany in June 1900.

See also Cuban Revolution; Hearst, William Randolph; Journalism; Pulitzer, Joseph; San Juan Hill, Charge up.

References and Further Readings

Angell, Roger. "The Greatest of the Boys: Like His Work, Stephen Crane's Life Reflects a Younger, More Adventurous America." *New Yorker,* September 7, 1998.

Davis, Linda H. *Badge of Courage: The Life of Stephen Crane.* Boston: Houghton Mifflin, 1998.

Stallman, F. R. *Stephen Crane: A Biography.* New York: George Braziller, 1968.

Creelman, James (1859–1915)

One of the best-known journalists of the Spanish-American War period, James Creelman was born in Montreal, Quebec, and moved to New York as a boy. A reporter at age 16 for the *Brooklyn Eagle,* he went on to join Joseph Pulitzer's *New York World.*

Creelman covered the Sino-Japanese War (1894), where his stunning eyewitness accounts of the Japanese massacre of thousands of Chinese elevated him to the ranks of journalism's elite. He was in Cuba during much of the next two years, reporting on the execution and otherwise brutal treatment of Cuban prisoners. His stories of conditions in Cuba resulted in powerful condemnatory editorials from the *World.*

Late in 1896, Creelman was hired away from the *World* by William Randolph Hearst's *New York Journal* to be the *Journal's* correspondent in Madrid. In 1897, he covered the Greco-Turkish War.

The outbreak of the Spanish-American War in 1898 found Creelman in Cuba with Gen. William Shafter's Fifth Corps. Wounded in the fighting at El Caney on 1 July 1898, he dictated his story to William Randolph Hearst himself while lying among the wounded. After the war, he published an account of his colorful and exciting journalistic experiences, entitled *On the Great Highway: The Wanderings and Adventures of a Special Correspondent.*

See also El Caney, Battle of; Hearst, William Randolph; Journalism; Pulitzer, Joseph.

References and Further Readings

Brown, Charles H. *The Correspondents' War: Journalists in the Spanish-American War.* New York: Charles Scribner's Sons, 1967.

Cosmas, Graham. *An Army for Empire: The United States Army in the Spanish-American War.* College Station: Texas A&M University Press, 1998.

Creelman, James. *On the Great Highway: The Wanderings and Adventures of a Special Correspondent.* Boston: Lothrop, 1901.

Cuba

Sometimes called the "Pearl of the Antilles," Cuba is the largest island in the West Indies, covering some 44,218 square miles. Located approximately 90 miles south of the Florida Keys, it has always held strategic value for the United States. Cuba's principal cities are Havana (the capital) and Matanzas on the north side of the island, Camagüey and Cienfuegos on the south side, and Guantánamo and Santiago de Cuba on the east. The island is divided into six major provinces: from west to east, Pinar del Rio, Havana, Matanzas, Santa Clara, Camagüey, and Oriente. Although the island contains three mountain ranges, it is essentially level and features a subtropical climate.

Cuba was discovered by Christopher Columbus in 1492 and colonized by Spain in 1511. The island soon became a thriving colony, used by Spain as an assembly point for New World expeditions. Long after the disappearance of Spain's North American possessions, Cuba remained an active colony, though unrest among the native population led finally to the Ten Years' War for independence from 1868 to 1878. Although Cubans did not gain independence as a result of that war, the spirit of the effort remained alive. In 1895, a new revolt generated a groundswell of public support among Americans for the plight of the Cubans, thereby forming the basis for the Spanish-American War.

See also Antilles; Cuban Campaign; El Caney, Battle of; Guantánamo, Battle of; Las Guásimas, Battle of; Santiago, Campaign and Siege of; Santiago de Cuba, Naval Battle of.

References and Further Readings

Ferrara, Orestes. *The Last Spanish War: Revelations in Diplomacy.* Translated from the Spanish by William E. Shea. New York: Paisley Press, 1937.

Musicant, Ivan. *Empire by Default: The Spanish-American War and the Dawn of the American Century.* New York: Henry Holt and Company, 1998.

Trask, David F. *The War with Spain in 1898.* Lincoln: University of Nebraska Press, 1996.

"Cuba Libre"

The American slogan "Free Cuba" (*Cuba libre*) became a cry heard across the country as an aroused U.S. public clamored for the release of Cuba from Spanish tyranny. Interestingly enough, *Cuba libre* later became the name of a drink made of rum and cola.

See also Cuba; Cuban Revolution.

References and Further Readings

Leech, Margaret. *In the Days of McKinley.* New York: Harper & Brothers, 1959.

Trask, David F. *The War with Spain in 1898.* Lincoln: University of Nebraska Press, 1996.

Cuba, U.S. Military Occupation of

Following the signing of the Protocol of Peace (cease-fire) in August 1898, Spanish forces slowly evacuated Cuba, and the United States delayed committing an army of occupation until the end of the malaria and yellow fever season.

On 1 January 1899, the United States established a military protectorate over Cuba and installed Gen. John R. Brooke as military governor of the island. The Seventh Army Corps was assigned as the army of occupation. Initially, the military force totaled 23,000 men, but it rapidly increased to nearly twice that number by spring. However, as Cuba remained relatively free of trouble, U.S. troops were gradually withdrawn, until only 11,000 remained at the end of 1899.

Compared to the troops who preceded them, the U.S. occupation forces in Cuba, Puerto Rico, and the Philippines were much better equipped and prepared for life in the Tropics, with improved clothing, cleaner camps, and stringent sanitary measures.

Brooke and the army of occupation faced a difficult challenge, as Cuba was a country in shambles after years of fighting and civil unrest. Initially, leaders of the Cuban revolutionary government were unhappy with the presence of U.S. troops while their own revolutionary army was still mobilized. This issue was resolved when President William McKinley offered a $75 bonus to each Cuban soldier who left the army. With this inducement attracting many soldiers, the army slowly disbanded.

The army of occupation undertook several social programs during its tenure in Cuba, including rebuilding roads and bridges and training native police to deal with outlaw bands. However, many U.S. commanders attempted to curtail traditional native practices while introducing American lifestyles to the Cuban populace. Moreover, U.S. troops were often drunk and disorderly and displayed racist attitudes toward the native people. Thus, most Cubans continued to resent the presence of U.S. soldiers.

In December 1899, General Brooke, who had been under some criticism for his administration of Cuban affairs, was transferred to the Department of the East. He was replaced by Gen. Leonard Wood, who promptly moved ahead with a vigorous program designed to establish an independent Cuban government. Wood's efforts bore fruit when the Republic of Cuba came into being in May 1902. Shortly thereafter, U.S. occupational forces left the island.

See also Brooke, John Rutter; Cuban Revolutionary Government; McKinley, William, Jr.; Wood, Leonard.

References and Further Readings

Cosmas, Graham. *An Army for Empire: The United States Army in the Spanish-American War.* College Station: Texas A&M University Press, 1998.

Leech, Margaret. *In the Days of McKinley.* New York: Harper & Brothers, 1959.

Cuban Campaign (June–July 1898)

At the outset, the war with Spain was seen as essentially a naval war, with the army playing a secondary role. Originally, it was decided that Maj. Gen. William R. Shafter, commanding the Fifth Corps, would land a force of 6,000 to 7,000 men on the south side of Cuba, with the intent of assisting the Cuban rebels. No one imagined that this force would remain for an extended period. However, the landing site was then changed to one near Havana, which, being only 90 miles from the Florida Keys, was more accessible. Scheduled for early May, the operation was postponed indefinitely when it was learned that the Spanish fleet had left the Cape Verde Islands and was presumably bound for the Caribbean.

When it was discovered that Adm. Pascual Cervera's Spanish fleet had slipped into the harbor of Santiago, plans to invade Cuba were renewed, this time with Santiago rather than Havana as the immediate objective. The invasion was slated to begin on 4 June, but Shafter was unable to meet that deadline due to matériel shortages, to say nothing of shortages of transports with which to ferry the expedition across the Caribbean to Cuba.

By 8 June, Shafter's staff had managed to squeeze some 17,000 men, more than 2,000 horses and mules, and 30 pieces of artillery aboard a motley collection of ships. Four more days passed, however, before the convoy actually sailed from the port of Tampa, Florida. On 14 June, the convoy picked up a naval escort and arrived off Santiago de Cuba—on the eastern tip of the island—on 20 June.

The Spanish had divined early on that the Americans would aim at Santiago, which, ironically enough, was also the headquarters of the Spanish Fifth Corps, commanded by Lt. Gen. Arsenio Linares, whose jurisdiction embraced all of Oriente Province. Linares had some 35,000 troops at his disposal, but only about one-third of them were immediately available to defend Santiago and its environs. The city and its garrison were under the command of Gen. José Toral y Vázquez.

The city of Santiago was well protected by both natural and man-made defenses. A fortified line of blockhouses and barbed wire covered any approach from the north and east and also protected a rail line and the city's water supply. The village of El Caney stood at the eastern end of this sector.

With the malaria and yellow fever season rapidly approaching, General Shafter believed it imperative to move on his objective quickly before his command was decimated by disease. The navy meanwhile had urged Shafter to capture the heavy guns around Santiago harbor, thereby allowing the U.S. ships to move against the Spanish fleet without having to contend with fire from those batteries.

After consulting with the leaders of the Cuban Revolutionary Army, Shafter decided to land his expedition at the small hamlet of Daiquirí, approximately 15 miles from Santiago. The Cubans promised to assist by attacking Spanish positions; the navy would provide some fire support.

The landing was as disorganized as the debarkation from Tampa had been. With little in the way of landing craft available, the operation had to be jury-rigged. Horses, for example, were pushed off the transports to swim ashore. Nevertheless, by nightfall of 22 June, 7,000 troops had landed and by 24 June, the entire expedition was ashore.

The Americans promptly took possession of Daiquirí, the small Spanish garrison having quickly fled. While the rest of the Fifth Corps was landing, the brigades of Brig. Gen. Henry W. Lawton and Brig. Gen. John C. Bates advanced on Siboney, which they occupied on 23 June.

Lawton's orders were to hold Siboney and cover the rest of the landing. However, soon after reaching Siboney, Maj. Gen. Joseph Wheeler joined Lawton and became the ranking officer on the scene. Wheeler—"Fighting Joe" Wheeler of Civil War fame—commanded the cavalry division of Shafter's Fifth Corps: nearly 3,000 troopers, including the Rough Riders, all sans horses. Having learned that the strong Spanish force at Las Guásimas might pose a threat to the expedition, Wheeler elected to advance on Las Guásimas on his own volition.

Wheeler directed Brig. Gen. S. B. Young to take his brigade plus the Rough Riders—some 1,300 men altogether—and attack Las Guásimas. In the early morning hours of 24 June, Young's men advanced on the Spanish position, defended by 1,500 troops. U.S. artillery provided some support, but the fire from the Spanish defenders, using their Mauser rifles and bullets propelled by smokeless powder, slowed the forward movement. Despite this, the Rough Riders managed to advance, along with the Ninth and Tenth (black)

The landing of the U.S. Fifth Corps at Daiquirí, Cuba, June 1898.

Cavalry Regiments (including Lt. John J. Pershing), driving the Spanish defenders from their positions.

The first phase of the Cuban Campaign had gone reasonably well for the Americans, though due less to U.S. organization and foresight than to the Spanish decision not to concentrate their resources against the invaders. Had General Linares made a stronger stand at Siboney, for example, it would surely have complicated Shafter's advance on Santiago.

Meanwhile, as Wheeler's troops were fighting at Las Guásimas, supplies and equipment were still coming ashore and the navy was ferrying Cuban insurgents to the invasion area, where it was hoped their added numbers would play a significant role in the campaign. Adm. William T. Sampson, commanding the U.S. fleet in Cuban waters, also learned that it was General Shafter's intent to move directly against the city of Santiago, rather than the heavy guns overlooking its harbor.

On 28 June, Shafter was informed that a heavy column of Spanish reinforcements was making its way toward Santiago, thus emphasizing the need to advance without delay. Shafter's plan called for Lawton to neutralize El Caney while the main body moved directly against San Juan Heights. The primary effort would be supported by Lawton after he took El Caney.

The attack began early on Saturday, 1 July. Lawton's two

brigades under Brig. Gen. Adna R. Chaffee and Brig. Gen. William Ludlow moved forward, supported by artillery that proved less than effective. Spanish resistance was strong, and it was not until late afternoon that Lawton finally secured his objective.

Just 2 miles east of El Caney rose San Juan Heights, which was composed of two prominent hills separated by a small valley: Kettle Hill and San Juan Hill. San Juan Heights controlled the approach to the city, which could not be taken without first securing that ground. To defend the heights, the Spanish had a series of trenches, barbed wire, and a few artillery pieces.

At 8 A.M. on 1 July, even as Lawton's men were going after El Caney, Shafter prepared to commit 8,000 men against San Juan Heights. The attack opened with U.S. artillery, which quickly drew counterfire from defenders armed with superior field pieces. U.S. casualties began to mount.

About midmorning, Lt. Col. Joseph Maxfield of the U.S. Signal Corps, together with a member of Shafter's staff, went aloft in a balloon to gather useful information about the battle. Unfortunately, when the balloon descended to a lower altitude to advance along with the troops, it was shot down.

As U.S. troops reached the area from which they would begin their assault—around midday—Spanish defenders laid down a heavy curtain of fire. Lawton had not yet arrived from El Caney, and Shafter was not present, being incapacitated with gout. However, his senior commanders agreed that the heights must be attacked immediately.

The Rough Riders, now commanded by Theodore Roosevelt (Col. Leonard Wood having been promoted to brigade commander) and flanked by the First, Ninth, and Tenth Cavalry Regiments, began their assault of Kettle Hill, so named because a huge cauldron used to process sugar was located there.

Storming up the slope on foot in what has become an American epic, Col. Theodore Roosevelt and his Rough Riders, along with their comrades from the other three regiments, gained the summit and took possession of Kettle Hill. They had little time in which to savor their accomplishment, however, for they were soon drawing fire from the Spanish defenders on San Juan Hill to the west. They could also see the brigade of Gen. Hamilton Hawkins struggling against heavy fire to take San Juan Hill.

Wasting no time, Roosevelt promptly directed his men to provide supporting fire. In due course, when Hawkins's men took the south end of San Juan Hill, Roosevelt led his command across the small valley that separated the two high points to attack the north end of the hill. The effort was actually a second try, the first having misfired. Originally, Roosevelt issued the order and started off for San Juan Hill believing the others were behind him. When he discovered that only a few had joined him, he returned to Kettle Hill, ready to accuse the regiment of cowardice. He quickly learned, however, that only a few men had actually heard the original order. After the mix-up was straightened out, Roosevelt led the second effort against the north end of San Juan Hill, this time successfully and with all hands.

Having lost the commanding ground, the Spanish withdrew into the city of Santiago. The loss of San Juan Heights effectively ended the Cuban Campaign. During the next six weeks, Shafter's Fifth Corps would cut off the city from outside help. There would be no more major confrontations between U.S. and Spanish troops, although sporadic firing and skirmishing would continue until Santiago's formal capitulation on 17 July.

See also El Caney, Battle of; Lawton, Henry Ware; Roosevelt, Theodore; San Juan Hill, Charge up; Shafter, William Rufus; Wheeler, Joseph "Fighting Joe."

References and Further Readings
Cosmas, Graham. *An Army for Empire: The United States Army in the Spanish-American War.* College Station: Texas A&M University Press, 1998.
Musicant, Ivan. *Empire by Default: The Spanish-American War and the Dawn of the American Century.* New York: Henry Holt and Company, 1998.
Nofi, Albert A. *The Spanish-American War, 1898.* Conshohocken, PA: Combined Books, 1998.
Trask, David F. *The War with Spain in 1898.* Lincoln: University of Nebraska Press, 1996.
Walker, Dale L. *The Boys of '98: Theodore Roosevelt and the Rough Riders.* New York: Forge Books, 1998.

Cuban Expeditionary Force, U.S.

Although small when compared to the expeditions of World Wars I and II, the U.S. Cuban Expeditionary Force was huge by the standards of its day. When the invasion force, officially the Fifth Corps, sailed for Cuba in June 1898, it was the largest military unit to leave the United States up to that time, a distinction it would retain until World War I.

The invasion fleet consisted of 35 vessels, transporting nearly 18,000 officers and men, plus some 2,300 horses and mules, 37 artillery pieces of various caliber, 4 Gatling guns, and 1 pneumatic dynamite gun. There were also 200 wagons and ambulances, together with a contingent of civilian teamsters, clerks, and others.

See also Army, U.S.; Cuban Campaign.
References and Further Readings
Cosmas, Graham. *An Army for Empire: The United States Army in the Spanish-American War.* College Station: Texas A&M University Press, 1998.
Musicant, Ivan. *Empire by Default: The Spanish-American War and the Dawn of the American Century.* New York: Henry Holt and Company, 1998.
Nofi, Albert A. *The Spanish-American War, 1898.* Conshohocken, PA: Combined Books, 1998.

Cuban Junta

In September 1895, the new Cuban revolutionary government established a junta in the United States under the leadership of Tomás Estrada Palma. As the governing council of the Cuban Revolutionary Party, the junta's mission was to establish diplomatic relations with other countries and encourage and solicit support from sympathetic Americans.

Headquartered in New York, the junta was composed mainly of nationalized Cubans. The junta also enjoyed considerable support from Americans such as Charles A. Dana, who supported the cause of Cuban independence, which had flourished for some time. For example, William O. McDowell, a New York businessman, had organized the Cuban League of the U.S. in 1892.

In addition to soliciting financial contributions for their cause, members of the junta also encouraged and supported filibustering expeditions whose objective was to provide the revolutionary army with weapons and ammunition.

See also Cuban Revolutionary Government; Dana, Charles Anderson; Estrada Palma, Tomás.
References and Further Readings
Foner, Philip S. *The Spanish-Cuban-American War.* 2 vols. New York: Monthly Review Press, 1972.
Leech, Margaret. *In the Days of McKinley.* New York: Harper & Brothers, 1959.
Quesada, Gonzalo de. *The War in Cuba: Being a Full Account of Her Great Struggle for Freedom.* Washington, DC: Liberty Publishing, 1896.

Cuban League of the U.S.

New York businessman William O. McDowell was attracted to the cause of Cuban independence after meeting the great patriot José Martí. McDowell was so impressed with Martí and his work that he formed the Cuban League of the U.S. in 1892 to provide support for the cause. Once the war began, the league could only continue to express vocal support for Cuban independence.

See also Cuban Junta; Cuban Revolutionary Government; Martí y Pérez, José.

References and Further Readings

Foner, Philip S. *The Spanish-Cuban-American War.* Vol. 1. New York: Monthly Review Press, 1972.

Thomas, Hugh. *Cuba: The Pursuit of Freedom.* New York: Harper & Row, 1971.

Cuban Revolution (Insurrection) (1895–1898)

During the last half of the nineteenth century, Cuba experienced two revolutions. The first, known as the Ten Years' War, lasted from 1868 to 1878 and did not achieve autonomy or independence. The second effort, sometimes called the Cuban Insurrection, began in 1895 and led to the U.S. intervention and war in 1898. Individuals such as Máximo Gómez, Antonio Maceo, and José Martí, who had been involved in the Ten Years' War, became key figures in the revolution of 1895.

The *insurrectos* received considerable aid from filibusters, who provided money and guns, among other things. The revolution received widespread attention in the United States, where reports of Spanish authorities abusing Cuban people generated sympathy for the latter and anger against the former. Cuba's desperate situation became an emotionally charged issue that was exacerbated by the press of the day. In addition, U.S. businesses were equally unhappy with the loss of profitable trade as a result of the revolution.

Spain's refusal to satisfactorily resolve the Cuban issue led to U.S. intervention and the Spanish-American War of 1898.

See also Cuba; McKinley, William, Jr.; Spain; Ten Years' War.

References and Further Readings

Gould, Lewis L. *The Spanish-American War and President McKinley.* Lawrence: University of Kansas Press, 1982.

Leech, Margaret. *In the Days of McKinley.* New York: Harper & Brothers, 1959.

Musicant, Ivan. *Empire by Default: The Spanish-American War and the Dawn of the American Century.* New York: Henry Holt and Company, 1998.

Portraits of five
Cuban heroes:
José Martí,
Máximo Gómez,
Antonio Maceo,
Salvador
Cisneros, and
Calixto García,
1896 (lithograph).

Quesada, Gonzalo de. *The War in Cuba: Being a Full Account of Her Great Struggle for Freedom.* Washington, DC: Liberty Publishing, 1896.

Cuban Revolutionary Army

Although the Cuban Army was structured along somewhat conventional lines, it was essentially a guerrilla force whose numbers fluctuated between 25,000 and 40,000 men. Gen. Máximo Gómez served as its commander in chief. Gómez's principal lieutenants were Gen. Antonio Maceo and Gen. Calixto García, who commanded the largest segment of the army, operating in Cuba's eastern Oriente Province. All three men were veterans of the ill-fated Ten Years' War (1868–1878). Subordinates at lower levels included planters and businessmen; the rank and file was composed mainly of tradesmen and laborers. As a rule, the army was well equipped with modern rifles that had been smuggled into the country by filibusters or captured from Spanish Army detachments. The machete, the ubiquitous tool of the sugarcane plantations, was also widely used by the army.

The revolutionary army was strongly supported by the native populace, which believed in the cause for which the army was fighting despite harsh measures brought to bear by the Spanish, especially against families of the army's known members. Most notable of these reprisals was the infamous *reconcentrado* policy of Gen. Valeriano Weyler.

The civil government did a fair job of keeping the army supplied. The army also created a system of gardens and cattle ranches in remote areas, and workshops were established to provide repairs and maintenance on weapons and equipment. Nevertheless, the army was often in need of food and supplies.

Correctly perceiving that his army of *insurrectos* could not hope to successfully wage traditional war with the Spanish forces, Gómez employed slash-and-run tactics, supported by a network of effective intelligence. The army would suddenly strike Spanish outposts and supply columns with small detachments, then quickly melt away into the hills and jungle. Sugarcane plantations provided a favorite target, the philosophy being that a serious interruption in the production of the highly profitable sugarcane would work an economic hardship on the Spanish. The idea was to harass the enemy as much as possible, wear down the Spanish will to resist, and induce U.S. intervention. Although Gómez's tactics did not secure total victory, they were successful enough to deny the use of the Cuban interior to the Spanish Army.

During the Spanish-American War, the revolutionary army did not play a major role in the Cuban land campaign, largely because U.S. commanders were loath to trust the reliability and competence of its troops. The army did, however, provide valuable intelligence service.

See also García Íñiguez, Calixto; Gómez Báez, Máximo; Maceo Grajales, Antonio; *Reconcentrado* System; Weyler y Nicolau, Valeriano "Butcher."

References and Further Readings

Cosmas, Graham. *An Army for Empire: The United States Army in the Spanish-American War.* College Station: Texas A&M University Press, 1998.

Quesada, Gonzalo de. *The War in Cuba: Being a Full Account of Her Great Struggle for Freedom.* Washington, DC: Liberty Publishing, 1896.

Russell, Henry B. *The Story of Two Wars.* Hartford, CT: Hartford Publishing Company, 1899.

Trask, David F. *The War with Spain in 1898.* Lincoln: University of Nebraska Press, 1996.

Cuban Revolutionary Government

In September 1895, representatives of the Cuban revolutionary movement met in Camagüey to organize a provisional government designed to function for two years and promote independence from Spain. Much soul searching had preceded the meeting. Earlier in 1895 at a conference convened by José Martí (the soul of Cuba's revolutionary movement), Antonio Maceo, another prominent figure in the freedom movement, supported a military junta as the best way to prosecute the revolution until independence was achieved. Maceo believed a civil government would undermine the revolution just as it had during the Ten Years' War. Martí, however, was convinced that the revolution needed a legitimate governing body in order to achieve international recognition. Unfortunately for the Cuban cause, Martí was killed in a firefight with Spanish troops shortly thereafter, leaving a vacuum in the revolutionary movement. In the absence of a civil government, other nations refused to recognize Cuba's belligerent status. As a consequence, Maceo stepped forward and reluctantly agreed to reverse his earlier position and support the creation of a civil government for two years.

Should independence be achieved sooner, a new formal government would be established at that time. The conference delegates agreed that the new revolution was, in fact, an extension of the 1868 struggle. The primary function of this new government was to prosecute the war to a successful conclusion; to this end, its powers would be extensive. The Cuban populace was expected to fully support the revolution. Foreigners, too, were obliged to support the cause by paying property taxes unless their country recognized Cuba's belligerency.

Delegates elected a president, vice president, and four secretaries. Salvador Cisneros Betancourt was elected president, Bartolomé Masó vice president, and Tomás Estrada Palma foreign representative. Máximo Gómez was appointed general in chief of the army, with Lt. Gen. Antonio Maceo appointed as second in command. To avoid governmental interference with the war effort, as had occurred during the

Ten Years' War, all military operations were to be controlled by the general in chief. A form of revolutionary government remained in place until U.S. occupation forces departed in 1902 and the new formal Cuban government emerged.

See also Cuban Junta; Gómez Báez, Máximo; Maceo Grajales, Antonio; Martí y Pérez, José; Ten Years' War.

References and Further Readings

Foner, Philip S. *The Spanish-Cuban-American War.* 2 vols. New York: Monthly Review Press, 1972.

Thomas, Hugh. *Cuba: The Pursuit of Freedom.* New York: Harper & Row, 1971.

Cuban Revolutionary Party (El Partido Revolucionario Cubano)

Created in the United States in 1892 by the father-patriot of Cuban independence, José Martí, the Cuban Revolutionary Party was pivotal in the Cuban independence movement. The influential Cuban junta, which played a key role in enlisting support for the Cuban cause, emerged from the Cuban Revolutionary Party.

Through Martí's untiring efforts, the party slowly acquired funds with which to promote the fight for independence. Tobacco workers, for example, agreed to contribute one day's earnings per week. Other, larger donations were also forthcoming, but the contributions of the tobacco workers testified to Martí's dedication to securing grassroot support. Interestingly, virtually all of South America was quite indifferent to the Cuban cause, although private organizations did provide some financial assistance to the Cuban Revolutionary Party.

See also Cuban Junta; Cuban Revolution; Martí y Pérez, José.

References and Further Readings

Foner, Philip S. *The Spanish-Cuban-American War.* 2 vols. New York: Monthly Review Press, 1972.

Thomas, Hugh. *Cuba: The Pursuit of Freedom.* New York: Harper & Row, 1971.

Cuban War of Independence

See **Ten Years' War**

Daiquirí Beachhead (Cuba)

See **Santiago, Campaign and Siege of**

Dana, Charles Anderson (1819–1897)

Born in New Hampshire, Charles Anderson Dana turned to a career in journalism after briefly experiencing the transcendentalist life at Brook Farm in Massachusetts. He joined the staff of Horace Greeley's *New York Tribune* in 1847 and became the paper's managing editor in 1849, a position he held until 1862. During the Civil War, Dana served as an official observer for Secretary of War Edwin M. Stanton and spent considerable time on the staff of Gen. Ulysses S. Grant. In 1868, Dana acquired the *New York Sun,* which soon became the instrument of his support for Cuban independence. His position on that issue, however, put him at odds with the Grant administration, which supported Spain and its colonial policies.

When a Spanish gunboat fired on the steamer *Allianca,* Dana decried the act and declared that the next time a similar incident occurred, the Spanish vessel should be destroyed. He was attracted to the writings of the great Cuban leader José Martí and published his work in the *Sun.* When Martí died, Dana wrote his obituary. He was also an active supporter of the Cuban junta during the Second Cuban Revolution in 1895. Indeed, there may have been no American more supportive of the Cuban cause than Charles A. Dana. Unfortunately, he did not live to see a free Cuba. When he died on 17 October 1897, his passing was mourned by the Cuban community.

> **See also** Cuban Junta; Cuban Revolutionary Government; Journalism; Martí y Pérez, José; Ten Years' War.
> **References and Further Readings**
> Brown, Charles H. *The Correspondents' War: Journalists in the Spanish-American War.* New York: Charles Scribner's Sons, 1967.

Davis, Charles Henry (1845–1921)

Born in Massachusetts to a naval officer who served with distinction in the Civil War, Charles Henry Davis graduated from the U.S. Naval Academy in 1864. Although his service thereafter was varied, he was particularly noted for his navigational skills and expertise with underwater oceanic cables. During the Spanish-American War, he was captain of the *Dixie,* a former transport vessel purchased by the navy for war service.

In the Puerto Rican Campaign, he commanded a small task force that included the gunboats *Annapolis* and *Wasp.* As the Puerto Rican Campaign developed, Davis expressed the belief that San Juan could be captured by the navy, a view that was shared by Adm. William T. Sampson and Capt. Alfred Thayer Mahan. However, General of the Army Nelson A. Miles opposed the plan, which subsequently became an issue of contention between the rival services. Eventually, the idea was scuttled.

Davis's Spanish-American War service also included actions off the shore of Cuba. In later life, he authored several books, including a biography of his father.

See also Interservice Relations; Naval Blockade of Cuba; Puerto Rican Campaign.

References and Further Readings

Chadwick, Rear Adm. French Ensor. *Relations of the United States and Spain: The Spanish American War.* 2 vols. New York: Charles Scribner's Sons, 1911 (reprinted in 1968).

Trask, David F. *The War with Spain in 1898.* Lincoln: University of Nebraska Press, 1996.

Richard Harding Davis. Perhaps the most renowned journalist of his day, Davis covered the Cuban and Puerto Rican Campaigns for the New York World *and* Scribner's Magazine.

Davis, Richard Harding (1864–1916)

A celebrated journalist and bon vivant, Richard Harding Davis was born in Philadelphia. The son of novelist Rebecca Harding Davis, he seems to have inherited his mother's literary bent and chose a career of words. Davis covered Cuba's fight for independence and the Spanish-American War during his journalism career.

In 1889, Davis joined the *New York Sun,* where he created a series of stories about a dashing fictional figure, Cortland Van

Bibber. The series was an overwhelming success and established Davis as one of the country's top journalists. In 1890, he was named managing editor of *Harper's Weekly*.

In 1896, with the Cuban Revolution gaining momentum, Davis traveled to Cuba, representing both *Harper's* and William Randolph Hearst's *New York Journal*. While in Cuba, he watched the execution of Cuban prisoners, which prompted him to write a powerful story entitled "The Death of Rodríguez." Later, one of his articles that appeared in the *Journal* was misrepresented by that paper. That deception so angered Davis that he never again worked for Hearst.

Following several European assignments, he returned to the United States in 1898 to cover the Spanish-American War for Joseph Pulitzer's *New York World*, the *Times* of London, and *Scribner's Magazine*. His reporting of the Santiago Campaign was frequently critical of U.S. military leadership, though he admired Theodore Roosevelt and wrote glowingly of the Rough Riders. He also covered the Puerto Rican Campaign.

Davis did not confine his criticism to the military, however. Early in the war, he denounced fellow reporter Poultney Bigelow, whose stories focused on the army's failure to provide proper living conditions, food, and equipment for the troops preparing to fight in Cuba. Davis believed such attacks were counterproductive to the war effort.

A natty dresser, Davis was aloof and something of a loner. Some of his fellow reporters saw him as overly romantic, but he was widely read and loved by the public. In addition to his newspaper work and a nonfiction work on the Spanish-American War, Davis authored nine works of fiction and three plays.

See also Bigelow, Poultney; Hearst, William Randolph; Journalism; Pulitzer, Joseph; Rough Riders.

THE BATTLE OF
SAN JUAN HILL

RICHARD HARDING DAVIS tells in the OCTOBER SCRIBNER'S how San Juan Hill was captured. His story of the battle is fully illustrated.

CAPTAIN ARTHUR H. LEE the British Military Attaché, gives a thrilling account of the fight of the Regulars at El Caney. Illustrated with photographs by the author.

SURRENDER OF SANTIAGO an illustrated article by J. F. J. Archibald, a correspondent present at the event.

Many other interesting features.

OCTOBER SCRIBNER'S
NOW READY   PRICE, 25 CENTS

Poster for an article in Scribner's Magazine, October 1898.

References and Further Readings

Brown, Charles H. *The Correspondents' War: Journalists in the Spanish-American War.* New York: Charles Scribner's Sons, 1967.

Chettle, John H. "When War Called, Davis Answered." *Smithsonian,* vol. 31, no. 1, April 2000.

Davis, Richard Harding. *The Cuban and Puerto Rican Campaigns.* New York: Charles Scribner's Sons, 1898.

Dawes, Charles Gates (1865–1951)

Born in Ohio, Charles Gates Dawes was a prominent attorney, influential Republican, and financier. He practiced law in Lincoln, Nebraska, until a series of financial setbacks forced him to move to Illinois. There, he became a key figure in that state's Republican machine, providing strong support for William McKinley and his actions during the Spanish-American War.

Following McKinley's election to the presidency, Dawes was appointed comptroller of the currency. As one of the nation's most knowledgeable individuals in fiscal matters, he was a confidante of President McKinley and the politically powerful senator from Ohio Marcus Hanna. An astute observer, Dawes provided valuable insights into the Washington scene and the presidency during the Spanish-American War in his *Journal of the McKinley Years.*

See also McKinley, William, Jr.; Spanish-American War, U.S. Public Reaction to.

References and Further Readings

Dawes, Charles G. *A Journal of the McKinley Years.* Chicago: Lakeside Press, 1950.

Leech, Margaret. *In the Days of McKinley.* New York: Harper & Brothers, 1959.

Day, William Rufus (1849–1923)

Born in Ravenna, Ohio, William Rufus Day was a longtime friend of William McKinley. A lawyer and jurist, Day was named assistant secretary of state to John Sherman in March 1897. Sherman's appointment was the result of political maneuvering by President McKinley. Hoping to create a senatorial vacancy in Ohio that could be filled by Marcus Hanna, McKinley persuaded the aging Sherman to relinquish his Senate seat and accept an appointment as secretary of state. During the year he served as Sherman's assistant, Day carried on the business of the department as the de facto secretary, and in April 1898, he succeeded Sherman as secretary of state. He served in this capacity throughout the war with Spain. His diplomatic skills were highly valued by President McKinley.

In September 1898, John Hay was named secretary of state, freeing Day to accept a presidential appointment to negotiate with Spain for the disposition of the Philippines. Day was opposed to the United States acquiring the entire archipelago but was overruled by McKinley.

> **See also** Hay, John Milton; McKinley, William, Jr.; Peace
> Commission; Philippine Islands, Acquisition of, by the United States.
> **References and Further Readings**
> Gould, Lewis L. *The Spanish-American War and President McKinley.*
> Lawrence: University of Kansas Press, 1982.
> Leech, Margaret. *In the Days of McKinley.* New York: Harper &
> Brothers, 1959.

Declaration of Paris (1856)

See **Naval Blockade of Cuba**

Derby, George McClellan (1856–1948)

Born at sea, George McClellan Derby was educated in Europe before returning to the United States and matriculating at West Point. After graduating in 1878, he was assigned to the Corps of Engineers, where he spent his entire military career. During the Spanish-American War, Derby served as chief engineer of the Fifth Corps in Cuba.

Derby conducted extensive reconnaissance missions between Santiago and the Fifth Corps landing area at Daiqurí. His efforts produced the first detailed maps of the area and provided valuable intelligence regarding Spanish troop positions. Derby was also actively involved in the Signal Corps's balloon survey during the advance on Santiago.

> **See also** Balloons; Santiago, Campaign and Siege of.
> **References and Further Readings**
> Cosmas, Graham. *An Army for Empire: The United States Army in the
> Spanish-American War.* College Station: Texas A&M University
> Press, 1998.
> Parkinson, Russell J. "United States Signal Corps Balloons,
> 1871–1902." *Military Affairs,* winter, 1960–1961.
> Wheeler, Joseph. *The Santiago Campaign, 1898.* Port Washington,
> NY: Kennikat Press, 1971.

Dewey, George (1837–1917)

Born in Montpelier, Vermont, on 26 December 1837, George Dewey graduated from the U.S. Naval Academy in 1858. During the Civil War, he served under Adm. David Farragut at New Orleans and Port Hudson, Mississippi. He was later assigned to the North Atlantic Squadron and participated in the campaign against Fort Fisher near Wilmington, North Carolina. As a result of his great victory at Manila Bay in the Philippines, Dewey was the most celebrated naval hero of the Spanish-American War.

Commodore George Dewey won instant renown for his great victory over the Spanish fleet at Manila Bay on 1 May 1898.

After the Civil War, he had a wide range of assignments that included service at sea as well as on shore, thus providing him with a broad naval background that ensured a steady rise in rank. Dewey's career was also furthered by his advocacy of the modern armored battleship. He was promoted to commander in 1872, captain in 1884, and commodore in 1896. He assumed command of the Asiatic Squadron at Nagasaki, Japan, on 3 January 1898. The assignment was one he had requested and one that had been pro-

moted and endorsed by then Assistant Secretary of the Navy Theodore Roosevelt. Acting on his own volition, Dewey moved his squadron to Hong Kong. Under orders from Roosevelt to be prepared to attack the Spanish fleet in Manila Bay if war was declared, he brought his squadron to a war-ready status.

In late April, Dewey was advised that a state of war existed between the United States and Spain. He was ordered to proceed to the Philippines and attack the Spanish fleet. The Asiatic Squadron, consisting of four cruisers—including the USS *Olympia,* Dewey's flagship—two gunboats, one revenue cutter, and a pair of supply vessels, sailed unobserved into Manila Bay on the night of 1 May 1898.

At 5:40 A.M., Dewey directed his flag captain, Charles Gridley, to "fire when ready." With that command, he commenced his attack on the seven smaller and inferior ships of the Spanish fleet, which were lying at anchor in the bay. Within a few hours, all Spanish ships were either sunk or burning and abandoned. Dewey's losses amounted to 7 wounded.

The Battle of Manila Bay was a signal victory for the U.S. Navy. Later, the Asiatic Squadron supported the landing of the American Expeditionary Force, which subsequently captured the city of Manila.

Dewey was promoted to rear admiral in honor of his magnificent victory and later was elevated to admiral of the navy, a special rank created just for him. Highly regarded as a thorough yet aggressive leader, Dewey served on the navy's General Board until his death in 1917.

See also Asiatic Squadron, U.S. Navy; Long, John Davis; Manila Bay, Battle of; Navy, U.S.; Roosevelt, Theodore.

References and Further Readings

Dewey, George. *Autobiography of George Dewey, Admiral of the Navy.* Annapolis, MD: Naval Institute Press, 1987.

Musicant, Ivan. *Empire by Default: The Spanish-American War and the Dawn of the American Century.* New York: Henry Holt and Company, 1998.

O'Toole, G. J. A. *The Spanish War: An American Epic, 1898.* New York: W. W. Norton, 1984.

Sargent, Nathan. *Admiral Dewey and the Manila Campaign.* Washington, DC: Naval Historical Foundation, 1947.

Trask, David F. *The War with Spain in 1898.* Lincoln: University of Nebraska Press, 1996.

Dick Act (1903)

See **Militia Act of 1903**

Diederich, Otto von

See **Germany**

Diseases

As in the Civil War, disease was as much to be feared as enemy fire during the Spanish-American War. Far more soldiers succumbed to the ravages of illness than to the effects of combat. Typhoid, typhus, and dysentery were widespread, particularly in stateside camps during the early weeks of the war. The U.S. Army Medical Corps, along with the rest of the army, was totally unprepared to deal with the rapid mobilization. Later, as the mosquito season reached its apex in

Cuba, yellow fever and malaria took an increasingly heavy toll on the troops. The more common communicable diseases such as mumps, chicken pox, and measles were also much in evidence. In U.S. camps and staging areas, nearly 21,000 cases of typhoid were reported, with 1,500 fatalities. During the course of the war, some 2,500 officers and men died from the effects of typhoid, compared to 281 battle-related deaths.

Spanish troops also suffered from the ravages of disease. Yellow fever claimed the lives of some 13,000 Spanish troops during the Cuban Revolution, ten times the number that died in combat. The Cubans, having developed some immunity, were less affected by the disease.

The rapid buildup of the army at the outset of the Spanish-American War resulted in overcrowded, unsanitary camps. These conditons were responsible for the spread of both typhus and typhoid. Although their names are phonetically similar, the two diseases are unrelated. Typhus is an acute infectious disease transmitted by fleas and lice; typhoid, also an acute infectious disease, is acquired by ingesting contaminated water, milk, and so forth.

Little could be done about mosquito-borne diseases such as yellow fever—called "yellow jack"—and malaria, other than to avoid campaigning during the summer when those fevers peaked. As summer approached, army leaders became fearful of an epidemic. A debilitating disease, yellow fever caused chills and fever, jaundice, internal hemorrhaging, and frequently death. Malarial symptoms were similar to those of yellow fever, but although debilitating, malaria was less deadly.

Both diseases were thought to be caused by poor sanitary conditions. It was not until 1904 that researchers learned that they were transmitted by mosquitoes. The female mosquito *Aedes aegypti* transmitted yellow fever; the *Anopheles* mosquito transmitted malaria.

As stories of the revolting camp conditions and the horrifying effects of these diseases spread across the United States, the War Department began to initiate reforms. Camps were moved to more healthful locations, stringent sanitation procedures were implemented, and facilities were improved, leading to a noticeable decline in hygiene-related diseases. More important, these reforms paved the way for a greater awareness of the need for proper sanitation and hygiene in the military.

See also Camps, Staging Areas, and Embarkation Points, U.S. Army; Casualties; Medical Department, U.S. Army; Sternberg, George Miller.

References and Further Readings

Cosmas, Graham. *An Army for Empire: The United States Army in the Spanish-American War.* College Station: Texas A&M University Press, 1998.

Gibson, John M. *Soldier in White: The Life of General George Miller Sternberg.* Durham, NC: Duke University Press, 1958.

Dodge, Grenville Mellen (1831–1916)

Born in Danvers, Massachusetts, Grenville Mellen Dodge served with distinction during the Civil War, rising to the rank of major general of volunteers. A civil engineer by training, he was active in railroading before the Civil War and returned to that field at the war's end. His skill as a railroad surveyor and builder soon moved him to the forefront of his profession. By 1866, he was a builder and chief engineer for the Union Pacific Railroad. A strong Republican and confidante to both President William McKinley and Secretary of War Russell Alger, Dodge encouraged a peaceful solution to the growing trouble with Spain.

When war was declared, Dodge was offered a senior command but rejected the offer. Throughout the war, however, he remained in close touch with McKinley and Alger, commenting on progress and new developments.

McKinley created a commission to investigate the notorious "beef scandal" and other controversies that surfaced during the war. The commission, officially called the War Department Investigating Commission, was chaired by Dodge and soon came to be known simply as the Dodge Commission.

See also Beef Scandal; McKinley, William, Jr.; Miles, Nelson Appleton; War Department Investigating Commission.

References and Further Readings

Alger, Russell A. *The Spanish-American War.* New York: Harper & Brothers, 1901.

DeMontravel, Peter R. *A Hero to His Fighting Men: Nelson A. Miles, 1839–1925.* Kent, OH: Kent State University Press, 1998.

Hirshon, Stanley P. *Grenville M. Dodge.* Bloomington: Indiana University Press, 1967.

Leech, Margaret. *In the Days of McKinley.* New York: Harper & Brothers, 1959.

Dodge Commission

See **War Department Investigating Commission**

Dorst, Joseph Haddox (1852–1915)

Born in Kentucky, Joseph Haddox Dorst graduated from West Point in 1873. After extensive service in the Fourth U.S. Cavalry during the Indian wars, he was promoted to captain in 1898. In May of that year, he was ordered to carry out a mission to resupply Cuban revolutionaries. Dorst and his detachment embarked on their mission aboard an old side-wheel steamer, the *Gussie*. Unfortunately, word of the mission was soon widely circulated by newsmen, and the advance publicity quickly robbed the expedition of the secrecy essential to its success. Nevertheless, the operation moved ahead as planned, and the detachment landed on Cuban soil. However, no revolutionaries were found. A force of Spanish Cavalry did compel Dorst and his men to return to Tampa, embarrassed and chagrined.

Later, in a second expedition, this one shrouded in proper secrecy, Dorst successfully landed troops, equipment, and supplies, thereby restoring a measure of pride to both himself and the army. Following his Cuban adventures, Dorst served in the Philippines.

See also Journalism.
References and Further Readings
Brown, Charles H. *The Correspondents' War: Journalists in the Spanish-American War*. New York: Charles Scribner's Sons, 1967.
Cosmas, Graham. *An Army for Empire: The United States Army in the Spanish-American War*. College Station: Texas A&M University Press, 1998.

Duffield, Henry Martyn (1842–1912)

Born in Michigan, Henry Martyn Duffield was an officer of volunteers during the Civil War. When the Spanish-American War broke out, Duffield, a successful attorney, was commissioned a brigadier general. He was appointed to lead a brigade of Michigan volunteers in Gen. William R. Shafter's Fifth Corps, the only separate unit of volunteers in Shafter's command.

During the Santiago Campaign, Duffield's brigade, supported by three naval vessels, was assigned to create a diversion at the Aguadores River while Shafter's main body advanced on El Caney and San Juan Heights. Only about half of Duffield's brigade had reached Cuba, so his command included some 1,200 men of the Thirty-third Michigan, augmented by Cuban revolutionaries.

Duffield's assignment was strategic. It was hoped that his movement would make the Spanish think that the U.S. objective was

Morro Battery, a key fort covering the east side of Santiago harbor. The ruse was unsuccessful. Following the Aguadores demonstration, Duffield's command was attached to the Independent Brigade of Gen. John C. Bates.

See also Aguadores River, Demonstration at; Santiago, Campaign and Siege of.

References and Further Readings

Nofi, Albert A. *The Spanish-American War, 1898*. Conshohocken, PA: Combined Books, 1998.

Trask, David F. *The War with Spain in 1898*. Lincoln: University of Nebraska Press, 1996.

Dunne, Finley Peter (1867–1936)

Born in Chicago, Finley Peter Dunne was one of the most influential U.S. journalists and humorist-satirists of the late nineteenth and early twentieth centuries. During the Spanish-American War, Dunne presented controversial personalities and issues of the times through a fictional Irish bartender named Mr. Dooley. Dooley's biting commentaries on Gen. Nelson A. Miles, Emilio Aguinaldo, and the Philippine-American War (or Philippine Insurrection, as it was then known) were widely read and might be likened to today's *Doonesbury* comic strip. Between 1898 and 1900, Dunne collected and published three volumes of Mr. Dooley's philosophy.

See also Journalism; Philippine-American War, U.S. Public Reaction to; Spanish-American War, U.S. Public Reaction to.

References and Further Readings

Dunne, Finley Peter. *Mr. Dooley in Peace and War*. Boston: Small, Maynard & Company, 1898.

———. *Mr. Dooley's Opinions*. New York: Harper & Company, 1901.

Musicant, Ivan. *Empire by Default: The Spanish-American War and the Dawn of the American Century*. New York: Henry Holt and Company, 1998.

Trask, David F. *The War with Spain in 1898*. Lincoln: University of Nebraska Press, 1996.

Dupuy de Lôme, Enrique (1851–1904)

Two incidents served to arouse and inflame the U.S. public in the weeks preceding the outbreak of war with Spain: the celebrated de Lôme letter and the destruction of the battleship *Maine* in Havana harbor. Of French extraction, Enrique Dupuy de Lôme, the Spanish ambassador to the United States, was a plenipotentiary of wide experience. He was regarded as arrogant and aloof by many in his Washington circles, but no one would deny his polished diplomatic skills.

Although thoroughly professional as the representative of the Spanish Crown, privately de Lôme abhorred the notion of Cuban autonomy and resented the U.S. refusal to crack down on activities of the Cuban junta. Had these views remained nothing more than his personal opinions, there would have been no incident. However, de Lôme committed the unpardonable faux pas (particularly for a diplomat of his experience) of expressing his views in a private letter. His letter was written to José Canalejas, editor of the *Heraldo de Madrid*, who was visiting Cuba at the time. Although undated, the letter was probably written in December 1897. De Lôme vented his full spleen in the missive, calling William McKinley a weak president who sought to pacify the "jingoes" in his party. Clearly, the ambassador was frustrated by U.S.-Spanish relations with respect to Cuba and needed to sound off to someone. Unfortunately for de Lôme, the letter was intercepted and read by Tomás Estrada Palma, representative of the Cuban Revolutionary Party in the United States. Estrada Palma promptly passed the letter on to the Cuban junta, which in turn contacted the State Department as well as William Randolph Hearst's vigorously pro-Cuban *New York Journal.*

When confronted by Assistant Secretary of State William R. Day, de Lôme admitted the letter was his and subsequently cabled his resignation to Madrid. The story broke first in the *Journal* and appeared soon thereafter in every major paper across the country. With its penchant for the sensational, Hearst's paper called it "the worst insult to the United States in its history," and others reported the incident with similar tones of outrage.

The U.S. government called for an apology. Defamation of the president's character could not be tolerated. Much diplomatic palavering ensued. Spain was properly regretful and eventually apologized, by which time, however, the destruction of the *Maine* resulted in new and far more sensational headlines.

See also Cuban Junta; Hearst, William Randolph; *Maine*; McKinley, William, Jr.; Spain.

References and Further Readings

Foner, Philip S. *The Spanish-Cuban-American War.* 2 vols. New York: Monthly Review Press, 1972.

Leech, Margaret. *In the Days of McKinley.* New York: Harper & Brothers, 1959.

Musicant, Ivan. *Empire by Default: The Spanish-American War and the Dawn of the American Century.* New York: Henry Holt and Company, 1998.

Wisan, Joseph Ezra. *The Cuban Crisis as Reflected in the New York Press (1895–1898).* New York: Columbia University Press, 1934.

Dynamite Gun

See **Weapons**

Eagan, Charles Patrick (1841–1919)

Charles Patrick Eagan moved to the United States with his Irish immigrant parents and was raised in the Washington Territory. After Civil War service as a volunteer, he remained in the army and saw action on the frontier during the Indian wars and was wounded in action during the Modoc Campaign. Eagan was a key player in the infamous "beef scandal" of the Spanish-American War.

In 1874, he transferred to the Subsistence Department, whose primary function was to feed the army. He was promoted to brigadier general in 1898 and appointed chief commissary officer of the army. As commissary general, Eagan worked tirelessly to improve the quality and distribution of rations to the army's field units.

The one significant change Eagan made, however, was destined to become his nemesis. In his zeal to improve the efficiency of distribution, he decided to replace the fresh beef given to troops in the field with processed beef packed in tins. Ostensibly, the beef could be consumed directly from the tins, though most troops did cook the meat. However, its appearance, odor, and taste made it a most unpalatable meal, whether cooked or not.

The use of tinned beef developed into the "beef scandal," which was the subject of an investigation by the Dodge Commission after the war. Then General of the Army Nelson Miles brought strong charges against the Commissary Department for its role in the scandal.

Stung by Miles's allegations, Eagan, who was known for his violent temper, lashed back with a virulent tirade, calling Miles a liar. As a result of his behavior, a court-martial ensued in which Eagan was found guilty of insubordination and suspended from duty for six years by President McKinley, though he was kept on full pay. At the end of the six years, Eagan retired.

In fairness, it should be noted that the problem with the tinned beef was not due to Eagan's dereliction or incompetence but rather to a poor, albeit well-intentioned, choice.

See also Beef Scandal; McKinley, William, Jr.; Miles, Nelson Appleton; War Department Investigating Commission.

References and Further Readings

Cosmas, Graham. *An Army for Empire: The United States Army in the Spanish-American War.* College Station: Texas A&M University Press, 1998.

DeMontravel, Peter R. *A Hero to His Fighting Men: Nelson A. Miles, 1839–1925.* Kent, OH: Kent State University Press, 1998.

Leech, Margaret. *In the Days of McKinley.* New York: Harper & Brothers, 1959.

Eastern Squadron, U.S. Navy

In late June 1898, with the Spanish-American War well under way, Secretary of the Navy John Long, acting on the recommendation of his Naval War Board, authorized the creation of a new naval force to be designated the Eastern Squadron. The decision was a strategic response designed to meet the threat posed by Adm. Manuel de la Cámara y Libermoore's fleet, which sailed from Cádiz, Spain, in mid-June to aid Spanish forces in the Philippines.

In response to the Spanish gambit, the navy, in a carefully planted intelligence ploy, let it be known that the Eastern Squadron might attack the coast of Spain. It was hoped that the news would result in the withdrawal of Cámara's fleet. In addition, the squadron was tabbed for eventual duty in the Philippines.

On 7 July, Commodore John C. Watson was appointed to command the Eastern Squadron, which was to include the battleships *Iowa* and *Oregon,* together with auxiliary vessels. Watson's ships would be taken from Adm. William T. Sampson's fleet, then carrying out the U.S. naval blockade of Cuba.

Meanwhile, Admiral Sampson had been directed to expand coverage of his blockade to include all of Cuba and Puerto Rico. Until that time, the blockade had focused on the northern coast of Cuba because the island's proximity to the Florida Keys facilitated refueling and because Sampson lacked enough ships to effectively monitor the entire island of Cuba, let alone Puerto Rico as well. Sampson protested Secretary Long's order, arguing that his fleet would be unduly weakened if those vessels were detached.

As the threat of Admiral Cámara's eastward sortie mounted, Secretary Long reinforced the Eastern Squadron with the armored cruiser *Brooklyn,* along with three auxiliary cruisers—the *Yosemite, Yankee,* and *Dixie.* In addition, Admiral Sampson was advised to be ready to detach the Eastern Squadron as circumstances dictated.

Again, Sampson protested, arguing that detachment of Watson's group would leave him without enough ships to enforce the blockade and cover the landing of Gen. William Shafter's Fifth Corps. Sampson was also thinking about the presence of Adm. Pascual Cervera's fleet in the harbor at Santiago de Cuba. He was concerned that if the Eastern Squadron was detached, he would lack the strength to deal with Cervera's fleet should it attempt to break out of the harbor. In view of this contingency, the Naval War Board directed that the *Oregon* and *Iowa* be retained by Sampson until replaced by ships from the East Coast.

The defeat of Admiral Cervera's fleet on 3 July 1898, coupled with the subsequent recall of Admiral Cámara's fleet to Spain, greatly reduced tensions within the navy and partially obviated the need for the Eastern Squadron. Nonetheless, the McKinley administration remained ready to send Watson's group to the Philippines to reinforce Commodore George Dewey's command against the Spanish or against any overt act by a European power (Germany was regarded as the most likely possibility).

Early in August, Sampson was directed to sail to the Philippines with a reinforced command that included the Eastern Squadron and seven additional cruisers. Once again, he expressed his disapproval, arguing for a concentration at San Juan, Puerto Rico. However, once peace negotiations with Spain were under way, Secretary Long rescinded the order, thereby bringing an end to the Eastern Squadron's role as a separate naval force.

See also Naval Strategy, U.S.; Sampson, William Thomas; Watson, John C.

References and Further Readings

Chadwick, Rear Adm. French Ensor. *Relations of the United States and Spain: The Spanish American War*. 2 vols. New York: Charles Scribner's Sons, 1911 (reprinted in 1968).

Trask, David F. *The War with Spain in 1898*. Lincoln: University of Nebraska Press, 1996.

Eighth Corps

See **Philippine Expeditionary Force**

El Caney (Cuba), Battle of (1 July 1898)

In his advance on Santiago, Cuba, Gen. William Shafter's strategy called for the seizure of San Juan Heights, preceded by the capture of El Caney, a key location 6 miles northeast of Santiago on the road

War council at Gen. William Shafter's headquarters, planning for the Battle of El Caney in San Juan.

to Guantánamo. El Caney was also important because of its proximity to a reservoir containing Santiago's water supply.

Shafter planned to attack San Juan Heights with one column while a second force struck El Caney and a third column executed a diversionary movement toward Aguadores. The attack on El Caney, slated to commence at dawn on 1 July, was to be carried out by the right wing of Shafter's Fifth Corps, commanded by Brig. Gen. Henry Ware Lawton. Shafter anticipated that no more than two hours would be needed to take El Caney, after which Lawton would march his command southwest to participate in the main effort against San Juan Heights. The heights attack would not commence until Lawton arrived.

Lawton's division was composed of two brigades commanded by Brig. Gen. Adna R. Chaffee and Brig. Gen. William Ludlow. Chaffee's brigade consisted of the Seventh, Twelfth, and Seventeenth Regulars; Ludlow had the Eighth and Twenty-second Regulars plus the Second Massachusetts Volunteers. In addition, there were two independent brigades under Brig. Gen. John C. Bates and Col. Evan Miles (no relation to Nelson A. Miles), for a total of about 6,600 men. Artillery support would be provided by a battery of four 3.2-inch guns commanded by Capt. Allyn Capron.

Despite the strategic location of El Caney, the Spanish commander at Santiago, Gen. Arsenio Linares y Pomba, had assigned only 500 men under Gen. Joaquin Vara del Ray to defend it. But if the garrison was small, the position was strong and well fortified, protected by two wooden blockhouses and a network of trenches, in addition to a stone fort located at El Viso, just southeast of El Caney.

Lawton marched his command over rough terrain through the night of 30 June so as to be in position to attack the next morning. Chaffee's brigade was located near the stone fort; Ludlow's brigade was positioned on the southwest. Bates and Miles were held in reserve.

Lawton began his attack between 6:30 and 7:00 A.M. Progress was slow from the start. Indeed, although Shafter had expected the entire position to be taken in two hours, it required that much time just to overcome the six wooden blockhouses. Gen. Vara del Ray was killed at about noon, but his troops continued their stubborn resistance well into the afternoon.

Although the Spanish defenders had no artillery, their Mauser rifles proved superior to the U.S. Krag-Jörgensen weapon. U.S. artillery was largely ineffective until Capron moved his battery closer to the action, at which time his guns were able to penetrate the stone fort at El Viso.

The unexpectedly long delay in subduing El Caney complicated Shafter's plan and caused him to direct Lawton to break off the attack and join the effort against San Juan Heights. Lawton protested, arguing that he was close to achieving his objective, and Shafter acquiesced.

As Capron's artillery began to make a difference in the fight, Lawton elected to commit his reserves. At about 3 P.M., he sent the Twelfth Infantry of Chaffee's brigade against El Viso, supported by the Twenty-fourth (black) Infantry of Bates's brigade. Although the Spanish defense of El Caney had been far more effective than Shafter and Lawton expected, by late afternoon, expiring ammunition and heavy casualties precluded a continuation of the battle. Of Vara del Ray's original garrison of 500 men, 235 were casualties, 125 were taken prisoner, and 80 escaped. Lawton's losses amounted to 81 killed and 360 wounded.

See also Aguadores River, Demonstration at; Chaffee, Adna Romanza; Lawton, Henry Ware; Ludlow, William; San Juan Hill, Charge up; Shafter, William Rufus.

References and Further Readings
Beede, Benjamin R., ed. *The War of 1898 and U.S. Interventions, 1898–1934*. New York: Garland Publishing, 1994.

Cosmas, Graham. *An Army for Empire: The United States Army in the Spanish-American War.* College Station: Texas A&M University Press, 1998.

Sargent, Herbert H. *The Campaign of Santiago de Cuba.* Chicago: A. C. McClurg and Company, 1907.

Trask, David F. *The War with Spain in 1898.* Lincoln: University of Nebraska Press, 1996.

El Pozo (Poso)

See **Santiago, Campaign and Siege of**

Escario, Federico

See **Santiago, Campaign and Siege of**

Estrada Palma, Tomás (1835–1908)

The Cuban Revolutionary Party, whose objective was Cuban independence, was represented in the United States by Tomás Estrada Palma. He had served as an army officer during the Ten Years' War.

Tomás Estrada Palma, president of the Cuban junta in New York. Here, Estrada, on the far right, is shown with his cabinet.

Following imprisonment for his role in the war, he went to the United States and became a citizen. When the Cuban Revolution began in 1895, he headed the Cuban junta in New York. Although he promoted Cuban independence, he also supported Cuba's annexation by the United States.

In December 1897, four months before the war between Spain and the United States broke out, Estrada Palma intercepted the famous de Lôme letter and sent it to the *New York Journal.* The letter, harshly critical of President William McKinley, might well have triggered a war with Spain then and there, rather than four months later.

After the declaration of war in April 1898, Estrada Palma staunchly supported U.S. efforts in Cuba and later served as the first president of the Cuban Republic from 1902 to 1906.

See also Cuban Junta; Cuban Revolution; Ten Years' War.

References and Further Readings

Foner, Philip S. *The Spanish-Cuban-American War.* 2 vols. New York: Monthly Review Press, 1972.

Musicant, Ivan. *Empire by Default: The Spanish-American War and the Dawn of the American Century.* New York: Henry Holt and Company, 1998.

Thomas, Hugh. *Cuba: The Pursuit of Freedom.* New York: Harper & Row, 1971.

Eulate y Ferry, Antonio (1845–1952)

A veteran Spanish officer, Antonio Eulate y Ferry joined the naval service at age 15. In the years preceding the Spanish-American War, he served in Cuba and fought the Carlist regime. Early in 1897, he was assigned to command the *Cristóbal Colón,* but by the time of the Spanish-American War, he had been transferred to the battleship *Vizcaya.*

During the fierce Battle of Santiago, which resulted from Adm. Pascual Cervera's attempt to escape from that harbor on 3 July 1898, Eulate, while in command of the *Vizcaya,* acquitted himself in the finest traditions of the Spanish Navy. Wounded several times, he was eventually captured and taken on board the U.S. battleship *Iowa,* where Capt. Robley Evans returned Eulate's saber in a gesture of friendship and respect. Eulate was later held as a prisoner of war in the United States before being returned to Spain.

See also Evans, Robley Dunglison; Santiago de Cuba, Naval Battle of.

References and Further Readings

Feuer, A. B. *The Spanish-American War at Sea.* Westport, CT: Greenwood Press, 1995.

Trask, David F. *The War with Spain in 1898*. Lincoln: University of Nebraska Press, 1996.

Evans, Robley Dunglison (1846–1912)

Born in Virginia, Robley Dunglison Evans graduated from the U.S. Naval Academy in 1863 in time to participate in Civil War naval action along the Atlantic seaboard and went on to serve with distinction during the Spanish-American War.

Although he came to be known as "Fighting Bob," Evans had a scientific bent. For example, in 1876, he invented a long-distance signaling lamp for use on naval vessels. A leading authority on the steel-making process, he played a key role in influencing the U.S. Navy's transition to steel ships.

During the Spanish-American War, Evans replaced Adm. William T. Sampson as commander of the battleship *Iowa*. In that capacity, Evans fired the first shot at Adm. Pascual Cervera's fleet during its sortie from Santiago harbor.

In 1901, Evans was promoted to rear admiral and named to command the Atlantic fleet. The capstone of his career was perhaps his assignment to command the U.S. Navy's "Great White" fleet on its historic round-the-world cruise in 1907.

See also Santiago de Cuba, Naval Battle of.

References and Further Readings

Bradford, James C., ed. *Admirals of the New Steel Navy*. Annapolis, MD: Naval Institute Press, 1996.

Evans, Robley D. *A Sailor's Log*. New York: D. Appleton & Company, 1901.

Feuer, A. B. *The Spanish-American War at Sea*. Westport, CT: Greenwood Press, 1995.

Expansionism

See Imperialism/Expansionism

Fifty Million Dollar Bill

After the battleship *Maine* was destroyed in February 1898 and with the likelihood of war with Spain looming, U.S. President William McKinley introduced legislation to help finance the war. The Fifty Million Dollar Bill, as it was known, allotted $50 million to upgrade the military services in preparation for war. The army-navy planners believed the conflict with Spain would be primarily a naval war, and emphasis was placed on preparing the U.S. fleet and reinforcing U.S. coastal defenses. Accordingly, $29 million of the $50 million went to the navy. The army's role at that early stage was more nebulous because McKinley withheld his plans for Cuba. If the U.S. objective was only to provide assistance to Cuban revolutionaries, the army's role would be far less demanding than if a conventional war was waged against Spain. In retrospect, it might seem that the army should have been given a larger portion of the $50 million, but at the time, the conflict was seen as a naval war.

See also Army, U.S.; McKinley, William, Jr.; Navy, U.S.; War, Spanish-American, U.S. Financing of.

References and Further Readings

Cosmas, Graham. *An Army for Empire: The United States Army in the Spanish-American War.* College Station: Texas A&M University Press, 1998.

Leech, Margaret. *In the Days of McKinley.* New York: Harper & Brothers, 1959.

Filibuster

The term *filibuster,* from the Spanish *filibustero* (free booter), refers to a private group or individual who aids a foreign nation at war or who participates in military action on foreign soil in violation of his or her own nation's neutral position.

Prior to the outbreak of the Spanish-American War, there was considerable activity in running guns, ammunition, and supplies to the Cuban revolutionaries. Although the U.S. Revenue Cutter Service (today's Coast Guard) intercepted many such expeditions, others managed to get through. Notwithstanding its protests, Spain did little to interfere with the expeditions, relying instead on the United States to control the situation. According to one authority, of some 67 filibustering expeditions launched between 1895 and 1898, the United States stopped 33, Spain intercepted 5 on the Cuban coast, 2 were halted by the British Navy, and 27 (40 percent) were successful.

These expeditions were almost entirely organized and funded by the Cuban junta, with a wide network of sympathizers in the United States ready and anxious to provide financial support. Efforts to aid the Cuban Revolutionary Army were, out of necessity, clandestine because such activities violated U.S. neutrality laws. Nevertheless, the Cuban cause relied on such outside support in order to fuel its struggle against the Spanish.

Filibustering produced a number of sensational stories and colorful characters during the Spanish-American War. Such stories include the notorious *Virginius* affair of 1873, in which a vessel with U.S. registry, carrying Cuban revolutionaries, arms, and munitions, was overtaken by the Spanish. The subsequent execution of its crew and passengers produced a storm of controversy, but diplomatic parleying helped to avoid a war at that time. Another story is that of the *Dauntless*, captained by "Dynamite" Johnny O'Brien. The *Dauntless* carried a Hotchkiss 12-pounder (artillery piece) with 800 shells; 1,300 Mauser and Remington rifles; 1,000 machetes; 800 pounds of dynamite; 460,000 rounds of small-arms ammunition; and various medical stores. Its mission interrupted by a Spanish patrol boat after landing some Cuban rebels, the *Dauntless* was forced to put back to sea, where it evaded the Spanish and returned to deposit its cargo on another occasion.

See also Crane, Stephen; Cuban Revolutionary Army; O'Brien, "Dynamite" Johnny.

References and Further Readings

Brown, Charles H. *The Correspondents' War: Journalists in the Spanish-American War.* New York: Charles Scribner's Sons, 1967.

Chadwick, Rear Adm. French Ensor. *Relations of the United States and Spain: The Spanish American War.* 2 vols. New York: Charles Scribner's Sons, 1911 (reprinted in 1968).

O'Toole, G. J. A. *The Spanish War: An American Epic, 1898.* New York: W. W. Norton, 1984.

Rickenbach, Richard V. "Filibustering with the *Dauntless*." *Florida Historical Quarterly,* 28, April 1950.

Smith, Horace. *A Captain Unafraid: The Strange Adventures of Dynamite Johnny O'Brien.* New York: Harper & Brothers, 1912.

Filipino Revolutionary Movement

New and harsh measures imposed by Spanish authorities in the Philippines led to a brief uprising of Filipino workers on Cavite in 1872. Although the authorities quickly suppressed the uprising, it served as a herald of things to come. As in Cuba, the unrest and uprisings in the Philippines reflected the steady disintegration of Spain's colonial empire, which would finally end with the Spanish-American War.

In 1892, José Rizal, a sometime poet, philosopher, artist, and writer whose inspiring works spoke of Filipino independence and nationalism, created the Liga Filipina (Philippine League). Rizal's reactionary novels ignited a spirit of rebellion among a large segment of the Filipino people. Rizal was eventually executed by the Spanish, along with hundreds of other native leaders, but the flame of rebellion that he had ignited continued to burn brightly after his death.

By 1896, the nationalist movement, known as the Katipunan (Patriot's League), numbered some 20,000, and its adherents fought the Spanish with varying degrees of success. The year 1896 also saw the emergence of Emilio Aguinaldo as the de facto leader of the revolutionary movement.

See also Aguinaldo y Famy, Emilio; Katipunan; Liga Filipina; Rizal, José.

References and Further Readings

Gates, John Morgan. *Schoolbooks and Krags: The United States Army in the Philippines, 1898–1902.* Contributions in Military History no. 3. Westport, CT: Greenwood Press, 1973.

Wolff, Leon. *Little Brown Brother: America's Forgotten Bid for Empire Which Cost 250,000 Lives.* New York: Kraus Reprint, 1970.

Flying Squadron, U.S. Navy

After the Spanish-American War broke out, the U.S. Navy was organized into five units, or squadrons. (Basically, a squadron is a group of naval vessels.) One of these was dubbed the "Flying Squadron," so called because it was expected to respond to any one of three possible contingencies: protecting the eastern seaboard, moving to the Caribbean to engage the Spanish fleet, or launching a strike against the Spanish homeland.

During the early weeks of the war, widespread fear of a Spanish strike against the East Coast dictated that the United States prepare for that eventuality. Accordingly, U.S. naval forces were deployed to cover the eastern seaboard from Maine to the Florida Keys. Based at Hampton Roads, Virginia, the Flying Squadron, commanded by Commodore Winfield Scott Schley, consisted of the battleships *Texas* and *Massachusetts* and the cruisers *Brooklyn, Columbia, Minneapolis,* and *New Orleans,* plus auxiliary vessels.

Once Adm. Pascual Cervera's Spanish fleet arrived in Cuban waters, fear of a Spanish attack against the East Coast subsided. Moreover, with Cervera's fleet ensconced in the harbor of Santiago de Cuba, the possibility of a sea battle near Puerto Rico appeared unlikely. Consequently, the Flying Squadron merged into the North Atlantic Squadron under Rear Adm. William T. Sampson and played a key role in the Battle of Santiago de Cuba on 3 July 1898.

See also Cervera y Topete, Pascual; Naval Strategy, U.S.; Naval Vessels, U.S., Auxiliary; Santiago de Cuba, Naval Battle of; Schley, Winfield Scott.

References and Further Readings

Chadwick, Rear Adm. French Ensor. *Relations of the United States and Spain: The Spanish American War.* 2 vols. New York: Charles Scribner's Sons, 1911 (reprinted in 1968).

Feuer, A. B. *The Spanish-American War at Sea.* Westport, CT: Greenwood Press, 1995.

Schley, Rear Adm. Winfield Scott. "Admiral Schley's Own Story." *Cosmopolitan Magazine,* December 1911.

Trask, David F. *The War with Spain in 1898.* Lincoln: University of Nebraska Press, 1996.

Food

See **Rations**

Foraker-Turpie Amendment

The Foraker-Turpie Amendment, introduced on 13 April 1898, was a congressional resolution that supported official recognition of the Cuban Republic. Cosponsored by Sen. Joseph Benson Foraker (1846–1917) of Ohio and Sen. David M. Turpie (1828–1909) of Indiana, the controversial amendment, which reflected congressional differences over the Cuban question and the president's authority to deal with the issue, was narrowly defeated on 16 April.

See also Cuban Revolution; Teller, Henry Moore.

References and Further Readings

Leech, Margaret. *In the Days of McKinley.* New York: Harper & Brothers, 1959.

Musicant, Ivan. *Empire by Default: The Spanish-American War and the Dawn of the American Century.* New York: Henry Holt and Company, 1998.

Fort San Antonio de Abad (Philippines)

A Spanish strong point on the Zapote Line, Fort San Antonio de Abad was southwest of Manila, close to the waters of Manila Bay. Before he was replaced in August 1898, Basilio Augustín Dávila, the Spanish governor-general of the Philippines, anticipating that Fort San Antonio de Abad would be a focal point of the U.S. effort to seize Manila, augmented its defense with three 3.6-inch guns and six 3.2-inch mountain guns.

During the First Battle of Manila Bay (in August 1898), Adm. George Dewey's ships in the bay provided covering fire while Gen. Francis Vinton Greene's brigade advanced and captured the fort, which the Spanish had by that time elected to abandon.

See also Dewey, George; Greene, Francis Vinton; Manila Bay, Battle of; Merritt, Wesley.

References and Further Readings

Linn, Brian McAllister. *The Philippine War, 1899–1902.* Lawrence: University Press of Kansas, 2000.

Trask, David F. *The War with Spain in 1898.* Lincoln: University of Nebraska Press, 1996.

France

See **Spanish-American War, International Reaction to**

Frye, William Pierce (1831–1911)

Born in Lewiston, Maine, William Pierce Frye studied law and in 1871 was elected to the U.S. House of Representatives, where he served for ten years. In 1881, he was elected to the U.S. Senate and in 1896 was named president pro tem of that body. An influential leader in the Senate, Frye was politically conservative and a supporter of President William McKinley's policies. Owing to his views and support for the McKinley administration, Frye was named a member of the Peace Commission during the negotiations with Spain at the end of the Spanish-American War.

An ardent expansionist, Frye favored acquisition of the entire Philippine Archipelago. At the same time, however, he believed that Spain needed to leave the bargaining table without feeling a loss of national pride and dignity. Thus, he supported a conciliatory payment to Spain in exchange for the archipelago. President McKinley and Congress accepted this proposal, and $20 million was eventually paid to Spain.

See also Peace Commission.

References and Further Readings

Leech, Margaret. *In the Days of McKinley*. New York: Harper & Brothers, 1959.

Morgan, H. Wayne, ed. *Making Peace with Spain: The Diary of Whitelaw Reid—September–December, 1898*. Austin: University of Texas Press, 1965.

Funston, Frederick (1865–1917)

Born in New Carlisle, Ohio, Frederick Funston was a filibuster as a young man, running guns and ammunition to Cuban rebels. In 1896, he joined the Cuban Revolutionary Army and participated in several campaigns as an artillery captain. When war with Spain broke out, Funston was appointed colonel in command of the Twentieth Kansas Volunteers and sent to the Philippines, where he served under Gen. Arthur MacArthur during campaigns on the island of Luzon.

When fighting erupted between U.S. troops and Filipino insurgents in February 1899, Funston's regiment was at the forefront of the action. A physically small man but possessed of boundless energy and self-assurance, Funston personally led charges against Filipino positions and swam rivers in pursuit of retreating enemies. Some alleged that such exploits were carried out to enhance his public image, and indeed, Funston never wasted an opportunity to see that his exploits were accorded proper coverage in the press.

His role in personally leading bayonet attacks and cavalry charges, which properly should have fallen to the command of a junior or noncommissioned officer, violated army regulations. However, that sort of daring and bravado made him a hero to the U.S. public, rivaled only by Theodore Roosevelt, George Dewey, and a handful of others. At Calacoon, for instance, Funston led a bayonet charge with three others, then swam the Bagbag River to capture what turned out to be an abandoned Filipino insurgent strong point.

When the Kansas Volunteers returned to the United States in the summer of 1899, some soldiers charged that Funston had approved murder and looting by the troops under his command. However, Gen. Elwell S. Otis, then military governor of the Philippines, chose not to press charges. Still other allegations described Funston as guilty of outrageous behavior, including stealing chalices from a church and conducting a mock mass for the amusement of his men. Funston responded with countercharges, including a suit against a San Francisco newspaper.

Despite the furor, Funston returned to the Philippines, where he was promoted to brigadier general and placed in command of three volunteer regiments. He made front-page news again when reports surfaced of his execution of Filipino prisoners, but once more, he avoided repercussions.

In 1901, Funston counted his biggest coup when he conceived and brought off a daring stratagem to capture the Filipino Nationalist leader Emilio Aguinaldo. Having learned of Aguinaldo's whereabouts

Gen. Frederick Funston. While serving in the Philippines, Funston, then a colonel, gained fame for his daring capture of the Filipino leader Emilio Aguinaldo.

through a captured courier, Funston organized a group of Filipino scouts who spoke the Tagalog dialect of Aguinaldo's followers. Then, disguising himself as a prisoner, Funston allowed himself to be taken into the insurgent camp, where he and his men overpowered and captured Aguinaldo.

As a result, Funston's popularity among the U.S. public soared. At Theodore Roosevelt's urging, he was appointed brigadier general in the regular army. However, his belief that Filipinos should be governed with a heavy hand and his criticism of U.S. policy to bring pacification and democracy to the Philippines also earned him several official reprimands. Despite this, he continued to escape serious censure or punishment.

The remainder of Funston's career was marked by several controversial clashes with the political administrations of Theodore Roosevelt and William Howard Taft. He continued to maintain a coterie of influential supporters who successfully persuaded President Woodrow Wilson to award him his second star in 1915. Funston died two years later while still on active duty.

See also Aguinaldo y Famy, Emilio; Atrocities; Filibuster; Otis, Elwell Stephen.

References and Further Readings

Crouch, Thomas W. *A Yankee Guerrillero: Frederick Funston and the Cuban Insurrection, 1896–1897.* Memphis, TN: Memphis State University Press, 1975

Funston, Frederick. *Memories of Two Wars.* New York: Charles Scribner's Sons, 1911.

Linn, Brian M. "Guerrilla Fighter: Frederick Funston in the Philippines, 1900–1901." *Kansas History,* no. 10, 1987.

Wolff, Leon. *Little Brown Brother: America's Forgotten Bid for Empire Which Cost 250,000 Lives.* New York: Kraus Reprint, 1970.

García Íñiguez, Calixto (1839–1898)

A Cuban revolutionary who had a significant impact on events that led to U.S. involvement in the Spanish-American War, Calixto García Íñiguez was one of the senior military leaders in the Cuban revolutionary movement, commanding the eastern, or "liberating," army.

When Gen. William R. Shafter's Fifth Corps was preparing to land in Cuba, García provided valuable intelligence data, suggesting that the U.S. troops land at Daiquirí. García's men also aided Shafter's campaign to capture Santiago.

The presence of his name in a verbal message from the U.S. War Department resulted in the creation of a myth surrounding García's role in events of 1898. The message, sent by Secretary of War Russell Alger and General of the Army Nelson Miles and delivered by a young intelligence officer, Andrew Rowan, in April 1898, confirmed to García the U.S. intention to aid the Cuban Revolution by providing military support. Inasmuch as war had not yet been declared, the message obviously had to be delivered orally rather than as a written communiqué. Subsequently known as the "message to Garcia," the communication was later the subject of a wildly inaccurate account of Rowan's mission by Elbert Hubbard that quickly captured the fancy of thousands of readers.

See also Cuban Revolutionary Army; Journalism; Spanish-American War, U.S. Public Reaction to.

References and Further Readings

Brown, Charles H. *The Correspondents' War: Journalists in the Spanish-American War.* New York: Charles Scribner's Sons, 1967.

Foner, Philip S. *The Spanish-Cuban-American War.* 2 vols. New York: Monthly Review Press, 1972.

Trask, David F. *The War with Spain in 1898.* Lincoln: University of Nebraska Press, 1996.

García, Pantaleon T. (1856–1936)

Born on Cavite, Philippine Islands, Pantaleon T. García was an influential member of the Filipino revolutionary movement known as the Katipunan. He fought Spanish forces in the Philippines for two years prior to the Spanish-American War. In December 1897, in compliance with the Pact of Biyak-na-Bató, García left the Philippines as a member of Emilio Aguinaldo's exiled political family.

He returned to the Philippines following the outbreak of the Spanish-American War and, after a brief stint in the legislative assembly, returned to soldiering. As a senior commander of the revolutionary forces, García attempted to arrange for the surrender of Manila, only to discover that the Spanish refused to capitulate to Filipino revolutionary forces, surrendering instead to U.S. forces in a contrived scenario.

In the war with the United States, which followed the Spanish-American War, García commanded insurgent forces in central Luzon. Captured in 1900, he swore allegiance to the United States and later held several positions in the new government. Ironically, he had earlier issued orders to his troops to "properly punish" pro-U.S. sympathizers.

> **See also** Aguinaldo y Famy, Emilio; Biyak-na-Bató, Pact of; Katipunan; Manila Bay, Battle of.
> **References and Further Readings**
> Greene, Maj. Gen. Francis V., U.S.V. "The Capture of Manila." *Century Magazine,* April 1899.
> Linn, Brian McAllister. *The Philippine War, 1899–1902.* Lawrence: University Press of Kansas, 2000.
> Wolff, Leon. *Little Brown Brother: America's Forgotten Bid for Empire Which Cost 250,000 Lives.* New York: Kraus Reprint, 1970.

Garretson, George Armstrong (1844–1916)

Born in Ohio, George Armstrong Garretson graduated from West Point in 1870 but resigned his commission three years later to enter the banking profession. When war with Spain broke out, he was appointed a brigadier general of volunteers, commanding the Second Brigade of the First Division.

After a brief assignment in Cuba, Garretson's brigade was assigned to the Puerto Rican Campaign as part of Gen. Guy V. Henry's division. Garretson's command fought a brief skirmish at Yauco on 26 July in the first confrontation between U.S. troops and Spanish forces in Puerto Rico.

> **See also** Puerto Rican Campaign.

References and Further Readings

Musicant, Ivan. *Empire by Default: The Spanish-American War and the Dawn of the American Century.* New York: Henry Holt and Company, 1998.

Trask, David F. *The War with Spain in 1898.* Lincoln: University of Nebraska Press, 1996.

German Asiatic Squadron

See **Germany**

Germany

During the Spanish-American War, Germany was the only major European power that presented the United States with any real cause for concern. Following Commodore George Dewey's victory at Manila Bay on 1 May 1898, Germany increased the strength of its Asiatic Squadron. Two German cruisers arrived in Manila shortly after the battle, followed on 12 June by Vice Adm. Otto von Diederich aboard the cruiser *Kaiserin Augusta.* Two additional vessels arrived a week later, giving Germany a numerical advantage in capital ships over the United States, which had but four.

The increase in German strength altered the balance of power in the area. Great Britain, by contrast, had only two ships in Philippine waters, and France and Japan only one each. For its part, Great Britain, fearing Germany's expansionist views, stood supportive of the U.S. position in the Philippines.

Dewey was concerned that Germany might interfere with operations in the Philippines before Spain surrendered, thereby ensuring itself a role in the peace negotiations and ultimate disposition of Spanish territory. He advised Washington of his concern, and as a result, the Navy Department felt that might be a compelling reason to dispatch the Eastern Squadron to the Philippines. However, due to the recall of Admiral Cámara's Spanish Squadron and the signing of the Protocol of Peace, the Eastern Squadron was never sent to the Philippines but remained in the Caribbean.

Germany's expansionist designs in the Pacific were no secret to military leaders in Washington, who had been kept apprised of such matters by the U.S. naval attaché in Berlin. Germany sought coaling stations and coveted parts of the Philippine Archipelago, as well as the Carolines and the Palaus, a subgroup of the Carolines.

When pressed by the U.S. State Department to explain its naval buildup in the Philippines, Germany asserted that it was merely protecting German nationals and property in the area. That explanation, however, was somewhat belied by Germany's actions.

According to one naval observer, the Germans behaved "as if Manila Bay were absolutely in their possession" (Musicant, p. 559). German ships roamed freely and even set up a station on Bataan Peninsula, where they landed a detachment of troops.

In the weeks following Dewey's 1 May victory, relations between the U.S. commodore and Admiral von Diederich grew uncomfortably strained. Dewey claimed that German ships interfered with the U.S. naval blockade of Manila, a charge that von Diederich stoutly denied, arguing that his intentions were in strict accord with international laws of neutrality. In a face-to-face confrontation with one of von Diederich's lieutenants, Dewey told the German officer that if Germany wanted war, it could have it. Perhaps the lieutenant was taken aback by the outburst; in any case, German behavior was less obtrusive thereafter.

When the first contingent of U.S. ground forces and three additional vessels arrived to bolster Dewey's squadron, tension between Dewey and the Germans began to ease. Following the capture of Manila and the subsequent signing of the Peace Protocol, ships belonging to foreign powers, including Germany, began to withdraw from Philippine waters. Germany, however, continued to manifest serious interest in the disposal of Spanish holdings in the Pacific and eventually agreed to pay Spain for rights to the Caroline, Pelew, and Ladrone Islands, excluding Guam.

See also Dewey, George; Manila Bay, Battle of; Philippine Islands, Acquisition of, by the United States; Spanish-American War, International Reaction to.

References and Further Readings

Morgan, H. Wayne, ed. *Making Peace with Spain: The Diary of Whitelaw Reid—September–December, 1898.* Austin: University of Texas Press, 1965.

Musicant, Ivan. *Empire by Default: The Spanish-American War and the Dawn of the American Century.* New York: Henry Holt and Company, 1998.

O'Toole, G. J. A. *The Spanish War: An American Epic, 1898.* New York: W. W. Norton, 1984.

Shippee, Lester B. "Germany and the Spanish-American War." *American Historical Review,* 30, July 1925.

Ghost Squadron

In June 1898, four Spanish naval vessels were sighted at night off the northern Cuban coast. The sighting raised fears in Washington that

Adm. Pascual Cervera's squadron had slipped out of Santiago de Cuba harbor undetected. If true, a powerful Spanish naval force was in the area and would need to be dealt with before any invasion of Cuba took place.

Accordingly, the departure of Gen. William R. Shafter's Fifth Corps from Tampa, Florida, for Cuba was delayed pending verification of the report. It was subsequently determined that Cervera's squadron was still at anchor in Santiago harbor and that three of the vessels in the reported sighting were actually U.S. ships and one was British—thus the name "Ghost Squadron."

> **See also** Cervera y Topete, Pascual; Naval Blockade of Cuba.
> **References and Further Readings**
> Trask, David F. *The War with Spain in 1898.* Lincoln: University of Nebraska Press, 1996.

Glass, Henry (1844–1908)

Born in Kentucky, Henry Glass was an 1863 graduate of the U.S. Naval Academy and a veteran of the Civil War. A career navy man, he received command of the cruiser *Charleston* in 1898. In this capacity, he commanded the escort of the first contingent of the expeditionary force to the Philippines in June 1898. En route, the force stopped at Guam, where Glass asked for and received the surrender of the island from its Spanish garrison. Later, Glass served as captain of the port of Manila. He was also a recognized authority on marine international law.

> **See also** Guam.
> **References and Further Readings**
> Portusach, F. "History of the Capture of Guam by the United States Man-of-War *Charleston* and Its Transports." *Proceedings of the United States Naval Institute,* 43, April 1917, pp. 707–718.
> Walker, L. W. "Guam's Seizure by the United States in 1898." *Pacific Historical Review,* 14, March 1945.

Gómez Báez, Máximo (1826–1905)

An important and influential Cuban revolutionary, Máximo Gómez Báez was born in Santo Domingo (Dominican Republic). He served in the Spanish Army both in his home country and later in Cuba, where he remained as a farmer after his military service. Gómez cooperated with Gen. William Rufus Shafter's command in the campaign against Santiago during the Spanish-American War.

During his years in Cuba, Gómez was drawn to the revolutionary cause and served in the insurgent army during the Ten Years' War from 1868 to 1878. His soldierly qualities did not go unnoticed. In the second revolution that began in 1895, the great Cuban patriot José Martí asked Gómez to lead an army. Although the two men differed philosophically in their approach to the revolution—Gómez, for example, believed the revolution could be won without U.S. aid—they both shared the dream of Cuban independence. Gómez's hit-and-run tactics proved highly effective against the Spanish, despite the latter's superiority in numbers. Totally dedicated to Cuban independence, Gómez refused to accept Spain's offer of autonomy for the island and also rejected a proposed arrangement to form a Spanish-Cuban alliance against the United States.

Martí's untimely death in May 1895 was followed by the creation of a new revolutionary government under Salvador Cisneros Betancourt, a haughty and aristocratic Cuban. Concerned that the revolution was being monopolized by the black Maceo brothers, Antonio and José, Betancourt insisted that Gómez replace the Maceos. When Gómez failed to comply, he was relieved of his command but refused to relinquish his military role in the revolution.

When the U.S. Fifth Corps landed at Daiquirí in June 1898, Gómez cooperated with General Shafter during the campaign against Santiago, despite his understandable resentment of the racism displayed by the U.S. troops. However, the joint operations failed to achieve the expected symbiosis.

See also Cuban Revolution; Maceo Grajales, Antonio; Martí y Pérez, José; Ten Years' War.

References and Further Readings

Foner, Philip S. *The Spanish-Cuban-American War.* 2 vols. New York: Monthly Review Press, 1972.

Musicant, Ivan. *Empire by Default: The Spanish-American War and the Dawn of the American Century.* New York: Henry Holt and Company, 1998.

Trask, David F. *The War with Spain in 1898.* Lincoln: University of Nebraska Press, 1996.

Gorgas, William Crawford (1854–1920)

Born near Mobile, Alabama, William Crawford Gorgas was the son of Josiah Gorgas, chief ordnance officer for the Confederacy during the Civil War. Unable to obtain an appointment to West Point, the young Gorgas joined the army's Medical Corps. By the time of the Spanish-American War, he was an army surgeon. Having survived a bout with yellow fever, Gorgas was placed in charge of the army's yellow fever camp in Cuba. Later (1898–1902), he served as chief sanitary officer for the city of Havana.

Following Walter Reed's discovery that yellow fever was transmitted by the mosquito, Gorgas instituted measures to eradicate the insects and successfully eliminated the disease from Havana. Later, his efforts to wipe out yellow fever in Panama were instrumental in the completion of the Panama Canal.

See also Diseases; Reed, Walter.

References and Further Readings

Hopkins, Joseph G. E., ed. *The Concise Dictionary of American Biography.* New York: Charles Scribner's Sons, 1964.

McCullough, David. *The Path between the Seas.* New York: Simon and Schuster, 1977.

Gorman, Arthur Pue (1839–1906)

Born in Maryland, Arthur Pue Gorman was elected U.S. senator from that state and served two terms: from 1881 to 1899 and from 1903 to 1906. A Democrat and an influential legislator, Gorman—who may have had his eye on the presidency as an Anti-Expansionist—was the driving force opposing ratification of the Treaty of Paris. Although Gorman was not alone, his was the loudest voice against ratification, rallying both conservative Democrats and radical Republicans in an effort to defeat the measure. Despite his machinations, the ratification passed, albeit by a single vote.

Defeated for reelection, Gorman left office in March 1899 but returned in 1903.

See also Treaty of Paris.

References and Further Readings

Gould, Lewis L. *The Spanish-American War and President McKinley.* Lawrence: University of Kansas Press, 1982.

Leech, Margaret. *In the Days of McKinley.* New York: Harper & Brothers, 1959.

Gray, George (1840–1925)

Born in Delaware, George Gray served first as attorney general of that state from 1879 to 1885 and then as a U.S. senator from 1885 to 1899. A veteran jurist (he served on the commission to adjudicate differences between the United States and Canada, for example), Gray was a logical choice to be on the commission to negotiate peace terms with Spain.

Although he was a conservative Democrat, Gray was a confidante of President William McKinley during the early days of the war with Spain. As an Anti-Expansionist, he opposed annexation of the Philippines on the grounds that to acquire the archipelago would run counter to U.S. political philosophy and would enmesh the United States in foreign affairs. However, he did sign the Treaty of Paris by which the United States acquired the Philippines, believing that it was better to have a signed treaty than to risk the outcome of continued deliberations and thereby compel the United States to further prosecute the war.

See also Treaty of Paris.

References and Further Readings

Leech, Margaret. *In the Days of McKinley.* New York: Harper & Brothers, 1959.

Morgan, H. Wayne, ed. *Making Peace with Spain: The Diary of Whitelaw Reid—September–December, 1898.* Austin: University of Texas Press, 1965.

Great Britain

Twice its foe in war, the United States found itself allied with Great Britain as the nineteenth century drew to a close. Great Britain, for its part, had grown increasingly concerned over Germany's alliance with Austria and Italy, as well as its colonial aspirations in the Pacific. As a consequence, it supported the U.S. position in the Philippines, although it professed to be completely neutral in the Spanish-American War. For example, Great Britain allowed Commodore George Dewey's Asiatic Squadron to prepare for its Philippine assignment at Hong Kong, a neutral port, after the official declaration of war between Spain and the United States. Later, Great Britain stood ready to assist Dewey when the situation was tense between Dewey and the German naval squadron in Manila Bay. Some historians see this period as the beginning of an Anglo-American alliance that continues to the present day.

See also Asiatic Squadron, U.S. Navy; Dewey, George; Germany; Spanish-American War, International Reaction to.

References and Further Readings

Bertram, Marshall. *The Birth of Anglo-American Friendship.* New York: University Press of America, 1992.

Leech, Margaret. *In the Days of McKinley.* New York: Harper & Brothers, 1959.

Musicant, Ivan. *Empire by Default: The Spanish-American War and the Dawn of the American Century.* New York: Henry Holt and Company, 1998.

Trask, David F. *The War with Spain in 1898.* Lincoln: University of Nebraska Press, 1996.

Greene, Francis Vinton (1850–1921)

Born in Rhode Island, Francis Vinton Greene graduated from West Point in 1870, first in his class. A brilliant man, Greene was an engineer and historian; he also served as Russian military attaché and was with the Russian Army in Turkey. Greene was named colonel of the Seventy-first New York Volunteers when war with Spain broke out.

Greene's assignment as a colonel proved short-lived. In May 1898, he was promoted to brigadier general, and at the request of Maj. Gen. Wesley Merritt, the commander of the Philippine Expeditionary Force (Eighth Corps), he was assigned to a brigade command under Merritt. Greene's brigade—which was the second segment of the Philippine Expeditionary Force—reached Manila on 17 July 1898, one month after its departure from San Francisco.

Because of Greene's diplomatic skills, General Merritt avoided involving Emilio Aguinaldo, leader of the Filipino revolutionary movement, in discussions regarding the capture and subsequent occupation of Manila. Largely as a result of Greene's efforts, the Filipino insurgents were persuaded to abandon a network of trenches facing Manila, allowing U.S. troops to occupy them.

In the subsequent attack on Manila (13 August 1898), Greene commanded the U.S. left flank and captured Fort San Antonio de Abad. In a carefully orchestrated plan to keep the Filipino revolutionaries from assuming control, Greene's troops outran the insurgents into the city to accept Manila's surrender from the Spanish. In the fall of 1898, Greene met with President William McKinley to provide valuable information about the Philippines. Greene strongly recommended that the United States retain all of the Philippines, rather than just a portion of the archipelago as was then being considered. At McKinley's request, Greene also conferred with Aguinaldo in the hope of avoiding hostilities with the Filipinos. Unfortunately, that effort came to naught when Aguinaldo explained to Greene that he (Aguinaldo) lacked the influence to prevent hostilities. In all likelihood, the Filipino leader was not inclined to aid the Americans, who clearly were no more committed to Filipino independence than the Spanish were.

Greene retired from the army in 1899 and went on to hold several important civilian positions, including that of New York City police commissioner. He also wrote several books on military affairs.

See also Aguinaldo y Famy, Emilio; Manila Bay, Battle of; Merritt, Wesley; Philippine Expeditionary Force.

References and Further Readings

Cosmas, Graham. *An Army for Empire: The United States Army in the Spanish-American War.* College Station: Texas A&M University Press, 1998.

Greene, Maj. Gen. Francis V., U.S.V. "The Capture of Manila." *Century Magazine,* April 1899.

Wolff, Leon. *Little Brown Brother: America's Forgotten Bid for Empire Which Cost 250,000 Lives.* New York: Kraus Reprint, 1970.

Greenleaf, Charles Ravenscroft

Born in Pennsylvania, Charles Ravenscroft Greenleaf later moved to Ohio, where he served as assistant surgeon of volunteers in the Civil War. He later transferred to the regular army and was promoted to colonel and assistant surgeon. In the early weeks of the Spanish-American War, Greenleaf reported on troop conditions in the U.S. staging areas. Later, he reported on conditions from aboard a ship when the Fifth Corps departed for Cuba in June 1898.

Greenleaf's reports noted the abominable conditions in U.S. camps and correctly predicted that health and sanitary problems would be even worse in the Tropics. During the siege of Santiago, he and his colleagues in the army's Medical Corps worked tirelessly to prevent an epidemic of malarial diseases, particularly yellow fever. Unfortunately, as the summer progressed, the incidence of those diseases rose at an alarming rate.

Veterans of the Fifth Corps who had been stricken by one of the tropical diseases and had not recovered sufficiently to be released to civilian life often collapsed in public. The frequency of such occurrences soon developed into something of a scandal. To deal with the situation, Greenleaf set up medical examining boards at various hospitals to ensure that the returning veterans were well enough to go home. Later, Greenleaf was appointed chief medical inspector, responsible for health and general hygiene at army posts and camps.

See also Diseases; Medical Department, U.S. Army.

References and Further Readings

Cosmas, Graham. *An Army for Empire: The United States Army in the Spanish-American War.* College Station: Texas A&M University Press, 1998.

Gibson, John M. *Soldier in White: The Life of General George Miller Sternberg.* Durham, NC: Duke University Press, 1958.

Trask, David F. *The War with Spain in 1898.* Lincoln: University of Nebraska Press, 1996.

Gridley, Charles Vernon (1844–1898)

A graduate of the U.S. Naval Academy at Annapolis, Charles Vernon Gridley first saw combat in the Civil War. By 1897, a veteran naval officer, he had been promoted to the rank of captain and placed in command of the cruiser *Olympia*, flagship of the Asiatic Squadron commanded by Commodore George Dewey. Gridley is best remembered as the recipient of Commodore Dewey's immortal order that opened the Battle of Manila Bay on 1 May 1898. At precisely 5:40 A.M., Dewey turned to him and said, "You may fire when you are ready, Gridley."

Despite his ill health prior to the outbreak of the Spanish-American War, Gridley insisted on retaining his command. Following the Battle of Manila Bay, his condition worsened, and he was ordered home but died en route.

See also Dewey, George; Manila Bay, Battle of.

References and Further Readings

Chadwick, Rear Adm. French Ensor. *Relations of the United States and Spain: The Spanish American War.* 2 vols. New York: Charles Scribner's Sons, 1911 (reprinted in 1968).

Musicant, Ivan. *Empire by Default: The Spanish-American War and the Dawn of the American Century.* New York: Henry Holt and Company, 1998.

Spector, Ronald. *Admiral of the New Empire: The Life and Career of George Dewey.* Greenville: University of South Carolina Press, 1988.

Trask, David F. *The War with Spain in 1898.* Lincoln: University of Nebraska Press, 1996.

Grito de Baíre

The Cuban Insurrection of 1895, which ultimately led to the Spanish-American War, arose from the village of Baíre. From there was sounded the *grito,* or cry, of the Cuban people.

See also Cuban Revolution; Gómez Báez, Máximo; Maceo Grajales, Antonio; Martí y Pérez, José.

References and Further Readings

Foner, Philip S. *The Spanish-Cuban-American War.* 2 vols. New York: Monthly Review Press, 1972.

Guam

Located in the western Pacific Ocean, Guam is an island of the northern Marianas chain. Also known as the Ladrones (from a word meaning thieves), the Marianas Islands were discovered by

Ferdinand Magellan in 1521 but not colonized until the seventeenth century. Guam was strategically positioned to provide a convenient coaling and resupply point for U.S. vessels en route to Pacific Rim countries, particularly the Philippines, during the Spanish-American War.

On 20 June 1898, the first of the U.S. expeditionary force bound for the Philippines arrived at Guam. Capt. Henry Glass, commanding the cruiser *Charleston,* opened fire on what proved to be a deserted fort. He proceeded to take control of the island from soldiers at a Spanish garrison who were as yet unaware that their country was at war with the United States. Glass, under a flag of truce and escorted by a marine detachment, then arranged for the formal surrender of the island and its garrison. After the surrender, the expeditionary force resumed its journey to the Philippines, leaving Guam unoccupied by a U.S. military unit. The United States formally acquired Guam as a result of the Treaty of Paris, which was signed in December 1898.

See also Glass, Henry; Philippine Expeditionary Force; Treaty of Paris.

References and Further Readings

Guam Visitor's Bureau. *Guam: Guam's Natural, Cultural and Historic Site Guidebook.* Tumon: Guam Visitor's Bureau, 1998.

Morgan, H. Wayne, ed. *Making Peace with Spain: The Diary of Whitelaw Reid—September–December, 1898.* Austin: University of Texas Press, 1965.

Portusach, F. "History of the Capture of Guam by the United States Man-of-War *Charleston* and Its Transports." *Proceedings of the United States Naval Institute,* 43, April 1917, pp. 707–718.

Walker, L. W. "Guam's Seizure by the United States in 1898." *Pacific Historical Review,* 14, March 1945.

Guantánamo (Cuba), Battle of (3–15 June 1898)

The city of Guantánamo is located on the southwestern coast of Cuba, approximately 46 miles east of Santiago. The city sits at the end of Guantánamo Bay, a body of water some 15 miles long that offers an excellent harbor. During the Spanish-American War, Guantánamo was attractive to the U.S. Navy as a coaling station and supply port because of its proximity to both the Florida Keys and the city of Santiago.

Accordingly, on 6 June 1898, less than six weeks after the declaration of war between the United States and Spain, a marine battalion received orders to seize Guantánamo. Four days later, on

10 June, a U.S. naval task force commanded by Comdr. Bowman H. McCalla and consisting of the cruisers *Marblehead* and *Yankee* shelled Spanish fortifications guarding the harbor. Following the naval bombardment, the First Marine Expeditionary Battalion, five infantry companies, and an artillery battery with three rapid-fire guns and a machine gun—a total of 650 officers and men under the command of Lt. Col. Robert W. Huntington—landed on the eastern shore of Guantánamo Bay and established Camp McCalla. The camp was a fragile position surrounded by jungle and brush, with the sea behind.

The villages of Guantánamo and Caimanera were defended by 6,000 Spanish troops commanded by Gen. Félix Pareja Mesa. A railroad connecting the two points was protected by blockhouses. After withdrawing from the positions now occupied by the marines, Pareja concentrated his forces at Cuzco Well, which was 6 miles away and the area's only fresh water supply.

Pareja wasted no time in challenging the invaders and attacked the newly landed marine battalion on the night of 11 June. Marine outposts were struck and the sentries killed and butchered. Huntington counterattacked, but the thick brush soon ruled out an effective response. That night, Spanish snipers harassed the defenders. Fighting continued for three days, in what the marines called "100 hours of fighting."

Finally on 14 June, Huntington, with some artillery now at his

Raising the U.S. flag at Guantánamo, 12 June 1898.

disposal, bombarded the Spanish positions. In addition, a small group of Cuban revolutionaries reinforced Huntington's defenders, along with a detachment of marines who arrived aboard the battleship *Texas*. After consulting with the Cubans, Huntington decided to attack the Spanish at Cuzco Well. Accordingly, at 9 A.M., a 160-man force under Capt. George F. Elliott and supported by Cuban revolutionaries advanced on Cuzco Well.

After securing the high ground overlooking Cuzco, the marines moved into the valley and, after a stiff fight, seized Cuzco and destroyed the well. On 15 June, the guns of the *Texas* blasted the Spanish fort at Caimanera; the following day, the battleship *Oregon,* on the scene after its magnificent voyage around Cape Horn, also fired on the fort. But with the destruction of the well, Spanish resistance was effectively ended, although scattered fighting continued for the next several days. The Spanish garrison, having been effectively cut off from other Spanish forces on the island and suffering from dwindling rations, illness, and a lack of fresh water, finally capitulated at the end of July.

During the two weeks of fighting, the marines inflicted some 160 casualties on the Spanish defenders and captured 18 men; 4 Cuban revolutionaries and 3 marines were killed in the fighting. Journalist Stephen Crane (author of *The Red Badge of Courage*) landed with the marines, wrote an account of the action, and was decorated for his part in the fighting.

With the capture of Guantánamo, the United States established its first position in Cuba, which also enabled it to maintain its naval blockade of the island. Guantánamo later served as a departure point for the Puerto Rican Expeditionary Force.

See also Crane, Stephen; Cuban Campaign; Marine Corps, U.S.; Naval Blockade of Cuba.

References and Further Readings

Feuer, A. B. "The U.S. Marines at Guantánamo Bay." *Military Heritage,* vol. 1, no. 3, December 1999.

Millett, Allan R. *Semper Fidelis: The History of the United States Marine Corps.* New York: Macmillan Publishing, 1982.

Trask, David F. *The War with Spain in 1898.* Lincoln: University of Nebraska Press, 1996.

Gullón y Iglesia, Don Pío (1835–1916)

A journalist by profession, Don Pío Gullón y Iglesia had been a Spanish government official during the Sagasta regime. However, he had no experience to qualify him for the challenge of serving as minister of state, the position he was named to in October 1897, during the crucial months preceding the declaration of war between Spain and the United States.

Gullón was strongly opposed to war with the United States, which he believed would be an exercise in futility for Spain. His strategy for dealing with the situation was to create a consensus among the major European powers as well as the Vatican in order to mediate the differences between the United States and Spain. His efforts proved unsuccessful, however, as the other powers chose not to intervene. Gullón was later criticized for having what was perceived as a conciliatory position toward the United States. He was replaced as minister of state by Almódovar del Rio in 1898.

See also Sagasta, Práxedes Mateo; Spanish-American War, International Reaction to.

References and Further Readings

Musicant, Ivan, *Empire by Default: The Spanish-American War and the Dawn of the American Century.* New York: Henry Holt and Company, 1998.

Trask, David F. *The War with Spain in 1898.* Lincoln: University of Nebraska Press, 1996.

Gunboat Operations, Philippines

As part of an overall strategy in dealing with revolutionaries during the Philippine-American War, U.S. military authorities imposed a blockade that prevented most interisland trade and communication as a means of isolating resistance.

With 7,000 islands covering some 500,000 square miles, the challenge was formidable. Additionally, the islands encompassed a wide variety of terrain, including mountains, swamps, and jungle. Penetrating the interior was difficult for ground troops; however, the miles of inland waterways were ideally suited for shallow-draft gunboats that could effectively enforce the blockade. The gunboats also pursued the smugglers and pirates who infested the islands.

At the outset of the Spanish-American War, the U.S. Navy's Asiatic Squadron included only one gunboat. By the end of the war, the navy had added to its fleet of gunboats and had captured a number of those vessels from the Spanish, who also found them ideally suited for interisland travel. By the time of the Philippine-American War (1899), the navy had twenty-five gunboats, ranging in size up to 900 tons and armed with cannons and machine guns.

The army had also acquired a number of gunboats, as well as a few smaller vessels capable of plying the inland waterways of the archipelago. The navy (and Adm. George Dewey in particular) did not take kindly to that intrusion into its domain. Eventually, a compromise was effected, in which the army retained some of its vessels to support land operations, while the navy was charged with enforcing the blockade.

Overall, gunboats proved a very effective tool for dealing with the revolutionary forces by almost totally shutting down the only avenue for outside supply.

See also Dewey, George; Interservice Relations; Philippine-American War, U.S. Public Reaction to.

References and Further Readings

Linn, Brian McAllister. *The Philippine War, 1899–1902.* Lawrence: University Press of Kansas, 2000.

Palmer, Frederick. *With My Own Eyes: A Personal Study of Battle Years.* Indianapolis, IN: Bobbs-Merrill, 1932.

Trask, David F. *The War with Spain in 1898.* Lincoln: University of Nebraska Press, 1996.

Gunboats

Gunboats were small, shallow-draft vessels designed to operate in coastal waters, bays, and estuaries. Although unarmored, gunboats filled a need in the Spanish-American War for both Spain and the United States. During the war, the Spanish Navy had twenty-six gunboats, compared to only sixteen for the United States.

Since there was no radio communication at the time of the Spanish-American War, gunboats often carried dispatches between ships, much as couriers did on land. They also served as pickets on the periphery of the fleet. Gunboats on Lake Lanao, Mindanao, played a key role in operations against the Moros and in enforcing the naval blockade elsewhere in the Philippines. Though unheralded, gunboats, along with torpedo boats, saw more action than any other class of naval vessel during both the Spanish-American War and the Philippine-American War.

See also Cienfuegos, Cutting the Cable at; Gunboat Operations, Philippines; Manila Bay, Battle of; Navy, Spanish; Navy, U.S.

References and Further Readings

Alden, John D. *The American Steel Navy.* Annapolis, MD: Naval Institute Press, 1972.

Feuer, A. B. "In 1899 the U.S. Army in the Philippines Was Supported by Utah Artillerymen aboard Spanish Gunboats." *Military History,* vol. 16, no. 5, December 1999.

Hitt, Parker. "Amphibious Infantry: A Fleet on Lake Lanao." *Proceedings of the United States Naval Institute,* 64, 1938.

Mead, Ernest E. "The Rescue of the *Winslow.*" *Harper's Monthly,* 1898.

Winslow, Cameron McRae. "Cable-cutting at Cienfuegos." *Century Magazine,* March 1899.

Gussie

See **Dorst, Joseph Haddox**

Hanna, Marcus (Mark) Alonzo (1837–1904)

Born in New Lisbon, Ohio, Marcus Alonzo Hanna served in the Union army during the Civil War. Later, as a businessman and politician, he became an influential figure in Ohio politics. Hanna supported William McKinley twice for governor of Ohio and also during the presidential campaign of 1896. Throughout the Spanish-American War, he remained one of President McKinley's most trusted advisers and an ardent supporter of his policies.

When President McKinley named the aging John Sherman secretary of state in 1897, he appointed Hanna to fill Sherman's vacated Senate seat. Hanna was later reelected through his own efforts, in a bitterly fought contest. Projecting a formidable presence in the Senate, he was opposed to war with Spain at the outset but later altered his views and championed U.S. overseas expansion.

> **See also** Anti-Imperialist League; Imperialism/Expansionism; McKinley, William, Jr.
>
> **References and Further Readings**
> Croly, Herbert David. *Marcus Alonzo Hanna: His Life and Work.* New York: Macmillan and Company, 1912.
> Leech, Margaret. *In the Days of McKinley.* New York: Harper & Brothers, 1959.

Havana (Cuba)

Located approximately 100 miles from the Florida Keys on Cuba's northwest side, Havana, with a population of nearly 200,000 in 1898, was the premier city in the West Indies. Possessing a fine natural harbor, it was well defended and served as headquarters of the Spanish government in Cuba throughout the Spanish-American War.

Although Havana felt the effects of the U.S. naval blockade, the city never felt the hand of war. U.S. troops did not occupy the city until December 1898, long after the Spanish-American War had ended. Interestingly, the destruction of the *Maine* while it was visiting

Havana was viewed by many as the event that triggered the war with Spain.

See also *Maine*; Naval Blockade of Cuba.
References and Further Readings
Chadwick, Rear Adm. French Ensor. *Relations of the United States and Spain: The Spanish American War.* 2 vols. New York: Charles Scribner's Sons, 1911 (reprinted in 1968).

Hawaiian Islands

An archipelago of eight islands located some 2,000 miles southwest of San Francisco, the Hawaiian Islands were a topic of considerable debate in the U.S. Congress during the closing years of the nineteenth century. After the Spanish-American War, the islands became strategically important to the United States, which was suddenly perceived as an international power in the Pacific, having acquired Guam and the Philippines as a result of the war.

Because of Hawaii's strategic location in the central Pacific, Expansionists wanted to bring the islands into the U.S. fold. President William McKinley endorsed the idea, believing that acquisition of Hawaii would open the door to Asia for U.S. commercial interests. However, voices of opposition in Congress were strong. Some members were concerned about what they saw as a burgeoning imperialist posture on the part of the United States. Others were concerned about the effect Hawaii's economy would have on the industry of certain states, for example, the sugarcane industry.

An 1897 resolution to annex the islands failed to qualify for congressional approval. However, a second resolution, introduced in May 1898, came hard on the heels of the declaration of war with Spain. With strong backing from President McKinley, the resolution overcame the opposition. Accordingly, the islands officially became a U.S. territorial possession on 7 July 1898, prompting McKinley to refer to the acquisition as "manifest destiny."

See also Imperialism/Expansionism; McKinley, William, Jr.; Philippine Islands, Acquisition of, by the United States.
References and Further Readings
Leech, Margaret. *In the Days of McKinley.* New York: Harper & Brothers, 1959.
Morgan, H. Wayne, ed. *Making Peace with Spain: The Diary of Whitelaw Reid—September–December, 1898.* Austin: University of Texas Press, 1965.
Traxel, David. *1898: The Birth of the American Century.* New York: Alfred A. Knopf, 1998.

Hawkins, Hamilton Smith (1834–1910)

Born in South Carolina, Hamilton Smith Hawkins later moved to New York and entered the U.S. Military Academy, graduating in 1855. A Civil War vetcran, he remained in the army and played an important role as brigadier general of volunteers and later major general in the Spanish-American War.

A tall, distinguished-looking white-haired officer, Hawkins commanded the First Brigade of Gen. J. F. Kent's First Division in the Santiago Campaign. During the approach to San Juan Hill, General Kent ordered one of Hawkins's regiments—the Seventy-first New York Volunteers—to move forward. The green, inexperienced New Yorkers broke under galling Spanish fire and fell back, making it impossible for the remainder of the brigade to move forward. General Kent then ordered the regiment to lie down so as to allow other units to advance.

After the Rough Riders secured the adjoining Kettle Hill, Hawkins's brigade advanced against the Spanish lines on San Juan Hill. When the Gatling gun detachment opened up on the Spanish positions, Hawkins, seemingly without fear of the deadly Spanish Mauser rifles, exhorted his men to move forward, waving his hat and crying, "Come on! Come on!" During the course of the action, Hawkins sustained a foot wound.

Promoted to brigadier general in the regular army in September 1898, he retired from active duty in October.

See also Kent, Jacob Ford; Rough Riders; San Juan Hill, Charge up.

References and Further Readings
Davis, Richard Harding. *The Cuban and Puerto Rican Campaigns.* New York: Charles Scribner's Sons, 1898.
Heitman, Francis B. *Historical Register and Dictionary of the United States Army, 1789–1903.* 2 vols. Urbana: University of Illinois Press, 1965.
Musicant, Ivan. *Empire by Default: The Spanish-American War and the Dawn of the American Century.* New York: Henry Holt and Company, 1998.
Samuels, Peggy, and Harold Samuels. *Teddy Roosevelt at San Juan: The Making of a President.* College Station: Texas A&M University Press, 1997.

Hay, John Milton (1838–1905)

Born in Salem, Indiana, John Milton Hay served as one of President Abraham Lincoln's two personal secretaries. An uncommonly brilliant man, Hay was a poet, journalist, historian, and statesman. Appointed assistant secretary of state in 1878, Hay and his superb negotiating skills proved especially valuable in resolving the volatile Venezuelan boundary dispute with Great Britain (1895). In 1897, he was named ambassador to Great Britain as a reward for his support of William McKinley during the 1896 presidential election. As ambassador, Hay proved to be President McKinley's European "eyes and ears" during the war with Spain.

Absolutely opposed to Spain's dominance of Cuba, Hay staunchly supported McKinley and his policies, including the acquisition of Puerto Rico and the Philippines. It was John Hay who wrote to Theodore Roosevelt in July 1898, calling the Spanish-American War "a splendid little war." Appointed secretary of state in 1898, Hay was largely responsible for creating the open door policy in China and resolving the Alaskan boundary dispute with Canada. He also orchestrated the Hay-Pauncefote Treaty of 1900, which led to the U.S. construction of the Panama Canal.

See also Great Britain; McKinley, William, Jr.

References and Further Readings

Gould, Lewis L. *The Spanish-American War and President McKinley.* Lawrence: University of Kansas Press, 1982.

Leech, Margaret. *In the Days of McKinley.* New York: Harper & Brothers, 1959.

O'Toole, G. J. A. *The Spanish War: An American Epic, 1898.* New York: W. W. Norton, 1984.

Trask, David F. *The War with Spain in 1898.* Lincoln: University of Nebraska Press, 1996.

Hearst, William Randolph (1863–1951)

William Randolph Hearst was born in San Francisco, the only child of Sen. George Hearst and Phoebe Apperson Hearst. Stories and illustrations of the Spanish-American War appeared in his newspapers throughout the war.

As a student at Harvard, Hearst acquired a taste for the newspaper business while working on the *Lampoon.* After expulsion from school for some sophomoric peccadilloes prior to graduation, Hearst joined the staff of Joseph Pulitzer's *New York World,* from which he launched his career as one of the legendary giants of journalism.

Given the *San Francisco Examiner* by his father in 1887, Hearst used his gift as a springboard from which to develop the colorful, theatrical style that was to become his trademark. His brand of journalism concentrated on the flashy and dramatic, sometimes at the expense of facts.

In 1895, Hearst moved into the New York market, buying the *New York Journal.* Using the family fortune, which had been made in mining, he proceeded to hire the best newspaper people he could find, including some from his competitor Joseph Pulitzer.

He arrived on the New York scene just as the Cuban Revolution was getting under way. Attracted to the story potential of the Cuban cause, Hearst focused the *Journal*'s efforts in support of the Cubans. Stories portrayed the Spanish rulers—especially the newly appointed military commander, Gen. Valeriano Weyler (dubbed "Butcher" by Hearst)—as ruthless tyrants. Although the *Journal* was not the only U.S. paper to take up the Cuban cause, it was the flashiest and arguably the most vocal.

Late in 1896, Hearst sent artist Frederic Remington to Cuba to sketch scenes depicting the inhumane treatment of Cubans. However, after two weeks, Remington grew tired of the assignment and cabled his publisher that he wished to come home; Remington stated that there would be no war. Hearst is alleged to have told him to provide the sketches and he (Hearst) would provide the war.

Hearst never missed an opportunity to undertake a scheme that promised an attractive return in publicity. One such plot was that to rescue political captive Evangelina Cisneros from a Cuban prison on the Isle of Pines. Evangelina had been jailed for helping her father, a revolutionary, escape from captivity. Calling her a Cuban Joan of Arc, Hearst launched a major campaign on Evangelina's behalf. Meanwhile, he dispatched reporter Karl Decker to rescue Evangelina, which the enterprising reporter managed to do.

Hearst himself traveled to Cuba as a war correspondent in June 1898. He personally witnessed the fighting and wrote accounts of the war for his own papers. He was particularly critical of the War Department for being so ill prepared to conduct a war.

William Randolph Hearst, one of the best known and most controversial newspaper publishers in U.S. history. Hearst's New York Journal *pressed for war with Spain after the battleship* Maine *was destroyed in Havana harbor on 15 February 1898.*

Along with Joseph Pulitzer, Hearst created what came to be known as "yellow journalism." The term came about because two comic strips from the competing *World* and *Journal* featured characters garbed in bright yellow. As competition between the two papers intensified, with one vying to outdo the other, the brand of journalism spawned by this competition was referred to as yellow journalism.

After the war, Hearst acquired numerous newspapers and periodicals, building an unrivaled empire. At the zenith of his power, he owned eighteen newspapers in a dozen cities and nine periodicals, including *Harper's Bazaar* and *Good Housekeeping*. Hearst did not limit himself to the printed word; he also acquired a motion picture studio, Cosmopolitan Productions.

In 1919, he began construction of his famous castle at San Simeon, California. The structure, which was completed in 1925, was given to the state of California in 1959, eight years after Hearst's death.

Hearst's flamboyant career was portrayed by Orson Welles in the classic film, *Citizen Kane*.

See also Cisneros, Evangelina; Journalism; Pulitzer, Joseph; Remington, Frederic Sackrider.

References and Further Readings

Musicant, Ivan. *Empire by Default: The Spanish-American War and the Dawn of the American Century*. New York: Henry Holt and Company, 1998.

Swanberg, W. A. *Citizen Hearst: A Biography of William Randolph Hearst*. New York: Charles Scribner's Sons, 1961.

Trask, David F. *The War with Spain in 1898*. Lincoln: University of Nebraska Press, 1996.

Hellings, Martin Luther (1841–1908)

A Pennsylvania veteran of the Civil War who mastered the science of telegraphy, Martin Luther Hellings prospered in that field. By the time of the Spanish-American War in 1898, he managed the International Ocean Telegraph (a subsidiary of Western Union) office in Key West, Florida. In this capacity, Hellings operated an intelligence network that provided the U.S. government with up-to-date information on Spanish activities in Cuba, both before and during the war with Spain.

Hellings, a resourceful individual, developed two independent systems for obtaining information. One method provided for the transmittal of confidential messages from the U.S. consul in Havana using steamships of the Plant Line. (Hellings had married into one of the wealthiest families in Florida and was acquainted with many of the area's prominent citizens and business officials, including H. B. Plant, owner of the steamship line.) Hellings's second channel of communication was through a Cuban telegrapher in Havana, Domingo Villaverde. Sympathetic to the Cuban revolutionary cause, Villaverde gladly cooperated in the endeavor, though telegraphic messages could only be sent during the hours when he alone was on duty.

Interestingly, Spain and the United States agreed to keep the lines between Havana and Key West open during the war. This allowed for a virtually uninterrupted flow of information, which was updated daily. The most significant piece of intelligence to be passed through the Hellings network pertained to the arrival of Adm. Pascual Cervera's Spanish Squadron in Santiago harbor.

The Hellings connection, which kept President William McKinley apprised of events in Cuba, was, surprisingly, unknown to many senior U.S. officials, including the secretaries of war and navy.

See also Cervera y Topete, Pascual; Communications; Military Intelligence, U.S.

References and Further Readings
O'Toole, G. J. A. *The Spanish War: An American Epic, 1898*. New York: W. W. Norton, 1984.

Henry, Guy Vernor (1839–1899)

Born at Fort Smith, Indian Territory, Guy Vernor Henry graduated from West Point in 1861. He saw extensive service in both the Civil War and the Indian wars and was awarded the Medal of Honor for his conduct in the Battle of Cold Harbor, Virginia, in 1864. In May 1898, he was promoted to brigadier general of volunteers and placed in command of the First Division of the Seventh Corps.

Henry's division (consisting of the Sixth Massachusetts and Sixth Illinois Infantry Regiments) landed in Cuba on 10 July. After the surrender of Santiago on 17 July, his command was assigned to the Puerto Rican Expedition, commanded by General of the Army Nelson Miles. After landing in Puerto Rico, Henry's seven-day march from Ponce to Utuado (6–13 August 1898) proved uneventful, with the Spanish offering no resistance.

After the war, Henry was promoted to brigadier general in the regular army and placed in command of the Military District of Ponce. Following this assignment, he succeeded Gen. John R. Brooke as military governor of Puerto Rico, a position he held until May 1899.

See also Puerto Rican Campaign.

References and Further Readings

Nofi, Albert A. *The Spanish-American War, 1898*. Conshohocken, PA: Combined Books, 1998.

Trask, David F. *The War with Spain in 1898*. Lincoln: University of Nebraska Press, 1996.

Hist (Gunboat)

See **Manzanillo, Actions at**

Hoar, George Frisbie (1826–1904)

Born in Concord, Massachusetts, George Frisbie Hoar graduated from Harvard Law School in 1846. He was deeply involved in the founding of the Republican Party in his home state. An influential U.S. senator at the time of the Spanish-American War, Hoar opposed war with Spain until the destruction of the *Maine* in Havana harbor. After the *Maine* disaster, he altered his stance and urged that the country adopt a united front in the war with Spain.

An avowed Anti-Imperialist, Hoar opposed the annexation of Hawaii on principle but eventually voted for the annexation measure in a gesture of support for President William McKinley. He was also unalterably opposed to acquisition of the Philippines, the only major issue on which he failed to support McKinley. He staunchly opposed the Treaty of Paris. Although Anti-Imperialist in spirit, Hoar refused to join the Anti-Imperialist League, believing that the most effective way to voice opposition was through party channels.

See also Anti-Imperialist League; Imperialism/Expansionism; McKinley, William, Jr.; Philippine Islands, Acquisition of, by the United States; Treaty of Paris.

References and Further Readings

Leech, Margaret. *In the Days of McKinley*. New York: Harper & Brothers, 1959.

Morgan, H. Wayne, ed. *Making Peace with Spain: The Diary of Whitelaw Reid—September–December, 1898*. Austin: University of Texas Press, 1965.

O'Toole, G. J. A. *The Spanish War: An American Epic, 1898*. New York: W. W. Norton, 1984.

Welch, Richard E., Jr. *George Frisbie Hoar and the Half-Breed Republicans*. Cambridge: Harvard University Press, 1971.

Hobson, Richmond Pearson (1870–1937)

A real hero of the Spanish-American War, Richmond Pearson Hobson was born in Greensboro, Alabama. He attended the U.S. Naval Academy, where he was an outstanding student, graduating first in his class in 1889.

Hobson's early naval career included three years in France and a tour with the Bureau of Construction and Repair. When war broke out between the United States and Spain, he was serving on the cruiser *New York* as assistant naval constructor for the fleet.

When Adm. William T. Sampson, commander of the U.S. fleet in Cuban waters, learned that Adm. Pascual Cervera's Spanish fleet was in Santiago harbor, destruction of that fleet became his primary objective. Sampson was confronted with the question of how this objective might best be accomplished. The harbor's entrance was guarded by several batteries of guns and electrical mines that could be detonated from shore-based locations. The mines were Sampson's greatest concern. The admiral believed the entrance to Santiago harbor could be blocked by scuttling the old collier *Merrimac,* thereby keeping the Spanish fleet bottled up until the army secured the batteries and eliminated the threat posed by the mines.

That assignment was given to Lieutenant Hobson, whose plan received Sampson's approval. Hobson proposed that he and a crew of six would take the *Merrimac* into the harbor's entrance, under cover of darkness. Once there, several torpedoes (or, more accurately for that time period, several underwater explosive devices) attached to the ship's port side would be set off. The vessel would then be maneuvered into a good blocking position and left to sink, with the crew being rescued by a lifeboat that had been towed behind the *Merrimac.* Since the narrowest part of the channel was approximately 350 to 450 feet and the *Merrimac* was 335 feet long, the ship, if scuttled in the right spot, would fill up most of the passageway. Although a hazardous undertaking, the plan held the promise of accomplishing exactly what Sampson wanted.

After several delays due to lighting conditions, Hobson got under way about 3 A.M. on 3 June 1898. All went smoothly at first, and the *Merrimac* was able to get well into the channel before being fired upon by Spanish shore batteries, which succeeded in

Lt. Richmond P. Hobson, one of the heroes of the Spanish-American War. Hobson and a volunteer crew scuttled the collier Merrimac *in the entrance to Santiago harbor in a vain effort to prevent the Spanish fleet from leaving. Hobson and his men were later captured by the Spanish and imprisoned for the remainder of the war.*

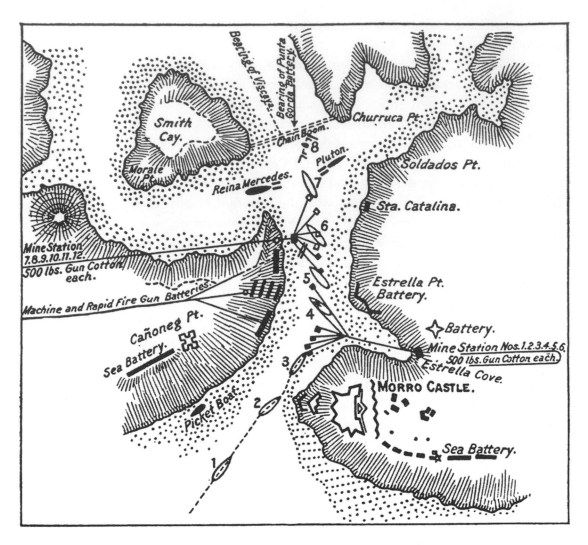

The scuttling of the U.S. Navy collier Merrimac *at the entrance to Santiago harbor, a Spanish view.*
Source: *Severo Gomez Nunez, "The Spanish-American War: Blockades and Coast Defense," in*
U.S. Navy, Office of Naval Intelligence, Notes on the Spanish-American War *(Washington, DC:*
Government Printing Office, 1900), p. 79.

damaging the ship's steering gear. As a result, Hobson had difficulty maneuvering the vessel. In addition, only two of the torpedoes detonated; consequently, the ship had to be scuttled at a point where its hulk offered little interference to traffic.

Hobson and his crew of six, plus a seventh man who had stowed away, abandoned the stricken vessel but were later captured by a Spanish steam launch carrying Admiral Cervera himself. The men were initially imprisoned in Morro Castle and later moved to Santiago. Freed after the war, Hobson and his crew became national heroes for their daring exploit.

See also Cervera y Topete, Pascual; Sampson, William Thomas; Santiago, Campaign and Siege of.

References and Further Readings

Feuer, A. B. *The Spanish-American War at Sea.* Westport, CT: Greenwood Press, 1995.

Hobson, Richmond Pearson. *The Sinking of the* Merrimac. New York: n.p., 1900.

———. "Sinking of the *Merrimac.*" *Century Magazine,* Four Parts, 1898–1899.

Trask, David F. *The War with Spain in 1898.* Lincoln: University of Nebraska Press, 1996.

Holguín (Cuba)

See **Santiago, Campaign and Siege of**

Hospital Corps

See **Medical Department, U.S. Army**

Howell, John Adams (1840–1918)

A U.S. Naval Academy graduate and career navy man, John Adams Howell had advanced to the rank of commodore by 1897. Recommended for command of the U.S. Asiatic Squadron, he was passed over in favor of George Dewey, for whom then Assistant Secretary of the Navy Theodore Roosevelt had lobbied vigorously. In the spring of 1898, Commodore Howell was appointed to command the Northern Patrol Squadron, whose territory embraced the Atlantic coast from Delaware to Maine. This assignment was followed by command of the European Squadron based at Lisbon, Portugal, with orders to monitor the movements of the Spanish fleet. Later, he commanded a squadron in Cuban waters and was promoted to rear admiral in August 1898.

In addition to his seagoing commands, Howell was also an inventor of some note. He designed the first U.S. torpedo around 1880, which remained in use until replaced by the Whitehead torpedo in circa 1898. His other inventions included a disappearing gun carriage.

See also Asiatic Squadron, U.S. Navy; Dewey, George; Navy, U.S.

References and Further Readings

Bradford, James C., ed. *Admirals of the New Steel Navy.* Annapolis, MD: Naval Institute Press, 1996.

Musicant, Ivan. *Empire by Default: The Spanish-American War and the Dawn of the American Century.* New York: Henry Holt and Company, 1998.

O'Toole, G. J. A. *The Spanish War: An American Epic, 1898.* New York: W. W. Norton, 1984.

Trask, David F. *The War with Spain in 1898.* Lincoln: University of Nebraska Press, 1996.

Hubbard, Elbert

See **García Íñiguez, Calixto**

Hull Bill

As the likelihood of war with Spain increased following the destruction of the battleship *Maine* in February 1898, discussions ensued regarding the U.S. Army's readiness for war. In March 1898, the Republican senator John A. T. Hull introduced legislation that would provide for an army that could be quickly expanded in a national emergency. The Hull Bill, as it came to be known, called for one battalion in each of the army's existing regiments to exist only as a framework unit, to which personnel could be quickly added when needed. This system would maintain the essential infrastructure without the actual rank and file.

The Hull Bill was vigorously opposed by the National Guard, which feared its role in the nation's military system would be greatly diminished under this proposal. Confronted by the guard's powerful lobby, Congress instead approved a bill that would allow National Guard units to be taken into federal service intact, rather than as a collection of individuals to be assigned to a unit of the War Department's choice.

See also Army, U.S.; Fifty Million Dollar Bill.

References and Further Readings

Cooper, Jerry. *The Rise of the National Guard: The Evolution of the American Militia, 1865–1920.* Lincoln: University of Nebraska Press, 1997.

Cosmas, Graham. *An Army for Empire: The United States Army in the Spanish-American War.* College Station: Texas A&M University Press, 1998.

Hull, John A. T.

See **Hull Bill**

Ilustrados

Ilustrados were Filipino Nationalists who embraced the teachings of the great José Rizal. Rizal advocated the Filipino cause be promoted through education and an increased awareness of Filipino self-identity. The term *ilustrados* refers to the "enlightened ones."

See also Aguinaldo y Famy, Emilio; Katipunan; Rizal, José.

References and Further Readings

Steinberg, David Joel. *The Philippines: A Singular and a Plural Place.* Boulder, CO: Westview Press, 1994.

Trask, David F. *The War with Spain in 1898.* Lincoln: University of Nebraska Press, 1996.

Wolff, Leon. *Little Brown Brother: America's Forgotten Bid for Empire Which Cost 250,000 Lives.* New York: Kraus Reprint, 1970.

Immunes

On 11 May 1898, as part of its military mobilization for the newly declared war with Spain, the U.S. Congress authorized the enlistment of 10,000 men from the southern states who were believed to be immune to tropical diseases, hence the term *immunes*. Of the 10 regiments authorized, 4—the Seventh, Eighth, Ninth, and Tenth U.S. Infantry Regiments—were composed of black soldiers.

See also Army, U.S.; Black American Soldiers; Diseases.

References and Further Readings

Cosmas, Graham. *An Army for Empire: The United States Army in the Spanish-American War.* College Station: Texas A&M University Press, 1998.

Trask, David F. *The War with Spain in 1898.* Lincoln: University of Nebraska Press, 1996.

Imperialism/Expansionism

The terms *imperialism* and *expansionism*, though sometimes used interchangeably, do not necessarily refer to the same thing. The terms tend to be fluid and elusive, and context is the key in making a distinction. With that in mind, imperialism may be defined as the political philosophy that advocates the expansion of a nation's political system, culture, and economic order into other parts of the world. As well, it usually implies sovereign rule over territory acquired by war or purchase. Expansionism, by contrast, may be used in the preceding context or may simply refer to the expansion of one nation's commercial trade interests or religious beliefs, for example.

As the United States approached the end of the nineteenth century, it found itself, for the first time in its brief history, no longer facing the challenges of taming the frontier. The United States had existed for some time as a coast-to-coast nation. The Indian problem had largely been resolved, at least in terms of being a threat to further settlement and travel. The open range was largely a thing of the past, and by 1897, only three territories (excluding Alaska) had yet to be awarded the mantle of statehood: Oklahoma (which became a state in 1907), Arizona (in 1912), and New Mexico (also in 1912). The land beyond the Mississippi and Missouri Rivers was vast and still lightly populated, but it was no longer the Wild West. Indeed, in his landmark essay, "The Significance of the Frontier in American History," published in 1893, Frederick Jackson Turner declared the frontier no longer existed.

In the years after the American Revolution, national expansion had not been totally ignored. The capture of Canada was a thwarted objective in the War of 1812 and again after the Civil War. Alaska was acquired in 1867, and President Ulysses Grant tried unsuccessfully to annex Santo Domingo in the 1870s. After much debate, Hawaii was annexed in 1898. Overall, however, the country was preoccupied with the trans-Mississippi West. But as the nineteenth century drew to a close, many in government and the private sector began to look beyond California to Asia as a market for the growing U.S. industrial output. Indeed, there was concern that the United States alone would not be able to absorb all that it produced. In addition, western expansion was seen by some as necessary to provide outer points of defense.

Interwoven among such arguments lay the notion of manifest destiny, that is, the philosophy that the United States was foreordained to reach out and spread its gospel of democracy among less-privileged countries. That same guiding star had drawn the nation westward to its Pacific shores. This idealistic notion also embraced the concept of social Darwinism, which argued that survival and growth belonged not only to the strongest individuals of a species but also to the strongest nations of the world.

Immediately after the war with Spain, expansion became a hotly debated topic as the United States dealt with the thorny issue of whether to acquire the Philippine Archipelago. The line between supporters and opponents of acquisition was clearly drawn. The debate spawned the Anti-Imperialist League which attracted some of the most prominent figures of the day, such as Andrew Carnegie and Samuel Gompers, allied against Theodore Roosevelt and Henry Cabot Lodge. In the end, those who supported Philippine acquisition had the stronger battalions, and for the first and only time in its history, the United States became a colonial power.

See also Anti-Imperialist League; Mahan, Alfred Thayer; McKinley, William, Jr.; Philippine Islands, Acquisition of, by the United States; Roosevelt, Theodore; Treaty of Paris.

References and Further Readings

Brands, H. W. *Bound to Empire: The United States and the Philippines.* New York: Oxford University Press, 1992.

Healy, David. *US Expansionism: The Imperialist Urge in the 1890s.* Milwaukee: University of Wisconsin Press, 1970.

LaFeber. *The New Empire.* Ithaca, NY: Cornell University Press, 1963.

Leech, Margaret. *In the Days of McKinley.* New York: Harper & Brothers, 1959.

May, Ernest R. *Imperial Democracy: The Emergence of America as a Great Power.* New York: Harcourt, Brace & World, 1961.

———. *American Imperialism: A Speculative Essay.* Chicago: Imprint Publications, 1991.

The Influence of Sea Power upon History

See **Mahan, Alfred Thayer**

Insular Affairs, Bureau of

As a result of the Spanish-American War, the United States found itself in the completely unfamiliar position of having to handle colonial issues and problems in the Philippines, Puerto Rico, and Guam. The government created the Bureau of Insular Affairs to deal with these problems.

First organized in 1898 as the Division of Customs and Insular Affairs within the War Department because the military occupied those territories, the division's name was changed to the Division of Insular Affairs in 1900 and then to the Bureau of Insular Affairs in

1902. However, operations remained under the overall control of the War Department.

The bureau's task was not a simple one, having to confront issues and problems with which the United States had no prior experience. Despite the nation's glaring lack of experience, the bureau carried out its mission in a creditable fashion. During the 1920s, the bureau was transferred to civilian control and then was abolished in 1939 when its usefulness declined.

See also Colonial Policies, U.S.; Philippine Commission.
References and Further Readings
Beede, Benjamin R., ed. *The War of 1898 and U.S. Interventions, 1898–1934.* New York: Garland Publishing, 1994.
Karnow, Stanley. *In Our Image: America's Empire in the Philippines.* New York: Random House, 1989.

Interservice Relations

At the time of the Spanish-American War, U.S. military planners believed that the nation's offensive striking capability resided in the navy. It was thought that, in the event of war, the most serious threat to U.S. security would come from an enemy attack against the coastline. The army was responsible for protecting the nation's coasts, but the navy was supposed to seek out and attack the enemy on the high seas. Although the war with Spain did not alter the traditional doctrine that focused on coastal defense, it did present U.S. military planners with the simultaneous challenge of conducting a large-scale military operation on foreign soil.

Rivalry among the different branches of the armed services, particularly the army and navy, has always been present, and it is more spirited at some times than at others. During the Spanish-American War, the rivalry and competition between the army and navy was often heated and disputatious enough to all but destroy any vestige of the harmony and cooperation needed to achieve a common goal. This was particularly true during the Cuban Campaign.

When it was learned that Adm. Pascual Cervera's Spanish fleet was in the harbor of Santiago de Cuba, Adm. William T. Sampson, commanding the U.S. fleet in Cuban waters, was confronted with a challenge—how best to get at the Spanish fleet. Since the harbor was mined and protected by several batteries of guns, Sampson wanted Gen. William R. Shafter's Fifth Corps (which was on Cuban soil by that time) to first secure the harbor defenses; this would allow the U.S. fleet to enter the harbor unimpeded. General Shafter, however, saw his mission as first defeating the Spanish Army and then securing the city of Santiago. A seeming inability to work out the details of this undertaking proved especially frustrating for Admiral Sampson. Fate intervened when Admiral Cervera elected to sortie from Santiago harbor. In the ensuing battle, the Spanish fleet was destroyed.

There were other examples of squabbling, such as that between Secretary of the Navy John Long and Secretary of War Russell Alger regarding lines of responsibility and accountability. During the Puerto Rican Campaign, President William McKinley finally had to issue a peremptory order to the navy to provide Gen. Nelson Miles with the vessels needed to execute the campaign.

See also Alger, Russell Alexander; Army, U.S.; Cuban Campaign; Hobson, Richmond Pearson; Long, John Davis; Navy, U.S.; Sampson, William Thomas; Shafter, William Rufus.

References and Further Readings

Cosmas, Graham. *An Army for Empire: The United States Army in the Spanish-American War.* College Station: Texas A&M University Press, 1998.

Millis, Walter. *The Martial Spirit.* Chicago: Ivan R. Dee, 1989.

Trask, David F. *The War with Spain in 1898.* Lincoln: University of Nebraska Press, 1996.

Weigley, Russell F. *History of the United States Army.* New York: Macmillan Publishing, 1967.

Jáudenes y Álvarez, Fermín

Fermín Jáudenes y Álvarez replaced Basilio Augustín as Spanish commander in the Philippines on 4 August 1898. The inheritor of a lost situation, Jáudenes was confronted by both Filipino revolutionaries and the United States. He was effectively trapped, for there was no hope of aid from Spain and surrender was not an option. Indeed, his predecessor was replaced because he had talked of surrendering to the Americans.

Through the efforts of the Belgian consul, Edouard André, Jáudenes communicated with Commodore George Dewey and later with Gen. Wesley Merritt, the U.S. commanders. On 13 August, unaware that an armistice had been signed the previous day and acting entirely on his own volition, Jáudenes opened surrender discussions with General Merritt. He subsequently agreed to surrender Manila to the Americans after mounting a token resistance to satisfy Spain's honor, providing that the Filipino revolutionary forces were excluded from participation. Jáudenes was later tried and castigated by his superiors for taking that action.

See also Augustín Dávila, Don Basilio; Manila, First Battle of; Merritt, Wesley.

References and Further Readings
Alberts, Don E. *Brandy Station to Manila Bay: A Biography of General Wesley Merritt.* Austin, TX: Presidial Press, 1980.
Musicant, Ivan. *Empire by Default: The Spanish-American War and the Dawn of the American Century.* New York: Henry Holt and Company, 1998.
Wolff, Leon. *Little Brown Brother: America's Forgotten Bid for Empire Which Cost 250,000 Lives.* New York: Kraus Reprint, 1970.

Jingoism

The precise origin of the word *jingo* is unclear. The exclamation "by jingo" has long been taken as an enthusiastic expression of assertiveness—as in "I can do it, by jingo!" Theodore Roosevelt was probably the most blatant example of a jingoist during the Spanish-American War.

Earlier, in 1878, war hawks in Great Britain who were urging their country to support the Turks against the Russians picked up the phrase and incorporated it into a song that expressed their view. "We don't want to fight, but by Jingo if we do, we've got the ships, we've got the men, we've got the money, too" (Bremner 1980, p. 215). As a result, the term *jingo* or *jingoism* has since come to characterize a blustering, chauvinistic form of patriotism.

See also McKinley, William, Jr.; Roosevelt, Theodore.
References and Further Readings
Brands, H. W. *TR: The Last Romantic.* New York: Basic Books, 1997.
Bremner, John B. *Words on Words: A Dictionary for Writers and Others Who Care about Words.* New York: MJF Books, 1980.
Leech, Margaret. *In the Days of McKinley.* New York: Harper & Brothers, 1959.
Millis, Walter. *The Martial Spirit.* Chicago: Ivan R. Dee, 1989.

Journalism

Despite its brevity (it lasted only three months), the Spanish-American War was the most intensely covered event in history up to that time. A conservative estimate is that some 300 correspondents covered the war; some estimates place the number at 500. Although correspondents from the New York newspapers, particularly the *Journal* and *World,* were most in evidence, other reporters from around the nation as well as Europe were also on the scene.

The turn of the century was the heyday of "yellow journalism." an expression that grew out of a cartoon in the *New York World* that was printed in yellow ink. William Randolph Hearst, publisher of the *New York Journal,* which was the *World*'s chief competitor, quickly adopted the idea for his paper. Eventually, the term came to embrace the sensationalized reporting that characterized the newspapers of that era.

Some reporters—such as Richard Harding Davis, Stephen Crane, and James Creelman—were as colorful as the newspapers they represented. Another member of that fraternity, Sylvester Scovel, attempted to punch Gen. William R. Shafter when the latter refused to include him in a victory photograph following the surrender of Santiago.

During the months leading up to the war, stories emanating from Cuba told of Spanish cruelties against Cubans, such as the har-

rowing tale of Evangelina Cisneros. These sensational stories were often exaggerated, but they nevertheless served to fuel an anti-Spanish attitude among the U.S. public. The tabloids found on today's newsstands might be seen as contemporary examples of sensational journalism, although carried to much greater lengths than the newspapers of the 1890s. The leading satirist of the day, Finley Peter Dunne, used his fictional creation Mr. Dooley to comment on the war and its political intrigues in much the same way that the modern character Doonesbury speaks to current events.

If U.S. newspapers were clearly anti-Spanish, the Spanish press was equally anti-American. The Spanish people resented U.S. interference in Cuba, and many believed that a break between the two countries was not far off.

The Spanish-American War proved expensive to cover. Although the United States and Spain had agreed to keep open the cable line between Havana and Key West, reporters covering the war had no access to Havana and had to send stories back to the United States via chartered dispatch boats, whose owners took advantage of the situation by charging exorbitant fees.

In addition to extensive coverage by the press, the war had the distinction of being the first to be captured on motion picture film. Stuart J. Blackton carried a 60-pound Vitagraph movie camera during the Santiago Campaign. Advances in photography also enabled a number of reporters (such as Richard Harding Davis) to carry their

"The Big Type War of the Yellow Kids," by Leon Barritt, 29 June 1898. Joseph Pulitzer and William Randolph Hearst, dressed as the yellow kids, push against opposite sides of a pillar of wooden blocks that spells WAR.

own still cameras, thereby providing a visual dimension to their stories that had never before been possible.

A coterie of well-known artists and illustrators also added their interpretations of the war to those of the reporters. Frederic Remington, Howard Chandler Christy, Walter Granville Smith, and others left a rich legacy of colorful, dramatic images of the Spanish-American War.

See also Benjamin, Anna Northend; Christy, Howard Chandler; Cisneros, Evangelina; Crane, Stephen; Creelman, James; Davis, Richard Harding; Hearst, William Randolph; Pulitzer, Joseph; Remington, Frederic Sackrider; Scovel, Henry Sylvester; Watkins, Kathleen Blake.

References and Further Readings

Bradford, James C., ed. *Crucible of Empire: The Spanish-American War and Its Aftermath.* Annapolis, MD: Naval Institute Press, 1993.

Brown, Charles H. *The Correspondents' War: Journalists in the Spanish-American War.* New York: Charles Scribner's Sons, 1967.

Dierks, Jack Cameron. *A Leap to Arms: The Cuban Campaign of 1898.* Philadelphia: J. B. Lippincott, 1970.

Harrington, Peter, and Frederic A. Sharf. *"A Splendid Little War": The Spanish-American War, 1898—The Artists' Perspective.* London: Greenhill Books, 1998.

Milton, Joyce. *The Yellow Kids: Foreign Correspondents in the Heyday of Yellow Journalism.* New York: Harper & Row, 1989.

Roth, Mitchel P. *Historical Dictionary of War Journalism.* Westport, CT: Greenwood Press, 1997.

Wisan, Joseph Ezra. *The Cuban Crisis as Reflected in the New York Press (1895–1898).* New York: Columbia University Press, 1934.

Katipunan

A Filipino Nationalist organization with secret rites giving it Masonic overtones, Katipunan was founded by Marcelo Pilar, although leadership of the group soon devolved to Andrés Bonifacio, who was later forced out of power and reportedly executed on the orders of Emilio Aguinaldo. Aguinaldo then seized control of the organization and became the most celebrated symbol of Filipino independence. The group's name was sometimes translated as "Sons of the People" or "Patriot's League."

Unlike José Rizal's Liga Filipina, which advocated advancement through education, the Katipunan philosophy was predicated on a violent overthrow of Spanish rule. As such, the organization attracted working-class Filipinos and at one time reportedly had nearly a quarter million members.

> **See also** Aguinaldo y Famy, Emilio; Bonifacio, Andrés; Filipino Revolutionary Movement; Rizal, José.
> **References and Further Readings**
> Steinberg, David Joel. *The Philippines: A Singular and a Plural Place.* Boulder, CO: Westview Press, 1994.
> Trask, David F. *The War with Spain in 1898.* Lincoln: University of Nebraska Press, 1996.
> Wolff, Leon. *Little Brown Brother: America's Forgotten Bid for Empire Which Cost 250,000 Lives.* New York: Kraus Reprint, 1970.

Kennan, George (1845–1924)

Born in Norwalk, Ohio, George Kennan learned military telegraphy during the Civil War. After accompanying a Western Union expedition to Siberia in 1865, he turned to writing and, during the Spanish-American War, covered the Cuban Campaign for *Outlook Magazine*. His coverage of the campaign was critical of army leadership, as was his book-length study of the campaign, entitled *Campaigning in Cuba,* which appeared in 1899. In that study, he censured the army for its failure to do a better job of combating the effects of the diseases that afflicted U.S. troops in Cuba. He was especially critical of Gen. William R. Shafter, commander of the Fifth Corps. Kennan himself came down with malaria and left Cuba in August but later returned to write about the U.S. occupation of the island. He was the father of the future diplomat George F. Kennan.

See also Casualties; Diseases; Journalism; Medical Department, U.S. Army; Santiago, Campaign and Siege of.

References and Further Readings

Brown, Charles H. *The Correspondents' War: Journalists in the Spanish-American War.* New York: Charles Scribner's Sons, 1967.

Carlson, Paul H. *Pecos Bill: A Military Biography of William R. Shafter.* College Station: Texas A&M University Press, 1989.

Kennan, George. *Campaigning in Cuba.* Reprint. Port Washington, NY: Kennikat Press, 1971.

Kent, Jacob Ford (1835–1918)

Born in Philadelphia, Jacob Ford Kent graduated from West Point in 1861. His Civil War service was followed by duty as a West Point instructor, then service on the western frontier. When war with Spain broke out, he was promoted to brigadier general of volunteers and appointed to command the First Infantry Division in Gen. William R. Shafter's Fifth Corps.

Kent's division was the main force in the assault on San Juan Hill, sustaining more than 500 casualties. Kent was one of the senior officers who signed the famous "Round Robin" letter, which called for removal of U.S. troops from Cuba because of the threat posed by tropical diseases such as yellow fever and malaria.

Shortly thereafter, Kent was promoted to major general of volunteers and later served briefly in the Philippines. He was promoted to the permanent rank of brigadier general in the regular army and retired in October 1898.

See also Diseases; "Round Robin" Letter; San Juan Hill, Charge up.

References and Further Readings

Chadwick, Rear Adm. French Ensor. *Relations of the United States and Spain: The Spanish American War.* 2 vols. New York: Charles Scribner's Sons, 1911 (reprinted in 1968).

Cosmas, Graham. *An Army for Empire: The United States Army in the Spanish-American War.* College Station: Texas A&M University Press, 1998.

Samuels, Peggy, and Harold Samuels. *Teddy Roosevelt at San Juan: The Making of a President.* College Station: Texas A&M University Press, 1997.

Kettle Hill (Cuba)

See **San Juan Hill, Charge up**

Key West, Florida

Strategically located 100 miles from Havana, Cuba, Key West played an important role in the Spanish-American War. In the months preceding the war, its port served as headquarters for the U.S. North Atlantic Squadron's winter exercises and was home to a wide assortment of naval vessels. Both the U.S. Navy and the U.S. Revenue Cutter Service (forerunner of the Coast Guard) expanded facilities at Key West as early as 1895 to monitor coastal waters for filibustering activities.

After war was declared, Key West's proximity to Cuba made it an ideal base from which to reinforce the naval blockade of the island. It provided coaling facilities and a communications center and also served as an embarkation point for some ground troops.

See also Filibuster; Naval Blockade of Cuba; Navy, U.S.; North Atlantic Squadron, U.S. Navy.

References and Further Readings

Chadwick, Rear Adm. French Ensor. *Relations of the United States and Spain: The Spanish American War.* 2 vols. New York: Charles Scribner's Sons, 1911 (reprinted in 1968).

Feuer, A. B. *The Spanish-American War at Sea.* Westport, CT: Greenwood Press, 1995.

Trask, David F. *The War with Spain in 1898.* Lincoln: University of Nebraska Press, 1996.

Kimball, William Warren (1848–1930)

An 1869 graduate of the U.S. Naval Academy, William Warren Kimball developed an early interest in submarines and torpedoes, becoming an authority on both. However, his most important contribution may have been as a naval strategist, particularly for the Spanish-American War.

In the three years preceding the war, a group of student officers at the newly formed Naval War College were directed to develop a naval strategy to be used in the event of war with Spain. Their ideas were turned over to Kimball, who concluded that U.S. interests could best be served by establishing and dispatching a naval force to capture Manila in the Philippine Islands. His recommendation, known as the Kimball Plan, was subsequently rejected because it failed to stress an aggressive strategy involving both the army and the navy.

During the war with Spain, Kimball commanded the Atlantic Squadron's torpedo boat flotilla.

See also Naval Strategy, U.S.

References and Further Readings

Musicant, Ivan. *Empire by Default: The Spanish-American War and the Dawn of the American Century.* New York: Henry Holt and Company, 1998.

Trask, David F. *The War with Spain in 1898.* Lincoln: University of Nebraska Press, 1996.

Ladrones

See **Guam**

Lake Lanao (Mindanao, Philippines) Campaigns (1901–1903)

During the years 1902 and 1903, the area around Lake Lanao, a large body of water in the western part of the island of Mindanao in the southern Philippine Archipelago, was the scene of hard fighting between U.S. troops and the Muslim inhabitants of the region. The Muslims of Mindanao and the nearby Sulu Archipelago, numbering perhaps 100,000, had been given the name *Moros* by the Spanish, who thought they resembled the Moors of North Africa. Perpetually troublesome to the Spanish, the recalcitrant Moros also posed a potential threat to U.S. efforts to pacify the region during the Spanish-American War.

In 1899, Gen. John C. Bates, in an effort to cultivate a climate of peace, signed a treaty with the sultan of Sulu, which, for the short term at least, was reasonably effective. By 1901, the army had established camps in Mindanao and begun moving into the Lanao region with a goal of civilizing the natives.

The Moros, meanwhile, had grown increasingly resentful. Although some Moro chieftains (*datus* or *dattos*) were on more or less friendly terms with the United States, many were overtly hostile, and attacks on small parties of U.S. soldiers grew more frequent.

In June 1901, Capt. John J. Pershing, who had demonstrated his soldierly qualities in leading the black Tenth Cavalry at San Juan Hill, was now in the Philippines at his own request. Pershing had been assigned to the remote army post of Iligan on the north-central coast of Mindanao, not far from the north shore of Lake Lanao. Pershing's orders were issued by Brig. Gen. George Davis, commander of the Department of Mindanao. His mission was to establish friendly relations with the

Moros. Again, as with his transfer from Cuba to the Philippines, Pershing volunteered for this assignment, despite the fact that it was regarded as a particularly difficult undertaking.

In May 1902, while Pershing was carrying out his assignment in the northern reaches of Lake Lanao, Col. Frank D. Baldwin, responding to Moro harassment of his working parties who were building a road inland from the coast to Lake Lanao, launched a punitive strike from Malabang. The subsequent campaign resulted in fierce fighting and the eventual destruction of Moro forts—called *cottas*—at Bayan and Binadayan.

Despite the success of his campaign, Baldwin's superiors, General George W. Davis and Maj. Gen. Adna R. Chaffee, military governor of the Philippines, thought Baldwin had acted too aggressively and failed to work hard enough to achieve harmonious relations with the Moros. Accordingly, Baldwin was replaced by Pershing. Although he was only a junior officer, Pershing seemed to have exactly the qualities Chaffee and Davis wanted for a leader in that especially challenging situation. Through patience and hard work, Pershing had demonstrated an ability to establish a good rapport with Moros on the north side of Lake Lanao. Whether he would be able to reprise his success around the southern shore of the lake remained to be seen.

In spite of his best efforts, when Pershing assumed command at Camp Vicars on the southern shore of Lanao, he found, as Baldwin had, that a strong element of Moros continued to ambush patrols and harass army camps. Ultimately, Pershing concluded that it was time to punish the Moros. In late September 1902, he conducted a campaign that subsequently destroyed several Moro *cottas* at Guaun and Bayabao. Pressing on toward Maciu, Pershing sent emissaries ahead to negotiate, but they were rebuffed. Pershing resumed his advance but was forced to pull back when he was unable to cross an inlet of Lake Lanao that separated Maciu, Sauir, and Talub.

Returning with engineers, Pershing ordered that a road be built around the inlet, and by 1 October, he confronted the *cottas*, from which flew the Moro red flags of war. The expedition's field pieces made short work of the Moro forts, and on 3 October, Pershing returned to Camp Vicars, having destroyed ten *cottas* and inflicted heavy casualties.

In November, Pershing renewed his efforts to persuade the Moro leaders, notably the sultan of Bacolod, to accept the U.S. terms. Although the terms were subsequently rejected, offensive operations did not resume until the following spring.

In April 1903, Pershing was authorized to move against the

intractable Bacolod leader, and on 3 April, he departed Camp Vicars with a strong column. Three days later, after much maneuvering over rugged terrain, Pershing surrounded the powerful Moro *cotta* at Bacolod, which was located on a ridge above Lake Lanao. On 7 April, he attacked amid a furious rainstorm. By dark, the *cotta* was ablaze from artillery fire. Again, Moro casualties were heavy, but Pershing also had allowed many to escape, hoping that, having witnessed his army's power, they might persuade other Moros that further resistance was futile.

In May, Pershing continued his sweep around Lake Lanao, defeating the Moros at Taraca and destroying more *cottas*. The expedition was supported by a fleet of gunboats that pursued and attacked the Moro *vintas* (a type of canoe). By 10 May, Pershing was back at Camp Vicars, holding the distinction of being the first to lead an expedition completely around Lake Lanao.

Pershing's honesty in dealing with the Moros and his readiness to inflict punishment when needed led to a resolution of the problem. Although some individuals continued to harass U.S. troops, the Moro threat was by and large eliminated as a result of these expeditions.

See also Baldwin, Frank Dwight; Chaffee, Adna Romanza; Moros; Pershing, John Joseph.

References and Further Readings

Beede, Benjamin R., ed. *The War of 1898 and U.S. Interventions, 1898–1934*. New York: Garland Publishing, 1994.

Hitt, Parker. "Amphibious Infantry: A Fleet on Lake Lanao." *Proceedings of the United States Naval Institute*, 64, 1938.

Linn, Brian McAllister. *The Philippine War, 1899–1902*. Lawrence: University Press of Kansas, 2000.

Miller, Stuart C. *Benevolent Assimilation: The American Conquest of the Philippines, 1899–1903*. New Haven, CT: Yale University Press, 1983.

Smythe, Donald. *Guerrilla Warrior: The Early Life of John J. Pershing*. New York: Charles Scribner's Sons, 1973.

Steinbach, Robert H. *A Long March: The Lives of Frank and Alice Baldwin*. Austin: University of Texas Press, 1989.

La Quasima

See **Las Guásimas**

Las Guásimas (La Quasima) (Cuba), Battle of (24 June 1898)

The second major land action between U.S. and Spanish forces in Cuba during the Spanish-American War occurred at Las Guásimas

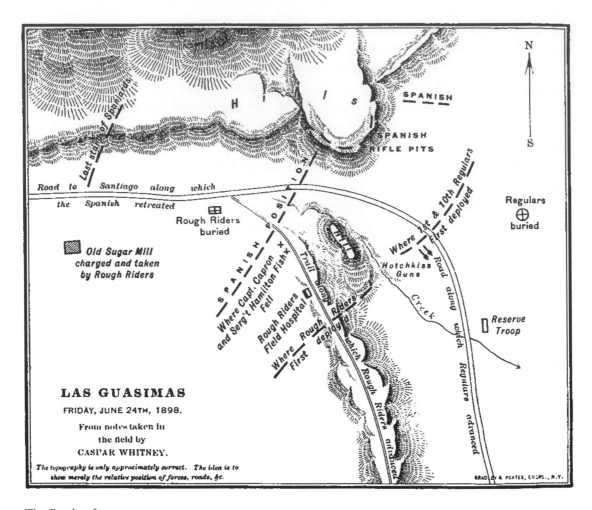

Inside the map:

N

S

SPANISH

SPANISH RIFLE PITS

Last stand of Spaniards

Road to Santiago along which the Spanish retreated

Rough Riders buried

Where 1st & 10th Regulars first deployed

Regulars buried

Old Sugar Mill charged and taken by Rough Riders

Where Capt. Capron and Serg't Hamilton Fish Fell

Hotchkiss Guns

Road along which Regulars advanced

Rough Riders Field Hospital

Where Rough Riders First deployed

Trail along Rough Riders

Creek

Reserve Troop

which Rough Riders advanced

LAS GUASIMAS

FRIDAY, JUNE 24TH, 1898.

From notes taken in the field by

CASPAR WHITNEY.

The topography is only approximately correct. The idea is to show merely the relative position of forces, roads, &c.

BRADLEY & POATES, ENGRS., N.Y.

The Battle of Las Guásimas, Cuba, 1898. Source: Harper's Pictorial History of the War with Spain (New York: Harper & Brothers Publishers, 1899), II, p. 329.

on 24 June 1898. (The first encounter took place 10 days earlier when a marine battalion secured Guantánamo after heavy fighting.)

Situated about 3 miles from Siboney, Las Guásimas sat at the junction of a narrow footpath and El Camino Real (the royal road), which led to Santiago de Cuba. After three years of fighting between the Cuban revolutionaries and Spanish forces, most of eastern Cuba had felt the heavy hand of war in one way or another. A small hamlet to begin with, Las Guásimas had been abandoned by June 1898, and now it was a rather nondescript place along the way to Santiago. Located along a high ridge, however, it offered the Spanish a strong defensive position.

Gen. William R. Shafter's Fifth Corps commenced its main advance on Santiago, moving inland from the landing site at Daiquirí on 22 June. Earlier that same day, Gen. Henry Ware Lawton's division began its independent movement toward Siboney, under orders to repel any Spanish attack that might come down El Camino Real. Lawton found Siboney abandoned by its Spanish defenders and advised Shafter accordingly. In view of that turn of events, Shafter directed Lawton to continue his advance toward Santiago.

Unfortunately, Shafter's orders were not directed specifically to Lawton; instead, they went to the senior officer present. As it turned out, that was Maj. Gen. Joseph "Fighting Joe" Wheeler, the ex-Confederate cavalry leader who had been appointed by President William McKinley to command the expedition's lone cavalry division. A Georgian turned Alabaman (he represented Alabama in Congress when war was declared), Wheeler was appointed by President McKinley as a gesture to help heal old North-South wounds. The Spanish-American War would produce two feisty bantam roosters: Joe Wheeler was one and Frederick Funston the other.

While Lawton was reporting to Shafter, Wheeler opted to take advantage of what seemed like a golden opportunity. Ranging far out in front with a small detachment of U.S. soldiers and Cuban guerrillas, Wheeler discovered that the Spanish, who had evacuated Siboney, were now digging in along a ridge at Las Guásimas, a few miles farther along El Camino Real.

Wheeler was anxious to fight. Shafter had wanted him to oversee the rest of the landing, but the restless, diminutive ex-Confederate believed he needed to see what the situation looked like up ahead. Given that Shafter's orders were directed to the senior officer present, Wheeler was more than willing to interpret those orders to meet the current situation—in other words, to attack, which he proposed to do the next day, 24 June.

Learning of Wheeler's plan, Lawton was angry at having been upstaged. He attempted to inform Shafter and have the attack called off, but the commanding general was still aboard ship and could not be contacted.

In the wake of the U.S. landing at Daiquirí, the Spanish commander at Santiago, Gen. Arsenio Linares, had ordered a withdrawal toward Santiago on 23 June. To facilitate this move, on 23 June Brig. Gen. Antero Rubín was directed to form a defensive position along the ridge at Las Guásimas. Pondering the situation, Linares became convinced that the Americans might well move along the coast to the San Juan River, then move up the river to Santiago. Fearing that such a move would cut off his troops at Las Guásimas, Linares ordered Rubín to retire to Santiago on 24 June.

As he evaluated the situation and made his plans to attack, Wheeler seems to have had some knowledge of the Spanish plans for withdrawal from intelligence supplied by Cuban revolutionaries under the command of Gen. Demetrio Castillo. Wheeler's plan called for Brig. Gen. Samuel B. M. Young's brigade, composed of the First and Tenth U.S. Regular Cavalry Regiments and the First U.S. Volunteer Cavalry (better known as the Rough Riders), together with a 4-gun battery of mountain field pieces, to attack Las Guásimas. The attack was to be further supported by some 800 revolutionaries, promised by General Castillo. The promised support, however, never materialized.

The approach to Las Guásimas, covered as it was with heavy brush and timber, afforded some concealment for Young's troops, who reached Las Guásimas at 5:40 A.M. on a hot and humid 24 June. At 8 A.M., Young's field pieces opened up but soon were silenced, and the artillerymen were forced to withdraw by the effective fire of the Spanish riflemen. The attack would have to proceed without artillery support. Young divided his brigade into two columns, with the First and Tenth Regular Cavalry Regiments under his personal command on the right flank and the Rough Riders, under Col. Leonard Wood and Lt. Col. Theodore Roosevelt, on the left. Four war correspondents, including Richard Harding Davis and Stephen Crane, also were on hand to cover the action.

The Spanish line was strong, with soldiers well positioned behind stone walls and wire fences, the salient point being a brick building. On the right, Young's regulars kept the defenders busy, but the Spanish riflemen were doing considerable damage with their Mauser rifles, firing smokeless powder and thereby rendering themselves almost impossible for U.S. soldiers to locate.

Wood directed Roosevelt to take three companies of the Rough Riders and work around behind the Spanish. In this situation, Roosevelt was truly in his element, as he would be later at Kettle Hill and San Juan Hill. At Las Guásimas, one correspondent described him as "the most magnificent soldier I have ever seen" (Samuels, p. 152). Alongside Roosevelt was arguably the most famous journalist of his era, Richard Harding Davis, having armed himself with a carbine and behaving more like soldier than correspondent.

Supported by fire from the other two regiments in Young's brigade, the Rough Riders advanced, with Roosevelt commanding on the left, Leonard Wood controlling in the center, and Wheeler himself, having arrived on the scene, taking personal charge on the right. In the heat of battle, Wheeler is reported to have shouted, "Come on—we've got the damn Yankees on the run" (Nofi, p. 128).

After two hours of fighting, General Rubín, in accordance with his orders, broke off the action and effected a clean withdrawal to Santiago. Although Young's brigade took possession of the ground and thus claimed a victory, the affair was of little strategic importance except as a tonic to the U.S. troops. Young's command incurred 16 casualties, including young Hamilton Fish, a New York socialite and grandson of the former secretary of state in President Ulysses Grant's administration. Fish probably was the first Rough Rider to die in action. Also killed was Capt. Allyn Capron Jr., whose father, Capt. Allyn Capron Sr., commanded an artillery battery in General Lawton's division.

> **See also** Davis, Richard Harding; Funston, Frederick; Roosevelt, Theodore; Rough Riders; Santiago, Campaign and Siege of; Wheeler, Joseph "Fighting Joe"; Wood, Leonard; Young, Samuel Baldwin Marks.

> **References and Further Readings**
> Davis, Richard Harding. *The Cuban and Puerto Rican Campaigns.* New York: Charles Scribner's Sons, 1898.
> Feuer, A. B. *The Santiago Campaign of 1898.* Westport, CT: Praeger Publishers, 1993.
> Nofi, Albert A. *The Spanish-American War, 1898.* Conshohocken, PA: Combined Books, 1998.
> Samuels, Peggy, and Harold Samuels. *Teddy Roosevelt at San Juan: The Making of a President.* College Station: Texas A&M University Press, 1997.

Lawton, Henry Ware (1843–1899)

Born in Ohio, Henry Ware Lawton enlisted in the volunteers during the Civil War and soon was appointed an officer. Later in the war, he was promoted to the rank of colonel and was awarded the Medal of Honor for his conduct during the Atlanta Campaign. Following the Civil War, he saw extensive service in the West during the Indian wars; Lawton was the man who finally captured Geronimo. When the Spanish-American War erupted, Lawton was promoted to brigadier general of volunteers. He was given command of the Second Division in Gen. William R. Shafter's Fifth Corps, comprising the Cuban Expeditionary Force.

In the advance on Santiago, Lawton, reinforced by Gen. John C. Bates's brigade, received an order from General Shafter to cover the landing at Daiquirí by advancing on Siboney. That order was changed by Gen. Joseph Wheeler, who, in Shafter's immediate absence, was the ranking commander on the field. Wheeler instead directed Lawton to attack at Las Guásimas and later at El Caney in support of the general movement on Santiago.

The fight at El Caney was expected to be relatively brief and simple, after which Lawton's command was to join the main attack

Gen. Henry Lawton with aides in Emilio Aguinaldo's former headquarters at Baliuag, 1899.

against San Juan Heights. El Caney, however, turned out to be a stiff, daylong fight that cost Lawton heavy casualties and delayed his participation in the attack on San Juan Heights.

After the Peace Protocol was signed in August 1898, Lawton served as military governor of Santiago. In March 1899, he was transferred to the Philippines, where he was killed the following December in action at San Mateo near Manila.

See also El Caney, Battle of; Manila Bay, Battle of; Santiago, Campaign and Siege of.

References and Further Readings
Cosmas, Graham. *An Army for Empire: The United States Army in the Spanish-American War.* College Station: Texas A&M University Press, 1998.
Musicant, Ivan. *Empire by Default: The Spanish-American War and the Dawn of the American Century.* New York: Henry Holt and Company, 1998.
Wolff, Leon. *Little Brown Brother: America's Forgotten Bid for Empire Which Cost 250,000 Lives.* New York: Kraus Reprint, 1970.

Lee, Fitzhugh (1835–1905)

A Virginian with an impressive family lineage, Fitzhugh Lee was the grandson of "Light-Horse" Harry Lee of Revolutionary War fame

Fitzhugh Lee, nephew of Confederate general Robert E. Lee, had a distinguished Civil War career. Prior to the Spanish-American War, he was U.S. ambassador to Cuba, and during the war, he served as major general of volunteers.

and the nephew of Robert E. Lee. After graduating from West Point in 1856, Fitzhugh Lee served on the frontier. Following the outbreak of the Civil War, he resigned his commission in the Union army to join the Confederacy. Lee went on to become one of the South's most celebrated cavalry leaders. Although he did not participate in any actions during the Spanish-American War, his command served as an occupational force in Cuba between 1899 and 1901.

After the Civil War, Lee entered politics and served one term as governor of Virginia. Although Lee was totally unfamiliar with Spanish language and customs, President Grover Cleveland appointed him U.S. consul general to Cuba in 1896. Lee's expansionist views ran counter to those of Cleveland, but he was a loyal Democrat. After William McKinley's election as president that same year, Lee retained his post in Havana and continued to monitor the Cuban situation for McKinley, as he had done for Cleveland.

At first overly sympathetic to the Cuban revolutionary cause (perhaps motivated by old Confederate feelings?), Lee later softened his position with respect to U.S. intervention. Interestingly, in the summer of 1896, he recommended to President Cleveland and Secretary of State Richard Olney that the United States have a warship with a contingent of marines ready to sail for Cuba. Yet in January 1898, when President McKinley ordered the battleship *Maine* to Havana, Lee opposed the move, fearing that the vessel's presence there would place additional stress on the already strained relations between Spain and the United States.

After the destruction of the *Maine* in February 1898, Lee returned to the United States. Following the declaration of war with Spain in April, he was commissioned a major general and placed in command of the Seventh Army Corps.

In addition to his service as a soldier and a diplomat, Lee wrote a biography of his uncle, Robert E. Lee, and a monumental study of Cuba's struggle with Spain.

See also Cuban Revolution; *Maine*; McKinley, William, Jr.
References and Further Readings
Lee, Fitzhugh. *Cuba's Struggle against Spain, with the Causes for American Intervention and a Full Account of the Spanish-American War, Including Final Peace Negotiations.* New York: American Historical Press, 1899.
Musicant, Ivan. *Empire by Default: The Spanish-American War and the Dawn of the American Century.* New York: Henry Holt and Company, 1998.
Nichols, James L. *General Fitzhugh Lee: A Biography.* Lynchburg, VA: H. E. Howard, 1989.
Trask, David F. *The War with Spain in 1898.* Lincoln: University of Nebraska Press, 1996.

León y Castillo, Fernando de (1842–1918)

A veteran lawyer and diplomat, Fernando de León y Castillo was three times Spanish ambassador to France—in 1887, in 1892, and from 1897 to 1910. As such, he was in a key position to influence events during the Spanish-American War.

In the summer of 1898, with the war going badly for Spain, León worked through the French ambassador to the United States,

Jules Cambon, to explore the possibilities for a cease-fire. Although he was not an official member of the Spanish negotiating committee during the discussions that led to the Treaty of Paris, León labored tirelessly behind the scenes to achieve a settlement that would be acceptable to the United States but not impose excessively harsh conditions on Spain. On one occasion, he importuned Whitelaw Reid, a member of the U.S. committee, to endorse a settlement whereby the United States would reimburse Spain for the expense of the Cuban Revolution, a recommendation that Reid rejected.

See also Treaty of Paris.

References and Further Readings

Morgan, H. Wayne, ed. *Making Peace with Spain: The Diary of Whitelaw Reid—September–December, 1898.* Austin: University of Texas Press, 1965.

Musicant, Ivan. *Empire by Default: The Spanish-American War and the Dawn of the American Century.* New York: Henry Holt and Company, 1998.

Liga Filipina

In 1872, harsh measures imposed on the working class of the Filipino populace by their Spanish rulers, especially the Roman Catholic priests, spawned a revolt that was quickly put down. Nevertheless, the effort gave birth to a new nationalistic movement among Filipinos living in Spain. The principal figure in this new movement was José Rizal, a writer and intellectual. Rizal's writings preached advancement and change through education, as opposed to violent overthrow.

When Rizal returned to the Philippines in 1892, he created the Liga Filipina (Philippine League) as an organization whose mission was to advance the cause of Filipino nationalism through education. The Liga Filipina failed to satisfy many Filipinos anxious for immediate results. This in turn led to the formation of the Katipunan, a secret society that advocated the overthrow of Spanish rule by force.

See also Katipunan; Rizal, José.

References and Further Readings

Karnow, Stanley. *In Our Image: America's Empire in the Philippines.* New York: Random House, 1989.

Steinberg, David Joel. *The Philippines: A Singular and a Plural Place.* Boulder, CO: Westview Press, 1994.

Trask, David F. *The War with Spain in 1898.* Lincoln: University of Nebraska Press, 1996.

Linares y Pomba, Arsenio (1848–1914)

A Spanish Army veteran of thirty years when the Spanish-American War was declared, Arsenio Linares y Pomba had seen service in Cuba and the Philippines and had fought against the Carlist regime in Spain. At the time of the Spanish-American War, he was back in Cuba as a lieutenant general and was charged with the defense of the eastern part of the island, including the city of Santiago de Cuba.

Linares had some 35,000 troops under his overall command. Of these, fewer than 10,000 were deployed to defend Santiago itself; the remainder were dispersed throughout the district to counter the strikes of the Cuban revolutionaries. Later criticized by the Cortes (the Spanish parliament) for failing to concentrate his command at Santiago, Linares nevertheless conducted a brave and determined defense of that city and was wounded at San Juan Hill.

Critics often fail to take into account that, in addition to dealing with Cuban revolutionaries throughout his jurisdiction, Linares lacked the supplies to sustain his entire command at Santiago had he concentrated at that point. More justified, perhaps, would be criticism of his failure to offer stout opposition to the landing of Gen. William Shafter's Fifth Corps at Daiquirí. Linares believed, however, that the landing would come at Santiago.

As the campaign progressed and it became apparent that Santiago could expect no relief, Linares, lacking the resources to turn back the Americans, strongly advised his superiors that surrender of the city was the only reasonable course of action. Accordingly, on 17 July 1898, Santiago de Cuba capitulated.

See also San Juan Hill, Charge up; Santiago, Campaign and Siege of.

References and Further Readings

Davis, Richard Harding. *The Cuban and Puerto Rican Campaigns.* New York: Charles Scribner's Sons, 1898.

Musicant, Ivan. *Empire by Default: The Spanish-American War and the Dawn of the American Century.* New York: Henry Holt and Company, 1998.

Samuels, Peggy, and Harold Samuels. *Teddy Roosevelt at San Juan: The Making of a President.* College Station: Texas A&M University Press, 1997.

Trask, David F. *The War with Spain in 1898.* Lincoln: University of Nebraska Press, 1996.

Lodge, Henry Cabot (1850–1924)

Born in Boston, Massachusetts, Henry Cabot Lodge was a descendant of one of the most distinguished lineages in New England.

Among the earliest Ph.D.'s to graduate from Harvard, he later taught history at that institution for three years. Lawyer, politician, and author, Lodge served in the U.S. House of Representatives from 1887 to 1893 and in the Senate from 1893 to 1924. His was a strong voice in support of the Spanish-American War.

A Republican, Lodge was a member of the powerful Foreign Relations Committee during his tenure in the Senate. Influential and articulate, he was a compelling force in Washington, always ready to express his views on foreign matters, which he frequently did through articles and essays published in the various intellectual journals of the day.

Like his friend and confidante Theodore Roosevelt, Lodge was a disciple of Alfred Thayer Mahan. An avowed Expansionist, Lodge firmly believed in and argued for the acquisition of new territory for the United States. He favored acquisition of Hawaii and believed in Cuban independence, to which end he argued for U.S. intervention.

After the destruction of the battleship *Maine,* Lodge was closely involved with President William McKinley and called for the expulsion of Spain from Cuba. During the Spanish-American War, he lent his Massachusetts home to the army for use as a signal station. He was a solid supporter of President McKinley's position regarding the acquisition of the entire Philippine Archipelago during the Treaty of Paris negotiations and later urged ratification of the treaty. In 1899, he published a history of the Spanish-American War.

See also Anti-Imperialist League; Imperialism/Expansionism; Philippine Islands, Acquisition of, by the United States; Roosevelt, Theodore; Treaty of Paris.

References and Further Readings

Leech, Margaret. *In the Days of McKinley.* New York: Harper & Brothers, 1959.

Lodge, Henry Cabot. *The War with Spain.* Reprint. New York: Arno Press, 1970.

Musicant, Ivan. *Empire by Default: The Spanish-American War and the Dawn of the American Century.* New York: Henry Holt and Company, 1998.

Widenor, William C. *Henry Cabot Lodge and the Search for an American Foreign Policy.* Berkeley: University of California Press, 1980.

Logistics

In a fundamental military context, logistics involves the procurement, storage, and transportation of troops and matériel from one point to another. During the Spanish-American War, especially at the outset, the U.S. War Department and its four principal bureaus or departments—Commissary, Ordnance, Quartermaster, and Medical—were ill prepared to meet the logistical demands imposed on them by the declaration of war.

Not since the Civil War, nearly 40 years in the past, had the army been asked to deal with numbers of the magnitude required by the Spanish-American War effort. Furthermore, the Civil War had been fought in the United States, not abroad. Now the War Department found itself confronted by the challenge of assembling and equipping an army that would fight on foreign soil. Not since the Mexican War (1848) had the army attempted an amphibious landing.

The sudden expansion of the army, brought on by the infusion of thousands of volunteer troops, found the army bureaus hard-pressed to furnish the newly created units with sufficient arms, equipment, medical supplies, and rations. As well, the means to transport troops to embarkation and staging areas such as Tampa, Florida, were wholly inadequate. Moreover, the ships needed to carry Gen. William Shafter's Fifth Corps to Cuba were simply unavailable and had to be purchased from private sources. As the war progressed, the flow of equipment and supplies improved dramatically.

See also Army, U.S.; Camps, Staging Areas, and Embarkation Points, U.S.

References and Further Readings

Cosmas, Graham. *An Army for Empire: The United States Army in the Spanish-American War.* College Station: Texas A&M University Press, 1998.

Musicant, Ivan. *Empire by Default: The Spanish-American War and the Dawn of the American Century.* New York: Henry Holt and Company, 1998.

Long, John Davis (1838–1915)

Along with President William McKinley, Secretary of State William R. Day, and Secretary of War Russell Alger (succeeded by Elihu Root), John Davis Long, as secretary of the navy, was one of the four key political figures in Washington during the Spanish-American War.

Born in Maine, Long studied law and entered politics, serving as governor of Massachusetts from 1880 to 1883. Following his tenure as governor, he was elected to the U.S. House of Representatives from that state, a position he held from 1883 to 1889.

Early in 1897, Long accepted an invitation to join President-elect McKinley's cabinet as secretary of the navy. A Republican and a longtime friend of McKinley, Long was a steady hand with a pleasant personality. Although not in the best of health, he was devoted and hardworking, to the extent that his physical condition allowed. He also was something of a poet.

Although Long completely lacked the credentials to head the Navy Department (most of the cabinet appointees were unequipped for their posts), he proved to be an able administrator. During his tenure as secretary, he made a genuine effort to see that the U.S. Navy was as prepared as budgetary limitations permitted.

As tensions between the United States and Spain grew increasingly strained in the months following Long's appointment, activity in the Navy Department picked up noticeably. In the event of war with Spain, the navy was expected to play the dominant role. Fortunately, Long had the good sense to utilize the expertise of his bureau chiefs and assistants and not interfere with their preparations.

John Davis Long, secretary of the navy during the Spanish-American War.

Long's most difficult challenge during the months preceding the outbreak of war may well have been that of managing his ebullient assistant secretary, Theodore Roosevelt. The hard-driving Roosevelt seemed to be something of a whirling dervish to Long, who never ceased to be amazed at Roosevelt's seemingly inexhaustible supply of energy. Long, however, thought Roosevelt served as a good counter to his own conservative approach to running the Navy Department. Accordingly, he became comfortable leaving the department in Roosevelt's hands when taking a day off or a long holiday, which he was prone to do for health reasons.

Long's absences, however, would prove to be troublesome. Late in February 1898, scarcely two weeks after the destruction of the *Maine,* Long took a day off only to find upon his return that his aggressive assistant secretary had not been content to simply oversee the department. To his horror, Long discovered that Roosevelt had issued several orders, the most significant of which was the one to Commodore George Dewey, commander of the U.S. Asiatic Squadron (for whose appointment Roosevelt had lobbied vigorously), directing him to be prepared to head to Manila and engage the Spanish fleet should war with Spain become a reality. Although the instructions per se were in accord with U.S. naval strategy, Roosevelt had exceeded his authority in issuing them.

Long's relationship with Secretary of War Russell Alger and the War Department itself was strained because of interservice rivalry and squabbling, which frequently made the task of conducting a war more difficult than necessary. For example, Long refused to risk his armored ships to support the army's Cuban Campaign until the Spanish fleet had been disposed of. In another instance, it took a presidential directive to pry loose enough vessels to execute the Puerto Rican Campaign.

Despite his rapport with President McKinley, Long was opposed to the U.S. acquisition of the Philippines. He retained his cabinet post until 1902 and later authored a two-volume history of the new navy.

See also Dewey, George; McKinley, William, Jr.; Navy, U.S.; Roosevelt, Theodore; Sampson, William Thomas; Schley, Winfield Scott.

References and Further Readings

Leech, Margaret. *In the Days of McKinley.* New York: Harper & Brothers, 1959.

Long, John D. *The New American Navy.* New York: Outlook, 1903.

Musicant, Ivan. *Empire by Default: The Spanish-American War and the Dawn of the American Century.* New York: Henry Holt and Company, 1998.

Trask, David F. *The War with Spain in 1898.* Lincoln: University of Nebraska Press, 1996.

Ludington, Marshall Independence (1839–1919)

Marshall Independence Ludington was born in Pennsylvania on the Fourth of July—hence the unusual middle name. He served throughout the Civil War as chief quartermaster of the Second Corps in the Army of the Potomac. After the war, he remained in the army as a quartermaster and developed a reputation as a first-rate administrator. In February 1898, he was named quartermaster general of the army. Ludington's experience and skills were sorely tried during the Spanish-American War as he sought to equip an army swollen by the influx of thousands of volunteers.

The Quartermaster Department had nowhere near the resources needed to accommodate such an expansion. Prewar preparations got under way in March as Ludington and Secretary of War Russell Alger met with wagon manufacturers and officers were sent to Saint Louis, Missouri, to see about the procurement of mules.

Lacking the necessary resources within his department, Ludington turned to outside contractors to fill the army's needs. But even with outside sources, the demand for clothing and tents, for example, simply could not be satisfied. Operating on the principle that something is better than nothing, Ludington authorized the use of substandard material. He tried to obtain the light cotton cloth called khaki, which the British had employed successfully, but no U.S. mills were able to produce the material.

Although the U.S. Army had many equipment deficiencies during the Spanish-American War, Ludington must be credited with doing all he could under the circumstances to meet the army's needs.

See also Alger, Russell Alexander; Army, U.S.

References and Further Readings

Cosmas, Graham. *An Army for Empire: The United States Army in the Spanish-American War.* College Station: Texas A&M University Press, 1998.

Ludlow, William (1843–1901)

William Ludlow was born in New York and graduated from West Point in 1864. An engineering officer, he had extensive service on the western frontier in the decades following the Civil War. With the outbreak of the Spanish-American War, Ludlow was promoted to brigadier general of volunteers and placed in command of the First Brigade in Gen. Henry Lawton's Second Division.

In addition to his duties as brigade commander, Ludlow served as chief engineering officer of the Fifth Corps. In this capacity, he was responsible for embarking Cuban revolutionary forces under Gen. Calixto García at Aseraderos during the Santiago Campaign.

Lawton was opposed to Gen. William Shafter's strategy for a direct advance on Santiago de Cuba, favoring instead the so-called Mariel Plan, which argued for seizure of that port, then an advance on Havana. Lawton commanded his brigade during the Battle of El Caney and later signed the famous "Round Robin" letter urging the removal of U.S. troops from Cuba because of the perceived threat of a tropical disease epidemic.

Ludlow was promoted to major general of volunteers in September 1898 and was military governor of Havana after the war. He also served for a time in the Philippines.

See also El Caney, Battle of; García Íñiguez, Calixto; Lawton, Henry Ware; Mariel.

References and Further Readings

Chadwick, Rear Adm. French Ensor. *Relations of the United States and Spain: The Spanish American War.* 2 vols. New York: Charles Scribner's Sons, 1911 (reprinted in 1968).

Cosmas, Graham. *An Army for Empire: The United States Army in the Spanish-American War.* College Station: Texas A&M University Press, 1998.

Lukban, Vicente (1860–1916)

Vicente Lukban was an important figure in the Filipino Revolutionary Army and one whose influence was felt in the Spanish-American War. After studying law in Manila, he returned to his home territory of Labo in the Camarines, where he served in various legal capacities. In 1896, he left the legal life and turned to farming for a time before returning to Manila, where he joined the revolutionary movement and eventually followed Emilio Aguinaldo to Hong Kong following Aguinaldo's surrender to the Spanish.

Upon the declaration of war between Spain and the United States, Aguinaldo returned to the Philippines accompanied by a retinue of followers, including Lukban, who was appointed colonel in the revolutionary army and assigned to his home territory, the Camarines. Later promoted to general, Lukban was sent to the Samar area in the southeastern part of the Philippine Archipelago, where he waged an effective guerrilla campaign against U.S. forces for some two years. Lukban may have been responsible for the notorious Balangiga Massacre, in which a detachment of U.S. soldiers was suddenly attacked and nearly wiped out.

Lukban was among the most respected of the Filipino revolutionary leaders—and among the most determined not to acquiesce. After Aguinaldo's capture, however, Lukban and other revolutionary leaders found themselves increasingly hard-pressed to maintain the integrity of their commands.

In February 1902, Lukban and his staff were finally captured, effectively ending the organized resistance to U.S. colonial rule. Following his imprisonment, Lukban accepted U.S. terms and eventually became an active figure in Filipino politics.

See also Aguinaldo y Famy, Emilio; Balangiga Massacre.

References and Further Readings
Beede, Benjamin R., ed. *The War of 1898 and U.S. Interventions, 1898–1934.* New York: Garland Publishing, 1994.
Gates, John Morgan. *Schoolbooks and Krags: The United States Army in the Philippines, 1898–1902.* Contributions in Military History no. 3. Westport, CT: Greenwood Press, 1973.
Linn, Brian McAllister. *The Philippine War, 1899–1902.* Lawrence: University Press of Kansas, 2000.
Wolff, Leon. *Little Brown Brother: America's Forgotten Bid for Empire Which Cost 250,000 Lives.* New York: Kraus Reprint, 1970.

Luna de St. Pedro, Antonio Narcisco (1866–1899)

A key figure in the Filipino revolutionary movement and the Spanish-American War, Antonio Narcisco Luna de St. Pedro was born in Manila to an upper-middle-class family. A scholar, he studied in Madrid and Paris and earned a doctorate in pharmacy. While in Spain, he became an associate of the prominent Filipino Nationalist José Rizal.

Luna wrote a number of scientific articles for which he achieved recognition. His political writings strongly advocated Philippine reform. In 1894, he returned to the Philippines as a chemist and joined the new revolutionary society known as the Katipunan. In 1896, Luna's revolutionary activities led to his arrest and imprisonment in the Philippines. One year later, he was sent to prison in Spain.

While Luna was in prison, José Rizal was executed, as was Andrés Bonifacio, leader of the Katipunan society. Rizal, however, was executed by the Spanish, whereas Bonifacio was killed by Filipino revolutionary followers of Emilio Aguinaldo, who had emerged as the new power figure in the Katipunan. Eventually, the uprising was put down by the Spanish, and Aguinaldo was forced to surrender and was subsequently exiled to Hong Kong.

Finally released from prison, Luna joined Aguinaldo in Hong Kong and offered his services to the revolutionary movement, which was still very much alive. Aguinaldo accepted the offer, albeit with a certain reserve. Although Luna was knowledgeable about military history and tactics, he had a reputation for being troublesome. Nevertheless, Aguinaldo appointed him a brigadier general in the revolutionary army.

During the Spanish-American War, Aguinaldo and his lieutenants returned to the Philippines to resume their fight against the Spanish. When the U.S. forces were preparing to attack Manila, Luna counseled Aguinaldo to ignore the restrictions placed on the Filipinos by the U.S. Army. Aguinaldo, however, chose to ignore this advice. Subsequently, the Spanish surrendered Manila to U.S. forces, completely excluding the Filipino Revolutionary Army from any participation.

During the period of treaty negotiations between Spain and the United States in the fall of 1898, Luna was named to command the Filipino Army. In reality, the appointment carried much less authority than the title implied, as Aguinaldo himself remained the true head of the army.

When fighting erupted between U.S. troops and the Filipino Nationalists in February 1899, heralding the start of the Philippine-American War (also called the Philippine Insurrection), Luna proved to be an active and aggressive field commander. But increasingly, he found himself at odds with Aguinaldo. A severe disciplinarian, Luna had many officers executed for minor violations, which earned him the sobriquet "General Article One."

In June 1899, Luna and his aide were assassinated, probably because Luna had become too difficult to deal with. The assassination may or may not have been carried out under Aguinaldo's orders. Certainly, it would not have been out of character for Aguinaldo to have issued such an order, and it could easily be argued that Luna had simply outlived his usefulness. Despite Luna's contribution to the cause of Filipino independence, Aguinaldo no longer could tolerate his presence.

See also Aguinaldo y Famy, Emilio; Manila Bay, Battle of; Manila, Second Battle of.

References and Further Readings

Beede, Benjamin R., ed. *The War of 1898 and U.S. Interventions, 1898–1934.* New York: Garland Publishing, 1994.

Gates, John Morgan. *Schoolbooks and Krags: The United States Army in the Philippines, 1898–1902.* Contributions in Military History no. 3. Westport, CT: Greenwood Press, 1973.

Linn, Brian McAllister. *The Philippine War, 1899–1902.* Lawrence: University Press of Kansas, 2000.

Wolff, Leon. *Little Brown Brother: America's Forgotten Bid for Empire Which Cost 250,000 Lives.* New York: Kraus Reprint, 1970.

Luzon (Philippine Islands)

Luzon is the largest and most populated island in the Philippine Archipelago, covering more than 40,000 square miles. A mountainous island, most of its population is located in and around Manila, capital city of the archipelago. Because of its size and central location and the presence of Manila, Luzon became the focal point of the Spanish defense system in the Philippines.

Except for the actions around Manila itself, Luzon saw little military activity during the Spanish-American War. After the Philippine-American War erupted in February 1899, however, it was the scene of hard campaigning as the U.S. forces sought to subjugate the Filipino revolutionary forces.

During the course of discussions between Spain and the United States that ultimately led to the Treaty of Paris in December 1899, there was talk of the United States retaining only the island of Luzon, which would provide a fine harbor and coaling station. In the end, though, the United States acquired the entire archipelago.

See also Aguinaldo y Famy, Emilio; Luna de St. Pedro, Antonio Narcisco; Luzon Campaigns; Manila Bay, Battle of; Philippine Archipelago; Treaty of Paris.

References and Further Readings

Linn, Brian McAllister. *The Philippine War, 1899–1902.* Lawrence: University Press of Kansas, 2000.

Morgan, H. Wayne, ed. *Making Peace with Spain: The Diary of Whitelaw Reid—September–December, 1898.* Austin: University of Texas Press, 1965.

Trask, David F. *The War with Spain in 1898.* Lincoln: University of Nebraska Press, 1996.

Wolff, Leon. *Little Brown Brother: America's Forgotten Bid for Empire Which Cost 250,000 Lives.* New York: Kraus Reprint, 1970.

Luzon Campaigns (Philippine Islands)

The Philippine-American War was ushered in by a series of hard-fought actions, covering a three-week period from 4 to 23 February 1899. Following these actions—which historian Brian Linn calls "the Second Battle of Manila"—the U.S. military commander in the Philippines, Maj. Gen. Elwell Otis, believed that the key to winning this newly erupted war, coming on the heels of the Spanish-American War, lay in securing that portion of Luzon north of Manila. Otis was convinced that the insurrection—as it was viewed—was rooted in the Tagalog population, concentrated in the provinces of southern Luzon. These areas, Otis reasoned, would be difficult to subjugate, but the ethnic groups north of Manila would welcome the Americans. This assessment was based on a misguided understanding of the Filipino opposition to the U.S. presence.

U.S. soldiers in the trenches, fighting the Filipinos, ca. 1899.

Otis's strategy had two parts. First, he decided to sever the Nationalists' supply line flowing north out of Manila. On 12 March 1899, Brig. Gen. Lloyd Wheaton, a tall Civil War veteran with a distinguished record in that conflict, struck east and south to Laguna de Bay with a provisional brigade. Wheaton's assignment was to clean out any pockets of Nationalist resistance and destroy crops that might be a source of supply to Aguinaldo's Army of Liberation. In

Filipino engineers completing the demolition of a bridge on Luzon.

the week that followed, Wheaton, supported by a gunboat and artillery, delivered a crippling blow to Nationalist forces south of Manila.

The second part of Otis's strategy was aimed at the capture of Malolos, newly proclaimed capital of the Philippine Republic. Phase two got under way on 25 March, when Brig. Gen. Arthur MacArthur's Second Division—9,000 men in three brigades under Gen. Harrison Otis (no relation to Elwell) and Gen. Irving Hale—moved north along the rail line from Caloocan. Wheaton, whose brigade had been assigned to the Second Division for this operation, made up the third element of MacArthur's command.

Otis and Hale drove north, supported by the artillery of the Utah Battery and a section of Colt machine guns. The advance was slow and the fighting fierce as the troops worked their way through nearly impenetrable brush. Meanwhile, Wheaton's brigade (called a "flying column"), which had gotten under way on 25 March, moved to the west of Otis and Hale. The idea was to catch the Army of Liberation—as Aguinaldo liked to call it—between the two forces. On 26 March, Wheaton's troops captured Malinta, though not in time to seal off Aguinaldo's withdrawing forces. Five days later, on 31 March, MacArthur's troops entered Malolos, which the departing Nationalists had burned and gutted. So the second phase of Otis's strategy was successful in a territorial sense, as Malolos now was in U.S. hands. But the Army of Liberation remained free.

Gen. Henry Ware Lawton was another colorful figure from the Civil War and Indian wars, as well as the Santiago Campaign in Cuba. While MacArthur and Wheaton moved against the Nationalists, Lawton's men captured Santa Cruz in Laguna Province. Through the combined efforts of the three commands, the Nationalist forces had been driven back some 25 miles from Manila, where active campaigning ceased temporarily with the arrival of summer monsoon rains.

By autumn 1899, the character of U.S. forces in the Philippines had changed. The term of service for Spanish-American War troops had expired. To replace them, the government created a force of

The Thirty-eighth U.S. Volunteers shortly after arriving in Manila in 1901.

two-year U.S. volunteer regiments (rather than state volunteer units), consisting of 1 cavalry and 24 infantry regiments.

The arrival of fall also heralded the beginning of the dry season and a resumption of campaigning. Three columns would take the field, with the primary objective of trapping Nationalist leader Emilio Aguinaldo, whose capture, it was believed, would destroy the Nationalist will to resist further.

While General Wheaton's column landed at Lingayen Gulf and moved east, Lawton and Gen. S. B. M. Young headed north up the Rio Grande de Pampanga, closing off the mountain passes of the Sierra Madres and thereby preventing the *insurrectos* from escaping. The plan called for Wheaton to rendezvous with Lawton at Dagupan. In the meantime, MacArthur advanced from San Fernando along a rail route that ran through the fertile valleys and plains of central Luzon.

Aguinaldo's army numbered perhaps as many as 80,000. Although they were not as well equipped as the U.S. forces and lacked a cadre of veteran leaders, the Nationalists were tough, courageous, and determined. They also had the advantage of being familiar with the territory.

Lawton's column made fair progress, considering the slow and cumbersome line of supply, which concerned Lawton greatly. Recognizing the importance of capturing Aguinaldo, he decided to send a mixed force of infantry and cavalry from San Isidro under General Young to push on in advance of the main column. Lawton also was concerned about Wheaton, from whom he had heard nothing. He feared that if their two commands did not unite as planned, Aguinaldo would have an opportunity to evade the net they were trying to drop over him.

Nevertheless, Lawton's command pursued the Nationalist forces aggressively, covering more than 100 miles of extremely harsh terrain over a six-week period. The group did manage to skirmish with Aguinaldo's rear guard but was unable to capture the Filipino leader. In addition to the army units involved in the campaign, a 400-man marine battalion assaulted Filipino entrenchments at Novaleta on 8 October.

Meanwhile, Wheaton, with a force of 2,500 infantry and artillery troops, had sailed north and reached San Fabian on 7 November, where he landed his troops after a naval bombardment. Once ashore, though, the normally aggressive Wheaton allowed himself to get bogged down. He took nineteen days to reach Dagupan—his rendezvous point with Lawton—though it was only 12 miles from San Fabian.

Even though some of Young's scouts had alerted Wheaton to the urgency of the situation, he seemed unable to act with much dispatch. Finally moved to action, Wheaton did manage to capture Aguinaldo's mother and infant son, but the Filipino leader himself escaped with about 1,000 followers. On 2 December, elements of Wheaton's command under Maj. Peyton March struck Aguinaldo's rear guard at Triad Pass, killing Gen. Gregorio del Pilar, Aguinaldo's close friend and adviser.

Gen. Henry Lawton with aides and Scott's Battery during the Battle of Baliuag, 1899.

The action at Triad Pass ended the U.S. Army's major campaigns in Luzon. To be sure, considerable fighting was yet to be done, but Aguinaldo recognized that he could not wage a conventional war against the United States with any real hope of succeeding. As a result, from December 1899 until Aguinaldo's capture in 1902, the U.S. Army was forced to fight a protracted guerrilla war.

See also Aguinaldo y Famy, Emilio; Lawton, Henry Ware; Luna de St. Pedro, Antonio Narcisco; MacArthur, Arthur; Otis, Elwell Stephen; Pilar, Gregorio del.

References and Further Readings

Gates, John Morgan. *Schoolbooks and Krags: The United States Army in the Philippines, 1898–1902.* Contributions in Military History no. 3. Westport, CT: Greenwood Press, 1973.

Linn, Brian McAllister. *The Philippine War, 1899–1902.* Lawrence: University Press of Kansas, 2000.

Millett, Allan R. *Semper Fidelis: The History of the United States Marine Corps.* New York: Macmillan Publishing, 1982.

Wolff, Leon. *Little Brown Brother: America's Forgotten Bid for Empire Which Cost 250,000 Lives.* New York: Kraus Reprint, 1970.

Macabebe (Maccabebe) (Filipino) Scouts

Members of the Macabebe tribe dwelling in Pampanga Province of central Luzon, like the Moros of Mindanao, were regarded as fierce and feared fighters. They were also the sworn enemies of the Tagalogs, the largest native tribe on Luzon. Emilio Aguinaldo, leader of the Filipino independence movement, was a Tagalog, and his tribe constituted the bulk of his following.

Having served Spain during the uprising in 1896 and again in 1898, the Macabebes offered to serve the United States when the Philippine-American War broke out in February 1899. The offer was accepted, and the Macabebe Scouts, as the group came to be known, served under Gen. Henry W. Lawton during the Luzon Campaigns. Although the scouts, whose numbers may have reached as high as

The Macabebe Scouts were fierce enemies of the Tagalogs (Emilio Aguinaldo's people). A detachment of scouts, under the command of Col. Frederick Funston, captured Aguinaldo.

5,000, demonstrated their fierce fighting qualities, they were also often guilty of perpetrating atrocities, especially on the Tagalogs, whether noncombatants or guerrillas. However, since the Tagalogs were perceived as the heart of what was then regarded as an insurrection, some U.S. military leaders were willing to overlook such behavior. Notably, a group of Macabebe Scouts accompanied Col. Frederick Funston on his daring mission to capture the Filipino Nationalist leader Emilio Aguinaldo.

See also Aguinaldo y Famy, Emilio; Funston, Frederick; Luzon Campaigns.

References and Further Readings

Beede, Benjamin R., ed. *The War of 1898 and U.S. Interventions, 1898–1934*. New York: Garland Publishing, 1994.

Gates, John Morgan. *Schoolbooks and Krags: The United States Army in the Philippines, 1898–1902*. Contributions in Military History no. 3. Westport, CT: Greenwood Press, 1973.

Miller, Stuart C. *Benevolent Assimilation: The American Conquest of the Philippines, 1899–1903*. New Haven, CT: Yale University Press, 1983.

MacArthur, Arthur (1845–1912)

Born in Massachusetts, Arthur MacArthur moved to Milwaukee with his family at an early age and there grew to manhood. At age 17, he joined the Wisconsin Volunteers and subsequently compiled a distinguished Civil War record. Following the war, he remained in the army and served on the western frontier. He continued his military career fighting in the Spanish-American War.

In May 1898, MacArthur was promoted to brigadier general and was assigned to the Eighth Corps, which arrived in the Philippines at the end of July. During the battle for Manila in August, two brigades were sent against the city's works: Gen. Francis V. Greene's brigade attacked from the north, and MacArthur's first brigade struck from the south.

According to a prior arrangement between Adm. George Dewey, Gen. Wesley Merritt, and the Spanish commander at Manila, Governor-General Fermín Jáudenes y Álvarez, the Spanish would offer only token resistance before surrendering to the United States in return for having the Filipino Nationalists prevented from entering Manila. Yet despite that agreement, MacArthur's troops encountered stiff resistance before breaching the Spanish lines. MacArthur then had to assume responsibility for turning back the Filipino Nationalists, who were determined to enter the city themselves.

Following the capture of Manila and the end of the war with Spain, MacArthur was placed in command of the Second Division of the newly reorganized Eighth Corps, commanded by Maj. Gen. Elwell Otis, who had replaced General Merritt.

MacArthur went on to play a key role in the subsequent campaigns against Emilio Aguinaldo and the Filipino Revolutionary Army. MacArthur's columns drove Aguinaldo's forces back from Manila, seizing the republican capital of Malolos and eventually capturing Aguinaldo himself.

From 1900 to 1901, MacArthur served as military governor of the Philippines. He retired from active duty in 1909. He was the father of Gen. Douglas MacArthur.

See also Aguinaldo y Famy, Emilio; Funston, Frederick; Manila, First Battle of; Merritt, Wesley; Philippine Expeditionary Force.

References and Further Readings

Gates, John Morgan. *Schoolbooks and Krags: The United States Army in the Philippines, 1898–1902.* Contributions in Military History no. 3. Westport, CT: Greenwood Press, 1973.

Linn, Brian McAllister. *The Philippine War, 1899–1902.* Lawrence: University Press of Kansas, 2000.

Wolff, Leon. *Little Brown Brother: America's Forgotten Bid for Empire Which Cost 250,000 Lives.* New York: Kraus Reprint, 1970.

Young, Kenneth Ray. *The General's General: The Life and Times of Arthur MacArthur.* Boulder, CO: Westview Press, 1994.

Maceo Grajales, Antonio (1845–1896)

Antonio Maceo Grajales, like José Martí and Máximo Gómez, was one of the pivotal figures of the Cuban revolutionary movement that preceded the Spanish-American War. Born in Majaguabo, San Luis, in the Province of Oriente, Cuba, he was called the "Bronze Titan." Maceo was a mulatto, and he sought as much to free blacks from bondage as to secure Cuban independence. He refused to sign the Treaty of Zanjón, ending the Ten Years' War (1868–1878), precisely because it failed to secure either of the those goals.

When Martí was organizing the Second Cuban War of Independence, he offered Maceo a key role in the revolutionary army. Originally Martí had planned to have Maceo command the expedition that would launch the war, but he later felt compelled to assign that task to Flor Crombet because Maceo demanded a better-equipped expedition than did Combet. Nevertheless, Martí wanted Maceo involved in the revolution, and he implored the Bronze Titan to place Cuba's needs above his own. Although disappointed at having

Antonio Maceo, the "Bronze Titan." A black Cuban patriot, Maceo was a military leader par excellence.

been bypassed for commander, Maceo could not ignore Martí's plea.

A natural leader, Maceo, whose brother José was also involved in the revolutionary movement, was a fierce and determined fighter. He could usually be found at the forefront of his command, and his troops, composed mainly of mounted blacks, were a persistent thorn in the Spanish side. His fast-moving forces consistently outmaneuvered the troops of Gen. Valeriano "Butcher" Weyler. Maceo's destruction of sugar plantations had a crippling effect on the Cuban/Spanish economy. Maceo died from wounds received in a surprise attack on his camp near Mariano, Cuba, on 5 December 1896. His death represented a severe loss to the Cuban cause.

See also Cuban Revolution; Gómez Báez, Máximo; Martí y Pérez, José; Weyler y Nicolau, Valeriano "Butcher."

References and Further Readings

Foner, Philip S. *The Spanish-Cuban-American War.* 2 vols. New York: Monthly Review Press, 1972.

———. *Antonio Maceo: The Bronze Titan of Cuba's Struggle for Independence.* New York: Monthly Review Press, 1977.

Thomas, Hugh. *Cuba: The Pursuit of Freedom.* New York: Harper & Row, 1971.

Macías y Casado, Manuel (1845–?)

A lieutenant general in the Spanish Army with a distinguished record of Caribbean service, Manuel Macías y Casado arrived in Puerto Rico on 9 February 1898 to assume his new duties as captain general of the island. He had been sent to install and oversee a policy of autonomy in Puerto Rico, which now would be essentially self-governing with a newly elected parliament. Unfortunately for Spain, such a move was much too late to salvage its crumbling colonial empire.

Unlike Cuba, where the local populace had been waging war against the Spanish since 1895, Puerto Rico had been a passive colony. As a result, the Spanish hoped that instituting the policy of autonomy would strengthen their relationship with Puerto Rico.

Upon the outbreak of war with the United States, however, the new program of autonomy was suspended and martial law was declared in Puerto Rico. Macías perceived correctly that the general populace lacked strong feelings about the war, though some evidence indicated that a portion of the population supported the U.S. position. Hoping to rally the people to his cause, Macías called upon them to resist any U.S. effort to take the island. Yet at the same time, doubting their loyalty, he refused to arm them. Learning of the impending U.S. invasion, Macías elected to disperse his limited forces at various strong points, mainly on the north end of the island. As a result, the Spanish were not strong enough to resist at any one position.

Gen. Nelson Miles's highly successful campaign, which began on 25 July 1898, quickly secured the island of Puerto Rico for the United States. Following Spain's capitulation, Macías remained on the island and assisted the United States in establishing its occupation forces before he returned to Spain in October.

See also Davis, Richard Harding; Miles, Nelson Appleton; Puerto Rican Campaign.

References and Further Readings

Davis, Richard Harding. *The Cuban and Porto Rican Campaigns.* New York: Charles Scribner's Sons, 1898.

Musicant, Ivan. *Empire by Default: The Spanish-American War and the Dawn of the American Century.* New York: Henry Holt and Company, 1998.

Rivero Méndez, Ángel. *Cronica de la Guerra Hispano Americana en Puerto Rico* (A chronicle of the Spanish-American War in Puerto Rico). New York: Plus Ultra, 1973.

Trask, David F. *The War with Spain in 1898.* Lincoln: University of Nebraska Press, 1996.

Mahan, Alfred Thayer (1840–1914)

One of the most influential figures of the late nineteenth century, Alfred Thayer Mahan had a profound impact on the development of the U.S. Navy and the shaping of U.S. foreign policy during the Spanish-American War.

Born at the U.S. Military Academy, Mahan was the son of the legendary Dennis Mahan, professor of mathematics and English at West Point. Alfred Thayer Mahan chose to walk a different path and attended the U.S. Naval Academy, from which he graduated, second in his class, in 1859. During the next three decades he enjoyed a singularly unimpressive naval career. He was not a good sailor and, indeed, did not even like the sea. Nonetheless, his contribution to maritime thinking would prove to be profound.

In 1885, Mahan was assigned to the newly formed Naval War College. Subsequently, he prepared a series of lectures, driven by what he perceived as a vital need to formulate a new doctrine of naval strategy by understanding the role of sea power in forging great nations throughout the course of history. This philosophy was translated into a book, *The Influence of Sea Power upon History, 1660–1783,* published in 1890. The book proved to be a huge success, although, ironically, the U.S. Navy itself was slow to perceive its significance. Elsewhere in the world—in Great Britain, Germany, and Japan, among others nations—the work found enthusiastic audiences.

Sea power, Mahan argued, was the path to greatness. Great Britain and Spain were classic examples. For a nation to have power at sea, he asserted, it needed not only a strong navy but also a large and energetic merchant marine system. And its people needed a seafaring tradition. Geography was important, too, said Mahan; a nation with strong fleets required plenty of adequate harbors. Finally, a nation had to have the resources to produce goods that its merchant marine system could carry across the oceans in trade. In short, if a nation was to be great, it needed to have an ambitious, vigorous naval and maritime program. As Mahan saw it, the United States possessed all of the requirements to become one of the world's great powers.

During the mid-1880s, the U.S. Navy had begun to emerge from the pit into which it had fallen after the Civil War. By 1898, under the guidance of energetic secretaries of the navy such as Benjamin Franklin Tracy, the navy had come to be regarded as among the most formidable in the world. A key role in the transformation was the Mahanian philosophy, which was embraced by many, including

Assistant Secretary of the Navy Theodore Roosevelt and other naval visionaries. *The Influence of Sea Power upon History* had an impact on naval and maritime thought that reached far beyond Mahan's day and is regarded by some as one of the most influential works of naval philosophy.

See also Naval Strategy, U.S.; Navy, U.S.; Roosevelt, Theodore.
References and Further Readings
Chadwick, Rear Adm. French Ensor. *Relations of the United States and Spain: The Spanish American War.* 2 vols. New York: Charles Scribner's Sons, 1911 (reprinted in 1968).
Mahan, Alfred Thayer. *Influence of Sea Power upon History, 1670–1783.* Boston: Little, Brown, 1890.
Musicant, Ivan. *Empire by Default: The Spanish-American War and the Dawn of the American Century.* New York: Henry Holt and Company, 1998.
Seager, Robert. *Alfred Thayer Mahan: The Man and His Letters.* Annapolis, MD: Naval Institute Press, 1977.

Maine (Battleship)

The introduction of the ironclads *Monitor* and *Merrimac* during the Civil War heralded the beginning of the "iron and steel navy." The U.S. Navy's shipbuilding program, which languished in the years immediately following the Civil War, was reborn in the 1880s. When completed in November 1890, the battleship *Maine*

The battleship Maine entering Havana harbor.

represented the navy's new look, featuring a belt of nickel steel armor around the waterline, as well as electrical lighting and motorized gun turrets.

The ship's powerful armament consisted of four 10-inch rifles and six 6-inch rifles forward and aft. These main batteries were supplemented by seven rapid-firing 6-inchers, plus a number of 1-pounders, Gatling guns, and torpedo tubes. Despite those state-of-the-art features, by the time of commissioning in September 1895, the *Maine* was rated a second-class battleship because newer and larger ships, such as those of the *Indiana* class, were already under construction.

Fully loaded, the *Maine* displaced 6,682 tons and carried 800 tons of coal in its fuel bunkers. It could cruise 7,000 miles with a full load of coal and was rated at a speed of 15 knots. The ship carried a crew of 26 officers and 326 men. At the time of construction, the *Maine* was the largest vessel ever built in the United States and, despite its second-class designation, was justly regarded as the navy's pride when it joined the fleet.

In late 1897, escalating riots and violence in Cuba precipitated growing concern for the safety of U.S. citizens and property there. As a precautionary measure, President William McKinley ordered that the *Maine* be sent to Port Royal, South Carolina, in October and then to Key West, Florida, in December, from which point it could quickly reach Cuba (90-odd miles distant) if needed.

During the next several weeks, tensions in Cuba ebbed and flowed. Finally, in January, McKinley advised the U.S. consul general in Havana, Fitzhugh Lee (a Civil War veteran and nephew of Robert E. Lee), that the *Maine* would arrive in Havana on 24 January. The rationale, McKinley explained, was to reestablish the practice of making goodwill visits to Cuban ports, which President Grover Cleveland had halted. Accordingly, to have the *Maine* visit Havana would stand as an act of international courtesy. Although Secretary of the Navy John D. Long claimed that the *Maine*'s visit was nothing more than a friendly call, in reality it was intended to emphasize U.S. concerns over the crisis on the island and to urge the granting of Cuban independence.

On 25 January 1898, the *Maine*, under the command of Capt. Charles Dwight Sigsbee, entered Havana harbor quietly and without incident. An 1863 graduate of the U.S. Naval Academy, Sigsbee, whose thirty-five-year career included service in the American Civil War, was an able and highly regarded officer, well qualified for his present command.

At 9:40 P.M. on 15 February, a sudden, violent explosion from the forward part of the ship wracked the *Maine,* lifting its bow out of the water. Bodies and debris were flung into the air as a blinding flash enshrouded the vessel. The explosion was catastrophic. Captain Sigsbee and most of the officers survived the blast because their quarters were in the aft (rear) section and thus escaped the full force of the explosion. Among the enlisted men, however, it was a far different story, as 252 were dead or missing and 8 others would die later. The stricken vessel itself settled slowly into the mud of Havana harbor, a portion of its superstructure rising above the murky waters as a grisly reminder of one of history's defining moments.

When news of the disaster reached the United States, the public was outraged. Many people were convinced that the explosion had been caused by a Spanish mine, though that theory had no supporting evidence. There was talk that the explosion had been the work of Cuban revolutionaries who wanted to encourage U.S. intervention, but American eyes focused mainly on Spain, despite Captain Sigsbee's caution about premature judgments.

Although war between the United States and Spain did not automatically follow in the wake of the disaster, the destruction of the *Maine* was the casus belli that ruled out any peaceful resolution of the Cuban issue. Fanned by the flames of a jingoistic press, the national sense of pride and honor would settle for nothing less than military satisfaction. "Remember the *Maine*" became a national rallying cry that united the country in the same way that "Remember Pearl Harbor" would forty-some years later.

The sunken Maine *in Havana harbor.*

On 20 February 1898, five days after the explosion, a hastily assembled naval court of inquiry headed by Capt. William Sampson convened in Havana to investigate the disaster. At the same time, Spain launched its own inquiry. The two courts were to arrive at completely different conclusions.

On 21 March 1898, the U.S. court concluded that the explosion had been caused by a submarine mine but was unable to assign responsibility for the act. In marked contrast, the Spanish investigating body determined that the explosion had been produced internally. There the matter rested for the moment.

In 1911, with Cuban permission, a cofferdam was constructed around the sunken battleship. The *Maine* was then brought to the surface and examined before being towed out to the open sea and reinterred in deep water. After examining the remains, a new board of inquiry, headed by Adm. Charles Vreeland, came to essentially the same conclusion as the Sampson court.

But the question of what happened to the *Maine* continued to invite speculation. In the 1970s, Adm. Hyman Rickover, father of the nuclear navy, became captivated by the mystery and launched his own study. His findings disagreed with those of the two earlier boards of inquiry. The explosion, Rickover concluded, had been caused by spontaneous combustion in the coal bunker. There was no mine.

More recently, in a 1995 study published by the Smithsonian Institution Press, authors Peggy and Harold Samuels made a compelling case for the culprit being a mine detonated by Spanish hardliners. Still, a definitive explanation most likely will elude us. What caused the *Maine* to explode is likely to remain an enduring mystery.

The *Maine*—or most of it—rests in peace on the ocean floor, but pieces of its once proud structure have survived. During the early 1900s, scrap metal from the ship supposedly was used to create a series of plaques commemorating Daniel Boone's westward passage, and Theodore Roosevelt, while leading his charge up Kettle Hill, carried a revolver salvaged from the ship. Other pieces can be found in the form of ashtrays, paperweights, and similar memorabilia. Thus, in one form or another, the *Maine* is still with us.

See also Lee, Fitzhugh; *Maine,* Inquiries into the Sinking of; Sigsbee, Charles Dwight.

References and Further Readings

Blow, Michael. *A Ship to Remember: The* Maine *and the Spanish-American War.* New York: William Morrow, 1992.

Faragher, John Mack. *Daniel Boone: The Life and Legend of an American Pioneer.* New York: Henry Holt and Company, 1992.

Musicant, Ivan. *Empire by Default: The Spanish-American War and the Dawn of the American Century.* New York: Henry Holt and Company, 1998.

Samuels, Peggy, and Harold Samuels. *Remembering the* Maine. Washington, DC: Smithsonian Institution Press, 1995.

Trask, David F. *The War with Spain in 1898.* Lincoln: University of Nebraska Press, 1996.

Weems, John Edward. *The Fate of the* Maine. New York: Henry Holt and Company, 1958.

Maine, Inquiries into the Sinking of

The destruction of the battleship *Maine* in Havana harbor on the night of 15 February 1898 is generally regarded as *the* incident that brought the United States to the brink of war with Spain. The destruction of the *Maine* generated a storm of angry rhetoric throughout the United States, calling for an immediate explanation of the cause. Whether Spain had been responsible was yet to be determined, though its guilt was established in the minds of many.

Recognizing the need to determine a cause as quickly as possible, Secretary of the Navy John D. Long on 16 February directed Adm. Montgomery Sicard to organize a court of inquiry to investigate the explosion. Subsequently appointed to the board were Capt. William T. Sampson as president and Lt. Comdr. Adolph Marix as judge advocate. Capt. French Ensor Chadwick and Lt. Comdr. William P. Potter completed the board.

The court convened on 21 February and, not surprisingly, was the subject of considerable newspaper attention. Testimony was taken from a number of individuals, including Capt. Charles Sigsbee, surviving commander of the ill-fated vessel. In addition, divers attempted to discern what had happened by examining the wreck. Murky waters, however, prevented a thorough assessment.

The court was in session for a month, at the end of which it concluded that the *Maine* had been sunk by two explosions, one of which had been caused by an underwater device—probably a mine—detonated by a person or persons unknown. This blast was followed by a second explosion in one of the ammunition bunkers. The court also considered but rejected the likelihood that the explosion was caused by spontaneous combustion in one of the ship's coal bunkers.

Although the court did not charge Spain with responsibility for the explosion, neither did it rule out Spain's involvement in the event. Anti-Spanish sentiment over Cuba had been building for some time, fueled by sensational press stories of Cuban atrocities. So when the *Maine* blew up, the public was outraged, and many believed Spain was responsible.

As the U.S. naval court was conducting its hearings, Spanish authorities were carrying out their own investigation. Given the tense nature of relations with the United States, Spain was anxious to prove, if possible, that it had had nothing to do with the disaster. Spanish divers, too, were unable to see much in the muddy waters of Havana harbor. The Spanish investigation offered the opinion that the *Maine* had been destroyed by an internal explosion.

By 1910, when the Spanish-American War was a dozen years in the past and emotions had cooled, the U.S. Congress undertook a more thorough investigation than had been possible in 1898. This time, it was decided to raise the hulk and conduct a scientific examination that would, it was hoped, settle the matter once and for all. In addition, this investigation would allow for any human remains to be brought back to the United States and buried in Arlington National Cemetery.

Accordingly, between May and October, Congress appropriated $650,000 and directed the chief of army engineers, Gen. William Bixby, to proceed with the project. Bixby appointed a three-man committee to raise the sunken *Maine* and undertake a thorough examination. The committee was headed by Col. William Black, who had been involved in building the Panama Canal; Maj. Mason Patrick, an officer of wide experience with harbor projects; and a Cuban expert, Harley Ferguson, who was to oversee the construction of a 350-foot × 170-foot cofferdam and the eventual raising of the *Maine*.

After considerable effort and notwithstanding the effects of a pair of hurricanes, the cofferdam finally was completed in June 1911. The engineers proceeded with raising the *Maine* and gradually removing water from the twisted and torn wreck. By late summer, much of the hulk had been brought to the surface and hosed clean for inspection.

In the meantime, President William Howard Taft appointed a new five-man board of inquiry to assess the evidence uncovered by the raising of the *Maine*. The new board was headed by Adm. Charles Vreeland, the navy's premier investigating official. Vreeland was joined by Col. William Black, Chief Naval Constructor Richard Watt, ordnance expert Joseph Strauss, and the recorder, Comdr. Charles Hughes. The Vreeland Board, as it came to be known, convened in Havana on 20 November 1911. After twelve days spent examining the wreck, the board adjourned to discuss and prepare its official report.

The Vreeland Report, issued in December 1911, agreed in part with the conclusions of the original court but went on to submit that the destruction of the vessel had been the result of an exterior explosion—at a different point than the Sampson court had thought— that in turn caused the magazines to detonate.

There the matter rested for sixty-odd years until, in 1974, Adm. Hyman Rickover, father of the U.S. nuclear navy, became intrigued by the *Maine* disaster and began his own, entirely unofficial investigation. The results of Rickover's study, published by the Department of the Navy under the title *How the Battleship* Maine *Was Destroyed,* concluded that the explosion or explosions were caused by a fire in one of the coal bunkers. There was, Rickover argued, no evidence of any mine.

Despite the investigations of two official boards of inquiry and one unofficial examination, the cause of the disaster that befell the *Maine* still has no definitive explanation. Speculation continues. Was the explosion set off by an underwater device? Or was it caused by fire resulting from spontaneous combustion in a coal bunker? If it was caused by a mine, who was responsible? Some have suggested that Cuban or Spanish hard-liners or perhaps filibusters caught up in the passions swirling around the issue of Cuban independence were responsible for destroying the *Maine,* knowing that it likely would result in U.S. intervention.

See also *Maine*; McKinley, William, Jr.; Navy, U.S.; Sampson, William Thomas; Sigsbee, Charles Dwight.

References and Further Readings

Blow, Michael. *A Ship to Remember: The* Maine *and the Spanish-American War.* New York: William Morrow, 1992.

Rickover, H. G. *How the Battleship* Maine *Was Destroyed.* Washington, DC: Department of the Navy, 1976.

Samuels, Peggy, and Harold Samuels. *Remembering the* Maine. Washington, DC: Smithsonian Institution Press, 1995.

Trask, David F. *The War with Spain in 1898.* Lincoln: University of Nebraska Press, 1996.

Weems, John Edward. *The Fate of the* Maine. New York: Henry Holt and Company, 1958.

Malolos (Philippines), Capture of (31 March 1899)

In February 1899, two months after the signing of the Treaty of Paris, the cease-fire that ended the Spanish-American War, fighting broke out between U.S. forces and Filipino Nationalists. To deal with this new threat, Maj. Gen. Elwell S. Otis, U.S. military commander in the Philippines, launched a campaign to seize the republican capital of Malolos, some 25 miles north of Manila, to where Emilio Aguinaldo's Nationalist Army had retreated.

On 25 March, U.S. forces under the command of Brig. Gen. Arthur MacArthur moved on Malolos. Fortunately for MacArthur, the town was located along a rail line, which greatly facilitated his advance. The U.S. column was forced to make a number of river crossings, where fighting was often heavy. In the face of MacArthur's costly but relentless forward movement, the Filipinos abandoned

U.S. troops entering Malolos, the newly proclaimed capital of the Filipino Republic, after capturing the city in 1899.

Malolos, and the town was occupied on 31 March 1899 by Kansas and Nebraska volunteers under the immediate command of Col. Frederick Funston.

Without the capture of Aguinaldo and the defeat of the Army of Liberation, the occupation of Malolos was much less significant than it might have been, particularly since MacArthur's command had incurred some 500 casualties during a campaign that had lasted but a week.

See also Aguinaldo y Famy, Emilio; Funston, Frederick; Luzon Campaigns; MacArthur, Arthur; Otis, Elwell Stephen.
References and Further Readings
Linn, Brian McAllister. *The Philippine War, 1899–1902.* Lawrence: University Press of Kansas, 2000.
Wolff, Leon. *Little Brown Brother: America's Forgotten Bid for Empire Which Cost 250,000 Lives.* New York: Kraus Reprint, 1970.

Mambises

During the First Cuban War of Independence (1868–1878)—which set the stage for the second revolution that led to U.S. involvement in the region at the end of the nineteenth century—Cuban guerrillas were called *Mambises,* a corruption of a term that originated in Santo Domingo when the inhabitants of that island rose up in revolt against Spain. The rebels there were led by a black man, former Spanish officer Juan Mamby. Spanish troops dubbed the insurgents the "men of Mamby." When the first Cuban revolt began, the Spanish soldiers, many of whom had come from Santo Domingo, bestowed the term on the Cuban rebels. The name also was used to identify Cuban revolutionaries during the Spanish-American War.

See also Cuban Revolution; Ten Years' War.

References and Further Readings

Foner, Philip S. *The Spanish-Cuban-American War.* 2 vols. New York: Monthly Review Press, 1972.

Quesada, Gonzalo de. *The War in Cuba: Being a Full Account of Her Great Struggle for Freedom.* Washington, DC: Liberty Publishing, 1896.

Manifest Destiny

The manifest destiny philosophy was based on the belief that the United States had a God-given mandate to implant the American way of life throughout the North American continent. Although the concept in one form or another had long been the province of all imperialist powers, the term as such seems to have been coined about 1845 by John L. O'Sullivan, editor of the *Democratic Review.*

Manifest destiny found new expression in the United States during the nineteenth-century westward march across the continent, and it influenced those who argued for expansion of U.S. power in Hawaii, Guam, and the Philippines.

See also Anti-Imperialist League; Imperialism/Expansionism; Roosevelt, Theodore.

References and Further Readings

Brands, H. W. *Bound to Empire: The United States and the Philippines.* New York: Oxford University Press, 1992.

Healy, David. *US Expansionism: The Imperialist Urge in the 1890s.* Milwaukee: University of Wisconsin Press, 1970.

LaFeber. *The New Empire.* Ithaca, NY: Cornell University Press, 1963.

Manila Bay, Battle of (1 May 1898)

On 27 April 1898, the U.S. Navy's Asiatic Squadron, commanded by Commodore George Dewey, sailed from Mirs Bay, China, under orders to attack the Spanish fleet in the Philippines. The Battle of Manila Bay, which followed, was a signal triumph for the navy and one of the most significant victories in U.S. history. In the space of a few hours, the balance of power in the Pacific shifted unalterably,

An artist's rendering of Dewey's victory at Manila Bay on 1 May 1898.

and the United States graduated from the status of a burgeoning force in the Western Hemisphere to that of an international power.

Dewey's squadron, originally composed of the cruisers *Olympia* (his flagship) and *Boston,* the gunboat *Petrel,* and the revenue cutter *McCulloch,* was reinforced by the cruisers *Raleigh, Baltimore,* and *Concord* before departing for the Philippines. One old paddle wheeler, the *Monocacy,* was left behind. All except the *Concord* and the *Petrel* were classified as "protected"—that is, they carried protective armor over their decks.

Dewey also had purchased a pair of supply ships before departing, to ensure an adequate store of coal and supplies for the coming campaign. He was, however, concerned about the squadron's supply of ammunition. At steaming time, his magazines carried only about 60 percent of their capacity.

Before leaving Mirs Bay, Dewey had rendezvoused with the former U.S. consul in the Philippines, Oscar Williams, who confirmed the commodore's belief that the U.S. squadron was superior to that of the Spanish and that an attack should be successful. Williams also reported that the Spanish fleet would be found in Subig (Subic) Bay, some 60 miles northwest of Manila Bay.

On 30 April, the Asiatic Squadron reached the Philippines, having completed its 600-mile journey from Mirs Bay. After a reconnaissance revealed that Williams's information was incorrect—that the Spanish fleet was not in Subig Bay—Dewey elected to move on to Manila Bay. As it turned out, Williams had been correct after all.

The Spanish fleet had in fact been at Subig the day before.

Meanwhile, Adm. Patricio Montojo, who commanded the Spanish naval forces in the area, had revised his strategy. After arriving at Subig Bay on 26 April, he learned that little had been done to prepare the area for defense. The promised shore batteries had not been emplaced, nor had the harbor entrance been mined. As a consequence, he concluded that he stood a better chance against the Americans in Manila Bay, where he intended to take advantage of shore-based batteries. In this, he was supported by his senior subordinates.

Montojo evidently was also motivated by the belief that his chances of victory were slim. Accordingly, he decided to move into the relatively shallow water—about 25 feet deep—of Cañacao Bay, a small inlet within greater Manila Bay where his men would have a better chance of escaping to the mainland if their ships were sunk or had to be scuttled.

As evening arrived, Montojo learned that the Americans had been at Subig Bay earlier. Despite that report and despite the sound of gunfire from the outer reaches of the bay, the Spanish commander apparently did not believe there was any urgency to the situation and went ashore for the night, along with most of his staff.

Hoping to catch the Spanish by surprise, Dewey decided to steam into Manila Bay after dark, with guns ready for action and the running lights of his vessels reduced to the absolute minimum. The entrance to the bay was guarded by two strong points and a pair of islands (one of which, Corregidor, would become famous during World War II). Although the Spanish had located a number of shore batteries in the area, some were antiquated and others were judged to be minimal threats because of their limited range. The batteries on Caballo Island and a point of rocks known as El Fraile did pose a potential danger, though, since the squadron would pass within 2 miles of the batteries' guns on its way into the bay. There was also some concern about the presence of mines, although Dewey regarded that threat as secondary, believing the Spanish lacked the technology to effectively mine deep waters.

As the U.S. vessels entered the bay, Dewey chose the larger of the two channels, Boca Grande. Steaming in a single file, the squadron escaped notice until it had passed El Fraile, when the Spanish opened fire with a few token rounds—the gunfire that Montojo had heard just prior to going ashore. Dewey's ships responded with several retaliatory rounds, but the duel was short-lived, and the Americans steamed on into the bay.

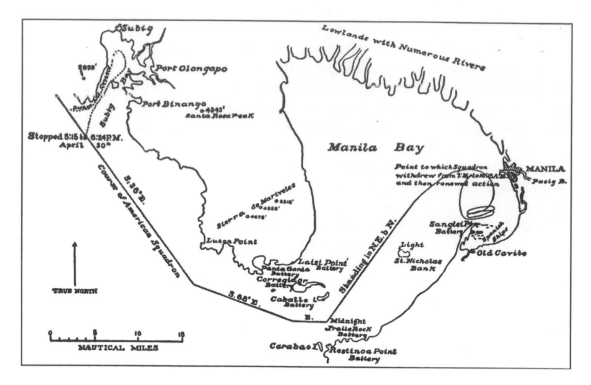

The battle of Manila Bay, showing the course of the U.S. Navy Squadron. Source: *Rear Adm. French Ensor Chadwick*, Relations of the the United States and Spain: The Spanish American War *(New York: Charles Scribner's Sons, 1911), I, p. 159.*

Having negotiated the most potentially dangerous part of the passage into Manila Bay with less trouble than feared, Dewey detached the two supply ships and the *McCulloch* from his main combat force and continued on, albeit slowly, for he did not wish to initiate action before dawn. Approaching the heart of Manila Bay, he halted and formed his squadron for battle.

The two opponents were not evenly matched, the Americans having a decided advantage. The U.S. squadron consisted of 6 warships—of which 4 were protected—mounting 53 heavy guns and manned by more than 1,600 sailors. By comparison, Montojo's force consisted of a pair of unprotected cruisers, the *Reina Cristina* and the *Castilla,* and the gunboats *Don Juan de Austria, Don Antonio de Ulloa, Isla de Cuba, Marqués del Duero,* and *Isla de Luzon.* Significantly, the Spanish vessels mounted only 37 heavy guns, and not only were these of smaller caliber than those on the U.S. ships but some were also of the old muzzle-loading variety. Finally, the U.S. crews were far better trained than those of the Spanish.

In one area, the Spanish did have an advantage—shore batteries, numbering more than 200, although many were equipped with old muzzle-loaders. But as subsequent events would show, Montojo's failure to effectively employ these guns negated his one advantage.

Montojo had anchored his fleet in a semicircular disposition in Cañacao Bay, just south of Manila. When dawn arrived, Dewey steamed past the city of Manila, pointing his squadron toward the anchored Spanish vessels. The *Olympia* led, followed by the *Baltimore, Raleigh, Petrel, Concord,* and *Boston.* A little after 5 A.M., the Manila batteries opened up, but poor aim by the Spanish gunners resulted in no damage to the U.S. ships. The *Boston* and *Concord* answered with passing counterbattery fire. Shortly thereafter, Montojo's ships opened fire.

As the U.S. vessels steamed toward the Spanish fleet in a single file, some 400 yards apart, two mines exploded, but they caused no damage. From a distance of about 5,000 yards, Dewey issued his famous order to Capt. Charles Gridley, commander of the *Olympia*: "You may fire when ready, Gridley." Shortly, the flagship of the U.S. squadron sent an 8-inch shell hurtling toward the Spanish.

At a distance of just over 2 miles, Dewey turned his ships toward the west, allowing his squadron to rake the Spanish fleet with full broadsides from all of his port (left side) guns as they passed by. After completing his run, Dewey reversed course, this time bringing his starboard batteries into action. During the next two hours, Dewey made four additional runs past the enemy, with telling effect.

Warned that the *Olympia* was running low on ammunition, Dewey broke off the attack to assess the situation. Although the report proved premature, he did not resume the attack immediately but instead allowed his crews to eat breakfast. In the meantime, Admiral Montojo directed all of his ships that were able to do so to withdraw south into Bacoor Bay to make a final stand.

About 11 A.M., Dewey resumed the attack, but Montojo was able to offer resistance from only one remaining gunboat. The guns on nearby Sangley Point might have helped had they been able to depress their barrels enough to allow them to fire at targets closer than 2,000 yards. For the Spanish, the situation had reached the hopeless stage. Shortly after noon Montojo surrendered.

During this decidedly one-sided battle, the Spanish ships either were sunk by gunfire or were set afire and scuttled. Three of the damaged ships were salvaged later and were used by the Americans. Dewey's ships sustained only minor damage. In addition to the destruction of the Spanish fleet, Montojo's crews suffered 371 casualties, in comparison to only 9 Americans wounded.

Although Dewey lacked the strength to extend his great victory ashore, he did remain in the area to provide support for a U.S. occupation force. The first elements reached the Philippines by the end of June.

See also Dewey, George; Montojo y Pasarón, Patricio; Roosevelt, Theodore.

References and Further Readings

Dewey, George. *Autobiography of George Dewey, Admiral of the Navy.* Annapolis, MD: Naval Institute Press, 1987.

Musicant, Ivan, *Empire by Default. The Spanish-American War and the Dawn of the American Century.* New York: Henry Holt and Company, 1998.

Trask, David F. *The War with Spain in 1898.* Lincoln: University of Nebraska Press, 1996.

Manila (Philippine Islands), First Battle of (13 August 1898)

The capital city of the Philippine Archipelago, Manila is located on the east side of Manila Bay on the island of Luzon. As the capital, it was the center of Spanish power in the archipelago and understandably was the focal point of Filipino Nationalist efforts to overthrow Spanish rule. Following his defeat of the Spanish naval squadron at Manila Bay on 1 May 1898, Commodore (later Rear Adm.) George Dewey realized that Manila could and should be seized, but he had no available landing force to undertake such a mission and therefore could only sit tight and await the army's arrival.

The Philippine Expeditionary Force—the Eighth Corps—reached the Philippines in three contingents, departing from San Francisco as ship availability permitted. The first contingent of 2,500, under Brig. Gen. Thomas Anderson, arrived at the end of June, followed in mid-July by 3,500 men under Brig. Gen. Francis V. Greene. The final contingent, numbering some 4,800 and commanded by Brig. Gen. Arthur MacArthur, reached the islands at the end of July, as did the overall commander of the Eighth Corps, Maj. Gen. Wesley Merritt.

At this juncture, the Spanish still controlled Manila and much of its environs. The city proper was split by the Pasig River, south of which stood the old walled city of Fort Santiago. The Spanish defensive line—called the Zapote Line—was located 1.5 miles to the south, from where a large blockhouse—Number 14—on the Pasay Road extended west to a stone structure known as Fort San Antonio de Abad, located near the shore of Manila Bay. Between these two strong points was a line of entrenchments.

Confronting the Spanish positions were some 10,000 Filipino Nationalist troops under the overall command of Gen. Emilio Aguinaldo, who had formally proclaimed the Republic of the Philippines on 12 June. Through the summer, the Nationalists had managed to effectively isolate Manila from its source of supplies, leav-

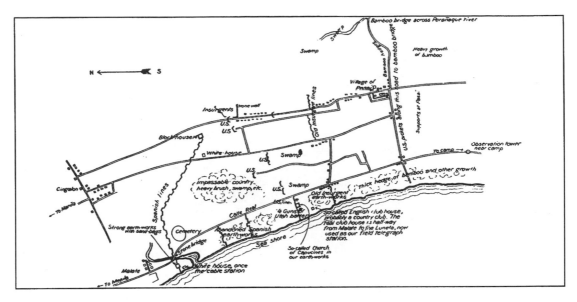

Positions of the U.S., Spanish, and Filipino forces early in the campaign against Manila, 1898.
Source: Harper's Pictorial History of the War with Spain *(New York: Harper & Brothers Publishers, 1899), II, p. 410.*

ing it, in effect, a city under siege. Food was scarce, consisting mainly of a little horseflesh and a little water buffalo. At night, the Nationalists and the Spanish defenders maintained lively fire between the two lines but undertook no serious offensive movements.

During the course of the U.S. buildup, General Greene's troops constructed a series of entrenchments and moved into some of the works created by the Nationalists, who abandoned these positions only reluctantly when General Greene persuaded them to do so. The arrangement was irregular. In places, the Nationalist forces actually occupied trench works in between the Americans and Spanish.

The two weeks preceding the attack on the city were marked by heavy rains—it was the monsoon season in the Philippines. The period also was characterized by frequent exchanges of artillery and rifle fire between the Americans and the Spanish, with Greene's units sustaining a number of casualties. In addition, relations between the Americans and Aguinaldo's Nationalists, at first cordial, had begun to deteriorate, as the latter had grown increasingly suspicious of U.S. intentions in the islands.

During the latter part of July, Admiral George Dewey became convinced that the Spanish would surrender Manila through negotiations. He met first with Capt. Gen. Basilio Augustín and later with his successor, Fermín Jáudenes y Álvarez, to explore what arrangements might be worked out.

General Greene, however, urged naval gunfire on Spanish

U.S. troops on the ramparts of Manila after the city's surrender in August 1898.

positions to relieve the pressure on his command. His troops had dug a line of trenches south of Fort Abad and were taking casualties from Spanish fire every day. General Merritt supported Greene in this request. Dewey, however, was reluctant to open fire, fearing that to do so might destroy any chance of securing the city by negotiation, which he still believed was entirely possible. Dewey suggested that perhaps the troops could be withdrawn from the trenches until a general attack became necessary. Nevertheless, the admiral did agree to support Greene if absolutely necessary. In that eventuality, Greene was to burn a blue light on the beach, and the ships would open fire. Dewey hoped that action would not be necessary.

General Merritt had arrived in the Philippines under orders from President William McKinley not to involve the Nationalists in taking Manila because to do so would be to involve them as partners in future treaty negotiations with Spain. Gen. Fermín Jáudenes, who had recently replaced Capt. Gen. Basilio Augustín as Spanish commander in Manila, had taken over with orders to hold the city. Inasmuch as peace negotiations were about to get under way, Spain's bargaining position would be weakened by a surrender of the city.

On 7 August, General Merritt and Admiral Dewey sent an ultimatum to General Jáudenes, demanding that either he surrender Manila within forty-eight hours or the United States would attack. In the meantime, through the efforts of the Belgian consul, Edouard André, Jáudenes agreed to consider surrendering Manila to U.S.

forces, but he insisted that it would have to appear that a genuine effort had been made to defend the city—Spain's honor had to be salvaged. Perhaps most important, the Filipinos could not be allowed to enter the city, as Jáudencs feared that the Nationalists would show no mercy to the Spanish defenders. Thus, Spain and the United States each had its reasons for wanting to keep Aguinaldo's people from entering Manila.

Finally, the two sides agreed that the Spanish would offer a token defense of their outer works but not of the walled city itself. However, neither of the U.S. commanders who were to lead the attack, Generals Greene and MacArthur, had been made aware of the pact because General Merritt feared that if they had known of the arrangements, their respective attacks would have lacked authenticity.

After the forty-eight-hour truce expired, Merritt's forces prepared to move. The axis of their attack would be south to north, in two essentially parallel columns. Greene's brigade would advance along the northern flank nearest Manila Bay, while MacArthur's brigade was to move along the southern flank. By prearrangement, Admiral Dewey's flagship, the *Olympia,* would fire a few token rounds at the heavy stone walls of Fort San Antonio de Abad before raising the international signal flag calling for Spain's surrender.

On the morning of 13 August, reveille was sounded amid a steady drizzle. Following the naval bombardment, directed against Fort San Antonio de Abad as agreed, the artillery opened fire and the assault moved forward, the troops advancing under what had turned into a drenching rain. The Spanish resistance turned out to be heavier than Merritt had expected, though not enough to thwart the advance. The Spanish defenders gradually fell back, and General Greene moved into the city unopposed to accept the Spanish surrender.

On the right flank, MacArthur found the going much tougher, exacerbated by Filipino Nationalists determined to be involved in the capture of the city. As MacArthur's troops moved north along the Singalong Road, Spanish infantry positioned in a blockhouse inflicted numerous casualties on a regiment of Minnesotans.

MacArthur's biggest challenge, however, was in keeping the Nationalists from entering the city. As his troops moved closer to Manila, their ranks became increasingly intermingled with those of the Filipinos, and MacArthur was compelled to have his commanders hold the Nationalists back from the city. By the end of the day, U.S. troops occupied all of Manila proper, but outside the city, Aguinaldo's troops, angry at being denied entrance, were in an ugly mood. Fortunately, the heavy tropical storm served to help defuse the hostile mob.

The capture of Manila yielded some 13,000 Spanish prisoners. In addition, the United States garnered 22,000 stands of small arms, 10 million rounds of ammunition, and 70 pieces of artillery.

At the time of the battle, the cable connection with Hong Kong was out of service. By the time it was restored on 16 August, it was learned that a peace protocol between the United States and Spain had been signed on 12 August—the day before the battle. This turn of events led Spanish peace negotiators to argue later that the U.S. capture of Manila was not valid, a point that the U.S. peace commissioners countered successfully.

See also Aguinaldo y Famy, Emilio; Dewey, George; Greene, Francis Vinton; Jáudenes y Álvarez, Fermín; MacArthur, Arthur; Merritt, Wesley.

References and Further Readings

Greene, Maj. Gen. Francis V., U.S.V. "The Capture of Manila." *Century Magazine,* April 1899.

Linn, Brian McAllister. *The Philippine War, 1899–1902.* Lawrence: University Press of Kansas, 2000.

Musicant, Ivan. *Empire by Default: The Spanish-American War and the Dawn of the American Century.* New York: Henry Holt and Company, 1998.

Wolff, Leon. *Little Brown Brother: America's Forgotten Bid for Empire Which Cost 250,000 Lives.* New York: Kraus Reprint, 1970.

Manila (Philippine Islands), Second Battle of (4–23 February 1899)

Relations between the United States and Emilio Aguinaldo's Philippine Revolutionary Army were strained almost from the moment the first elements of the Eighth Corps arrived in the Philippines in late June 1898. In large part, the friction resulted from the lack of a clear Philippine policy on the part of President William McKinley, who was undecided as to exactly what the U.S. role in the archipelago ought to be once Spain was defeated. Interwoven into this political tapestry was a racial bias on the part of U.S. troops against the Filipino people, whom many soldiers regarded as inferior and referred to as "niggers." In addition to vague political directives, then, there was an attitudinal problem that did not bode well for future relations.

For his part, Aguinaldo sought U.S. recognition of the Philippine Republic and a full partnership in defeating Spain. The McKinley administration, however, was unwilling to recognize any republican government. Indeed, Gen. Wesley Merritt, commanding the Philippine Expeditionary Force, was specifically directed not to enter into any political arrangements with Aguinaldo. Although Merritt's instructions were otherwise ambiguous, President McKinley was clear on that point.

During the summer of 1898, however, both sides were largely occupied with the task of defeating Spanish forces around Manila. During the First Battle of Manila on 13 August, the relationship between the forces of Aguinaldo and Merritt deteriorated further when the Americans denied the revolutionary army access to the old walled city of Manila; their aim was to shut out the Army of Liberation (as Aguinaldo referred to it) from any role in determining the ultimate disposition of the Philippines during later treaty negotiations.

Nonetheless, in the nearly five months following the Spanish surrender of Manila in August and the signing of the Treaty of Paris in December 1898, U.S. occupation troops and the Philippine Army of Liberation managed to more or less coexist, though the situation clearly was a volatile one.

In the aftermath of Manila's surrender, the United States insisted that the Filipino Army retract its lines from in front of the capital city as a preventive measure, to avoid possible exchanges with U.S. troops. Aguinaldo grudgingly acceded to the U.S. demands, but there were frequent verbal exchanges between Americans and Filipinos, suggesting that a full-scale eruption perhaps was not far off.

That eruption occurred on the night of 4 February 1899. Exactly who fired the first shot remains a matter of dispute. The evidence suggests that the fighting was simply the result of an explosive situation, awaiting only the spark needed to ignite a war that was inevitable. At any rate, in the Santa Mesa District northeast of Manila, a patrol of Nebraska troops fired on some Filipino troops, supposedly as retaliation against the latter's incursion into what had been agreed to as a neutral zone. The exchange set off what would prove to be a three-year war between the United States and Aguinaldo's republican forces.

The U.S. response to the fighting was swift. On Sunday, 5 February 1899, Gen. Arthur MacArthur attacked along his Second Division front. Supported by artillery and naval gunfire, some elements of the division advanced through rice paddies, encountering minimal opposition and seizing Nationalist positions. Other units had to contend with more difficult terrain and heavy fire from the enemy. By the end of the second day of fighting, on 6 February, MacArthur's troops had driven the Nationalists back and secured the high ground north of Manila.

Meanwhile, also on 6 February, Brig. Gen. Thomas Anderson's division attacked Army of Liberation positions south of Manila. Anderson's troops—composed largely of volunteers from the western states—were also supported by artillery as they steadily advanced. At an old Spanish position on the Pasig River, strong enemy fire stalled Anderson's advance until supporting cross fire from a California regiment got things moving again, and in short order, the Army of Liberation forces were in full retreat.

As the Filipinos fled, the U.S. attack lost its cohesiveness in the melee of the pursuit. Units became mixed, and organizational control was temporarily lost. General Anderson had intended to corner the Filipinos between his two brigades, but the strategy fell apart when the attack splintered. As well, there was a breakdown in communications all the way down the chain of command.

The fighting of 5 and 6 February was heavy, and by the end of the second day, the U.S. forces—Anderson's in particular—were widely dispersed. Although the area over which much of the action of 6 and 7 February had taken place was largely secured, pockets of resistance remained, with considerable fighting. On 16 February, for example, the Filipinos attacked one of Anderson's brigades in grand style—trim ranks, bugles, flags flying—only to be devastated by the Americans' disciplined fire. On 19 February, California and Washington troops, supported by fire from the gunboat *Laguna de Bay,* devastated enemy positions south of Manila.

In the wake of the fighting of 5 and 6 February, most of the Army of Liberation had fallen back to Caloocan, a dozen miles north of Manila. MacArthur's plan to strike Caloocan had to be postponed, however, because of an anticipated uprising in the city of Manila itself. Finally, on 10 February, MacArthur's division, supported by Dewey's naval guns, attacked the Filipino positions in Caloocan and by day's end had secured that important rail center on the line to Malolos, the newly proclaimed capital of the Philippine Republic.

Meanwhile, the uprising in Manila, which the United States had learned about through captured Nationalist documents, enabled the provost guard of Maj. Gen. Elwell S. Otis to shut down the revolt before it really got started by arresting known revolutionaries. Although some street fighting ensued, it fell far short of a full-scale revolt. The failure of the revolt to materialize—some said because of poor organization within the Army of Liberation—effectively ended the Second Battle of Manila. The next phase of General Otis's effort to defeat Aguinaldo's Army of Liberation would begin with a spring campaign against the capital of Malolos.

See also Aguinaldo y Famy, Emilio; Anderson, Thomas McArthur; Dewey, George; MacArthur, Arthur; Otis, Elwell Stephen.

References and Further Readings

Gates, John Morgan. *Schoolbooks and Krags: The United States Army in the Philippines, 1898–1902.* Contributions in Military History no. 3. Westport, CT: Greenwood Press, 1973.

Linn, Brian McAllister. *The Philippine War, 1899–1902.* Lawrence: University Press of Kansas, 2000.

Wolff, Leon. *Little Brown Brother: America's Forgotten Bid for Empire Which Cost 250,000 Lives.* New York: Kraus Reprint, 1970.

Young, Kenneth Ray. *The General's General: The Life and Times of Arthur MacArthur.* Boulder, CO: Westview Press, 1994.

Manzanillo (Cuba), Actions at (30 June–1 July, 18 July, and 12 August 1898)

The dispersal of Spanish forces in Oriente Province proved to be a factor in the U.S. advance on Santiago. In June 1898, Gen. Arsenio Linares y Pomba, commander of the Spanish forces in Oriente Province, had dispersed his troops—some 35,000 men—to cover various strategic points in the province. About 10,000 of these troops were concentrated at Santiago, and another 6,000 were at the port city of Manzanillo. It has been argued, retrospectively, that Linares would have been wiser to concentrate his entire command at Santiago, but to have done so would have placed an additional burden on the limited resources of a city that was already unable to meet the needs of the garrison and its own inhabitants.

By late June 1898, when Gen. William R. Shafter's Fifth Corps began its advance on Santiago, Manzanillo could receive supplies only through the efforts of runners who effectively penetrated the U.S. naval blockade. And with the surrounding countryside controlled largely by Cuban revolutionaries, Manzanillo was, for all intents and purposes, an isolated community.

As Shafter's campaign advanced, a relief column of some 3,800 men under the command of Col. Federico Escario left Manzanillo to reinforce the garrison at Santiago. Escario's column did manage to reach Santiago, though not before fighting some 40 engagements with the revolutionary forces of Gen. Calixto García and sustaining nearly 400 casualties during the course of its 150-mile march. Escario's arrival at Manzanillo proved to be a mixed blessing at best, as it meant more mouths to feed with inadequate food supplies.

By late June, Adm. William T. Sampson moved to tighten the noose still further by sending shallow-draft vessels into the narrow waters around Manzanillo in order to thwart the efforts of blockade runners. Accordingly, on 30 June, the armed yacht *Hist,* the gunboat

Hornet, and the armed tug *Wompatuck,* under orders to seize any blockade runners they found, encountered instead the Spanish launch *Centenila.* During the exchange of fire that ensued, the Spanish vessel was sunk, though it would later be raised and reused by the Spanish. The United States sustained no casualties.

Later that day, the U.S. vessels entered Manzanillo harbor and shelled a troop-carrying sloop, driving it to shore. More significantly, though, they found a large torpedo boat and eight gunboats prepared to receive them. This greeting committee was supported by an old smoothbore coastal gun located on Caimanera Point, as well as several pieces of field artillery and guns mounted on pontoons.

Fighting began at 3:20 P.M. and continued for an hour and a half, with heavy exchanges of fire. Both sides scored hits. The *Hist* was struck eleven times, and the *Hornet* also sustained several hits, as did the *Wompatuck.* The U.S. ships, for their part, disabled the torpedo boat, sank one of the gunboats, and destroyed one of the pontoons. The only U.S. casualties were 3 men who were scalded by escaping steam on the *Hornet.* Spanish losses were unknown.

Despite the damage inflicted on the Spanish ships, the U.S. vessels had not really neutralized the harbor's defenses. The following day, therefore, the *Scorpion* and the *Osceola* arrived to knock out the Spanish shore batteries, but after a sharp, though brief, encounter, they were forced to withdraw.

With the defeat of Adm. Pascual Cervera's squadron in the Battle of Santiago, the navy was free to dispatch a stronger force to finish the job at Manzanillo. Accordingly, on 18 July, two gunboats, the *Wilmington* and the *Helena,* led the *Hist, Hornet, Wompatuck, Scorpion,* and *Osceola* back to Manzanillo, where they proceeded to vanquish the remaining Spanish ships.

A month later, on 12 August, a still stronger force arrived in the harbor. After the Spanish commander refused to surrender, the ships' guns pounded the city and its defenses. Unfortunately, the signing of an armistice that same day negated the need for the fighting of 12 August.

See also Linares y Pomba, Arsenio; Naval Blockade of Cuba; Santiago, Campaign and Siege of.

References and Further Readings

Chadwick, Rear Adm. French Ensor. *Relations of the United States and Spain: The Spanish American War.* 2 vols. New York: Charles Scribner's Sons, 1911 (reprinted in 1968).

Feuer, A. B. *The Spanish-American War at Sea.* Westport, CT: Greenwood Press, 1995.

Trask, David F. *The War with Spain in 1898.* Lincoln: University of Nebraska Press, 1996.

María Cristina, Queen Regent of Spain (1858–1929)

The daughter of Archduke Charles Ferdinand of Austria, María Cristina married Alfonso XII of Spain in 1879. The marriage was short-lived, however, lasting only six years until Alfonso's death in 1885. Following the birth of their son Alfonso XIII in 1886, María became queen regent of Spain, a position she would hold until her son came of age in 1902.

María was a gracious and tactful ruler, and her reign was largely peaceful, though it was marred by unrest during the Spanish-American War. Politically conservative, she sought to preserve Spain's disintegrating colonial empire. As a ruler who was active in her nation's foreign policy, María wrote to her cousin, Queen Victoria of England, with the hope of enlisting the queen's help in mustering international support for Spain's position. In this endeavor, however, María was unsuccessful. Despite her hope of maintaining a colonial empire, she recognized and accepted Spain's weak bargaining position in the aftermath of the war. Over the objections of her advisers, she ratified the Treaty of Paris in March 1899.

See also Alfonso XII; Alfonso XIII; Spanish-American War, International Reaction to.

References and Further Readings

Bécker, Jerónimo. *Historia de las relaciones exteriores de España durante el siglo XIX* (The history of Spanish foreign relations during the nineteenth century). Vol. 3. Madrid: J. Rates, 1926.

Ferrara, Orestes. *The Last Spanish War: Revelations in Diplomacy.* Translated from the Spanish by William E. Shea. New York: Paisley Press, 1937.

Gould, Lewis L. *The Spanish-American War and President McKinley.* Lawrence: University of Kansas Press, 1982.

Trask, David F. *The War with Spain in 1898.* Lincoln: University of Nebraska Press, 1996.

Mariana Islands

See **Guam**

Mariel (Cuba)

Located in western Cuba, about 26 miles southwest of Havana, Mariel originally was to have played a key role in the U.S. invasion of Cuba during the Spanish-American War. Subsequent events, however, redefined U.S. strategy.

Early plans focused on Havana as the primary U.S. objective. Because of the proximity of Mariel to Havana, the initial plans proposed by a joint army-navy board called for a landing at Mariel, from which a drive on Havana then could be launched. At a White House conference held in early May 1898, President William McKinley, in company with Secretary of War Russell Alger, Navy Secretary John Long, General of the Army Nelson Miles, and Adm. Montgomery Sicard, hammered out the early strategy.

The navy favored an immediate invasion, as did President McKinley. Strangely, Secretary of War Alger also supported the idea and spoke as though the army were ready to execute an immediate invasion of Cuba when in fact it was far from prepared for such an undertaking, as pointed out by General of the Army Miles.

Behind-the-scenes squabbling between Alger and Long made interservice cooperation difficult at best. Secretary Long, probably feeling a bit smug because he knew the navy's state of readiness was much higher than that of the army, made a point of prodding Alger. Exasperated and stung by Long's accusations, Alger directed Miles to assemble a force of 70,000 to take Havana. As historian David Trask has noted, there is no clear explanation for such an order, except possibly to embarrass General Miles, with whom Alger was feuding constantly.

In any event, the two-stage plan called for an expedition of regular troops to quickly seize Mariel and establish a base camp. Once this objective was accomplished, a large force of volunteers would land, and the drive on Havana would begin. Gen. William R. Shafter's Fifth Corps, then assembling in Florida, was reported near readiness, and on 9 May 1898, he was directed to execute the Mariel strategy.

The plan soon self-destructed, however, when it became apparent that the volunteers were much further from being ready to take the field than had been supposed. Then, too, the huge logistic problems of arming and equipping a large army soon began to manifest themselves. Finally, the arrival in Caribbean waters of the Spanish fleet under Adm. Pascual Cervera altered the picture completely. The proposed invasion of Cuba would have to wait until the Spanish fleet was destroyed or otherwise neutralized. Once Cervera's squadron was isolated in Santiago harbor, the Cuban invasion went forward, though the objective had by then shifted to Santiago rather than Havana via Mariel.

See also Alger, Russell Alexander; Cervera y Topete, Pascual; Long, John Davis; McKinley, William, Jr.; Miles, Nelson Appleton; Santiago, Campaign and Siege of; Shafter, William Rufus.

References and Further Readings

Cosmas, Graham. *An Army for Empire: The United States Army in the Spanish-American War.* College Station: Texas A&M University Press, 1998.

O'Toole, G. J. A. *The Spanish War: An American Epic, 1898*. New York: W. W. Norton, 1984.

Trask, David F. *The War with Spain in 1898*. Lincoln: University of Nebraska Press, 1996.

Marinduque (Philippine Islands)

Located about 11 miles from the large island of Luzon, Marinduque comprises some 400 square miles. At the time of the Spanish-American War, it was home to about 50,000 individuals, mainly concentrated in five coastal communities connected by a network of roads or paths. A rugged, mountainous interior made cross-country travel difficult. The island's agricultural economy produced hemp and rice.

The small island of Marinduque played an important role in the Philippine-American War. It served as a training ground for the development of the pacification techniques the U.S. Army used to control guerrilla activities elsewhere in the archipelago.

The U.S. Army arrived on Marinduque in April 1900. Concerned that Filipino guerrillas might use the strategically located island as a base of operations, Gen. John C. Bates, commanding the U.S. forces in southern Luzon, decided to take control of the island. The largely passive population of Marinduque, while outwardly receptive to the Americans, was at the same time secretly supporting guerrilla forces on the island. Some 250 active resistance fighters were aided by perhaps as many as 2,000 part-time guerrillas.

Over the next two years, the island was occupied by various army units. The units conducted a number of campaigns that moved into the rough terrain of the island's interior but seldom were accorded an opportunity to catch and engage the guerrilla forces of Col. Maximo Abad, who sought to avoid contact with U.S. forces.

One exception occurred on 13 September 1900, when a detachment of the Twenty-ninth U.S. Volunteers under the command of Capt. Devereux Shields was ambushed in the mountains by a large guerrilla contingent. After a fighting retreat, the detachment surrendered to the guerrillas near the barrio (town) of Massiquisie. The event provoked retaliatory action as the army promptly reinforced the island garrison and launched a number of stronger punitive expeditions, which met with varying degrees of success. Casualties were inflicted on the guerrillas, and some stocks of supplies were destroyed, but these efforts did little to significantly cripple guerrilla activities.

Because of their failure to end guerrilla activities using traditional methods, army commanders sometimes turned to harsh means to establish firm control. Most notable was the concentration policy, wherein all civilians were brought together in six communities in an effort to isolate them from the guerrillas. Any individuals who failed to comply or were found guilty of aiding the guerrillas were treated as enemies. Ironically, this was essentially the very policy that Gen. Valeriano "Butcher" Weyler had instituted in Cuba, where it was known as the *reconcentrado* and helped to arouse U.S. public opinion against Spain. Although the army's version of "concentration" on Marinduque fell far short of Weyler's methods in Cuba, it did underscore the difficulty the military faced in its efforts to separate noncombatants from guerrillas.

By 1901, increasing pressure on guerrilla forces throughout the archipelago, including the capture of Emilio Aguinaldo, compelled Abad to surrender. His surrender ended the army's counterinsurgency program on the island.

Unsettled conditions remained on Marinduque, however. Civil unrest and rumors of revolt within the recently established Philippine Constabulary brought about a renewal of military action to locate cached guerrilla weapons and to arrest malcontents. Finally, in 1902, the Philippine-American War officially ended, and the army left the island.

Overall, the U.S. Army's performance on Marinduque left much to be desired. Leadership varied from weak to mediocre. However, patrols suffered minimal casualties because of a lack of real aggressiveness on the part of the Filipino guerrillas. During its tenure on Marinduque, the army sustained some 27 casualties, and nearly twice that number were taken captive, though most were released later. The guerrillas, by contrast, suffered 100 casualties, and perhaps as many as 200 were taken prisoner. Despite these losses, Abad seemed able to replenish his ranks.

See also Aguinaldo y Famy, Emilio; Benevolent Assimilation; "Civilize 'em with a Krag"; Philippine Constabulary.

References and Further Readings

Birtle, Andrew J. "The U.S. Army's Pacification of Marinduque, Philippine Islands, April 1900–April 1901." *Journal of Military History,* vol. 61, no. 2, April 1997.

Linn, Brian McAllister. *The U.S. Army and Counterinsurgency in the Philippine War, 1899–1902.* Chapel Hill: University of North Carolina Press, 1989.

———. *The Philippine War, 1899–1902.* Lawrence: University Press of Kansas, 2000.

Marine Corps, U.S.

The Spanish-American War period was important in helping to set the tone for the future development of the U.S. Marine Corps. The two decades preceding the war were a transitional period for the Navy Department, including the Marine Corps. Both sought a new identity within a navy that was changing from wood and sails to steel and steam.

At that juncture in its history, the Marine Corps was a much smaller organization than it would eventually become. As a result of increased appropriations, the full-strength allotment of the corps was increased from 3,000 to 4,600 men, and its commandant, Lt. Col. Charles Haywood, was promoted to brigadier general.

The role of the corps as the fleet marine force was yet to be defined, though its function during the Spanish-American War would bring that role into sharper focus. Prior to the war with Spain, the primary duties of the corps were to provide gunners and guards for navy vessels, function as naval landing parties, and provide guard service at naval shore installations.

During the Santiago Campaign, a specially formed 6-company battalion, consisting of 24 officers and 633 men under the command of a Civil War veteran, Lt. Col. Robert W. Huntington, landed at Guantánamo Bay. Following what came to be known as "one hundred hours of fighting," including the Battle of Cuzco, the battalion secured the area. Although it represented the first serious ground action of the war, the fighting was of only minor importance to the overall Santiago Campaign. Nevertheless, it was of great importance to the future development of the Marine Corps. Most senior army and navy officers had viewed the corps as strictly a "seagoing military service," but the action at Guantánamo Bay demonstrated that it was capable of fulfilling a larger role.

Later, at Adm. George Dewey's request, a battalion of marines was sent to the Philippines. Later, a second and a third battalion were added, and the units were subsequently reorganized as a regiment, marking the first time the Marine Corps had a regimental-size force in the field. Although a good portion of the regiment continued to perform its traditional function of guarding naval facilities, one battalion joined an army expedition as it moved against Filipino insurgents on Cavite. The battalion attacked and captured the town of Novaleta and later secured Olongapo on Subig (Subic) Bay.

The Marine Corps's otherwise exemplary record in Cuba and the Philippines was tarnished in the aftermath of the notorious Balangiga Massacre. Sent to assist the army in punishing those responsible for the incident at Balangiga, a battalion under the command of Maj. Littleton W. T. Waller, following the directive of the area army commander, Gen. Jacob Smith, set out to lay the heavy hand of war on the Island of Samar. In the three weeks that followed, Waller's battalion did exactly that.

Pursuing guerrilla forces, the marines attacked a nearly impregnable guerrilla stronghold situated on a high mountainside and, after a fierce fight, secured the position. Waller then took a mixed force of marines and Filipino scouts on a horrendous trek, searching for a suitable route to erect a telegraph line. By the time the scouts reached their destination, a dozen had died and the others, including Waller, had to be hospitalized.

Along the way, some of the natives employed to carry supplies apparently attacked one of the marine officers. Enraged, Waller ordered a dozen natives summarily shot. As a result of that incident, Waller was court-martialed. However, the court-martial was instituted by the army, which lacked official jurisdiction in the matter; the Marine Corps itself took no action. Nevertheless, the incident was a blemish on the record of the corps.

See also Balangiga Massacre; Crane, Stephen; Guantánamo, Battle of; Smith, Jacob Hurd.

References and Further Readings

Feuer, A. B. "Spanish Fleet Sacrificed at Santiago." *Military History*, vol. 15, no. 2, June 1998.

———. "The U.S. Marines at Guantánamo Bay." *Military Heritage*, vol. 1, no. 3, December 1999.

Linn, Brian McAllister. *The Philippine War, 1899–1902*. Lawrence: University Press of Kansas, 2000.

Millett, Allan R. *Semper Fidelis: The History of the United States Marine Corps*. New York: Macmillan Publishing, 1982.

Moskin, J. Robert. *U.S. Marine Corps Story*. New York: McGraw-Hill, 1977.

Shulimson, Jack. "Marines in the Spanish-American War." In James C. Bradford, ed. *Crucible of Empire: The Spanish-American War and Its Aftermath*, pp. 127–157. Annapolis, MD: Naval Institute Press, 1993.

Martí y Pérez, José (1853–1895)

Sometimes called "the Apostle" because he preached the gospel of Cuban independence, José Martí was the beacon that attracted all those who believed in the cause of liberating Cuba. Born in Havana, Martí was the son of a professional soldier. Although he was too young to participate in the Ten Years' War, which began in 1868, that futile struggle had an enormous impact on Martí, who cultivated and nurtured democratic ideals and the goal of Cuban independence. He began to write inflammatory essays and plays that were critical of Spanish authority and promoted Cuban independence, for which he was arrested and imprisoned.

Paroled and sent to Spain, Martí studied law and earned a degree in 1873. A true intellectual, he discovered a number of kindred spirits who also were devoted to the concept of a free and independent Cuba.

When the Ten Years' War ended, Martí returned to Havana, where he continued to agitate for Cuban independence. Arrested and deported once more, he went to New York City, which he found to be a fertile field in which to cultivate assistance for the Cuban cause. He remained in New York until 1895, raising money and organizing the Cuban Revolutionary Party. His efforts made him the central figure in the Cuban revolutionary movement. An idealist and visionary whose life was dedicated to the Cuban cause, Martí believed that Cuba should be built on democratic principles—principles that applied regardless of an individual's race. He drew to his ranks other notable Cuban revolutionaries, including Máximo Gómez and Antonio Maceo, the "Bronze Titan."

The Cuban War of Independence began with the *Grito de Baíre* in February 1895. In May, Martí arrived in Cuba from Florida, only to be killed in a battle at Dos Rios on 19 May. His loss was a tremendous blow to the revolutionary cause, but due in no small part to his unceasing labors on its behalf, the revolution was able to carry on without its most eloquent and determined spokesman.

See also Cuban Junta; Cuban Revolution; Gómez Báez, Máximo; Maceo Grajales, Antonio; Ten Years' War.

References and Further Readings

Foner, Philip S. *The Spanish-Cuban-American War.* 2 vols. New York: Monthly Review Press, 1972.

Gray, Richard B. *José Martí, Cuban Patriot.* Gainesville: University of Florida Press, 1962.

Kirk, John M. *José Martí: Mentor of the Cuban Nation.* Tampa: University Presses of Florida, 1983.

Thomas, Hugh. *Cuba: The Pursuit of Freedom.* New York: Harper & Row, 1971.

Martínez de Campos, Arsenio (1831–1900)

Arsenio Martínez de Campos was a veteran Spanish soldier and politician with a distinguished career. He achieved notable success in quelling the insurrection of the Ten Years' War. As a consequence, when revolution flared up again in 1895, he was sent back to Cuba as governor-general.

Believing that reform was Spain's only answer to the Cuban problems, Martínez fought for an end to slavery and a general softening of the stance toward the Cuban populace. He offered amnesty to the *insurrectos* and attempted to contain the revolution by establishing a line of trenches called *trochas*. Martínez believed he could win by distributing sufficient stocks of supplies at key points on the island and concentrating his forces in such a way as to isolate the revolutionaries. The strategy, however, failed, and Martínez was replaced by the notorious Gen. Valeriano "Butcher" Weyler.

See also Cuban Revolution; Ten Years' War; *Trocha*; Weyler y Nicolau, Valeriano "Butcher."

References and Further Readings

Foner, Philip S. *The Spanish-Cuban-American War.* 2 vols. New York: Monthly Review Press, 1972.

Musicant, Ivan. *Empire by Default: The Spanish-American War and the Dawn of the American Century.* New York: Henry Holt and Company, 1998.

Trask, David F. *The War with Spain in 1898.* Lincoln: University of Nebraska Press, 1996.

Massiquisie (Philippines), Battle of

See **Marinduque**

Matanzas (Cuba)

Matanzas, Cuba, a city in Matanzas Province, is located approximately 50 miles east of Havana on Matanzas Bay. In April 1898, following the declaration of war with Spain, the U.S. Navy blockaded the city; later, the city was bombarded by the *New York,* the *Puritan,* and the *Cincinnati.* Spanish batteries returned the fire. Although neither side inflicted any real damage on the other, the incident marked the first exchange of fire between the two countries.

See also Naval Blockade of Cuba; Naval Strategy, U.S.

References and Further Readings

Chadwick, Rear Adm. French Ensor. *Relations of the United States and Spain: The Spanish American War.* 2 vols. New York: Charles Scribner's Sons, 1911 (reprinted in 1968).

Musicant, Ivan. *Empire by Default: The Spanish-American War and the Dawn of the American Century.* New York: Henry Holt and Company, 1998.

Trask, David F. *The War with Spain in 1898.* Lincoln: University of Nebraska Press, 1996.

Maxfield, Joseph Edwin

See **Balloons**

Mayagüez (Puerto Rico), Battle of (10 August 1898)

One of the three largest cities in Puerto Rico, Mayagüez is located about 70 miles west of San Juan. During the Spanish-American War, the Spanish had not created any defensive works around Mayagüez, even though it was one of the key cities in Puerto Rico. At the outset of the Puerto Rican Campaign, Mayagüez was the target of Brig. Gen. Theodore Schwan's column, composed of elements of the Nineteenth Infantry and Fifth Cavalry and two batteries of artillery.

After landing at Yauco, Schwan advanced on Mayagüez. On 10 August 1898, his column captured the city after a brief engagement with the Spanish, who incurred some 50 casualties. U.S. losses amounted to 17.

> **See also** Miles, Nelson Appleton; Puerto Rican Campaign; Schwan, Theodore.
> **References and Further Readings**
> Beede, Benjamin R., ed. *The War of 1898 and U.S. Interventions, 1898–1934.* New York: Garland Publishing, 1994.
> Hermann, Karl S. *A Recent Campaign in Puerto Rico.* Boston: E. H. Bacon & Company, 1907.
> Musicant, Ivan. *Empire by Default: The Spanish-American War and the Dawn of the American Century.* New York: Henry Holt and Company, 1998.

McClernand, Edward John (1848–1926)

Born in Illinois, Edward John McClernand graduated from the U.S. Military Academy at West Point in 1870. He saw extensive service on the western frontier during the Indian wars and was awarded the Medal of Honor for action in the Battle of Bear Paw Mountains, Montana, in 1877.

By 1898, McClernand had risen to the rank of lieutenant colonel and was assigned to the staff of Gen. William Shafter, commanding the Fifth Corps in Cuba. During the Santiago Campaign, when Shafter, suffering from heat prostration and gout, was too ill to be at the front, McClernand was given the task of keeping the commander apprised of progress and developments.

In the attack on San Juan Heights, at least one of the senior officers, Gen. Jacob Kent, thought McClernand was indecisive. McClernand, however, was in an awkward situation because serving as Shafter's representative did not automatically mean he was fully deputized to issue orders on Shafter's behalf. Considering the circumstances, his caution might well be excused.

Later, when Shafter was contemplating a withdrawal from his position at Santiago because of the onset of the tropical disease season, McClernand, reasoning that the United States had nothing to lose, suggested first demanding the surrender of Santiago. After considering the idea, Shafter agreed to try that approach, and the Spanish eventually did surrender the city, though it proved to be a drawn-out process.

After the war, McClernand was promoted to brigadier general. He retired in 1912.

See also Kent, Jacob Ford; Santiago, Campaign and Siege of; Shafter, William Rufus.

References and Further Readings

McClernand, E. J. "The Santiago Campaign." *U.S. Infantry Journal,* vol. 21, no. 3, September 1922.

Musicant, Ivan. *Empire by Default: The Spanish-American War and the Dawn of the American Century.* New York: Henry Holt and Company, 1998.

Trask, David F. *The War with Spain in 1898.* Lincoln: University of Nebraska Press, 1996.

McCoy, Frank Ross (1874–1954)

An 1897 graduate of West Point, Frank Ross McCoy was a career army officer who proved equally adept as administrator, field commander, and diplomat. When the Spanish-American War erupted, McCoy was posted to the Tenth Cavalry, which was assigned to Gen. William R. Shafter's Fifth Corps—the Cuban Expeditionary Force. In the fighting for Kettle Hill during the Santiago Campaign, McCoy sustained a leg wound. Quite by chance, he was assisted in ministering to his wound by Col. Leonard Wood. McCoy was sent back to the United States to recover. He returned to Cuba in 1899 as part of the U.S. occupation force.

A second chance encounter with Leonard Wood (now a major general), who had returned to Cuba as military governor of Havana, led to McCoy's appointment as Wood's aide-de-camp. The relationship flourished. McCoy served his general well, and Wood became one of McCoy's career mentors.

In 1903, McCoy, now a captain, accompanied Wood to the Philippines. There, he was appointed intelligence officer in the Department of Mindanao and often participated in campaigns against the recalcitrant Moros. Three years later, in 1906, having gathered sufficient information from his various sources, McCoy led a small, elite force against the Moros, capturing the evasive leader Datu Ali.

An able, energetic officer, Frank Ross McCoy went on to serve in a number of responsible positions, both military and nonmilitary.

See also Moros; San Juan Hill, Charge up; Wood, Leonard.

References and Further Readings

Bacevich, A. J. *Diplomat in Khaki: Major General Frank Ross McCoy and American Foreign Policy, 1898–1949.* Lawrence: University Press of Kansas, 1989.

McKinley, William, Jr. (1843–1901)

The pivotal figure of the Spanish-American War, William McKinley Jr. was born in Niles, Ohio. His Civil War service as a young Ohio Volunteer officer had a profound impact on McKinley's life. Like many if not most soldiers, he developed a deep hatred of war. Nevertheless, he performed his duty ably and emerged from the war as a brevet major of volunteers.

After the Civil War, McKinley studied law and was admitted to the Ohio bar. In 1876, he ran for and was elected to the U.S. Congress as a Republican, and later, he served two terms as governor of Ohio. In 1896, he defeated William Jennings Bryan to become the twenty-fifth president of the United States.

In the century since the Spanish-American War, historians have debated and sharply differed over McKinley's presidency. In the first two decades following the war, scholars largely supported the McKinley administration for its able prosecution of the war and for the results of the Treaty of Paris, by which the United States acquired its first territorial possessions. Beginning about 1920, however, opinions began to diverge. Some saw McKinley as a reluctant expansionist, but others viewed him as a president who employed clever means to expand U.S. interests—a crafty politician who adroitly managed the acquisition of territorial possessions seemingly without wanting to do so.

The controversy is attributable in large part to the fact that historians have little knowledge of McKinley as a man. He left behind almost nothing in the way of personal correspondence, memos, or a diary through which historians might gain some access to his inner

President William McKinley (on the right) *and his advisers during the Spanish-American War.*

thoughts and feelings. Instead, to evaluate his presidency, scholars have had to rely on the recollections and observations of those with whom he worked closely. As a consequence, he remains something of an enigma, a controversial occupant of the White House during the transitional period when the United States moved onto the stage of international affairs.

When William McKinley took the oath of office in 1897, the Cuban War of Independence was already two years old and rapidly becoming a popular issue. Although the press of the day painted increasingly negative pictures of Spain's terrible treatment of the Cubans, McKinley moved cautiously in forming an official position about Spain.

By June 1897, McKinley, who had come to favor Cuban independence, officially demanded of Spain that Cubans be treated in a humane way. In so doing, the president departed from the position of strict neutrality to which his predecessor, Grover Cleveland, had adhered. As a result of McKinley's prodding, Spain did make an effort to improve relations with the Cubans by offering autonomy and repealing the hated *reconcentrado* policy. Neither McKinley nor the Cuban revolutionaries, however, were willing to accept anything less than full independence.

During the ensuing months, as tensions mounted, McKinley ordered the navy's Atlantic Squadron to Key West, Florida, as a signal to the Spanish government that the United States regarded the situation as serious. In addition, he directed the War and Navy Departments to prepare war plans.

The month of February 1898 saw publication of the famous de Lôme letter. Enrique de Lôme, Spanish ambassador to the United States, wrote a letter highly critical of McKinley, which was intercepted by the Cuban junta and turned over to the *New York Journal*. In the letter, de Lôme called McKinley a spineless politician, a president with no backbone. This was a careless and utterly foolish thing for the Spanish ambassador to do, and upon publication of the letter he promptly tendered his resignation . Amazingly, McKinley himself remained remarkably composed about de Lôme's remarks— undoubtedly more so than his successor, Theodore Roosevelt, would have done. Publication of the de Lôme letter was followed by the second provocative event that month, when the battleship *Maine* blew up in Havana harbor on the night of 15 February, further inflaming public opinion against Spain.

After the destruction of the *Maine,* McKinley pushed through legislation known as the Fifty Million Dollar Bill. The bill was designed to prepare the nation's military services for war.

On 11 April, with negotiations to resolve the Cuban crisis clearly having failed, McKinley requested a declaration of war from Congress, which authorized armed intervention in Cuba on 19 April. Three days later, on 22 April, the president initiated a naval blockade of Cuba, and Congress thereupon officially declared war on Spain, effective as of 21 April.

Overall, McKinley's conduct of the war was efficient, especially in the area of communications. He created the nation's first official war room in the White House. President Abraham Lincoln had spent hours in the military telegraph office, keeping himself updated on the progress of the Civil War. McKinley took that concept to the next stage. The war room was set up to accommodate 25 telegraph lines and 15 special telephone lines, through which McKinley kept close personal tabs on developments in Cuba.

With the exception of Secretary of War Russell Alger, McKinley's relationship with his cabinet was generally harmonious. Alger, who performed well enough in a prewar bureaucratic environment, proved to be a poor choice to manage the War Department under the stress of conflict. McKinley came to rely on him less and less. He also came to avoid General of the Army Nelson Miles, whose frequent squabbling with Alger caused McKinley to turn increasingly to Adj. Gen. Henry Corbin for military advice. By contrast, McKinley worked well with Secretary of the Navy John D. Long.

Militarily, the war proved to be far less challenging than negotiating the final peace treaty with Spain. The Philippines turned out to be the sticking point. Had it not been for the U.S. acquisition of the Philippines, McKinley's role in history surely would be much less controversial. At one point early on, McKinley professed to not know the exact location of the Philippines—a remark he perhaps did not intend to be taken literally. He seems to have agonized a great deal as to whether the United States should retain just the port city of Manila, the island of Luzon, or the entire Philippine Archipelago.

Also, a strong argument arose against the United States taking *any* part of the Philippines because to do so would run counter to U.S. constitutional philosophy. In the end, McKinley reasoned that the islands should not be returned to Spain and that if the United States did not take them, Germany or Japan surely would. Thus, he concluded that the United States should take all of the Philippines, and he instructed his peace commissioners in Paris to stand firm on that point. Because Spain had little bargaining power, it had no choice but to accede to U.S. demands. In addition to the Philippines, the United States acquired Puerto Rico and Guam in the Marianas Islands. The terms of the Treaty of Paris further required Spain to evacuate Cuba and called for the United States to oversee that island's preparation for independent government.

If William McKinley was not the most controversial occupant of the White House, he is certainly one of the most difficult presidents to know. Pleasant and affable, with a wry sense of humor and a fondness for cigars, he somehow appeared more like a country judge than a president of the United States. For all that, however, he was an astute politician, who, if he seemed at times indecisive, was fully in charge. His office was open to nearly everyone who wished to see him, and he was the first president to establish a regular format for providing the media with White House news.

McKinley was shot on 6 September 1901 during his second term of office by anarchist Leon Czolgosz. He died eight days later. This tragic event ruled out the possibility of his further elaborating on some of the controversial issues of his presidency, such as the acquisition of the Philippines.

See also Alger, Russell Alexander; Dupuy de Lôme, Enrique; Long, John Davis; Philippine Islands, Acquisition of, by the United States; Spanish-American War, U.S. Public Reaction to; Treaty of Paris.

References and Further Readings

Gould, Lewis L. *The Spanish-American War and President McKinley.* Lawrence: University of Kansas Press, 1982.

Leech, Margaret. *In the Days of McKinley.* New York: Harper & Brothers, 1959.

Morgan, H. Wayne, ed. *Making Peace with Spain: The Diary of Whitelaw Reid—September–December, 1898.* Austin: University of Texas Press, 1965.

Musicant, Ivan. *Empire by Default: The Spanish-American War and the Dawn of the American Century.* New York: Henry Holt and Company, 1998.

Smith, Ephraim K. "William McKinley's Enduring Legacy." In James C. Bradford, ed. *Crucible of Empire: The Spanish-American War and Its Aftermath,* pp. 205–250. Annapolis, MD: Naval Institute Press, 1993.

Media Coverage

See **Journalism**

Medical Department, U.S. Army

At the time of the Spanish-American War, the U.S. Army found itself overwhelmed in responding to the needs of a rapidly expanding force. The Medical Department stands as a striking example of the War Department's lack of preparedness to meet the challenge.

Doctors were not highly regarded within the military hierarchy. Indeed, they did not even carry military rank until the 1880s. Many senior commanders tended to see doctors as wanting to mollycoddle the troops. In camp and in the field, army surgeons had no real authority to insist that sanitary standards be maintained.

As the nineteenth century drew to a close, the medical profession was still largely ignorant about the real cause of typhoid fever and tropical diseases. As a consequence, the medical treatment provided for soldiers stricken with these illnesses was totally ineffective.

To make matters worse, the army's top medical man, Surgeon General George Sternberg, was ill suited to the task of running the Medical Department. As one historian has observed, Sternberg was an outstanding research scientist but lacked the administrative skills necessary to manage his department effectively.

Along with the other bureaus in the War Department, the Medical Department completely lacked the resources to provide the supplies required by the army's mobilization to wartime strength. Moreover, the infrastructure for getting the supplies and equipment to the new

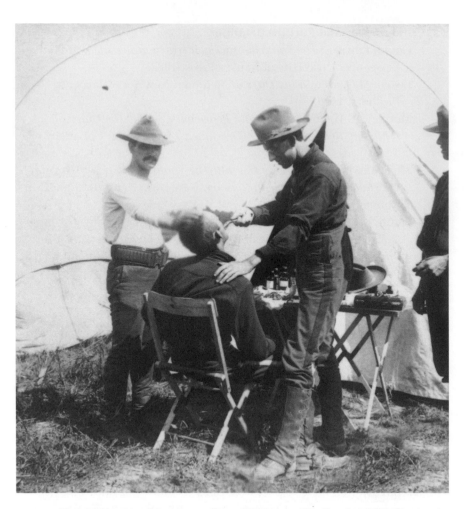

assembly camps and later to Gen. William Shafter's Fifth Corps in Cuba simply did not exist. Also, there was a critical shortage of surgeons, which compelled General Sternberg to employ civilian doctors on a contract basis, often without a close enough look at their qualifications.

In 1898, the Medical Department included a Hospital Corps of some 700 well-trained field aides, who functioned as the medics and corpsmen of that day. They were trained to administer first aid, bear stretchers, drive ambulances, and perform other medically related duties as needed. The rapid expansion of the army in 1898 also was felt in the Hospital Corps, whose numbers increased rapidly to nearly 6,000. During the Spanish-American War, the army employed female nurses in field hospitals for the first time.

Although the establishment of division field hospitals had worked well enough for the army in the Civil War, the system broke down during the Spanish-American War because of the shortage of equipment, surgeons, and other trained medical personnel. Like the rest of the army, the Medical Department performed about as well as could be expected given the conditions of the time and the limitations under which it operated. To its credit, the department was eminently successful in setting up a first-rate hospital ship, the *Relief,* which saw service in the Caribbean.

See also Diseases; Sternberg, George Miller.

References and Further Readings

Ashburn, Percy M. *A History of the Medical Department of the United States Army.* Boston: Houghton Mifflin, 1929.

Cosmas, Graham. *An Army for Empire: The United States Army in the Spanish-American War.* College Station: Texas A&M University Press, 1998.

Sternberg, George M. *Sanitary Lessons of the War.* Washington, DC: Byron S. Adams, 1912.

Meriwether, Walter Scott

See Maine

Merrimac

Named after the famous Civil War ironclad, the *Merrimac* was a naval collier—a ship that carried coal to resupply other ships. Originally named the *Solveig,* it was one of a number of privately owned vessels the U.S. Navy purchased to augment its fleet when war with Spain seemed imminent. At the time of its purchase, it was renamed the *Merrimac.*

When the U.S. fleet moved into Cuban waters, the *Merrimac* had to be towed because of persistent mechanical problems. Later, when a plan was devised to block Adm. Pascual Cervera's Spanish Squadron in Santiago harbor by scuttling a ship in the harbor entrance, the *Merrimac* was chosen for the mission, for it was considered expendable. Its last commander was Lt. Richmond Pearson Hobson who, with a crew of seven, entered the harbor in the early morning hours of 3 June. Fire from Spanish shore batteries subsequently disabled the *Merrimac,* and it had to be scuttled, though short of the spot where it would have blocked passage of the Spanish ships out of Santiago harbor.

See also Hobson, Richmond Pearson; Santiago de Cuba, Naval Battle of.

References and Further Readings

Chadwick, Rear Adm. French Ensor. *Relations of the United States and Spain: The Spanish American War.* 2 vols. New York: Charles Scribner's Sons, 1911 (reprinted in 1968).

Feuer, A. B. *The Spanish-American War at Sea.* Westport, CT: Greenwood Press, 1995.

Hobson, Richmond Pearson. *The Sinking of the* Merrimac. New York: n.p., 1900.

Merritt, Wesley (1834–1910)

Wesley Merritt was born in New York and at age 15 moved to southern Illinois with his family. Entering the U.S. Military Academy at West Point in 1855, he graduated in 1860. Merritt's was the only class to spend five years at the academy. Following a distinguished career as a Civil War cavalry leader, Merritt served with further distinction on the western frontier during the Indian wars. By the time of the Spanish-American War in 1898, Merritt, now a major general, had become the army's number two soldier, second only to General of the Army Nelson Miles.

Gen. Wesley Merritt, center, and staff aboard the steamer Newport, *en route to Manila, 1898.*

In May of 1898, Merritt was appointed to command the Eighth Corps, slated for duty in the Philippines. The Philippine Expeditionary Force sailed in three sections, as ships were available. Merritt himself arrived in late July with the third contingent.

By the time of Merritt's arrival, Spanish forces in the Manila area were effectively contained on land by troops from the first two contingents of his Eighth Corps and by the Filipino Nationalist forces of Emilio Aguinaldo. In addition, the ships of Adm. George Dewey's Asiatic Squadron controlled the waters of Manila Bay, where they had scored their great victory on 1 May 1898.

Merritt arrived in the Philippines under orders not to recognize or make arrangements with the Filipino Nationalists. President William McKinley wanted to avoid involving the Nationalists in treaty negotiations with Spain.

After discussing the situation, Merritt and Dewey agreed that the attack on Manila should commence as soon as possible. How to neutralize Aguinaldo's army, however, was another matter. The question was resolved during a secret meeting between Merritt, Dewey, and the Spanish commander, Gen. Fermín Jáudenes. Jáudenes, recognizing the hopelessness of his position, agreed to surrender after a token fight in which Spanish honor would be salved, provided that Dewey's warships did not bombard Manila and that Aguinaldo's troops were not allowed to enter the city.

Merritt did not reveal the terms of the agreement to his field commanders, Gen. Francis Greene and Gen. Arthur MacArthur, because he wanted the efforts to appear genuine rather than staged. The attack was brought off successfully on 13 August, although the fighting proved real enough, especially in MacArthur's sector, where the United States suffered nearly 50 casualties. And with few exceptions, Aguinaldo's men were prevented from entering Manila despite angry protests by the Filipinos. Merritt was unaware that the Protocol of Peace (cease-fire) between the United States and Spain actually had been agreed to the day before.

General Merritt subsequently was named military governor of Manila, but at his own request he was replaced in the fall by his deputy, Gen. Elwell Otis. At President McKinley's direction, Merritt proceeded to Paris, where he was to provide U.S. peace commissioners with his views on the Philippines and recommendations regarding the U.S. acquisition thereof.

Merritt retired from active duty in 1900. He was an able and energetic soldier, whose career bridged the half century between the Civil War and America's emergence as a world power.

See also Aguinaldo y Famy, Emilio; Dewey, George; Greene, Francis Vinton; MacArthur, Arthur; Manila Bay, Battle of; Manila, First Battle of; Philippine Expeditionary Force.

References and Further Readings

Alberts, Don E. *Brandy Station to Manila Bay: A Biography of General Wesley Merritt.* Austin, TX: Presidial Press, 1980.

Musicant, Ivan. *Empire by Default: The Spanish-American War and the Dawn of the American Century.* New York: Henry Holt and Company, 1998.

Wolff, Leon. *Little Brown Brother: America's Forgotten Bid for Empire Which Cost 250,000 Lives.* New York: Kraus Reprint, 1970.

"A Message to Garcia"

See **Rowan, Andrew Summers**

Miles, Evan

See **El Caney, Battle of**

Miles, Nelson Appleton (1839–1925)

One of the celebrated military figures in U.S. history and a key individual in the Spanish-American War, Nelson Appleton Miles was born on a farm near Westminster, Massachusetts. At the outbreak of the Civil War, he was appointed a lieutenant of volunteers but rose quickly in rank, demonstrating a natural capacity for battlefield leadership. After the war, he served with equal distinction on the western frontier during the Indian wars. By 1895, he had risen to the post of general of the army, and he was the nation's number one soldier when war with Spain was declared.

Miles was opposed to war, believing that diplomacy could have resolved the differences between Spain and the United States. Like most professional military men, he held the strong opinion that the job of conducting a war was best left to the regular army rather than to an army of volunteers—an interesting perspective, as Miles had himself risen from the volunteer ranks.

Although not opposed per se to the use of volunteers, Miles thought an invasion of Cuba ought to be carried out by regular troops, with volunteers replacing the regulars at home. There, they would garrison the coast defense works, which were deemed an essential part of U.S. strategy because of the concern that Spain would attack the coastline. Miles also objected to an invasion of Cuba during the summer, the tropical disease season.

Originally, U.S. strategy focused on Havana, but Miles persuaded President William McKinley that the city was not a good choice because it was the strongest Spanish position on the island. The revised strategy that finally emerged settled on Santiago de Cuba, which made far more sense to Miles. He had argued, however, for postponing an invasion of Cuba until the Spanish fleet was destroyed. Unlike his boss, Secretary of War Russell Alger, with whom he was continually at odds throughout the war, Miles recognized the inherent impracticality of expanding the nation's army to several times its prewar strength and expecting to employ it virtually overnight.

Miles seemed to have a realistic understanding of the problems to be overcome in creating and organizing a large army. At his recommendation, regulars were assembled at New Orleans, Mobile, and Tampa. Volunteers were first brought together at staging areas in their respective states, then moved to federal camps, such as Camp Thomas, Chickamauga.

Miles supported the choice of Gen. William R. Shafter to command the Cuban Expeditionary Force (the Fifth Corps). In July 1898, Miles, undoubtedly chafing at not having a more active role in the war, visited Shafter in Cuba. To Miles's credit, he did not interfere in the operations there, even though, as commanding general, he was Shafter's superior.

Once Santiago capitulated, Miles was given the green light to proceed with the invasion of Puerto Rico, an assignment he had coveted early on. Indeed, Miles had originally argued for an invasion of Puerto Rico before attempting to seize Cuba.

Originally, Miles had planned to land at Fajardo on the east coast of Puerto Rico, but en route, he changed his mind because of anticipated heavy losses. On 25 July 1898, his forces landed instead at Guánica on the southwest coast. The campaign proved virtually bloodless, and the island was secured in three weeks. The end of the war brought an end to the campaign.

In the aftermath of the war, Miles was the central figure in the notorious beef scandal. He alleged that the Commissary Department had issued spoiled beef to the troops, but others claimed that the

Lt. Gen. Nelson Appleton Miles. He served with great distinction in the Civil War and Indian wars and was eventually named commanding general of the army, a post he held at the time of the Spanish-American War.

meat was safe, just not very palatable. Testimony was presented to the Dodge Commission, headed by former Civil War general and railroad builder Grenville Dodge.

Miles's allegations stung and elicited a fiery response from Commissary General Charles P. Eagan, who launched a tirade against Miles. Eagan was severely reprimanded for his outburst. However, Miles himself did not emerge unscathed. He, too, was reprimanded by the Dodge Commission for making charges that were proven to be substantially unfounded. Miles's old enemy, Secretary of War Alger, sought to take advantage of the situation by requesting that Miles be relieved of his command—a request that President McKinley denied.

In 1901, Miles was promoted to lieutenant general and retired two years later. Vain, ambitious to a fault, and contentious, Miles, despite his leadership qualities on the field of battle, was a commanding general who displayed little political savvy. Because of his continual squabbling with Alger and others, President McKinley came to rely on his counsel less and less. Theodore Roosevelt, who also crossed swords with Miles, called him "a brave peacock."

See also Alger, Russell Alexander; Army, U.S.; Beef Scandal; Eagan, Charles Patrick; McKinley, William, Jr.; Puerto Rican Campaign; Roosevelt, Theodore; Shafter, William Rufus.

References and Further Readings

Cosmas, Graham. *An Army for Empire: The United States Army in the Spanish-American War.* College Station: Texas A&M University Press, 1998.

DeMontravel, Peter R. *A Hero to His Fighting Men: Nelson A. Miles, 1839–1925.* Kent, OH: Kent State University Press, 1998.

Johnson, Virginia. *The Unregimented General: A Biography of Nelson A. Miles.* Boston: Houghton Mifflin, 1962.

Miles, Nelson A. *Personal Recollections and Observations of General Nelson A. Miles.* 2 vols. Lincoln: University of Nebraska Press, 1992.

Miley, John David (1862–1899)

Born in Illinois, John David Miley graduated from West Point in 1883. His first assignment was in the field artillery. During the Spanish-American War, he served as aide to Gen. William R. Shafter in Cuba.

In the advance on Santiago, when Shafter was too ill to travel, Miley was chosen to carry Shafter's orders to the front. Later, he served as Shafter's representative a second time. On that occasion, Miley met with foreign nationals to discuss the evacuation of civilians from Santiago.

Miley served as a commissioner during the negotiations that led to the release of Lt. Richmond P. Hobson, captured by the Spanish after his ill-fated attempt to scuttle the collier *Merrimac* and thereby block the entrance to Santiago harbor. Along with Gen. Joseph Wheeler and Gen. Henry Lawton, Miley was a signatory to the Capitulation Agreement of Santiago and received the surrender of other Spanish commanders.

Miley was promoted to lieutenant colonel and inspector general of volunteers in September 1898. He died in December 1899.

See also Capitulation Agreement, Santiago de Cuba; Santiago, Campaign and Siege of; Shafter, William Rufus.

References and Further Readings

Chadwick, Rear Adm. French Ensor. *Relations of the United States and Spain: The Spanish American War.* 2 vols. New York: Charles Scribner's Sons, 1911 (reprinted in 1968).

Heitman, Francis B. *Historical Register and Dictionary of the United States Army, 1789–1903.* 2 vols. Urbana: University of Illinois Press, 1965.

Miley, John D. *In Cuba with Shafter.* New York: Charles Scribner's Sons, 1899.

O'Toole, G. J. A. *The Spanish War: An American Epic, 1898.* New York: W. W. Norton, 1984.

Military Intelligence, U.S.

The acquisition of information about enemy movements and the application of that knowledge to strategic and tactical aims played a pivotal role in the U.S. prosecution of the Spanish-American War. Although espionage tactics were not considered ethical during peacetime, there was a concerted effort to collect and evaluate information regarding Spain's prosecution of the war. Indeed, even before the declaration of hostilities, the United States sought and received information about Spain through military attachés and foreign office consuls.

The navy had created the Office of Naval Intelligence (ONI) in 1882, and the army founded its own Military Information Division (MID) in 1889. Neither agency, however, could be thought of as a sophisticated intelligence-gathering department as that term is understood today.

The ONI was the older and larger of the two agencies and the most aggressive as well; it worked to decipher Spanish cable transmissions and planted false information about U.S. intentions and ship movements. The ONI also had the advantage of having the information it collected assessed by the Naval War College, which had been created in 1884 to provide an intellectual forum for officers to analyze, study, and debate naval strategy and tactics. By contrast, the MID had no comparable institution with which to work. As war with Spain became imminent and the navy recognized the need for more ships, ONI operators worked to purchase foreign vessels.

The navy also had in place a unique system to receive intelligence information out of Cuba. Through Martin Hellings, manager of the International Ocean Telegraph in Key West, and through a Cuban patriot in Havana, Domingo Villaverde, valuable information regarding Spanish activities in Cuba was made available to the United States. Interestingly enough, only President William McKinley and a handful of others had access to that information.

See also Hellings, Martin Luther; Naval Strategy, U.S.

References and Further Readings

O'Toole, G. J. A. *The Spanish War: An American Epic, 1898.* New York: W. W. Norton, 1984.

Trask, David. "American Intelligence during the Spanish-American War." In James C. Bradford, ed. *Crucible of Empire: The Spanish-American War and Its Aftermath,* pp. 23–46. Annapolis, MD: Naval Institute Press, 1993.

Militia

See **Army, U.S.; Militia, Naval**

Militia Act of 1903

The confusion that accompanied the call-up of volunteers during the Spanish-American War underscored a fundamental weakness in the U.S. system of wartime mobilization. That weakness led to the passage of the Militia Act of January 1903, also known as the Dick Act for its author, Sen. Charles W. Dick of Ohio. The 1903 act replaced the old Militia Act of 1792, which had been in effect at the time of the Spanish-American War.

Elihu Root, who replaced Russell Alger as secretary of war, was the driving force behind the new militia act, as well as other army reform measures. The new act created a militia system that was set up in two parts: the Reserve Militia and the Organized Militia. Although both were operated by the states, the Organized Militia received federal funding and could be activated by the president for a nine-month term of service.

The act of 1903 was a step in the right direction and sought to eliminate confusion about state militia units and how they best fit in with the army's needs in time of national emergency. But the confusion would not be completely eliminated until the Armed Forces Reserve Act of 1952 introduced a clear and coherent picture of how reserves and the National Guard could be utilized most effectively.

See also Alger, Russell Alexander; Army, U.S.; Hull Bill; Root, Elihu.

References and Further Readings

Cooper, Jerry. *The Rise of the National Guard: The Evolution of the American Militia, 1865–1920.* Lincoln: University of Nebraska Press, 1997.

Cosmas, Graham. *An Army for Empire: The United States Army in the Spanish-American War.* College Station: Texas A&M University Press, 1998.

Militia, Naval

Although the bulk of mobilization for the Spanish-American War involved ground forces, the U.S. Navy also reinforced its cadre of regulars. Late in March 1898, state naval militias were requested to supply crews and officers for duty. Approximately 2,600 men eventually were called up. Most of these individuals were assigned to some kind of coastal defense duty, including an auxiliary force known as the Mosquito Squadron, which helped patrol the eastern U.S. coastline. Later, some individuals also served in Cuban waters. Interestingly, of all the states, Illinois had the largest contingent of naval militiamen serving in Cuban waters.

See also Auxiliary Squadron, U.S. Navy.

References and Further Readings

Chadwick, Rear Adm. French Ensor. *Relations of the United States and Spain: The Spanish American War.* 2 vols. New York: Charles Scribner's Sons, 1911 (reprinted in 1968).

Trask, David F. *The War with Spain in 1898.* Lincoln: University of Nebraska Press, 1996.

Mindanao (Philippine Islands)

The southernmost and second largest island in the Philippine Archipelago, Mindanao covers about 36,000 square miles, most of which is mountainous and heavily forested. At the time of the Spanish-American War, approximately one-third of the people on Mindanao were Muslims—called *Moros* by the Spanish.

During the Paris Peace Talks, opinion was divided among the U.S. representatives. For example, Sen. William P. Frye and Sen. George Gray held the opinion that the southern portion of the Philippine Archipelago—Mindanao and the Sulu Islands—should be left to Spain or ceded to Holland (which already had colonies in that part of the world and, it was thought, would not prove to be an unfriendly neighbor). But when President William McKinley elected to acquire all of the Philippines, the U.S. commissioners supported his position. This ultimately resulted in the United States assuming control of the entire archipelago.

During the years 1902 and 1903, Mindanao was the scene of severe fighting between the U.S. Army and rebellious Moros, who proved to be the most difficult of all the Filipinos to subjugate.

> **See also** Baldwin, Frank Dwight; Lake Lanao Campaigns; Moros; Pershing, John Joseph; Treaty of Paris.
>
> **References and Further Readings**
>
> Linn, Brian McAllister. *The Philippine War, 1899–1902.* Lawrence: University Press of Kansas, 2000.
>
> Morgan, H. Wayne, ed. *Making Peace with Spain: The Diary of Whitelaw Reid—September–December, 1898.* Austin: University of Texas Press, 1965.
>
> Smythe, Donald. *Guerrilla Warrior: The Early Life of John J. Pershing.* New York: Charles Scribner's Sons, 1973.

Monroe Doctrine

The Monroe Doctrine, one of the best-known policy statements in U.S. history, was first promulgated during the administration of President James Monroe. The doctrine essentially warned European nations that the era of colonization in the Western Hemisphere was over and that the United States would not tolerate either colonization or interference in that part of the world. The Monroe Doctrine did not bear directly on the Spanish-American War, but its existence as a statement of U.S. policy in the Western Hemisphere was always acknowledged.

Although President William McKinley did not feel obliged to invoke the Monroe Doctrine during the Spanish-American War, his fear that an independent Cuba might prove irresistible to some European nation compelled him to take the position that before Cuba would be granted full independence, it must be ready to function as a stable, democratic nation.

Unlike Cuba, Puerto Rico had remained largely quiet and untroubled. Expansionists in the United States argued for the acquisition of Cuba, but they were outnumbered by those who favored Cuban independence. Despite all of the rhetoric about the Philippines, the Anti-Expansionists were rather blasé about the acquisition of Puerto Rico, although it, too, might have proved a tempting target to a European nation looking to expand. Thus, the guiding precepts of the Monroe Doctrine played a role in the negotiations that led to the final dispositions of Cuba and Puerto Rico.

See also Anti-Imperialist League; Imperialism/Expansionism; McKinley, William, Jr.

References and Further Readings

Leech, Margaret. *In the Days of McKinley.* New York: Harper & Brothers, 1959.

O'Toole, G. J. A. *The Spanish War: An American Epic, 1898.* New York: W. W. Norton, 1984.

Montero Ríos, Don Eugenio (1832–1914)

Born near Madrid, Don Eugenio Montero Ríos was one of the most influential members of Spain's Liberal Party. A jurist and a former minister, he was a man of great refinement and wide experience. It was clear to Montero Ríos that Spain could not hope to win a war with the United States, and shortly after the declaration of hostilities, he proposed to Premier Práxedes Mateo Sagasta that Spain enter into immediate negotiations, with the hope of arranging a more favorable settlement than would be the case if it were to lose the war. Montero Ríos's proposal was rejected.

After the hostilities ceased, Montero Ríos was appointed president of the Spanish commission during the Paris Peace Talks. In an effort to wrest more favorable terms for his country, he employed delaying tactics. He was willing to offer up Cuba, the Philippines, and Puerto Rico, provided that the United States agree to pay for the entire cost of the war—a proposal the U.S. commissioners rejected. A hard bargainer, Montero Ríos was displeased with the final treaty.

Upon the death of Sagasta in 1905, Montero Ríos became premier of Spain and leader of the country's Liberal Party.

See also Philippine Archipelago; Spain; Treaty of Paris.

References and Further Readings

Montero Ríos, Don Eugenio. *El Tratado de Paris* (The Treaty of Paris). Madrid: Valesco, 1947.

Morgan, H. Wayne, ed. *Making Peace with Spain: The Diary of Whitelaw Reid—September–December, 1898.* Austin: University of Texas Press, 1965.

Montgomery

See **Naval Vessels, U.S., Auxiliary**

Montojo y Pasarón, Patricio (1839–1917)

A veteran naval officer, intellectual, novelist, and essayist, Adm. Patricio Montojo y Pasarón commanded the Spanish fleet in the Philippines. Like other Spanish commanders, both in Cuba and the Philippines, Montojo had few options from which to choose in prosecuting the Spanish-American War. Although his contingent outnumbered Commodore George Dewey's Asiatic Squadron, most of the vessels under Montojo's command were small and lightly armed, being employed mainly for interisland traffic. Of the ships under his command, seven were capable of offering a real defense against Dewey, whose ships were better protected and mounted more powerful batteries.

Originally, Montojo's strategy was to challenge Dewey in Subig (Subic) Bay, about 60 miles west of Manila. But when a personal reconnaissance revealed the lack of preparedness in that area, he revised his strategy and elected to confront Dewey in Manila Bay.

Following the virtual destruction of his fleet in the 1 May 1898 Battle of Manila Bay, during which he was wounded in the leg, Montojo withdrew to the city of Manila. There, he continued to exercise his command responsibilities until the surrender of the city on 13 August.

Montojo returned to Spain, where he subsequently was court-martialed for having allowed the destruction of his squadron, and was ordered to retire from active duty. Montojo later wrote an account of the Battle of Manila Bay.

See also Asiatic Squadron, U.S. Navy; Dewey, George; Manila Bay, Battle of.

References and Further Readings

Chadwick, Rear Adm. French Ensor. *Relations of the United States and Spain: The Spanish American War.* 2 vols. New York: Charles Scribner's Sons, 1911 (reprinted in 1968).

Montojo, Patricio. "El desastre de Cavite, sus causas y sus efectos" (The cause and effect of the disaster at Cavite). *La España Moderna,* 1909.

Trask, David F. *The War with Spain in 1898.* Lincoln: University of Nebraska Press, 1996.

Moret y Prendergast, Segismundo (1838–1913)

An attorney and veteran politican, Segismundo Moret y Prendergast came from a distinguished Spanish family and was educated in England. In October 1897, he was appointed *ministro de ultramar* (colonial minister) during the regime of Práxedes Mateo Sagasta, replacing Valeriano "Butcher" Weyler. However, when the war broke out, he was himself replaced because of his opposition to the conflict. A steadfast believer in Cuban autonomy, Moret sought to turn around the situation on the island by offering the Cubans a wide range of freedoms and reforms. Under his proposal, the Cubans would elect their own governing councils and parliament and would have complete control of internal affairs, including education, public works, agriculture, and industry. Spain would continue to exercise control of the military and the judicial system, as well as the relationship between church and state.

Moret also believed that peace with the United States could be achieved through negotiation. Because of his strong pacification position, he fell out of favor after the declaration of war with the United States and was replaced by Vicente Romero Girón. After Sagasta's death in 1903, Moret served as prime minister.

See also Cuban Revolution; Sagasta, Práxedes Mateo; Spain; Weyler y Nicolau, Valeriano "Butcher."

References and Further Readings

Foner, Philip S. *The Spanish-Cuban-American War.* 2 vols. New York: Monthly Review Press, 1972.

Musicant, Ivan. *Empire by Default: The Spanish-American War and the Dawn of the American Century.* New York: Henry Holt and Company, 1998.

Morgan-Cameron Resolution (April 1896)

Although the U.S. Congress passed the Morgan-Cameron Resolution two years prior to the outbreak of hostilities with Spain, the measure was nevertheless significant in that it served as an indicator—a barometer—of the congressional mood with respect to Spain and the events in Cuba.

In February 1896, Sen. John T. Morgan of Alabama, a Democrat and Expansionist, and Sen. Donald Cameron of Pennsylvania, a Republican, joined forces to propose a resolution recognizing Cuban "belligerency" (which meant to recognize its status among nations). The resolution further sought to achieve peace in Cuba through Cuban independence.

The Morgan-Cameron Resolution was passed on 6 April 1896, following two months of debate. Though it did not carry the force of law, the resolution did serve notice to President Grover Cleveland's administration that the situation in Cuba had become a national issue. It also gave the president evidence how Congress felt about the matter.

See also Cuban Revolution; Spanish-American War, U.S. Public Reaction to.

References and Further Readings

Foner, Philip S. *The Spanish-Cuban-American War.* 2 vols. New York: Monthly Review Press, 1972.

O'Toole, G. J. A. *The Spanish War: An American Epic, 1898.* New York: W. W. Norton, 1984.

Moro Campaigns (Philippines)

See **Lake Lanao Campaigns**

Moros

The Muslim tribes of Mindanao and the Sulu Archipelago were called *Moros* by the Spanish, who thought they bore a strong resemblance to the Moors of North Africa. Of all the native inhabitants of the Philippines, the Moros perhaps were the fiercest and most recalcitrant. From the time of the earliest Spanish arrivals, the Moros had resisted, waging a continuous jihad, or holy war, against Christians, whom they were sworn to kill. That attitude carried over to the Americans when they arrived in the Philippines during the Spanish-American War. Wearing gaudy turbans and often attacking in mass waves, bran-

Native Moros, Zamboanga Province, Mindanao, 1900.

dishing knives and spears, the Moros presented a fearsome appearance.

In the so-called Bates Treaty of 1899, Gen. John C. Bates established a more or less harmonious relationship with the Moros by promising financial rewards and religious freedom in exchange for an end to the Moros slave trade and pirate activities. The treaty worked well enough until it was repealed by Gen. Leonard Wood in 1902. Wood believed that a stricter, more disciplined approach was needed in dealing with the Moros.

From 1902 to 1903, U.S. forces under Col. Frank D. Baldwin and Capt. John J. Pershing fought a series of fierce battles with the Moros in the Lake Lanao region of Mindanao. These actions effectively ended Moro resistance to U.S. rule.

See also Baldwin, Frank Dwight; Bates, John Coalter; Bates Treaty; Bud Bagsak, Battle of; Bud Daju, Battle of; Lake Lanao Campaigns; Pershing, John Joseph.

References and Further Readings

Karnow, Stanley. *In Our Image: America's Empire in the Philippines.* New York: Random House, 1989.

Smythe, Donald. *Guerrilla Warrior: The Early Life of John J. Pershing.* New York: Charles Scribner's Sons, 1973.

Steinbach, Robert H. *A Long March: The Lives of Frank and Alice Baldwin.* Austin: University of Texas Press, 1989.

Steinberg, David Joel. *The Philippines: A Singular and a Plural Place.* Boulder, CO: Westview Press, 1994.

Morro Castle (Cuba)

See **Morro Heights**

Morro Heights (Cuba)

The narrow channel leading into the harbor at Santiago de Cuba—at one point only 350 feet wide—was mined. It was also guarded by the lower and upper Socapa batteries on the west side and on the east by the Punta Gorda, Estrella, and Morro batteries. The eastern batteries were situated on the high ground known as Morro Heights. The Morro battery was adjacent to Morro Castle, from which it drew its name. During the Spanish-American War, the overall defense of Morro Heights was the responsibility of the Spanish Army. The U.S. Navy wanted Gen. William R. Shafter's Fifth Corps to secure the heights and clear the mines from the channel, following which the navy would be able to enter the harbor and attack Adm. Pascual Cervera's Spanish fleet.

General Shafter, however, concluded that a more effective strategy would be to attack Santiago directly, at the same time deceiving the Spanish into believing that his target was Morro Heights.

As a sidelight, Lt. Richmond P. Hobson, a naval constructor (one whose specialty is naval architecture) was captured and temporarily imprisoned in Morro Castle by the Spanish after his ill-fated attempt to blockade Santiago harbor by scuttling the collier *Merrimac* in the channel.

See also Hobson, Richmond Pearson; *Merrimac*; Sampson, William Thomas; Santiago de Cuba, Naval Battle of; Shafter, William Rufus.
References and Further Readings
Sampson, Rear Adm. William T. "The Atlantic Fleet in the Spanish War." *Century Magazine,* April 1899.
Shafter, Maj. Gen. William R., U.S.V. "The Capture of Santiago de Cuba." *Century Magazine,* February 1899.
Trask, David F. *The War with Spain in 1898.* Lincoln: University of Nebraska Press, 1996.

Mosquito Squadron, Navy

See **Auxiliary Squadron, U.S. Navy**

National Guard

See **Army, U.S.**

Naval Blockade (U.S.) of Cuba

On 23 April 1898, Spain declared war on the United States. Forty-eight hours later, on 25 April, President William McKinley asked Congress for a formal declaration of war against Spain. Congress promptly granted the request, making the declaration retroactive to 21 April.

Meanwhile on that same day (21 April), McKinley ordered a naval blockade of major Cuban ports on the north side of the island, which was all that the navy's immediate resources could handle. In accordance with that directive, Capt. William T. Sampson, commanding the U.S. Navy's North Atlantic Squadron, sailed from Key West, Florida, for Cuba on 22 April. On the following day, Sampson directed his ships to close off the ports of Matanzas, Cárdenas, Mariel, and Cabañas. A lack of vessels prohibited Sampson from sealing off Cuba's southern ports or the easternmost harbors along its north shore or those on the island of Puerto Rico until late June. At the outset, Sampson's task was formidable, given that he had only 26 ships with which to patrol 2,000 miles of coastline. Later, that number grew to 124, but even at that, it was but one-fifth as many ships as the U.S. Navy used to blockade approximately the same amount of Confederate coastline during the Civil War.

The blockade was conducted in accordance with traditional maritime rules, governed by the 1856 Declaration of Paris. Neutrality on the high seas was honored. Ships that had left Spain prior to the official declaration of war were granted immunity from search. Any Spanish vessel docked in a U.S. port at the time of the declaration was given until 21 May to depart but was allowed to carry only enough coal to reach its home port.

Steamships captured by U.S. vessels on 22 April 1898, three days before the start of the Spanish-American War. The Spanish ship Pedro *was captured by the* New York, *and the Spanish steamer* Buena Ventura *was captured by the gunboat* Nashville *17 miles off Key West, Florida (drawing by Carlton T. Chapman for* Harper's Weekly*).*

The intent of the blockade was to shut down commercial trade with Cuba, as well as the movement of troops and supplies from Spain. As Sampson's resources permitted, vessels were halted and inspected. Contraband was confiscated and later distributed according to maritime law, a process that continued to as late as 1900.

In addition to intercepting ships en route to Cuba, the blockade engaged in more than a dozen clashes with Spanish shore batteries. One such clash occurred at Matanzas on 27 April when U.S. ships were fired on for the first time in the war. Another took place on 11 May when detachments from the USS *Marblehead* and *Nashville* cut the underwater cable near Cienfuegos. Later that day, the torpedo boat *Winslow* was disabled in Cárdenas harbor.

The blockade's effectiveness is somewhat debatable. At the time, the Spanish government claimed that the blockade was an illegal, albeit ineffective, act of war. After the war, however, Spain admitted that only a few ships had managed to slip through the cordon. It seems clear that the blockade imposed a definite hardship, not only on the Spanish forces but also—and probably more acutely—on the civilian population. One historian has suggested that a longer war would have had a severe effect on Cuban life.

See also Cárdenas; Cienfuegos, Cutting the Cable at; North Atlantic Squadron, U.S. Navy; Sampson, William Thomas.

References and Further Readings
Bernadou, Lt. J. B. "The 'Winslow' at Cardenas (May 11, 1898)." *Century Magazine*, March 1899.
Feuer, A. B. *The Spanish-American War at Sea.* Westport, CT: Greenwood Press, 1995.

Sampson, Rear Adm. William T. "The Atlantic Fleet in the Spanish War." *Century Magazine*, April 1899.

Trask, David F. *The War with Spain in 1898*. Lincoln: University of Nebraska Press, 1996.

Winslow, Cameron McRae. "Cable-cutting at Cienfuegos." *Century Magazine*, March 1899.

Naval Strategy, Spanish

At the highest level, Spain's naval strategy during the 1898 war with the United States may best be described as completely unrealistic. In the late fall of 1897, Rear Adm. Segismundo Bermejo was appointed to the post of minister of marine (equivalent to the U.S. secretary of the navy). As war with the United States became more imminent, Bermejo, together with other high-ranking Spanish officials in the government and the navy, began considering Spain's naval response in the event of war.

Bermejo envisioned a division of the Spanish fleet, with one squadron posted around Cádiz to defend the Iberian Peninsula and another, composed of battleships and five armored cruisers together with torpedo boats and destroyers, posted to reinforce the ships at Havana. This squadron's mission would be to attack and defeat the U.S. fleet and destroy Key West, Florida, a base for U.S. naval operations. With this accomplished, the Spanish fleet would proceed to blockade the eastern U.S. seaboard.

A more unrealistic strategy could scarcely be imagined. Adm. Pascual Cervera, appointed to command the Spanish fleet in October 1897 and later charged with executing this dreamlike plan, tried to point out that the U.S. fleet was far stronger than the Spanish and that a defensive strategy would be more practical for Spain to pursue. Indeed, Cervera was convinced that Spain had no hope of competing with the U.S. Navy. Spain, argued Cervera, had less tonnage, fewer guns, and its ships-of-the-line were in an abysmal state of readiness.

Also, Spain had to consider its Pacific holdings. José Sobral, naval attaché in Washington, thought that, in the event of war, the United States was likely to take offensive action in the Philippines and that Spain was not prepared to adequately defend both the Philippine Archipelago and Cuba.

Despite his impressive marshaling of facts in opposition, Cervera was unable to dissuade Bermejo from pursuing his unrealistic strategy. Even the destruction of the battleship *Maine* in Havana harbor in February 1898 failed to alter the Spanish ministry's perception of how war with the United States should best be conducted.

Accordingly, on 7 April 1898, Cervera's squadron departed Cádiz for the Cape Verde Islands. By 19 April, his unit had been reinforced by a pair of cruisers from Havana, which had arrived by way of San Juan, Puerto Rico. Still, his squadron was in dreadful shape. Some ships were badly in need of repair, others lacked ammunition, and in one case, that of the *Cristóbal Colón,* main batteries were missing. From here Cervera was subsequently ordered to Puerto Rico.

With the declaration of war on 23 April, Spanish naval officials reviewed Bermejo's strategy. Although Cervera's compelling arguments were recognized, the only modification to the strategy was to allow Cervera to choose his own destination, in accordance with circumstances as he found them. Ultimately, Cervera sought sanctuary in the harbor of Santiago de Cuba, where his force was subsequently destroyed by the powerful U.S. fleet when he attempted to sortie on 3 July 1898.

Meanwhile, recognizing that the United States was likely to attack the Philippines, Spain centered its defense of the archipelago around Manila, Cavite, and Subig (Subic) Bay, under the overall command of Adm. Patricio Montojo. Although both Cervera and Montojo carried out their missions as best they could, neither received the support they needed, mainly because Spain simply lacked the resources. Montojo was subsequently defeated by Commodore George Dewey in the Battle of Manila Bay on 1 May 1898.

Following Montojo's defeat at Manila Bay, Adm. Manuel Cámara left Spain in June 1898, ostensibly under orders to relieve Spanish forces in the Philippines. Spain hoped that Cámara's squadron would be perceived as enough of a threat to compel the United States to send a portion of its fleet, then in Cuban waters, to Admiral Dewey's assistance. The strategy did worry U.S. naval authorities, who were concerned that Dewey's squadron would not be strong enough to deal with Admiral Cámara's fleet. However, Cervera's defeat at Santiago forced Cámara's recall to Spain, thereby negating that threat.

In summary, Spanish naval strategy was predicated on the belief that it would be better to suffer a glorious defeat, in which the empire could take justifiable pride, than to submit meekly to superior U.S. naval forces. The Spanish people, it was believed, wanted Spain's honor preserved above all else.

> **See also** Cámara y Libermoore, Manuel de la; Cervera y Topete, Pascual; Manila Bay, Battle of; Montojo y Pasarón, Patricio; Naval Strategy, U.S.; Santiago de Cuba, Naval Battle of.

References and Further Readings

Chadwick, Rear Adm. French Ensor. *Relations of the United States and Spain: The Spanish American War.* 2 vols. New York: Charles Scribner's Sons, 1911 (reprinted in 1968).

Feuer, A. B. *The Spanish-American War at Sea.* Westport, CT: Greenwood Press, 1995.

Trask, David F. *The War with Spain in 1898.* Lincoln: University of Nebraska Press, 1996.

Naval Strategy, U.S.

The U.S. Navy began developing a strategy for prosecuting a war with Spain several years before the Spanish-American War was declared. At the Naval War College (established at Newport, Rhode Island, in 1884), students began work on such plans in 1894 as a training exercise; the plans underwent numerous modifications during the next four years. One plan actually accounted for the possibility of France and the United States being allied in a war against Spain and England. Developing events, however, soon compelled such planning to focus on war between the United States and Spain.

Planners differed in their strategic views. Then Assistant Secretary of the Navy Theodore Roosevelt envisioned a blockade of Cuba while a select naval squadron attacked the Spanish coast and the Asiatic Squadron seized Manila in the Philippine Islands. Another planner imagined a Spanish fleet sailing from Cádiz to Cuban waters while the United States secured Nipe Bay on the northeast coast of Cuba as a coaling station. This victory would be followed by a blockade of the main Cuban ports and a confrontation with the Spanish fleet when it arrived in the area.

Subsequent plans called for an attack on the Iberian Peninsula as well as Spanish possessions in the Pacific, but it was recognized that these actions alone would probably not compel Spain to yield. Attacks on Cuba and Puerto Rico not only would force Spain to respond, but they also would give the United States a logistic advantage. A scenario for a Caribbean offensive included an expeditionary force landing in Cuba to capture Havana in what was predicted to be a month-long campaign aided by Cuban revolutionary forces.

The first complete plan was created in 1896 by Lt. William Kimball of the Office of Naval Intelligence. The plan was predicated on a belief that a war with Spain would be waged mainly at sea and that any land operation would be strictly secondary. Kimball recommended naval strikes against Spain itself as well as the Philippines. It was hoped that the combined result of these efforts would compel Spain to release its hold on Cuba.

Meanwhile, the Naval War College continued to develop a strategy that presupposed war with Spain and Great Britain. The Navy Department, however, apparently not fully satisfied with what had been put forth by either the War College or Lieutenant Kimball, began to explore various strategic possibilities on its own.

Ideas on how to conduct a war with Spain included sending a combined fleet to battle the Spanish fleet in its home waters. As for Cuba, which remained the crux of the problem between the United States and Spain, a strong Cuban Revolutionary Army would eliminate or greatly reduce the need for a U.S. expeditionary force.

By 1897, the Navy Department had begun to look favorably on strategic ideas that favored a strike against the Iberian Peninsula as a means of keeping the Spanish fleet in home waters. At the same time, U.S. forces would seize Puerto Rico, while the Asiatic Squadron attacked the Philippines. This strategy also included sending some ground troops to both Cuba and Puerto Rico. At the same time, Navy Department planners were developing a plan that took into account the possibility of war with Spain with Japan as Spain's ally. This combination required taking preventive measures to protect Hawaii and the West Coast of the United States.

In March 1898, Secretary of the Navy John D. Long convened a naval war board to advise him on matters of naval importance. Originally, the board was composed of Assistant Secretary of the Navy Theodore Roosevelt, Adm. Montgomery Sicard, Capt. Arent Crowinshield, and Capt. Albert S. Barker. However, in May, Roosevelt resigned his post to enter the army, and shortly thereafter, Capt. Alfred Thayer Mahan was appointed to the group. Thus, for all practical purposes, the board was composed of Sicard, Crowinshield, Barker, and Mahan. The board recommended that the United States blockade Cuban ports and attack the Spanish fleet in the Philippines. It was thought that this would eventually lead to a confrontation with the Spanish fleet, in which the United States would emerge triumphant, thereby paving the way for an expeditionary force to seize both Cuba and Puerto Rico.

When war was finally declared in the spring of 1898, U.S. naval strategy had largely settled on a four-point plan: (1) a blockade of Cuba, (2) a concentration of naval power in the Caribbean, which included bringing the battleship *Oregon* from the Pacific Coast, around Cape Horn, to join the rest of the Atlantic Squadron, (3) an expeditionary force with Havana as an objective, and (4) an attack on the Spanish fleet in the Philippines.

U.S. defensive preparations included safeguarding the eastern seaboard by strengthening key coastal fortifications. In addition, provisions were made for an increased surveillance of the coastline by two of the navy's five operational squadrons.

See also Long, John Davis; Mahan, Alfred Thayer; Naval Blockade of Cuba; Naval Vessels, U.S., Auxiliary; Naval War Board, U.S.; Navy, U.S.; Roosevelt, Theodore.

References and Further Readings

Chadwick, Rear Adm. French Ensor. *Relations of the United States and Spain: The Spanish American War.* 2 vols. New York: Charles Scribner's Sons, 1911 (reprinted in 1968).

Cosmas, Graham. *An Army for Empire: The United States Army in the Spanish-American War.* College Station: Texas A&M University Press, 1998.

Musicant, Ivan. *Empire by Default: The Spanish-American War and the Dawn of the American Century.* New York: Henry Holt and Company, 1998.

O'Toole, G. J. A. *The Spanish War: An American Epic, 1898.* New York: W. W. Norton, 1984.

Trask, David F. *The War with Spain in 1898.* Lincoln: University of Nebraska Press, 1996.

Naval Vessels, U.S., Auxiliary

In preparation for war with Spain, the U.S. Navy was divided into five operational squadrons. The heart of the navy's fleet was concentrated in or near Caribbean and Philippine waters. However, an auxiliary force of eight monitors, seven yachts, and two tugs was charged with defending the East Coast of the United States. This unit, nicknamed the "Mosquito Squadron," was manned primarily by naval cadets. Commanded by Rear Adm. Henry Erben, the Mosquito Squadron was headquartered in New York.

See also Naval Strategy, U.S.; Navy, U.S.

References and Further Readings

Chadwick, Rear Adm. French Ensor. *Relations of the United States and Spain: The Spanish American War.* 2 vols. New York: Charles Scribner's Sons, 1911 (reprinted in 1968).

Trask, David F. *The War with Spain in 1898.* Lincoln: University of Nebraska Press, 1996.

Naval War Board, U.S.

The Naval War Board was organized by Secretary of the Navy John D. Long to provide guidance and make recommendations on naval matters and to formulate strategy. The board was quite active during the Spanish-American War. The board was composed of

Adm. Montgomery Sicard (the chair), Capt. Arent S. Crowinshield, Capt. Albert S. Barker, and Capt. Alfred Thayer Mahan. In his capacity as assistant secretary of the navy, Theodore Roosevelt was one of the original members of the board but resigned in May 1898 to serve in the Rough Riders.

Alfred Thayer Mahan, the most outspoken advocate of sea power, believed the board was a sham but continued to serve nevertheless. Mahan was of the opinion that one officer vested with the proper authority would serve more effectively than a board.

The board provided Secretary Long with advice on strategy and tactics and disposition of the fleet. Thus, Long was able to report to President McKinley as an informed secretary of the navy. Perhaps the most significant recommendation made by the board was to develop a naval blockade of Cuba, while having Commodore George Dewey neutralize the Spanish fleet in the Philippines and secure a base of operations there.

The army, unfortunately, lacked a counterpart to the Naval War Board.

See also Long, John Davis; Mahan, Alfred Thayer; Naval Strategy, U.S.

References and Further Readings

Long, John D. *The New American Navy.* New York: Outlook, 1903.
Trask, David F. *The War with Spain in 1898.* Lincoln: University of Nebraska Press, 1996.

Navy, Spanish

At the time of the Spanish-American War in 1898, the Spanish Navy was a far cry from its famed armada of the sixteenth century. Although the Spanish fleet had grown in the decades preceding the war with the United States, little had been done to maintain the ships in a high degree of readiness. It was not until the mid-1890s that Spain began to upgrade and modernize its navy. Some progress was made, but financial support was weak—there was no money for gunnery practice or even for routine maintenance, such as scraping the bottom of ships to remove marine growth.

In 1898, the Spanish Navy consisted of 45 ships, which included 1 first-class battleship, 1 second-class battleship, 5 armored cruisers, 5 protected cruisers, and 12 unprotected cruisers, plus a number of destroyers, gunboats, and torpedo boats. In armament, armor, and overall tonnage, the Spanish fleet ranked far behind the U.S. fleet, which had 79 ships. In terms of personnel, the Spanish Navy numbered some 1,400 officers and 14,000 enlisted men. Overall command of the navy was vested in the minister of marine, Segismundo Bermejo, the counterpart to U.S. Secretary of the Navy John D. Long.

Despite the clear deficiencies of the Spanish fleet, some Europeans believed that Spain was not without advantages—one being the speed and maneuverability of its destroyers and torpedo boats, which, it was thought, would more than offset the advantages of the more powerful but slower U.S. battleships. Finally, it was believed that Spain's new, fast, armored cruiser, *Cristóbal Colón*, had no peer in the U.S. Navy.

See also Navy, U.S.

References and Further Readings

Chadwick, Rear Adm. French Ensor. *Relations of the United States and Spain: The Spanish American War.* 2 vols. New York: Charles Scribner's Sons, 1911 (reprinted in 1968).

Feuer, A. B. *The Spanish-American War at Sea.* Westport, CT: Greenwood Press, 1995.

Nofi, Albert A. *The Spanish-American War, 1898.* Conshohocken, PA: Combined Books, 1998.

Trask, David F. *The War with Spain in 1898.* Lincoln: University of Nebraska Press, 1996.

Navy, U.S.

The years immediately following the Civil War saw the U.S. Navy sink into decline and neglect. Well into the 1880s, most of the navy still consisted of wooden sailing vessels armed with antiquated smoothbore cannons. The picture began to change in the late 1880s, spurred by a burgeoning coterie of intellectuals in the new Naval War College who lobbied for modernization of the navy. Their efforts were supported by a succession of visionary secretaries of the navy—William E. Chamberlain, William C. Whitney, and Benjamin Franklin Tracy—who argued for and received congressional approval to create a modern steam-powered steel navy. The publication in 1890 of Alfred Thayer Mahan's *Influence of Sea Power upon History* also helped enormously to create an environment favorable to a rebirth of the U.S. Navy.

As a result of the modernization program, the U.S. Navy was transformed into a comparatively small (sixth in the world) but very powerful naval force. By the time of the Spanish-American War in 1898, the heart of the navy consisted of four first-class battleships—the *Indiana, Iowa, Massachusetts,* and *Oregon*—all of which featured heavy armor, powerful batteries, and a cruising range of more than 5,000 miles. A pair of second-class battleships, the *Maine* and *Texas,*

The U.S. Navy's gunboat Nashville *at the time of the Spanish-American War.*

were also part of the new navy. Slower and lacking the armor of the *Indiana*-class ships, these battleships were nonetheless powerful vessels, possessing 8- and 13-inch rifled batteries. Monitors carried armament nearly equal to that of the battleships but were much slower. Of the U.S. battleships, the *Maine* and *Oregon* are best known. The former achieved immortality when it was destroyed in Havana harbor in February 1898. Its destruction served as a rallying cry for the United States to go to war with Spain. The *Oregon* became noted because of its historic voyage from the West Coast of the United States around Cape Horn to join the Atlantic fleet in the Caribbean following the declaration of war with Spain.

The ships were supported by a strong force of armored and protected cruisers, the former having more and heavier armor than the protected cruisers. There was also a variety of smaller auxiliary vessels, consisting of gunboats, torpedo boats, revenue cutters, and yachts. Gunboats, which were smaller well-armed ships, were not well suited to work on the high seas. They were most effective in inland waterways, such as those in the Philippines. Revenue cutters were small, fast, and lightly armed vessels designed for coastal patrol. The fleet also included an experimental dynamite cruiser, the *Vesuvius,* which mounted three pneumatic tubes on its deck capable of firing 100-pound projectiles of guncotton, a highly explosive substance made of cotton treated with nitric and sulfuric acid.

As war with Spain became increasingly likely, the navy bought civilian ships to supplement the fleet, including yachts that were converted to serve as ships of war. In preparing for war, the navy spent some $18 million of its $29 million allocation from the Fifty Million Dollar Bill authorized by Congress.

The U.S. Navy had 196 ships totaling 116,000 tons, as opposed to Spain's 45 ships of 56,000 tons. In June 1898, the navy consisted of 1,751 officers and 13,750 enlisted men. By the end of the war, those numbers increased to 24,000 total, of which some 4,400 were naval militiamen from various states. Overall, U.S. naval crews were better trained than their Spanish counterparts, particularly in gunnery skills.

The navy operated as part of the Navy Department, the overall umbrella under which the U.S. Navy, U.S. Marine Corps, and various bureaus such as Navigation and Yards and Docks are found. At the time of the Spanish-American War, the Navy Department was presided over by Secretary of the Navy John D. Long. The command structure did not include a chief of naval operations (CNO) who reported to the secretary of the navy; that post was not created until 1915.

See also Long, John Davis; Mahan, Alfred Thayer; Naval Strategy, U.S.; Navy, Spanish; *Oregon*; Roosevelt, Theodore.

References and Further Readings

Chadwick, Rear Adm. French Ensor. *Relations of the United States and Spain: The Spanish American War.* 2 vols. New York: Charles Scribner's Sons, 1911 (reprinted in 1968).

Feuer, A. B. *The Spanish-American War at Sea.* Westport, CT: Greenwood Press, 1995.

Nofi, Albert A. *The Spanish-American War, 1898.* Conshohocken, PA: Combined Books, 1998.

Trask, David F. *The War with Spain in 1898.* Lincoln: University of Nebraska Press, 1996.

Newspapers

See **Journalism**

Nipe Bay (Cuba)

Located on the northeast coast of Cuba, Nipe Bay played a key role in early U.S. naval planning for a war with Spain. One plan that emerged from the Naval War College anticipated a movement of the Spanish fleet to Cuban waters, with the United States responding by capturing Nipe Bay. The bay would then be used as a coaling station and as a launching point for sorties against the Spanish fleet.

Although this plan did not come to pass, Nipe Bay did play a role in the war. Later plans called for the Puerto Rican Expedition to use Nipe Bay as a staging area. Accordingly, the *Annapolis,* the *Wasp,* and the armed tug *Leyden* entered Nipe Bay in July 1898 and took possession of it after a short-lived fight with an old Spanish gunboat, the *Jorge Juan,* which was later scuttled by its crew. Subsequently, Guantánamo Bay was selected as the staging area for Gen. Nelson Miles's Puerto Rican Campaign.

See also Miles, Nelson Appleton; Naval Strategy, Spanish; Naval Strategy, U.S.

References and Further Readings

Chadwick, Rear Adm. French Ensor. *Relations of the United States and Spain: The Spanish American War.* 2 vols. New York: Charles Scribner's Sons, 1911 (reprinted in 1968).

Trask, David F. *The War with Spain in 1898.* Lincoln: University of Nebraska Press, 1996.

North Atlantic Fleet

See **North Atlantic Squadron, U.S. Navy**

North Atlantic Squadron, U.S. Navy

The North Atlantic Squadron was one of the U.S. Navy's five operational units at the time of the Spanish-American War; it was transferred to Key West, Florida, during the winter of 1897–1898. Ostensibly, the purpose of the move was to conduct winter exercises, but it was also intended to alert Spain to a strong U.S. naval presence less than 100 miles from Cuba. Virtually all ships later employed in the naval blockade of Cuba were from this squadron.

The North Atlantic Squadron, under the command of Rear Adm. William T. Sampson, constituted the heart of the U.S. Navy's fighting power in 1898. The fleet's newest and largest vessels, including the battleships *Iowa* and *Indiana* and the armored cruiser *New York,* were in the squadron and would later be joined by the battleship *Oregon,* following its record-breaking cruise from the West Coast of the United States around Cape Horn to the Caribbean.

The squadron was redesignated the North Atlantic Fleet in June 1898. Neither designation should be confused with the Northern Patrol Squadron.

See also Naval Blockade of Cuba; Naval Strategy, U.S.; Navy, U.S.; *Oregon*; Sampson, William Thomas.

References and Further Readings

Chadwick, Rear Adm. French Ensor. *Relations of the United States and Spain: The Spanish American War.* 2 vols. New York: Charles Scribner's Sons, 1911 (reprinted in 1968).

Sternlicht, Sanford. *McKinley's Bulldog: The Battleship Oregon.* Chicago: Nelson-Hall, 1977.

Trask, David F. *The War with Spain in 1898.* Lincoln: University of Nebraska Press, 1996.

Northern Patrol Squadron, U.S. Navy

One of five operational groups of the U.S. Navy in 1898, the mission of the Northern Patrol Squadron was to monitor the coastline between Maine and Delaware. The squadron was created in response to public fear that Spain would attack the East Coast. Commanded by Commodore John A. Howell, the Northern Patrol Squadron included the protected cruiser *San Francisco* and the auxiliary cruisers *Yankee, Yosemite, Prairie,* and *Dixie.*

See also Howell, John Adams; Naval Strategy, U.S.; Navy, U.S.

References and Further Readings

Chadwick, Rear Adm. French Ensor. *Relations of the United States and Spain: The Spanish American War.* 2 vols. New York: Charles Scribner's Sons, 1911 (reprinted in 1968).

Trask, David F. *The War with Spain in 1898.* Lincoln: University of Nebraska Press, 1996.

Nuevitas (Cuba)

A port city on Cuba's eastern coast, Nuevitas is worth noting for two reasons. On 16 August 1896 (two years before the Spanish-American War), a filibustering expedition led by the legendary "Dynamite" Johnny O'Brien landed near Nuevitas with arms and ammunition for the Cuban revolutionaries. Discovered by a Spanish gunboat, O'Brien, in character with his elusive nature, evaded capture. Nuevitas was also targeted by Gen. Nelson Miles as a staging center for the army's advance on Havana. His plan, however, did not win the approval of President William McKinley.

See also Cuban Campaign; Miles, Nelson Appleton; O'Brien, "Dynamite" Johnny.

References and Further Readings

O'Toole, G. J. A. *The Spanish War: An American Epic, 1898.* New York: W. W. Norton, 1984.

Trask, David F. *The War with Spain in 1898.* Lincoln: University of Nebraska Press, 1996.

O'Brien, "Dynamite" Johnny (1837–1917)

A legendary filibuster, John O'Brien was born of Irish immigrant parents in the dry dock area of Manhattan. As a young man, he carried arms to the Confederacy but also worked for the Union cause on occasion. After the Civil War, he became a harbor pilot and was christened "Daredevil" for his boldness and skill in taking boats through the treacherous waters of Hell Gate, connecting Long Island Sound and the East River. But it was as a filibuster—running arms and ammunition to revolutionaries in Central America and Cuba— that O'Brien forged his real reputation and earned the lasting sobriquet "Dynamite Johnny," so christened because in 1888 he carried a cargo of dangerous explosives to insurgents in Panama.

In the years preceding the Spanish-American War, O'Brien, supported by the Cuban junta and U.S. businessmen, ran contraband to the Cuban rebels, claiming sympathy for the revolutionary cause. Because filibusters operated outside national neutrality laws, they were constantly sought by the U.S. Revenue Cutter Service (forerunner of the U.S. Coast Guard) as well as by authorities of the countries to which they were bringing contraband. O'Brien proved unusually adept at eluding traps set for him, including those devised by the famed Pinkerton detective agency to catch him when he was not at sea. In 1896, O'Brien's vessel, the *Dauntless,* carried a young adventurer named Frederick Funston to Cuba to serve as artillery chief to the revolutionary army. Funston would later gain fame as an army officer in the Philippines.

After the Spanish-American War, O'Brien was made chief of pilots in Havana harbor as a reward for his efforts in supporting the revolution. In 1911, he was chosen to be at the helm of the resurrected battleship *Maine* as it was towed to deep water and sent to its final resting place. One of the most colorful characters of the period, O'Brien, despite a life of hazard, lived to the ripe old age of 80, dying in New York in 1917.

See also Cuban Junta; Cuban Revolution; Funston, Frederick; *Maine,* Inquiries into the Sinking of; Naval Blockade (U.S.) of Cuba; Revenue Cutter Service, U.S.

References and Further Readings

Funston, Frederick. *Memories of Two Wars.* New York: Charles Scribner's Sons, 1911.

O'Toole, G. J. A. *The Spanish War: An American Epic, 1898.* New York: W. W. Norton, 1984.

Smith, Horace. *A Captain Unafraid: The Strange Adventures of Dynamite Johnny O'Brien.* New York: Harper & Brothers, 1912.

O'Donnell y Abréu, Carlos (1834–1903)

Although of Irish descent, Carlos O'Donnell y Abréu's ancestors had been Spanish citizens for several generations. O'Donnell himself was duke of Tetuán and Spanish foreign minister from 1895 to 1897. As foreign minister during the critical months preceding the Spanish-American War, O'Donnell worked to defeat the Cuban rebellion and at the same time argued for Cuban autonomy. He also took the position that the Spanish monarchy would collapse if Spain were defeated by the United States and that this in turn would jeopardize other European monarchies. He articulated this belief in a document that came to be known as the O'Donnell Memorandum, which he wrote during the summer of 1896. O'Donnell hoped to enlist European support for the Spanish position through the argument set forth in his memorandum—particularly the support of European powers who recognized the vulnerability of their own positions.

Although President Grover Cleveland's administration was not opposed to Spanish rule in Cuba per se, the president did seek an end to the Cuban rebellion and restoration of peace. In any case, the United States, standing by the tenets of the Monroe Doctrine, would not tolerate the presence of another European power in Cuba other than Spain. When O'Donnell was advised that his memorandum would not sit well with the United States and that President Cleveland's offer (extended through Secretary of State Richard Olney in April 1896) to mediate the differences between Spain and the Cuban rebels should be accepted, O'Donnell withdrew the memorandum from consideration. A key argument in support of his reasoning had been the strong possibility that William Jennings Bryan, known to be anti-Spanish, would be elected the next president of the United States. However, William McKinley's victory at the polls made the point academic.

After the Spanish-American War, O'Donnell refused invitations to serve as a member of the Spanish peace treaty commission.

See also Cleveland, Grover; Cuban Revolution; Olney, Richard; Spain.
References and Further Readings
O'Toole, G. J. A. *The Spanish War: An American Epic, 1898.* New York: W. W. Norton, 1984.
Trask, David F. *The War with Spain in 1898.* Lincoln: University of Nebraska Press, 1996.

Olney, Richard (1835–1917)

Born in Boston, Richard Olney, a Democrat, held two posts in President Grover Cleveland's administration, serving first as attorney general from 1893 to 1895 and then just prior to the Spanish-American War as secretary of state from 1895 to 1897. As secretary of state, the most challenging issue facing Olney was the situation in Cuba, just as it would be for his successors.

In 1895, Olney reaffirmed a basic tenet of the Monroe Doctrine—namely, that the United States stood as the principal power in the Western Hemisphere. However, he also supported Spain's efforts to end the revolution in Cuba. As the lead spokesperson on foreign matters in the Cleveland administration, Olney was opposed to Cuban independence, believing it would create chaos on the island. His offer to have the United States mediate a settlement between Spain and the Cuban revolutionaries was rejected.

See also Cleveland, Grover; Cuban Revolution; O'Donnell y Abréu, Carlos; Spain.
References and Further Readings
Eggert, Gerald G. *Richard Olney: Evolution of a Statesman.* University Park: Pennsylvania State University Press, 1974.
Musicant, Ivan. *Empire by Default: The Spanish-American War and the Dawn of the American Century.* New York: Henry Holt and Company, 1998.
Trask, David F. *The War with Spain in 1898.* Lincoln: University of Nebraska Press, 1996.

O'Neill, William Owen "Buckey" (1860–1898)

The colorful captain of the Rough Riders' A Troop, which saw action in Cuba during the Spanish-American War, William Owen "Buckey" O'Neill had done just about everything prior to joining the Riders: He had been a newsman; an explorer; sheriff of Yavapai County, Arizona Territory; and the mayor of Prescott, Arizona. He was also famed for his gambling exploits in Prescott, where he earned the sobriquet "Buckey" because of his penchant for "bucking the tiger," or going broke in faro.

Resolved to gain military honors for himself in Cuba, he joined the Rough Riders. He was in the forefront of action during the Santiago Campaign. While fighting in front of San Juan Heights, he refused to take cover from Spanish sniper fire. Warned to stay down, he pronounced that the bullet that would kill him had not yet been made; a split second later, he was struck in the mouth and killed instantly.

Brave to a fault, O'Neill had earlier tried unsuccessfully to rescue two drowning black soldiers during the U.S. landing at Daiquirí and had led his company with distinction in the fight at Las Guásimas. Perhaps because he exemplified the colorful man of action of the western frontier, O'Neill was a particular favorite of Theodore Roosevelt.

See also Roosevelt, Theodore; Rough Riders; San Juan Hill, Charge up; Santiago, Campaign and Siege of.

References and Further Readings

Samuels, Peggy, and Harold Samuels. *Teddy Roosevelt at San Juan: The Making of a President.* College Station: Texas A&M University Press, 1997.

Walker, Dale L. *Death Was the Black Horse: The Story of Rough Rider Buckey O'Neill.* Austin, TX: Madrona Press, 1975.

———. *The Boys of '98: Theodore Roosevelt and the Rough Riders.* New York: Forge Books, 1998.

Open Door Policy

Late 1899 found President William McKinley's administration focusing considerable attention on Asia. In addition to the Philippine-American War, China was a subject of concern and discussion. The United States and the European powers regarded China as a lucrative market for exports and agreed that access to China should remain unrestricted.

The United States had acquired Spanish possessions following the Spanish-American War and the Treaty of Paris, yet the U.S. Constitution contained no provisions for governing colonies. In establishing a colonial policy, President McKinley's wish was that the Philippines be free of any constitutional mandates.

As part of that picture, the United States proposed an "open door" trade policy between itself and European nations, especially with respect to China. The United States would be required to extend the same open door courtesy to European countries regarding the Philippines. The McKinley administration was successful in opening Chinese and other Asian markets to U.S. industrial exports.

The orchestration of this trade strategy is sometimes said to have been the hallmark of McKinley's Asian policy.

See also Boxer Rebellion; Imperialism/Expansionism.

References and Further Readings

Gould, Lewis L. *The Spanish-American War and President McKinley.* Lawrence: University of Kansas Press, 1982.

LaFeber. *The New Empire.* Ithaca, NY: Cornell University Press, 1963.

Leech, Margaret. *In the Days of McKinley.* New York: Harper & Brothers, 1959.

Oregon (Battleship)

The battleship *Oregon* is one of the most famous ships in U.S. naval history. During the Spanish-American War, its reputation was equaled only by that of the *Maine.*

The *Oregon*'s niche in history was secured for all time with its internationally famous voyage around Cape Horn. In a record-breaking journey, the *Oregon* departed San Francisco on 14 March 1898 and steamed around Cape Horn to join the North Atlantic Squadron's blockade of Cuba. The ship traveled 14,000 nautical miles in 66 days, an extraordinary feat that captured the world's attention. Perhaps most significantly, the voyage dramatically reinforced the need for an isthmian canal.

An *Indiana*-class battleship, the *Oregon* was launched in 1893 and commissioned in 1896. When it joined the fleet, it was the navy's third modern steel battleship and one of the finest warships in the world. Officially, the *Oregon* was designated BB3, or Battleship 3, the *Indiana* and the *Massachusetts* being BB1 and BB2, respectively. At the time of the famed voyage around the horn, the *Oregon*'s commander was Capt. Charles E. Clark, appointed to the post in March 1898.

The hull of the *Oregon* was protected by 18 inches of armor at the waterline. Its main batteries consisted of four 13-inch breech-loading rifles, eight 8-inch breechloaders, and four 6-inch breechloaders. Additionally, it mounted twenty 6-pounder, rapid-fire guns, plus a pair of Gatling guns and six torpedo tubes.

The *Oregon* carried 1,800 tons of coal in its bunkers, which gave it a cruising range of 16,000 nautical miles at a speed of 10 knots. When called upon to do so, the *Oregon* could cut through the water at a maximum speed of 18 knots. The ship carried a crew of 30 officers and 438 men.

Forward deck of the famed battleship Oregon. *The ship's unprecedented voyage around Cape Horn, sailing from California to join the Atlantic fleet in Cuban waters, made history.*

After joining Adm. William T. Sampson's squadron on 24 May 1898, the *Oregon* supported the landing of Gen. William R. Shafter's Fifth Corps at Daiquirí. During the great naval battle of Santiago Bay on 3 July, it was the *Oregon,* with its boilers on line, that gave prompt pursuit to Adm. Pascual Cervera's Spanish Squadron, mortally wounding the *Infanta Maria Teresa* in the ensuing battle.

Later, the *Oregon* provided naval support during the Boxer

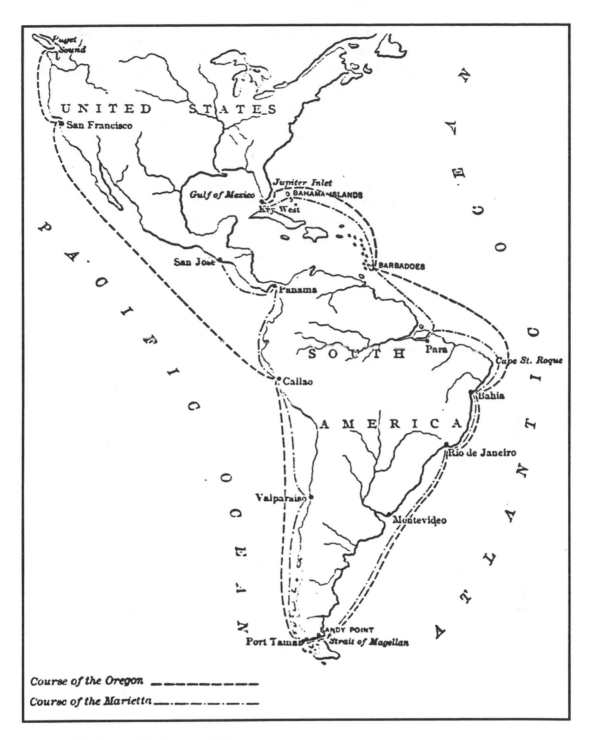

Voyage of the battleship Oregon, *1898.*

Source: *Edgar Stanton Maclay,* A History of the United States Navy from 1775 to 1902 *(New York: D. Appleton and Company, 1902), III, p. 76.*

Rebellion. In 1920, it was set up as a monument in the city of Portland, Oregon. By World War II, although in the process of being scrapped, the navy still found a use for the ship. With its superstructure gone, the hull was towed to Guam, where it served the navy's Seabees as a dynamite-stowage barge.

See also Boxer Rebellion; Naval Blockade of Cuba; Navy, U.S.; Santiago de Cuba, Naval Battle of.

References and Further Readings

Beardsley, Rear Adm. C. A. "The Trial of the *Oregon*." *Harper's New Monthly Magazine*, 98, 1899, pp. 699–707.

Braistead, William Reynolds. *The United States Navy in the Pacific, 1897–1909*. Austin: University of Texas Press, 1958.

Sternlicht, Sanford. *McKinley's Bulldog: The Battleship* Oregon. Chicago: Nelson-Hall, 1977.

Trask, David F. *The War with Spain in 1898*. Lincoln: University of Nebraska Press, 1996.

Otis, Elwell Stephen (1838–1909)

Born in Maryland and educated as a lawyer, Elwell Stephen Otis served as a volunteer officer during the Civil War. Like a number of other volunteer soldiers, Otis found military life to his liking and remained in the army after the war, later serving on the western frontier during the Indian wars. By 1893, he had been promoted to brigadier general.

Following the outbreak of war with Spain in 1898, Otis was appointed major general of volunteers and sent to the Philippines as second in command to Maj. Gen. Wesley Merritt. In August 1898, he succeeded Merritt as commander of the Eighth Corps and military governor of the Philippines when Merritt was relieved of the command at his own request.

A thirty-six-year army veteran when he arrived in the Philippines, Otis, sporting an impressive set of Dundreary whiskers, resembled a professor of philosophy more than an army general. In any case, he had the misfortune to direct affairs in the Philippines during the initial stages of U.S. involvement in the archipelago. In this capacity, he had to make critical decisions when there were no clear guidelines as to U.S. policy, except for President William McKinley's desire to see the Philippines pacified in a kind and compassionate manner. "Benevolent assimilation," as it came to be known, was not, however, an easy policy to implement.

A conservative officer by nature, Otis's refusal to acknowledge the limitations of his military resources, particularly the troop strength to respond effectively to the movements of the Filipino Nationalist Army, exacerbated a difficult situation. For example, Otis's field commanders had to execute his directives while being compromised by the logistic problems of campaigning in extremely difficult conditions, against an elusive foe, and without sufficient manpower.

Otis also had to deal with the problem posed by volunteer troops who wanted to go home once the war with Spain had ended. These men had volunteered to fight the Spanish, not the Filipinos. He had difficulty dealing with the volunteers, despite the fact that he had once been a volunteer soldier himself and indeed had led volunteer troops with distinction during the Civil War. The state volunteer units were eventually sent home, but until replacements arrived, Otis had to make do with the regular army units that were available.

Perhaps the most controversial of all Philippine commanders, he was sharply criticized by some of his senior subordinates. Adm. George Dewey, his naval counterpart, thought him "a pincushion of an old woman" (Linn, pp. 29–30). His strict censorship of news stories did not endear him to the press, and reporters often painted Otis in a critical light. Indeed, the so-called feud between Otis and Brig. Gen. Henry Lawton, his most outspoken critic, may have been largely the creation of the press. Otis was succeeded as military governor of the Philippines in May 1900 by Gen. Arthur MacArthur.

See also Aguinaldo y Famy, Emilio; Benevolent Assimilation; Lawton, Henry Ware; MacArthur, Arthur; McKinley, William, Jr.; Merritt, Wesley.

References and Further Readings

Gates, John Morgan. *Schoolbooks and Krags: The United States Army in the Philippines, 1898–1902.* Contributions in Military History no. 3. Westport, CT: Greenwood Press, 1973.

Linn, Brian McAllister. *The Philippine War, 1899–1902.* Lawrence: University Press of Kansas, 2000.

Wolff, Leon. *Little Brown Brother: America's Forgotten Bid for Empire Which Cost 250,000 Lives.* New York: Kraus Reprint, 1970.

Pacification Program (Philippine Islands)

The United States acquired control of the Philippines, Guam, and Puerto Rico as a result of the Spanish-American War. The U.S. colonial policy in the Philippines was initially predicated on President William McKinley's idea of benevolent assimilation, a concept whereby U.S. troops were to treat the native population in a firm but kind manner, demonstrating respect for both human and property rights. It should be noted that in the early years of U.S. involvement in the Philippines, control of the archipelago was vested in the principal military authority, that is, the military governor of the islands.

Although McKinley's policy did produce some positive results, as illustrated by reforms in the educational system and the introduction of democratic government at the local level, it also proved a challenge to implement. Racial bias and a condescending attitude toward the native inhabitants on the part of many U.S. soldiers were often stumbling blocks. The problem was compounded by a growing anti-American attitude on the part of the Filipino revolutionary forces of Emilio Aguinaldo, once it became clear that the United States had simply replaced Spain as the governing power. Caught between the two groups was the great block of Filipino people, many of whom welcomed the U.S. presence in the archipelago, particularly the more affluent Filipinos who sought to preserve their wealth and positions. As the Philippine-American War progressed, many natives felt compelled to assist whichever faction seemed to offer the most protection and assistance.

Six months after the war with Spain ended, the situation in the Philippines changed dramatically. During the Philippine-American War (sometimes called the Philippine Insurrection), which began in February 1899, the U.S. military had to operate under an entirely new set of circumstances. Confronted with a conflict in which it was often impossible to distinguish guerrillas from peaceful villagers, the army sought to carry out the president's pacification policy by issuing General Order (GO) 100. This order had its roots in the Civil War and had originally been issued as a guide for the conduct of troops in the field.

Fundamentally, GO 100 was intended to provide soldiers with a standard for moral behavior that would respect human and property rights and dispense justice fairly. However, if natives continued their resistance or assisted guerrilla forces, they were to be treated as criminals and punished accordingly, even with summary execution in some instances. Local Filipinos were not the only ones subject to disciplinary action. U.S. newspapers also ran the risk of having action taken against them if they carried stories that were considered seditious.

The strategy was to isolate the revolutionary forces (guerrillas), composed of full-time fighters and part-time guerrillas, from those not resisting U.S. authority. Moreover, the intent was to make clear that, although the earlier policy of benevolent assimilation had not been abandoned, U.S. authorities would not be trifled with.

The 1900 presidential campaign, pitting incumbent William McKinley against William Jennings Bryan, also shaped the political-military climate in the Philippines. Aguinaldo's followers believed that McKinley's reelection would persuade many Filipinos to recognize U.S. authority rather than continue to fight.

As the Philippine-American War dragged on, it became increasingly difficult for the troops to deal with the natives in a kindly way, especially when they found comrades who had suffered unspeakable tortures at the hands of guerrillas before being killed. In retaliation, U.S. troops carried out their own form of reprisal, when they could do so. However, military directives continued to specify kindly treatment of Filipinos, drawing a line that was difficult to walk.

See also Aguinaldo y Famy, Emilio; Benevolent Assimilation; MacArthur, Arthur; McKinley, William, Jr.; Otis, Elwell Stephen.

References and Further Readings

Gates, John Morgan. *Schoolbooks and Krags: The United States Army in the Philippines, 1898–1902.* Contributions in Military History no. 3. Westport, CT: Greenwood Press, 1973.

Leech, Margaret. *In the Days of McKinley.* New York: Harper & Brothers, 1959.

Linn, Brian McAllister. *The U.S. Army and Counterinsurgency in the Philippine War, 1899–1902.* Chapel Hill: University of North Carolina Press, 1989.

———. *The Philippine War, 1899–1902.* Lawrence: University Press of Kansas, 2000.

Papal Mediation

As war between Spain and the United States moved closer to reality, Germany grew increasingly concerned that European monarchies would be negatively affected if the United States was to win, which seemed likely. Consequently, Germany urged the Vatican to propose papal mediation. Accordingly, in the spring of 1898, John Ireland, the archbishop of Minneapolis and a personal friend of President William McKinley, journeyed to Washington to broach the idea of papal mediation to the president.

Ireland came away from his meeting with the president with the mistaken understanding that McKinley desired peace and sought assistance in achieving that objective. As a consequence, the Vatican offered arbitration to Spain. The queen regent and her government were receptive and agreed to cease hostilities against the Cuban rebels, providing the U.S. Navy left Cuban waters.

Once the proposal was presented to the United States, the misunderstanding became clear. McKinley had not requested papal mediation but instead had hoped that, through Archbishop Ireland and the Vatican, Spain might be persuaded to accept his (McKinley's) earlier offer calling for Cuban independence. The White House summarily rejected the papal proposal and Spain's offer. President McKinley made it clear that he would recognize and accept only the proposal he had submitted to Spain in March 1898.

See also McKinley, William, Jr.; Spanish-American War, International Reaction to.

References and Further Readings

Foner, Philip S. *The Spanish-Cuban-American War.* 2 vols. New York: Monthly Review Press, 1972.

Leech, Margaret. *In the Days of McKinley.* New York: Harper & Brothers, 1959.

Musicant, Ivan. *Empire by Default: The Spanish-American War and the Dawn of the American Century.* New York: Henry Holt and Company, 1998.

Trask, David F. *The War with Spain in 1898.* Lincoln: University of Nebraska Press, 1996.

Paredes, José de

See **Santiago de Cuba, Naval Battle of**

Paterno, Pedro Alejandro (1858–1911)

A leader of the Filipino revolt against Spanish rule, Pedro Alejandro Paterno was the son of a well-to-do Philippine businessman who was able to provide his son with a university education in Spain, where Pedro studied law. His ancestry together with his fine education made Paterno a good example of a rising social class in the Philippines known as the *ilustrados,* or enlightened ones.

As a member of Emilio Aguinaldo's political family, Paterno offered to mediate the differences between Spain and the Filipino revolutionaries. This offer led to the famous and controversial Pact of Biyak-na-Bató of 14 December 1897, in which Aguinaldo agreed to leave the Philippines and live in exile in Hong Kong in exchange for indemnities paid to the revolutionaries. Paterno accompanied Aguinaldo into exile.

With Commodore George Dewey's victory at Manila Bay in May 1898, the Aguinaldo entourage returned to the Philippines, where Paterno later served as the first president of the new Philippine Republic and played a key role in drafting the Malolos Constitution. He was captured by the United States during the Philippine-American War and subsequently negotiated an armistice with the United States, for which he was charged with treasonous behavior by Aguinaldo, but by that time, Aguinaldo lacked the power to take action against Paterno.

See also Aguinaldo y Famy, Emilio; Biyak-na-Bató, Pact of; Dewey, George; Manila Bay, Battle of; Philippine-American War, U.S. Public Reaction to; Primo de Rivera, Fernando.

References and Further Readings

Gates, John Morgan. *Schoolbooks and Krags: The United States Army in the Philippines, 1898–1902.* Contributions in Military History no. 3. Westport, CT: Greenwood Press, 1973.

Linn, Brian McAllister. *The Philippine War, 1899–1902.* Lawrence: University Press of Kansas, 2000.

Steinberg, David Joel. *The Philippines: A Singular and a Plural Place.* Boulder, CO: Westview Press, 1994.

Wolff, Leon. *Little Brown Brother: America's Forgotten Bid for Empire Which Cost 250,000 Lives.* New York: Kraus Reprint, 1970.

Peace Commission

Following the signing of the Peace Protocol, which brought an end to hostilities between the United States and Spain, President William McKinley appointed a peace commission to negotiate terms of a formal and permanent peace agreement. Former Secretary of State William R. Day headed the U.S. contingent, which also included Whitelaw Reid, Cushman Davis, William P. Frye, George Gray, and John Bassett Moore. The Spanish negotiators included Eugenio Montero Ríos who headed the group, Bonaventura Abarzuza, José Garnica y Díaz, Rafael Cerero y Sáenz, Wenceslao Ramirez de Villaurruta, and Emilio de Ojeda.

The two groups began negotiating in Paris in October 1898 and concluded deliberations in December. The more prominent provisions of the agreement, known appropriately enough as the Treaty of Paris, provided for U.S. acquisition of the Philippine Archipelago, Guam, and Puerto Rico. The treaty was not ratified by the U.S. Congress until February 1899.

See also Day, William Rufus; Gray, George; Protocol of Peace; Reid, Whitelaw; Treaty of Paris.

References and Further Readings

Leech, Margaret. *In the Days of McKinley.* New York: Harper & Brothers, 1959.

Morgan, H. Wayne, ed. *Making Peace with Spain: The Diary of Whitelaw Reid—September–December, 1898.* Austin: University of Texas Press, 1965.

Peanut Club

Horatio Rubens, legal counsel to the Cuban junta (a U.S.-based group of Cuban patriots who worked on behalf of Cuban independence), always kept a plentiful supply of peanuts available in the junta's New York office; thus, the headquarters came to be called the "Peanut Club" by some reporters.

See also Cuban Junta; Estrada Palma, Tomás; Journalism.

References and Further Readings

Milton, Joyce. *The Yellow Kids: Foreign Correspondents in the Heyday of Yellow Journalism.* New York: Harper & Row, 1989.

Pearl of the Antilles

See Cuba

Pershing, John Joseph (1860–1948)

One of the most celebrated figures in U.S. military history, John Joseph Pershing was born in Missouri. After graduating from the U.S. Military Academy at West Point in 1882, he was assigned to the Sixth Cavalry and served in the West during the closing phase of the Indian wars. Later, he was commandant of cadets at the University of Nebraska, earned a law degree, and was promoted to first lieutenant. During the Spanish-American War, Pershing served in Cuba with the Tenth (black) Cavalry, which he led during the Santiago Campaign, participating in the battles of El Caney, Las Guásimas, and Kettle Hill. As a result of his staunch advocacy for black troops, he earned the sobriquets "Black Jack" and "Nigger Jack." Felled by malaria in 1898, he was sent home from Cuba and assigned to the Insular Bureau of the War Department.

In 1899, he requested and received a transfer to the Philippines, where he served with distinction against Moro insurgents on the island of Mindanao until 1903. An extraordinarily able officer, Pershing possessed great skill as a negotiator. Though only a captain, he was frequently assigned to field commands that normally would have been given to a colonel. Pershing conducted successful campaigns against Moro strongholds at Bud Daju and Bud Bagsak.

Recalled to Washington in 1903, he was given his second tour of staff duty, during which he married Helen Francis Warren, daughter of powerful Wyoming senator Francis E. Warren. Later, he was appointed military attaché to Japan and acted as an official observer during the Russo-Japanese War. His leadership abilities, reinforced by the backing of his influential father-in-law, persuaded President Theodore Roosevelt to promote Pershing from captain to brigadier general, jumping him over some 800 senior officers. He went on to command the celebrated punitive expedition into Mexico after Pancho Villa in 1915 and was then named to command the American Expeditionary Force in France during World War I.

See also Bud Bagsak, Battle of; Bud Daju, Battle of; Lake Lanao Campaigns; Moros; San Juan Hill, Charge up.

References and Further Readings
Linn, Brian McAllister. *The U.S. Army and Counterinsurgency in the Philippine War, 1899–1902*. Chapel Hill: University of North Carolina Press, 1989.
———. *The Philippine War, 1899–1902*. Lawrence: University Press of Kansas, 2000.
Sanford, Wayne L. "Battle of Bud Daju: 6 March 1906." *Indiana Military History Journal*, no. 7, May 1982.
Smythe, Donald. *Guerrilla Warrior: The Early Life of John J. Pershing.* New York: Charles Scribner's Sons, 1973.
Vandiver, Frank E. *Black Jack: The Life and Times of John J. Pershing.* 2 vols. College Station: Texas A&M University Press, 1977.

Philippine-American War, U.S. Public Reaction to

The close proximity of Cuba to the United States and the intense newspaper coverage on the Spanish treatment of Cubans led to a heightened public awareness of and sympathy for the Cuban people. Thus, when the battleship *Maine* mysteriously blew up in Havana harbor on the night of 15 February 1898, the American public clamored for retaliation against Spain. Commodore George Dewey's stunning victory over the Spanish fleet on the waters of Manila Bay was applauded from one end of the country to the other as the first U.S. triumph of the Spanish-American War.

In marked contrast, the Philippine-American War, which erupted in February 1899, just two days before the signing of the Treaty of Paris officially ended the war between Spain and the United States, was not a popular undertaking with the American public. Unlike Cuba, which was less than 100 miles from Key West, Florida, the Philippines lay thousands of miles beyond the western horizon. Few Americans, reportedly including President William McKinley himself, knew exactly where the islands were located or anything about their inhabitants. In addition, the Philippine-American War underscored divisive debate about imperialism and the United States as a colonial power.

When fighting broke out between U.S. troops and the republican forces of Emilio Aguinaldo, public opinion regarding the continued U.S. presence in the Philippines was sharply divided. The war against Spain, with Cuba as a focal point, had been a uniting cause. The only cause in the Philippines was U.S. imperialism and the nation's new role as a colonial power, which many Americans diametrically opposed. Those in the United States who strongly supported the war, however, also were vocal, and the issue almost certainly played a role in President McKinley's reelection in 1900. Moreover, the U.S. War Department had little difficulty recruiting more than 30,000 volunteers specifically for service in the Philippines.

On the international front, the Roman Catholic Church stood solidly behind President McKinley's acquisition of the Philippines. The church had large property holdings in the archipelago and felt that they would be more secure under U.S. rule than under that of another nation.

See also Philippine Islands, Acquisition of, by the United States.

References and Further Readings

Beede, Benjamin R., ed. *The War of 1898 and U.S. Interventions, 1898–1934.* New York: Garland Publishing, 1994.

Leech, Margaret. *In the Days of McKinley.* New York: Harper & Brothers, 1959.

May, Ernest R. *American Imperialism: A Speculative Essay.* Chicago: Imprint Publications, 1991.

Philippine Archipelago

The Philippine Archipelago, which the United States acquired as a result of the Spanish-American War, comprises more than 7,000

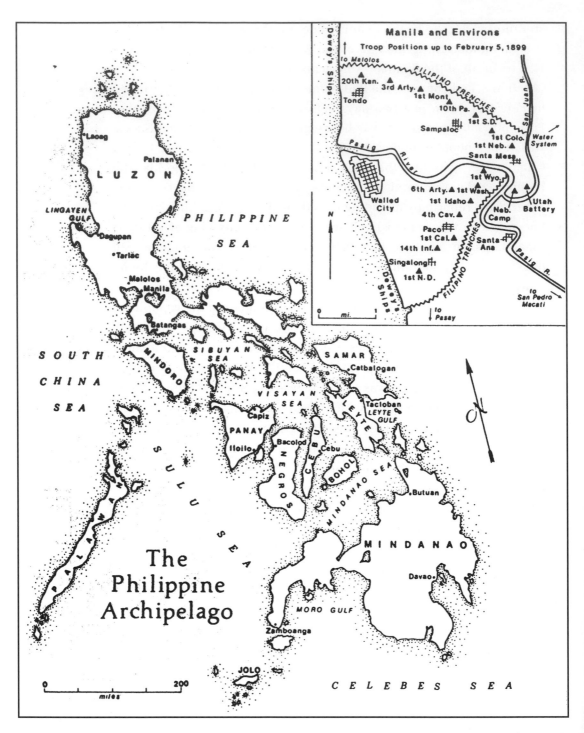

The Philippine Archipelago during the Philippine-American War, with insert of the Manila area in 1899.

Source: *Stuart C. Miller,* Benevolent Assimilation: The American Conquest of the Philippines, 1899–1903 *(New Haven, CT: Yale University Press, 1983), p. 45. Copyright Yale University Press.*

tropical islands, totaling some 500,000 square miles. Luzon, in the north, and Mindanao, in the south, are the two largest islands in the archipelago. Other principal islands include Cebu, Leyte, Negros, Panay, and Samar. The archipelago's terrain is rugged, consisting of mountains, swamps, and jungle, cut by numerous watercourses. The islands are subject to earthquakes and frequent volcanic eruptions. At the time of the Spanish-American War, the people who inhabited the islands were more or less isolated from one another, which gave birth to a variety of languages that made campaigning in the archipelago difficult.

The Spanish explorer Ferdinand Magellan discovered the archipelago in 1521 and claimed it for Spain, thereby ushering in nearly four centuries of Spanish rule. The northern and central islands were well indoctrinated with Spanish customs and Roman Catholicism, the religion of Spain, but the southern islands—that is, Mindanao and the Sulu Archipelago—were inhabited primarily by the Moros. The Moros stubbornly refused to accept a Christian intrusion into their region, first by the Spanish and later by the Americans.

The Spanish-American War of 1898 freed the Philippines from Spanish rule, only to be replaced by U.S. authority. The Philippine-American War of 1899 to 1902 ended Filipino resistance to the United States. In 1934, the Philippine Commonwealth was officially established; the archipelago was granted full independence in 1946.

See also Aguinaldo y Famy, Emilio; Philippines Islands, Acquisition of, by the United States.
References and Further Readings
Linn, Brian McAllister. *The Philippine War, 1899–1902*. Lawrence: University Press of Kansas, 2000.
Steinberg, David Joel. *The Philippines: A Singular and a Plural Place*. Boulder, CO: Westview Press, 1994.

Philippine Commission

In an effort to formulate an effective colonial policy for the Philippine Islands, which the United States acquired as a result of the Spanish-American War, President William McKinley created an advisory body known as the Philippine Commission. The first of two such commissions was created in late 1898. Consisting of five members, the first commission was headed by Jacob G. Schurman, president of Cornell University; Dean C. Worcester, from the University of Michigan's Zoology Department; and Col. Charles Denby, former U.S. minister to China. Because they were intimately acquainted with day-to-day events in the Philippines, Adm. George Dewey, hero of the Battle of

Manila Bay, and Maj. Gen. Elwell Otis, military commander in the Philippines, were also included in the commission.

Interestingly, all of the members were opposed to annexation of the Philippines and were specifically appointed by McKinley, who felt that their Anti-Expansionist views would be more useful than those of individuals who favored U.S. acquisition of the archipelago.

In January 1899, the commission arrived in the archipelago with a mandate to examine the problems and the growing issues of disagreement between the United States and the Filipino Nationalists. Although well intentioned, the commission was largely ineffective in its efforts to end Filipino resistance. The commission was technically composed of five members, but only Schurman, Worcester, and Denby actually carried out the group's work, as both Dewey and Otis regarded the body as useless and seldom attended meetings.

In 1901, following Schurman's resignation, President McKinley appointed William Howard Taft to head up a second commission. The second commission was scarcely more effective than its predecessor, hamstrung again by personality clashes. Taft's relationship with Otis's successor, Gen. Arthur MacArthur, was strained at best; neither liked or respected the other.

See also Dewey, George; MacArthur, Arthur; McKinley, William, Jr.; Otis, Elwell Stephen; Taft, William Howard.

References and Further Readings

Leech, Margaret. *In the Days of McKinley.* New York: Harper & Brothers, 1959.

Linn, Brian McAllister. *The Philippine War, 1899–1902.* Lawrence: University Press of Kansas, 2000.

Philippine Constabulary

When the United States began its military occupation of the Philippines at the end of the Spanish-American War in August 1898, martial law was imposed as a means of maintaining law and order. With the end of martial law in July 1901, civil affairs in the Philippines were administered by the Philippine Commission. On 18 July 1901, the commission created the Philippine Constabulary to serve as the law enforcement body for the Philippines. In this capacity, members of the constabulary functioned as a form of national police, whose job was to maintain law and order throughout the archipelago. Their role in carrying out that assignment was anything but uneventful. During 1901, for example, constabulary members killed or captured more than 3,000 *ladrones* (bandits) in fulfilling their mission.

Although they participated to some extent with the Philippine Scouts and the U.S. Army, their principal function was to deal with the many bandits who flourished in the islands. The rank and file of the constabulary was composed of Filipinos between 18 and 25 years of age, in good health, and fluent in both Spanish and English. The officer corps was composed of U.S. Army officers, known as constables. Uniforms were similar to those of the U.S. Army and the Philippine Scouts. The constabulary differed from the Philippine Scouts in that the scouts served directly under the U.S. Army but the constabulary was an arm of the civil government.

Although not highly regarded by the U.S. Army at the outset, the Philippine Constabulary did evolve into a highly effective police force. By late 1902, the constabulary numbered some 6,000 men and garrisoned more than 200 stations throughout the archipelago. Units were stationed in the areas from which they had enlisted. The normal duty of the constabulary was to cover an area in small patrols, maintaining law and order. The constabulary was active until World War II, when it merged with the Philippine Army.

See also Lake Lanao Campaigns; Philippine-American War, U.S. Public Reaction to; Philippine Commission; Philippine Scouts.

References and Further Readings

Coats, George Yarrington. "The Philippine Constabulary: 1901–1917." Ph.D. diss., Ohio State University, 1968.

Hurley, Vic. *Jungle Patrol: The Story of the Philippine Constabulary.* New York: E. P. Dutton, 1938.

Linn, Brian McAllister. *The Philippine War, 1899–1902.* Lawrence: University Press of Kansas, 2000.

Smith, Cornelius C., Jr. *Don't Settle for Second: Life and Times of Cornelius C. Smith.* San Rafael, CA: Presidio Press, 1977.

Philippine Expeditionary Force

As a follow-up to Adm. George Dewey's victory over the Spanish on Manila Bay on 1 May 1898 (he was promoted from commodore to rear admiral on 7 May), President William McKinley directed that an expeditionary force be sent to the Philippines. General of the Army Nelson Miles initially recommended a mixed force of regulars and volunteers, composed of 5,000 infantry, cavalry, and artillery troops.

Maj. Gen. Wesley Merritt, veteran of the Civil War and the Indian wars and the second-ranking soldier in the army, was appointed to command the expeditionary force, which was designated the Eighth Army Corps. Maj. Gen. Elwell S. Otis, like Merritt another veteran of the Civil War and Indian wars, was named second in command.

Although the War Department later increased the strength of the expedition to 20,000 men, Merritt argued for a stronger representation of regulars than Miles was willing to allot. Further, Merritt believed his assignment embraced the entire Philippine Archipelago, whereas Miles saw only the city of Manila and its port facilities as the objective. The fact that the army's two ranking soldiers differed to such an extent with regard to the expedition's role underscores the ambiguity surrounding the U.S. mission in the Philippines, about which President McKinley had been vague at best. In any event, a mixed force of 5,000 regulars and 15,000 volunteers was earmarked for the Eighth Corps.

San Francisco was the assembly and embarkation point for the Eighth Corps. As the various regiments arrived there, they were issued weapons and supplies and given training in simulated battle exercises. Compared to the confusion experienced by the Fifth Corps at Tampa, preparations at San Francisco proceeded smoothly. Unfortunately, there were not enough ships to accommodate Merritt's entire command in one convoy, so the corps was divided into three contingents. The first, consisting of 2,500 men under Brig. Gen. Thomas Anderson, sailed on 25 May 1898; a second group, 3,500 strong, under Brig. Gen. Francis Greene, departed on 15 June. The third and largest contingent, some 4,800 men commanded by Brig. Gen. Arthur MacArthur, sailed on 27 June. Merritt and Otis followed two days later.

All three contingents reached the Philippines by July, where General Merritt's first task was to capture the city of Manila. The capture took place on 13 August, although Merritt was unaware that Spain and the United States had agreed to the Protocol of Peace (cease-fire) the previous day.

At his own request, General Merritt was relieved of command in the fall of 1898, and command of the Philippine Expeditionary Force devolved to General Otis. Initially, Otis was faced with the difficult task of maintaining peace and order among recalcitrant Filipino revolutionaries who resented the U.S. presence in their islands. Then, in February 1899, war broke out between the United States and the Filipino Republican Army, headed by Emilio Aguinaldo.

Otis then had to deal with Aguinaldo as well as with increasingly disgruntled state volunteers. Once the war with Spain ended, these volunteers, who had been mustered into federal service to fight Spain, saw no reason to remain in the Philippines and fight a war against Filipino insurgents. Eventually, these volunteers were shipped back to the United States and replaced with U.S. volunteer regiments recruited specifically for fighting in the Philippines. The Philippine

Expeditionary Force that sailed from San Francisco in the early summer of 1898 had undergone an almost complete transformation by early 1900.

See also Aguinaldo y Famy, Emilio; Anderson, Thomas McArthur; Army, U.S.; Greene, Francis Vinton; MacArthur, Arthur; McKinley, William, Jr.; Manila Bay, Battle of; Merritt, Wesley; Otis, Elwell Stephen.

References and Further Readings

Alberts, Don E. *Brandy Station to Manila Bay: A Biography of General Wesley Merritt.* Austin, TX: Presidial Press, 1980.

Cosmas, Graham. *An Army for Empire: The United States Army in the Spanish-American War.* College Station: Texas A&M University Press, 1998.

Linn, Brian McAllister. *The Philippine War, 1899–1902.* Lawrence: University Press of Kansas, 2000.

Philippine Islands, Acquisition of, by the United States

President William McKinley's decision to annex the Philippine Archipelago as part of the settlement with Spain after the Spanish-American War ranks as one of the most controversial moves in U.S. history. Congressional leaders, politicians, businessmen, and military leaders of the day were sharply divided over the issue of annexation. And in the years since, historians have been equally divided in their assessment of McKinley's decision.

During the negotiations in Paris that eventually led to the Treaty of Paris, McKinley gave some consideration to annexing only Manila, with its port facilities. However, in the event of war, the city by itself would have been nearly impossible to defend. Another option was to annex the entire island of Luzon, including Manila. Also considered was annexation of the entire archipelago, save for the southernmost island of Mindanao. However, any of these options would surely have invited other European nations, most likely Germany, and possibly Japan to share in the division of the archipelago, and that did not bode well for the future. Nor could McKinley simply return the islands to the control of Spain. The possibility of the Philippines becoming a protectorate also seemed a poor choice, since the United States would have no real authority but would bear all of the responsibility. As a consequence, McKinley concluded that since the Filipinos were not yet ready for self-rule, the only real option was for the United States to annex the entire archipelago.

The Expansionists, led by Theodore Roosevelt and Henry Cabot Lodge, expounding the philosophy of social Darwinism—that is, that only superior people and cultures were able to gain ground and flourish—argued that the United States had a responsibility, indeed an obligation, to take U.S. democratic principles and know-how abroad.

During the negotiations in Paris, the U.S. commissioners heard a strong argument from the naval attaché, Comdr. Royal Bradford, a dyed-in-the-wool Expansionist who favored acquisition of all Spanish territories, including Cuba, as well as a bit of China.

Anti-Expansionists such as Andrew Carnegie feared that if the Philippines became a U.S. possession, citizenship might one day be conferred on Filipinos, an inferior race of people. And there were commercial concerns on the part of the opposition, born out of fear that the home labor market would be affected by cheap labor in the Philippines.

Perhaps the strongest argument put forth by the Anti-Expansionists was that annexation was contrary to U.S. policy. Not only was there no precedent for annexation in the nation's history but the United States had also never had colonial aims; furthermore, there was no provision in the Constitution for acquiring and administering colonies.

McKinley is alleged to have said that he never wanted the Philippines, and when they came as "a gift from the Gods" (Smith, p. 207), he did not know what to do with them, an observation that may have contained more than a germ of truth. But no one really knows exactly how McKinley felt about the Philippines because of the lack of personal papers to explain his views on the issues that confronted his presidency.

See also McKinley, William, Jr.; Philippine Archipelago; Treaty of Paris.

References and Further Readings

Alfonso, Oscar M. *Theodore Roosevelt and the Philippines, 1897–1909.* Quezon City: University of the Philippines Press, 1970.

Leech, Margaret. *In the Days of McKinley.* New York: Harper & Brothers, 1959.

May, Ernest R. *American Imperialism: A Speculative Essay.* Chicago: Imprint Publications, 1991.

Morgan, H. Wayne, ed. *Making Peace with Spain: The Diary of Whitelaw Reid—September–December, 1898.* Austin: University of Texas Press, 1965.

Musicant, Ivan. *Empire by Default: The Spanish-American War and the Dawn of the American Century.* New York: Henry Holt and Company, 1998.

Smith, Ephraim K. "William McKinley's Enduring Legacy." In James C. Bradford, ed. *Crucible of Empire: The Spanish-American War and Its Aftermath,* pp. 205–250. Annapolis, MD: Naval Institute Press, 1993.

Philippine Islands, Blockade of

Part of the U.S. strategy in combating the Filipino guerrilla forces during the Philippine-American War (1899–1902) was to impose a naval blockade that effectively shut down interisland commerce. The principal tool was the shallow-draft gunboat, which was able to ply the inland waterways of the archipelago's more than 7,000 islands. In addition to making it all but impossible for the guerrillas to obtain needed supplies, the blockade imposed a hardship on those Filipinos who were not resisting U.S. authority.

Strict regulations prohibited anyone from taking more than 2 pounds of rice out of Manila at any one time, thereby depriving guerrilla forces of what was the single most important food item in the archipelago. War matériel—weapons, ammunition, clothing, anything that might be regarded as being of legitimate use to the revolutionary forces—was considered illegal trade and prohibited from being exported to any part of the archipelago.

The navy's blockade, confined to the inland waterway system, was complemented on land by the army's effort to defeat the guerrillas.

> **See also** Gunboat Operations, Philippines; Otis, Elwell Stephen.
> **References and Further Readings**
> Linn, Brian McAllister. *The Philippine War, 1899–1902*. Lawrence: University Press of Kansas, 2000.
> Palmer, Frederick. *With My Own Eyes: A Personal Study of Battle Years*. Indianapolis, IN: Bobbs-Merrill, 1932.
> Trask, David F. *The War with Spain in 1898*. Lincoln: University of Nebraska Press, 1996.

Philippine Scouts

During the Philippine-American War, U.S. military forces in the archipelago were confronted with hostile terrain, elusive revolutionary forces, and the daunting challenge of communicating with a native population that spoke in many dialects. Thus, local commanders had to be imaginative and resourceful if they were to be at all effective. To address such problems, an auxiliary force of Filipinos was created to support U.S. military efforts, in much the same way as the army had enlisted the services of friendly Indian scouts during Indian wars on the frontier.

In July 1900, Lt. Matthew Batson organized a company of Macabebe scouts to serve in what was probably the first official Filipino scout detachment. It was logical to choose the Macabebes as the first native auxiliaries because they had been loyal to Spain and were antirepublican. Perhaps most important, the Macabebes were fierce enemies of the Tagalogs, who constituted the main tribal group on Luzon and provided most of the manpower for the Filipino Republican Army.

Using their intimate knowledge of the local terrain as well as the guerrilla forces they pursued, the Macabebes moved through jungle and swamp, securing information on guerrilla movements and positions. The Macabebes also effectively hunted down the *ladrones* (bandits) who infested the region.

The Macabebean experiment was so successful that Maj. Gen. Elwell Otis, commanding U.S. forces in the Philippines, ordered two more 100-man native scout units organized in September and October 1900.

Despite this initial success, many army officers were skeptical as to the effectiveness of the native scouts. Their attitude was due, in part, to a lack of faith in the trustworthiness of the scouts. Also, many officers (as well as enlisted men) harbored a deep racial bias toward the Filipino people, whom they considered inferior in much the same way that they regarded blacks and Indians as inferior.

Nevertheless, the Filipino scout organizations not only survived but grew and expanded to more than 15,000 in number. By early 1901, Gen. Arthur MacArthur, who had replaced General Otis and who had been among those most adamantly opposed to native scouts, was forced to acknowledge their contribution and ordered the creation of more scout units. MacArthur's recognition of the scouts' success was no doubt encouraged by his concern for troops to replace the volunteer units being returned to the States.

See also Macabebe Scouts; MacArthur, Arthur; Otis, Elwell Stephen; Philippine-American War, U.S. Public Reaction to.

References and Further Readings

Gates, John Morgan. *Schoolbooks and Krags: The United States Army in the Philippines, 1898–1902.* Contributions in Military History no. 3. Westport, CT: Greenwood Press, 1973.

Linn, Brian McAllister. *The Philippine War, 1899–1902.* Lawrence: University Press of Kansas, 2000.

Wolff, Leon. *Little Brown Brother: America's Forgotten Bid for Empire Which Cost 250,000 Lives.* New York: Kraus Reprint, 1970.

Pilar, Gregorio del (1877–1899)

A former university student, Gregorio del Pilar, brother of Pio del Pilar, embraced the cause of Filipino nationalism with youthful passion. His courage and zeal brought him to Emilio Aguinaldo's attention. When Aguinaldo accepted exile as part of the Pact of

Biyak-na-Bató, Pilar was in the retinue of followers who accompanied Aguinaldo to Hong Kong. Although the Spanish had won a temporary victory with the pact, the cause of Filipino nationalism remained alive and well, demonstrating in the Philippines, as well as in Cuba, that the reign of Spanish colonialism was drawing to a close.

When Aguinaldo returned to the Philippines following the outbreak of war between Spain and the United States, Pilar was appointed brigadier general in the Filipino Republican Army, despite his youth. A natural field commander, Pilar conducted a brilliant rearguard defense at Tirad Pass during the Philippine-American War, thereby allowing Aguinaldo's main army to escape. The battle is sometimes called the "Filipino Thermopylae" because it resembled the heroic Spartan defense at Thermopylae in 480 B.C. Throughout the fierce fight, Pilar, mounted on a white horse, continually exhorted his troops. He was eventually killed by sniper fire, becoming in death a martyred hero—the Filipino Roland.

See also Aguinaldo y Famy, Emilio; Biyak-na-Bató, Pact of; Pilar, Pio del.

References and Further Readings

Kalaw, Tedoro M. *An Acceptable Holocaust: Life and Death of a Boy General.* Translated by M. A. Foronda. Manila: National Historical Commission, 1974.

LeRoy, James. *Americans in the Philippines.* 2 vols. Boston: Houghton Mifflin, 1914.

Linn, Brian McAllister. *The Philippine War, 1899–1902.* Lawrence: University Press of Kansas, 2000.

Wolff, Leon. *Little Brown Brother: America's Forgotten Bid for Empire Which Cost 250,000 Lives.* New York: Kraus Reprint, 1970.

Pilar, Pio del (1860–1931)

Older brother of Gregorio del Pilar, Pio del Pilar was both politically and militarily active in the Philippine revolutionary movement, which was very much alive even after the Spanish won a temporary victory with the Pact of Biyak-na-Bató. As a major general, he was one of Emilio Aguinaldo's senior commanders during the siege of Manila. His dislike of Americans was intense. Following the end of the war with Spain in August 1898 and the beginning of the Philippine-American War in February 1899, Pilar, a cruel sort, provoked U.S. retaliation with obstructionist tactics and illegally held U.S. soldiers captive. He was also a member of the Philippine National Assembly and helped draft the Malolos Constitution. After the outbreak of the Philippine-American War, Pilar waged guerrilla warfare against the United States. He was subsequently captured and sent into exile on the island of Guam.

See also Manila Bay, Battle of; Pilar, Gregorio del.
References and Further Readings
Kalaw, Tedoro M. *The Philippine Revolution.* Manila: Vargas Filipiana Foundation, 1969.
LeRoy, James. *Americans in the Philippines.* 2 vols. Boston: Houghton Mifflin, 1914.
Linn, Brian McAllister. *The Philippine War, 1899–1902.* Lawrence: University Press of Kansas, 2000.

Plant Railroad and Steamship Company

Transportation played an important part in the U.S. war effort during the Spanish-American War. In the years following the Civil War, Henry Bender Plant (1819–1899), a Connecticut man, acquired a number of southern railroad properties, as well as steamship lines and hotels, all of which were managed and operated under the Plant System umbrella. These rail lines ran south from Georgia to the city of Tampa, Florida, which Plant was rapidly developing into a major port city. In Tampa, freight arriving on his rail lines could be loaded aboard his waiting steamships.

Those facilities and proximity to Havana made Tampa a logical point for assembling and embarking the Cuban Expeditionary Force. Unfortunately, Plant's Tampa facilities were not yet ready to accommodate the Fifth Corps in the spring of 1898. As a result, there was much confusion and overcrowding as the troops poured into the city.

See also Army, U.S.; Camps, Staging Areas, and Embarkation Points, U.S. Army; Cuban Campaign; Cuban Expeditionary Force, U.S.
References and Further Readings
Cosmas, Graham. *An Army for Empire: The United States Army in the Spanish-American War.* College Station: Texas A&M University Press, 1998.
Leech, Margaret. *In the Days of McKinley.* New York: Harper & Brothers, 1959.
O'Toole, G. J. A. *The Spanish War: An American Epic, 1898.* New York: W. W. Norton, 1984.

Platt Amendment

See **Platt, Orville Hitchcock**

Platt, Orville Hitchcock (1827–1905)

Born in Washington, Connecticut, Orville Hitchcock Platt studied law and then entered politics, serving as U.S. senator from Connecticut from 1879 to 1905. Although an active participant in the debate over Cuban independence during the 1890s, Hitchcock, a firm supporter of President William McKinley, argued for a peaceful solution to the growing disagreement between the United States and Spain over the Cuban question. As a strong advocate of expansionism, he favored acquisition of Hawaii and the Philippines.

Platt later served as chair of the Committee on Cuban Relations and is best known for the Platt Amendment, which he introduced in 1901 when the United States was withdrawing its occupation force from Cuba, preparatory to granting Cuban independence. In effect, the Platt Amendment stipulated that the new Cuban government was initially to be bound by certain restrictions. It could not, for example, enter into treaties with any other nation without U.S. approval. The amendment also guaranteed the United States the right to operate military stations on the island and the right to intervene in Cuban affairs when such action was judged necessary.

See also Anti-Imperialist League; Cuba, U.S. Military Occupation of; Imperialism/Expansionism.

References and Further Readings

Foner, Philip S. *The Spanish-Cuban-American War.* 2 vols. New York: Monthly Review Press, 1972.

Leech, Margaret. *In the Days of McKinley.* New York: Harper & Brothers, 1959.

Thomas, Hugh. *Cuba: The Pursuit of Freedom.* New York: Harper & Row, 1971.

Post, Charles Johnson (1873–1956)

Charles J. Post, a former illustrator for the *New York Journal,* served with the Seventy-first New York Volunteers in Cuba during the Santiago Campaign, where he sketched his various impressions of the war. These drawings later served as the basis for a popular memoir of the Spanish-American War, entitled *The Little War of Private Post,* a book that has been in and out of print since it first appeared.

See also Artists and Illustrators; Santiago, Campaign and Siege of.

References and Further Readings

Post, Charles Johnson. *The Little War of Private Post.* Boston: Little, Brown, 1960.

Trask, David F. *The War with Spain in 1898.* Lincoln: University of Nebraska Press, 1996.

Walker, Dale L. *The Boys of '98: Theodore Roosevelt and the Rough Riders.* New York: Forge Books, 1998.

Powelson, Wilfred Van Nest (1872–1960)

Born in Middleton, New York, Powelson studied naval architecture in Glasgow, Scotland, after graduating from the U.S. Naval Academy at Annapolis. He had a standing personal interest in the battleship *Maine,* although he had never actually served on the vessel. Powelson had expected to be transferred to the *Maine* and had, accordingly, carefully studied its construction. In a rather unusual twist, Powelson found himself on the dispatch steamer *Fern,* which reached Havana harbor the day after the *Maine* blew up.

Owing to his background in naval architecture, Powelson, though only an ensign, was regarded as something of an expert in an uncrowded field. During the first court of inquiry's investigation into the *Maine* disaster, he studied the evidence and was particularly successful in building a rapport with the divers who surveyed the ship's wreckage. Later, Powelson testified as an expert witness, stating that the explosion had been external in nature, which suggested that someone had deliberately blown up the *Maine.*

See also *Maine*; *Maine,* Inquiries into the Sinking of.

References and Further Readings

Blow, Michael. *A Ship to Remember: The* Maine *and the Spanish-American War.* New York: William Morrow, 1992.

O'Toole, G. J. A. *The Spanish War: An American Epic, 1898.* New York: W. W. Norton, 1984.

Rickover, H. G. *How the Battleship* Maine *Was Destroyed.* Washington, DC: Department of the Navy, 1976.

Samuels, Peggy, and Harold Samuels. *Remembering the* Maine. Washington, DC: Smithsonian Institution Press, 1995.

Pratt, E. Spencer

Early in 1898, just before the outbreak of the war with Spain, U.S. Consul E. Spencer Pratt met in Hong Kong with the exiled leader of the Filipino revolutionary movement, Emilio Aguinaldo, and encouraged Filipino resistance against Spain. Aguinaldo later charged that Pratt and Commodore George Dewey, who had also talked with him, had promised Philippine independence in exchange for Aguinaldo's cooperation against Spain. Both Pratt and Dewey denied making such an offer, and, in view of President William McKinley's attitude toward the Philippines, it seems highly unlikely that either Pratt or Dewey would have made such a commitment. Some measure of support may have been offered, which Aguinaldo chose to interpret in accordance with his own political objective.

See also Aguinaldo y Famy, Emilio; Biyak-na-Bató, Pact of; Dewey, George; McKinley, William, Jr.; Philippine-American War, U.S. Public Reaction to.

References and Further Readings

Leech, Margaret. *In the Days of McKinley.* New York: Harper & Brothers, 1959.

Primo de Rivera, Fernando (1831–1921)

Fernando Primo de Rivera was governor and captain general of the Philippines from April 1897 to 9 April 1898, just days before the war with the United States broke out. When his offer to pardon Filipino insurgents failed to end the revolution, Primo de Rivera turned to stronger tactics, realizing all the while that he lacked the necessary resources to quash the rebellion. He hoped that a harsher hand might encourage the insurgents to reconsider his offer of amnesty. This led him to accept Pedro Paterno's offer to mediate the differences between Spain and the Filipino Revolutionary Army, which ultimately led to the pact of Biyak-na-Bató and Emilio Aguinaldo's subsequent exile to Hong Kong.

When Primo de Rivera learned that the U.S. Asiatic Squadron was preparing to attack the Philippines if war broke out, he directed Adm. Patricio Montojo, who was commanding Spanish naval forces in the Philippines, to prepare to confront the United States in Subig (Subic) Bay. However, on 9 April, just two weeks before war was declared, Primo de Rivera was replaced by Lt. Gen. Basilio Augustín Dávila. Believing that the Spanish naval squadron in the Philippines could win a battle with the U.S. Asiatic Squadron, Augustín Dávila refused to allow Admiral Montojo to disperse his squadron, thereby contributing to Commodore Dewey's victory on Manila Bay.

See also Aguinaldo y Famy, Emilio; Augustín Dávila, Don Basilio; Manila Bay, Battle of; Montojo y Pasarón, Patricio; Paterno, Pedro Alejandro.

References and Further Readings

Musicant, Ivan. *Empire by Default: The Spanish-American War and the Dawn of the American Century.* New York: Henry Holt and Company, 1998.

Wolff, Leon. *Little Brown Brother: America's Forgotten Bid for Empire Which Cost 250,000 Lives.* New York: Kraus Reprint, 1970.

Prisoners of War

Very few U.S. soldiers were taken prisoner by the Spanish during the Cuban Campaign of the Spanish-American War, but Gen. William R. Shafter's Fifth Corps captured some 26,000 Spanish soldiers.

After the Protocol of Peace was signed in August, the Spanish prisoners were transported to the United States and held in custody before eventually being returned to Spain at U.S. expense. Owing to the guerrilla nature of the Philippine-American War, prisoner-of-war formalities were seldom observed. There were numerous instances of torture and mutilation of prisoners by both U.S. troops and Filipino insurgents.

See also Atrocities; Balangiga Massacre; Santiago, Campaign and Siege of.

References and Further Readings

Linn, Brian McAllister. *The U.S. Army and Counterinsurgency in the Philippine War, 1899–1902.* Chapel Hill: University of North Carolina Press, 1989.

———. *The Philippine War, 1899–1902.* Lawrence: University Press of Kansas, 2000.

Musicant, Ivan. *Empire by Default: The Spanish-American War and the Dawn of the American Century.* New York: Henry Holt and Company, 1998.

Welch, Richard E., Jr. "American Atrocities in the Philippines: The Indictment and the Response." *Pacific Historical Review,* vol. 43, no. 2, May 1974.

Proctor, Redfield (1831–1908)

Commodore George Dewey, famous for his victory over the Spanish at Manila Bay, was a protégé of Vermont senator Redfield Proctor. Born in Proctorsville, Vermont, Redfield Proctor was the son of a successful merchant and manufacturer. After graduating from Dartmouth, he studied law and began his legal practice in Boston in 1860. During the Civil War, he served as colonel of the Fifteenth Vermont Volunteers.

After the Civil War, Proctor entered politics in Vermont, serving first as state senator, then as lieutenant governor, and finally as governor. Appointed secretary of war in President Benjamin Harrison's cabinet, he resigned in 1891 to enter the U.S. Senate and was subsequently reelected three times.

Known as the "Marble King" because the Vermont Marble Company of which he was president was the largest company of its kind in the country, Proctor was a powerful and influential member of the Senate, where he had a reputation for thoroughness and being a steady

hand. It was Proctor who sponsored the appointment of Commodore George Dewey to command the Asiatic Squadron. Proctor made a fact-finding visit to Cuba prior to the war, and as a result of his personal observations, he lobbied persuasively for U.S. intervention in Cuba.

> **See also** Dewey, George; McKinley, William, Jr.; Roosevelt, Theodore.
> **References and Further Readings**
> Leech, Margaret. *In the Days of McKinley.* New York: Harper & Brothers, 1959.
> Musicant, Ivan. *Empire by Default: The Spanish-American War and the Dawn of the American Century.* New York: Henry Holt and Company, 1998.

Protocol of Peace

On 12 August 1898, the United States and Spain signed the Protocol of Peace that officially brought an end to hostilities and permitted the two nations to proceed with formal treaty negotiations at a neutral location. Paris was selected as the site of the negotiations, and there, after several months of discussion, a formal treaty was entered into in December 1898.

Today, a protocol of peace would be termed a cease-fire agreement.

President William McKinley (standing right, next to table) and members of his official family watch as French ambassador Jules Cambon signs the Protocol of Peace, a document preceding the formal peace negotiations ending the Spanish-American War.

See also Treaty of Paris.

References and Further Readings

Leech, Margaret. *In the Days of McKinley.* New York: Harper & Brothers, 1959.

Musicant, Ivan. *Empire by Default: The Spanish-American War and the Dawn of the American Century.* New York: Henry Holt and Company, 1998.

O'Toole, G. J. A. *The Spanish War: An American Epic, 1898.* New York: W. W. Norton, 1984.

Trask, David F. *The War with Spain in 1898.* Lincoln: University of Nebraska Press, 1996.

Puerto Rican Campaign (21 July–12 August 1898)

Initially, both General of the Army Nelson Miles and his predecessor, Gen. John Schofield, who acted as a military adviser to President William McKinley during the early weeks of the Spanish-American War, favored a Puerto Rican campaign over an invasion of Cuba. Miles thought it more strategically sound to strike Puerto Rico first, wait until the fever season in Cuba ended, and then send the navy to defeat the Spanish fleet. In late May 1898, when Adm. Pascual Cervera's Spanish fleet sailed into the harbor of Santiago de Cuba, thereby surrendering its strategic initiative, Miles again pressed for a Puerto Rican campaign, to be followed by an invasion of Cuba. However, President William McKinley chose to invade Cuba first as a means of supporting the navy in its effort to destroy the Spanish fleet, which remained the primary strategic objective. This move, it was reasoned, would have a more immediate and compelling effect on Spain.

Although the destruction of Admiral Cervera's fleet on 3 July 1898 was a stunning victory for the United States, the campaign for Santiago had bogged down, and Miles was directed to proceed to Cuba with an additional 3,400 troops to support Gen. William Shafter's campaign if needed. But on 17 July, Santiago capitulated, and Miles received authorization on the following day to proceed with an invasion of Puerto Rico.

Miles's opposition to a Cuban invasion during the fever season was well founded. By the time Santiago surrendered, General Shafter's Fifth Corps was riddled with yellow fever and malaria. Miles had originally planned to include a part of the Fifth Corps in his Puerto Rican Campaign, but the men were in no shape for more campaigning. Miles had wisely kept his troops with him on ship so as not to expose them to tropical fevers. Now, with authorization finally in hand, Miles sailed for Puerto Rico with a force of 3,400, to be followed by an additional 13,000 men and supporting artillery.

Interservice bickering and rivalry, present throughout the campaign in Cuba, was not absent from the Puerto Rican Campaign. Miles, who never avoided a conflict if he could help it, argued with Adm. William T. Sampson about the size of his naval escort. President McKinley, the soul of patience, finally tired of the wrangling and directed the navy to provide Miles with whatever ships he needed. But the bickering and underhandedness did not end there. In early August, Comdr. Charles Davis recommended to Admiral Sampson that the navy take San Juan alone, without the army's participation. Miles learned of the scheme and promptly nipped the plan in the bud, securing assurance from Washington that the navy would do no more than deliver troops to the island.

Initially, the plan called for Miles to land at Cape Fajardo on the north coast of Puerto Rico. Once at sea, however, he changed the objectives to Ponce and Guánica on the south coast. From intelligence reports provided him, Miles knew the Spanish were expecting him to land at Fajardo and had prepared accordingly. The city of Ponce, by contrast, was the largest on the island, only 70 miles from San Juan, and it offered a ready source of supplies.

Meanwhile, Manuel Macías, Governor-General of Puerto Rico, was fully aware of the U.S. intent to invade his island, though the point of landing was unknown. Macías's orders were to offer stout resistance, as it was hoped that doing so would strengthen Spain's bargaining position. As he saw it, he had the option of either concentrating most of his military resources around San Juan, the capital, or dispersing his forces so as to cover key positions. Although there were other strong points on the island, the bulk of the Spanish defenses were around San Juan.

On 25 July, a naval landing party captured Guánica, a small but good deep-water harbor 15 miles west of Ponce, without resistance. On 27 July , a detachment from Guánica advanced on Ponce and was joined the following day by troops under the command of Brevet Maj. Gen. James H. Wilson, whose force had sailed from Charleston on 20 July. The combined force compelled the Spanish to surrender the city. Also on 28 July, a column under Brig. Gen. George Garretson moved on Yauco, a few miles north of Guánica. After a brief skirmish with Spanish troops, Garretson and his troops captured the town and nearby railroad.

Although the population of Puerto Rico had not risen up against Spanish rule, as was the case in Cuba, they did not strongly support the Spanish. Indeed, when in Ponce, Miles proclaimed the Americans had come as liberators and found that the population responded enthusiastically.

By 5 August, the columns of Maj. Gen. John R. Brooke and Brig. Gen. Theodore Schwan had landed on the island with 5,000 and 3,000 men, respectively, so that combined with General Wilson's force, Miles now had some 17,000 troops at his disposal. Unlike William Shafter's Fifth Corps, the various elements of Miles's command left the United States fully equipped to conduct their campaign.

Miles learned that the Spanish were organizing their defenses in the low mountainous area separating the northern half of the island from the southern half. A key position in this plan was the strong point at Aibonito, which guarded a gateway through the mountains leading to San Juan, Mile's goal. To attain that objective, he decided to advance with four columns of troops, sweep across the island, and converge at San Juan.

General Schwan was to move from Ponce, northwest along the left flank, to Mayagüez and Arecibo. Garretson's course was due north to Adjuntas and then Arecibo, where he and Schwan would form one column under Brig. Gen. Guy Henry and move directly on San Juan. Meanwhile, a third column under General Wilson was to march northeast from Ponce to Aibonito, the only Spanish strong point on the route to San Juan. Finally, General Brooke was directed to march to Cayey, at which point he would be behind the Spanish defenders at Aibonito. It was believed his presence would compel the defenders to retire, leaving the route from Aibonito open.

Schwan got under way on 6 August, aiming to clear western Puerto Rico of any Spanish forces, but he discovered that few troops were there to offer any real resistance. In the course of an eight-day march, Schwan's column captured nine towns and had a sharp fight near Mayagüez, suffering some 17 casualties in the process.

General Brooke commenced his advance, moving west on 8 August from Arroyo toward Guyama, where he encountered significant resistance and sustained several casualties before finally capturing the position.

On 9 August, Wilson had a stiff fight at Coamo, a few miles southwest of Aibonito. This hard-fought action ended when the Sixteenth Pennsylvania moved around the Spanish and flanked the defenders out of position before inflicting heavy casualties. Some 40 Spanish were killed and wounded, and 170 were captured. Wilson's losses were 6 men wounded.

The entire campaign was being conducted amid an impending cease-fire. As Wilson was preparing to attack Aibonito after a request for surrender was rejected, Miles received word that the Protocol of

Peace had been signed, thereby concluding the campaign.

Brief though it was, the Puerto Rican Campaign moved along smartly, far more so than General Shafter's effort in Cuba. There were no tropical diseases to debilitate the troops, and the various columns made surprisingly good time marching over rough terrain. During the campaign, Miles and his field commanders fought six engagements and suffered only 30 casualties.

Although conducted successfully, the Puerto Rican Campaign unfortunately had little effect on the final terms of the peace negotiations of 1898, except to reaffirm that Spain had little bargaining power at the conference table. Had the campaign taken longer and proven costlier, it might well have worked to Spain's advantage.

See also Brooke, John Rutter; McKinley, William, Jr.; Miles, Nelson Appleton; Protocol of Peace; Santiago, Campaign and Siege of; Schwan, Theodore; Wilson, James Harrison.

References and Further Readings

Cosmas, Graham. *An Army for Empire: The United States Army in the Spanish-American War*. College Station: Texas A&M University Press, 1998.

Leech, Margaret. *In the Days of McKinley*. New York: Harper & Brothers, 1959.

Trask, David F. *The War with Spain in 1898*. Lincoln: University of Nebraska Press, 1996.

Wilson, James Harrison. *Under the Old Flag: Recollections of Military Operations in the War for the Union, the Spanish War, the Boxer Rebellion, etc.* Vol. 2. New York: D. Appleton & Company, 1912.

Pulitzer, Joseph (1847–1911)

Joseph Pulitzer was one of the most influential voices in the history of U.S. journalism, and his paper, the *New York World*, aggressively covered both the Spanish-American War and the subsequent war in the Philippines. Pulitzer was born in Hungary, the son of a Catholic mother and a Jewish father. As a young man, he emigrated to the United States sometime before the Civil War, settling in the Saint Louis area. Tall and an excellent horseman, his poor eyesight probably would have kept him out of military service had it not been for the fact that an aggressive recruiter signed him up for the Union army.

After the Civil War, Pulitzer began his newspaper career with the *St. Louis Post-Dispatch*. After moving to New York in 1883, he took over the *New York World*, making it a voice for reform and speaking out against corporate interests. Pulitzer believed that sensational stories sold newspapers, and the *World* came to reflect that philosophy.

In the years preceding the outbreak of the Spanish-American

War, Cuba was a fertile field in which to exploit sensationalism. The plight of the Cuban people under the thumb of Spanish tyranny made marvelous copy. Between them, Pulitzer and his archrival, William Randolph Hearst and his *New York Journal,* were largely responsible for introducing a sensationalist style of reporting that came to be known as yellow journalism (so nicknamed because of the yellow ink on the cartoon strips of the *World* at first and later the *Journal*).

Pulitzer, however, did earn bad publicity during the Santiago Campaign in Cuba when one of his reporters, Sylvester Scovel, threatened to punch Fifth Corps commander Gen. William R. Shafter over the latter's refusal to let him appear in a victory photo. Then, when a Stephen Crane story implied cowardice on the part of the Seventy-first New York Volunteers, the *World* lost face. Pulitzer backed away from war as a focal point of his coverage, adopting a more sedate style of news reporting.

Nervous and high-strung, Pulitzer scarcely knew an idle moment during his 64 years of life.

See also Hearst, William Randolph; Journalism.

References and Further Readings

Brown, Charles H. *The Correspondents' War: Journalists in the Spanish-American War.* New York: Charles Scribner's Sons, 1967.

Milton, Joyce. *The Yellow Kids: Foreign Correspondents in the Heyday of Yellow Journalism.* New York: Harper & Row, 1989.

Punta Gorda (Cuba)

A small peninsula north of the main channel leading into the harbor of Santiago, Punta Gorda was part of the Spanish defensive system designed to guard the harbor. There, a battery of four modern breechloaders and a pair of old howitzers were located. The Punta Gorda battery, along with others, posed a real threat to any naval vessels that attempted to enter the harbor. It was this threat that caused U.S. Adm. William T. Sampson to reject the idea of sending his squadron into the harbor to attack Adm. Pascual Cervera's Spanish Squadron until the army had neutralized the threat.

See also Santiago, Campaign and Siege of; Santiago de Cuba, Naval Battle of.

References and Further Readings

Feuer, A. B. *The Spanish-American War at Sea.* Westport, CT: Greenwood Press, 1995.

O'Toole, G. J. A. *The Spanish War: An American Epic, 1898.* New York: W. W. Norton, 1984.

Trask, David F. *The War with Spain in 1898.* Lincoln: University of Nebraska Press, 1996.

Rations

Feeding the U.S. Army during the Spanish-American War, whether it was at home or actively campaigning in the field, was the responsibility of the Army Subsistence Department, which probably did a good job overall, considering its resources and the prevailing attitude toward nutrition at that time. Troops in garrison (at a permanent duty station) were fed a standard bill of fare, which consisted of fresh beef and sometimes pork, as well as bread, green coffee, and fresh vegetables in season. The usual condiments such as salt, pepper, sugar, and vinegar also were available.

Troops in the field were issued fatty bacon, hardtack, canned beef, canned beans, and canned tomatoes, which frequently were in a state of fermentation. The C rations and K rations known to soldiers of World War II and Korea did not exist at the time of the Spanish-American War. The Subsistence Department had been working on an emergency ration consisting of bacon, pea meal, hardtack, coffee, and seasoning, plus some tobacco, but in 1898, that ration was still in the experimental stage, so few troops used it.

The only really significant change in the army's diet during the Spanish-American War was the use of fresh roast beef that had been processed and stored in tins. Introduced by Commissary General Charles P. Eagan, this processed beef later became the subject of the notorious "beef scandal." The meat was intended to be cooked before being consumed, but troops in the field often did not have time to cook the beef and frequently ate it directly from the tin—or tried to. The odor of the preservative and the taste of the beef itself turned many a hungry soldier's stomach.

Aside from the tinned beef, the troops seemed to fare well enough on army rations, notwithstanding the monotony of the diet. The men did complain about the unground green coffee, however, because they had no way to conveniently grind the beans.

Although the Subsistence Department did a good job of distributing rations to field commands, it played no part in meal preparation. The department was responsible only for providing the regiments with rations every ten days. The rations then were distributed to the various companies, where some individual or section was detailed to prepare the meals.

The system began to break down at the company level, for the commanders did not always follow through on the requisitioning of supplies or on ensuring that a reliable meal system was set up. Although some company cooks were good, many were not. Others did a poor job of using rations to the best advantage. As a result, meals often were generous at the beginning of the issuance period and slim at the end.

In response to Commissary General Eagan's efforts, the U.S. Congress in July 1898 finally authorized army companies to have trained cooks. The change, however, did not come about in time to have a noticeable impact on the army during the Spanish-American War.

See also Beef Scandal; Eagan, Charles Patrick.

References and Further Readings

Cosmas, Graham. *An Army for Empire: The United States Army in the Spanish-American War.* College Station: Texas A&M University Press, 1998.

Seaman, Louis Livingston. "The United States Army Ration in the Tropics." Open letter. *Century Magazine,* February 1899.

Rea, George Bronson (1869–1936)

An electrical engineering graduate of Stevens Institute of Technology, George Bronson Rea arrived in Cuba about 1890 to pursue his career. In 1896, a year after the beginning of the Cuban War of Independence, Rea, who also studied military history and who had been drawn to the Cuban revolutionary movement, joined the *New York Herald* as a reporter. He traveled with the celebrated Cuban revolutionary leaders Máximo Gómez and Antonio Maceo, the "Bronze Titan." Rea considered the former to be overrated but regarded the latter as a superb field commander. During the Spanish-American War, he covered the Santiago Campaign. Later, because of his engineering background, he was assigned to study the Spanish fortifications in San Juan, Puerto Rico.

Because Rea was an on-the-spot reporter, his stories to the *Herald* were firsthand accounts. These reports usually painted a far different picture than did the stories by other reporters, who relied on the information circulated by the revolutionaries themselves. Later, Rea published a book in which he exposed the exaggerations—about the atrocities and casualties—in much of the writings about the Cuban War of Independence (*Facts and Fakes about Cuba*).

See also Cuban Revolution; Gómez Báez, Máximo; Journalism; Maceo Grajales, Antonio.

References and Further Readings

Brown, Charles H. *The Correspondents' War: Journalists in the Spanish-American War.* New York: Charles Scribner's Sons, 1967.

Milton, Joyce. *The Yellow Kids: Foreign Correspondents in the Heyday of Yellow Journalism.* New York: Harper & Row, 1989.

Rea, George Bronson. *Facts and Fakes about Cuba.* New York: George Monro's Sons, 1897.

Reconcentrado (Reconcentration) System

Following his appointment as Spanish commander in Cuba, Gen. Valeriano Weyler initiated a policy of shifting the native populations to central locations, where they were under military control—a policy so oppressive that it served to bring the plight of the Cuban people to the attention of sympathetic Americans. Weyler's strategy was to isolate the rebels from the nonrebels and thereby cut them off from local support. Accordingly, the people found outside these designated areas were deemed to be rebels. Control of the populace was tightened further by means of a series of *trochas* (trenches) that divided the island.

Although Weyler's *reconcentrado* policy had some success, it worked a great hardship on the nonrebel population. Living conditions were like those in a concentration camp: crowded, with shortages of food and medical supplies. As reports describing these conditions began to appear in U.S. newspapers, the public outcry against Spanish treatment of the Cuban people increased. Eventually, Weyler was replaced.

Interestingly, in an effort to deal with Filipino guerrillas, U.S. Army officers later employed a similar policy in the Philippines by attempting to isolate the insurgents from the civilian population.

See also Cuban Revolution; Weyler y Nicolau, Valeriano "Butcher."

References and Further Readings

Foner, Philip S. *The Spanish-Cuban-American War.* 2 vols. New York: Monthly Review Press, 1972.

Linn, Brian McAllister. *The Philippine War, 1899–1902.* Lawrence: University Press of Kansas, 2000.

Trask, David F. *The War with Spain in 1898.* Lincoln: University of Nebraska Press, 1996.

Reed Commission

See **Reed, Walter**

Reed, Walter (1851–1902)

Born in Virginia, Walter Reed studied medicine, graduating from Bellevue Hospital Medical College. In 1875, he entered the U.S. Army Medical Corps. After fifteen years of service on the western frontier, he was named curator of the Army Medical Museum as well as professor of bacteriology and microscopy at the Army Medical College in Washington. During the Spanish-American War, Reed and several other surgeons visited a number of army camps to see firsthand the atrocious living conditions. These inspections resulted in significant improvements in sanitary conditions—but not in time to prevent more than 20,000 cases of typhoid fever. Surgeon General George Miller Sternberg then appointed Reed to head up a commission to investigate the reasons that such conditions had been allowed to exist.

Surgeon General Sternberg, himself an authority on tropical fevers, recognized Reed's interest in studying and researching the cause of these fevers and appointed Reed to head a yellow fever commission. The commission subsequently determined that the *Aedes aegypti* mosquito transmitted the dreaded fever.

Reed died of appendicitis in 1902. The Walter Reed Army Hospital in Washington, DC, is named in his honor.

> **See also** Camps, Staging Areas, and Embarkation Points, U.S. Army; Diseases; Medical Department, U.S. Army; Sternberg, George Miller.
> **References and Further Readings**
> Bean, William B. *Walter A. Reed: A Biography.* Charlottesville: University Press of Virginia, 1982.

Reid, Whitelaw (1837–1912)

An influential journalist, Whitelaw Reid graduated from Miami University in 1856. As a newspaperman, he reported extensively on the Civil War for the *Cincinnati Gazette.* He later was named managing editor of the *Washington Tribune.* An active member of the Republican Party and an avowed Expansionist, Reid was a strong supporter of President William McKinley and his decisions relating to the Spanish-American War.

In the fall of 1898, while assembling the U.S. commission to negotiate a peace settlement with Spain, McKinley chose Reid, knowing full well that he was an Expansionist who favored acquisition of the Philippines. McKinley, however, sought to have the commission balanced equally between Expansionists and Anti-Expansionists. Reid's diary of the commission's deliberations later served as the basis for a book about the Treaty of Paris, *Making Peace with Spain.*

See also Journalism; McKinley, William, Jr.; Philippine Islands, Acquisition of, by the United States; Treaty of Paris.

References and Further Readings

Cortissoz, Royal. *The Life of Whitelaw Reid.* New York: Charles Scribner's Sons, 1921.

Leech, Margaret. *In the Days of McKinley.* New York: Harper & Brothers, 1959.

Morgan, H. Wayne. *America's Road to Empire: The War with Spain and Overseas Expansion.* New York: John Wiley & Sons, 1965.

———. *Making Peace with Spain: The Diary of Whitlaw Reid— September–December, 1898.* Austin: University of Texas Press, 1965.

"Remember the *Maine*"

In addition to "Remember the Alamo" and "Remember Pearl Harbor," famous war slogans in U.S. history include "Remember the *Maine,* to hell with Spain." The slogan emerged out of the Spanish-American War and referenced the destruction of the well-known battleship that some thought was blown up by the Spanish, though that finding was never confirmed. The origin of the slogan is unclear, but it may have been part of a poem or a cartoon caption that appeared in the *New York World* newspaper immediately after the *Maine* was destroyed.

See also *Maine.*

References and Further Readings

Blow, Michael. *A Ship to Remember: The* Maine *and the Spanish-American War.* New York: William Morrow, 1992.

Remey, George Collier (1841–1928)

Born in Iowa, George Collier Remey graduated from the U.S. Naval Academy at Annapolis in 1859. He served in the U.S. Navy during the Civil War and by 1898 had risen to the rank of commodore, in command of the naval base at Key West, Florida. There, he efficiently managed the navy's key base during the Spanish-American War. After hostilities in Cuba ended, Remey commanded the Asiatic Squadron in Philippine waters. He was promoted to rear admiral in 1898, and during the Boxer Rebellion, he transferred his headquarters to China to coordinate naval activities in that area.

See also Boxer Rebellion; Naval Blockade of Cuba; Navy, U.S.

References and Further Readings

Chadwick, Rear Adm. French Ensor. *Relations of the United States and Spain: The Spanish American War.* 2 vols. New York: Charles Scribner's Sons, 1911 (reprinted in 1968).

Linn, Brian McAllister. *The Philippine War, 1899–1902.* Lawrence: University Press of Kansas, 2000.

Trask, David F. *The War with Spain in 1898.* Lincoln: University of Nebraska Press, 1996.

Remington, Frederic Sackrider (1861–1909)

Born in Canton, New York, Frederic Sackrider Remington was one of the best-known illustrators of the western American frontier. In 1880, Remington went to the West, where he created numerous sketches and paintings of cowboys, soldiers, and Indians. By 1895, with the Wild West having mostly disappeared, Remington returned to the East, where he went to work for William Randolph Hearst's *New York Journal.* It was for the *Journal* that Remington illustrated the scenes from the Spanish-American War.

In 1896, Hearst sent the young illustrator to Cuba to record his impressions of the revolution and the sufferings of the Cuban people. Remington was discouraged by the conditions he saw; he also believed there would be no war with Spain—and so informed his boss. Hearst reportedly replied that if Remington would provide the drawings, he (Hearst) would provide the war. Many of Remington's drawings were featured in the stories of Richard Harding Davis, who at the time also worked for Hearst.

Despite Hearst's words, Remington soon returned to the United States. After the outbreak of war with Spain in April 1898, he went to Tampa, Florida, where he recorded impressions of camp life, and he later covered the Cuban Santiago Campaign.

See also Artists and Illustrators; Cuban Revolution; Davis, Richard Harding; Hearst, William Randolph; Santiago, Campaign and Siege of.

References and Further Readings

Allen, Douglas. *Frederic Remington and the Spanish-American War.* New York: Crown Publishers, 1971.

Harrington, Peter, and Frederick A. Sharf. *"A Splendid Little War": The Spanish-American War, 1898—The Artists' Perspective.* London: Greenhill Books, 1998.

Revenue Cutter Service, U.S.

Forerunner of the U.S. Coast Guard, the Revenue Cutter Service had its origin in the aftermath of the Revolutionary War with Great Britain when fast ships—known as cutters—patrolled the coastline, enforcing maritime laws and collecting tariffs. At the time of the Spanish-American War in 1898, some thirteen revenue cutters and crews were attached to the Navy Department for duty. Eight cutters were assigned to the North Atlantic Squadron and saw action in Caribbean waters. Four cutters were sent to the Pacific coast, and the cutter *McCulloch* joined the Asiatic Squadron.

See also Naval Strategy, U.S.; Navy, U.S.

References and Further Readings

Chadwick, Rear Adm. French Ensor. *Relations of the United States and Spain: The Spanish American War.* 2 vols. New York: Charles Scribner's Sons, 1911 (reprinted in 1968).

Musicant, Ivan. *Empire by Default: The Spanish-American War and the Dawn of the American Century.* New York: Henry Holt and Company, 1998.

U.S. Coast Guard. *Coast Guard History.* Washington, DC: Department of Transportation, U.S. Coast Guard, 1982.

U.S. Revenue Cutter Service in the War with Spain, 1898. Washington, DC: U.S. Government Printing Office, 1800.

Rizal, José (1861–1896)

One of the great heroes of Philippine independence, José Rizal was born into an affluent family of a Filipino father and a Chinese mother. Following a university education at Saint Thomas in Manila, Rizal went to Madrid to do postgraduate work. Despite their affluence, the family was excluded from the top rung of Philippine society, which was composed largely of Spanish blue bloods. Excluded as they were, the Rizal family developed an intense dislike both for the Spanish and for the Catholic religious orders, whose priests treated Filipino workers like slave labor. Rizal's family was involved in the Filipino independence movement, which preceded the Spanish-American War.

In Madrid, young Rizal soon found himself in the forefront of the university liberals opposed to Spanish rule in the Philippines. Later, he traveled throughout Europe honing his political philosophy. A true intellectual, Rizal also studied medicine and wrote a novel on Filipino freedom. Upon returning to Spain, his writings continued to further his reputation as the foremost exponent of Filipino nationalism.

In 1892, Rizal returned to the Philippines and established the Liga Filipina (Filipino League), an organization that advocated a nonviolent approach to Filipino freedom. Nonetheless, Spanish authorities regarded him as a subversive and eventually exiled him to the island of Mindanao, southernmost in the archipelago, where he continued to write and practice medicine.

Meanwhile, the Filipino independence movement had departed from Rizal's nonviolent approach to freedom, advocating the overthrow of the Spanish government. Although Rizal was diametrically opposed to this philosophy, Spanish authorities continued to regard him as a dangerous political enemy. In 1896, Rizal was arrested and executed for sedition. The act was a serious blunder on Spain's part because Rizal in death became a martyr and father figure of Filipino independence.

See also Aguinaldo y Famy, Emilio; Bonifacio, Andrés; Katipunan.

References and Further Readings

Linn, Brian McAllister. *The Philippine War, 1899–1902.* Lawrence: University Press of Kansas, 2000.

Steinberg, David Joel. *The Philippines: A Singular and a Plural Place.* Boulder, CO: Westview Press, 1994.

Wolff, Leon. *Little Brown Brother: America's Forgotten Bid for Empire Which Cost 250,000 Lives.* New York: Kraus Reprint, 1970.

Roosevelt, Theodore (1858–1919)

Theodore Roosevelt was easily the most colorful U.S. figure of the Spanish-American War period. Born in New York City, he graduated from Harvard in 1880. Physically weak and asthmatic as a child, he built himself up through hard work and sheer determination. Following the deaths of his mother and his first wife on the same day, Roosevelt headed west and spent two years ranching in North Dakota. The hard life of the frontier seemed to be exactly the tonic he needed to regenerate his spirit.

Eventually, Roosevelt returned to the East and entered politics, serving as a member of the U.S. Civil Service Commission and president of the New York City Board of Police Commissioners. He earned a reputation as a hard-driving reformer. Also a prolific writer, Roosevelt's *Naval History of the War of 1812* is still regarded as an outstanding work.

In 1897, President William McKinley appointed Roosevelt assistant secretary of the navy under Secretary John D. Long. An avowed Expansionist and a jingoist, Roosevelt championed Commodore George Dewey's appointment as commander of the U.S. Navy's Asiatic Squadron, believing that Dewey was exactly the right man to have in the western Pacific in the event of war with Spain, which seemed increasingly likely.

On one occasion, when Secretary Long was away from the office on a brief holiday, Roosevelt took it upon himself to issue a directive to Dewey to keep his ships "coaled up." In the event of war, Dewey was to steam directly to the Philippines and there engage the Spanish fleet. Although Roosevelt has been criticized for taking it upon himself to issue such an order, the strategy governing Dewey's movements had already been decided by the president and Secretary Long. Nevertheless, Roosevelt exceeded his authority in issuing a directive that ought to have come directly from the secretary.

After the declaration of war with Spain, Roosevelt resigned from the Navy Department and, together with his friend Leonard Wood, organized the First U.S. Volunteer Cavalry, which eventually would be known as the Rough Riders, one of the best-known units in U.S. military history. Initially, Roosevelt was offered command of the regiment, but he deferred to his friend Wood, who then was appointed colonel of the regiment, with Theodore as his lieutenant colonel and second in command.

Col. Theodore Roosevelt at the time of the Spanish-American War.

Roosevelt probably recognized that, given his total lack of military experience, he would be wise to let Wood command the regiment. Being second in command would give Roosevelt an opportunity to observe without having to bear the burden of command—at least until he had acquired some experience.

Roosevelt's penchant for publicity was irksome at times for Wood, who could not help but feel that, although he was the regimental commander, the regiment really had become Roosevelt's. Indeed, one of the nicknames by which the regiment was known was "Teddy's Terrors." The two men nevertheless remained good friends during their service together.

When Gen. William R. Shafter's Fifth Corps sailed for Cuba in June 1898, there was room enough to accommodate only two-thirds of the Rough Riders—and even that was largely a result of the aggressiveness of Wood and Roosevelt, who were determined that their regiment not be left behind, though there was room for only a few horses.

President Theodore Roosevelt reading his message to his cabinet before sending it to Congress, 1903 (left to right: George B. Cortelyu, Philander C. Knox, Henry C. Payne, William Henry Moody, John Hay, Roosevelt, Ethan Allen Hitchcock, Elihu Root, Leslie Mortier Shaw, and James Wilson).

During the stiff fight at Las Guásimas at the outset of the Santiago Campaign, Roosevelt acquitted himself well. The Spanish defenders were well concealed, so it was not easy to see the enemy, but Roosevelt later claimed he would simply advance toward the sound of the guns. One reporter accompanying the advance declared that Roosevelt was the "most magnificent soldier I have ever seen" (Samuels and Samuels, p. 152). Roosevelt never lost an opportunity to air his views to the press. Reporters were in abundance in Cuba, and Roosevelt made good copy. He developed an especially strong rapport with the noted journalist Richard Harding Davis.

As the Fifth Corps continued its movement toward Santiago, illness necessitated changes in command. Gen. Joseph Wheeler, who was commanding the cavalry division, took ill with a fever, as did one of his two brigade commanders, Gen. Samuel Young. Subsequently, his other brigade commander, Gen. Samuel Sumner, took over temporary command of the division, Leonard Wood moved up to brigade command, and Theodore Roosevelt, now a full colonel, assumed command of the Rough Riders.

On 1 July 1898, in the advance on San Juan Heights, the cavalry, including Roosevelt's Rough Riders, was assigned the task of taking a high point known as Kettle Hill (so named because of the large iron kettles located there that were used in refining sugar). Meanwhile, on the left, Gen. Jacob Kent's division would assault San Juan Hill. In the face of heavy fire, Roosevelt—on horseback and brandishing a navy pistol that was retrieved from the sunken battleship *Maine* and presented to him by his brother-in-law, Comdr. William S. Cowles—led the Rough Riders in a successful charge, overcoming the Spanish defenders on the crest.

Then, noting that General Kent's troops were struggling to attain their objective, Roosevelt exhorted his men to follow him across the intervening ground between the high points to support Kent's effort. Thus, although the Rough Riders did in fact assault San Juan Hill, the famous charge for which they are known was really up Kettle Hill.

After the capitulation of Santiago on 17 July, with an alarming number of U.S. troops succumbing to tropical fevers—especially the dreaded yellow fever—Roosevelt participated in signing the famous "Round Robin" letter. This letter contained the signatures of the senior commanders and was sent to General Shafter, urging immediate withdrawal of the Fifth Corps from Cuba. Shortly thereafter, orders were issued for the Fifth Corps to return to Montauk Point, New York.

Following the Cuban Campaign, Roosevelt returned to the political life he loved, running as William McKinley's vice presidential nominee in the 1900 election. After McKinley's reelection and assassination in 1901, Roosevelt became the twenty-sixth president of the United States and was reelected in 1904.

It was and is hard to dislike Theodore Roosevelt and his ebullient ways. A man of definite ideas and opinions, he was unabashedly American in an era when nationalism was popular.

See also Dewey, George; Long, John Davis; McKinley, William, Jr.; Rough Riders; San Juan Hill, Charge up; Santiago, Campaign and Siege of; Wood, Leonard.

References and Further Readings
Leech, Margaret. *In the Days of McKinley*. New York: Harper & Brothers, 1959.
Samuels, Peggy, and Harold Samuels. *Teddy Roosevelt at San Juan: The Making of a President*. College Station: Texas A&M University Press, 1997.
Trask, David F. *The War with Spain in 1898*. Lincoln: University of Nebraska Press, 1996.
Walker, Dale L. *The Boys of '98: Theodore Roosevelt and the Rough Riders*. New York: Forge Books, 1998.

Root, Elihu (1845–1937)

Born in New York, Elihu Root was an attorney and politician. Although he did not play a key role in the Spanish-American War, Root, who replaced Russell Alger as secretary of war in August 1898, occupied that important position during the Philippine-American War. An energetic, hardworking man, he brought a sense of efficiency and discipline to the War Department that had been notably lacking during Alger's tenure. Root is generally credited with introducing the U.S. Army to a modern military system.

See also Alger, Russell Alexander; Army, U.S.; McKinley, William, Jr.; War Department, U.S.

References and Further Readings

Cosmas, Graham. *An Army for Empire: The United States Army in the Spanish-American War.* College Station: Texas A&M University Press, 1998.

Jessup, Philip C. *Elihu Root.* 2 vols. New York: Dodd, Mead & Company, 1938.

Leech, Margaret. *In the Days of McKinley.* New York: Harper & Brothers, 1959.

Rough Riders

The Rough Riders were perhaps the most unusual aggregation of soldiers in the history of the U.S. Army; certainly, this regiment was the most famous and colorful of the Spanish-American War. Included in its ranks were cowboys, eastern society lads, college students, policemen, and Texas Rangers, among others.

As part of the nation's military mobilization for the recently declared war with Spain, congressional authorization granted President William McKinley the power to enlist special regiments composed of individuals who possessed unique (or at least special) skills. This mandate led to the formation of the First U.S. Volunteer Cavalry Regiment, which came to be known as the Rough Riders.

Initially, command of the regiment was offered to Theodore Roosevelt. He declined, however, saying that he would agree to serve as second in command to his friend Leonard Wood. The gesture most likely was not made out of modesty but because Roosevelt recognized that he had no experience in commanding troops and that his own position, as well as that of the regiment, would be far better served if he accepted the rank of lieutenant colonel, second in command.

Once formation of the regiment was announced on 25 April 1898, applications began to pour in. The press wasted no time focus-

Col. Theodore Roosevelt and the Rough Riders after their successful charge up Kettle and San Juan Hills.

ing on Roosevelt as a story source. Though Leonard Wood was regimental commander and an officer of considerable army experience on the western frontier, he was scarcely mentioned in their reports. But the undue attention accorded Roosevelt seemed not to overly disturb Wood, who left Washington, DC, for San Antonio, Texas, in early May to prepare for the regiment's training. Roosevelt followed two weeks later.

Throughout the month of May, companies from New Mexico, Arizona, and Indian Territory, along with those from the East, arrived in San Antonio. The regimental headquarters was set up in the Menger Hotel, the oldest hotel in Texas (which is still operating and proud of its heritage as home of the Rough Riders). Accompanying the men were arms, equipment, and horses. Actual training ground for the regiment was at Riverside Park on the San Antonio River, south of the city.

On 27 May, the regiment received orders to move to Tampa, Florida, where Gen. William R. Shafter's Fifth Corps was assembling for its forthcoming invasion of Cuba. The appellation *Rough Riders* was coined early on, though several names were bandied about before the regiment was finally and forever known by its historical sobriquet. Among those suggested were "Teddy's Terrors," "Teddy's Terriers," and "Teddy's Texas Tarantulas." Insofar as the press was concerned, at least, the unit clearly was Theodore Roosevelt's regiment.

Finally, on 30 May 1898, the Rough Riders boarded a train for the journey to Tampa, arriving on 1 June. The next week was spent preparing for the upcoming Cuban Campaign, before orders finally came down to board ship. Lack of space on the transport permitted Wood and Roosevelt to take only 8 of their 12 troops. Moreover, there was no room for horses, except personal mounts for the senior officers.

On 13 June 1898, the Rough Riders sailed from Tampa. Upon the regiment's arrival in Cuba, it was assigned to Gen. Samuel Young's brigade of Gen. Joseph Wheeler's cavalry division. When General Young fell ill, Colonel Wood was assigned to command the cavalry brigade, which led in turn to Roosevelt's appointment as colonel and commander of the Rough Riders.

The regiment participated in the Battles of Las Guásimas and San Juan Heights, with which its name will forever be linked. Contrary to popular belief, the Rough Riders did not actually charge up San Juan Hill but rather charged up nearby Kettle Hill. After securing Kettle Hill, Roosevelt led the regiment across the intervening ground to assist Gen. Jacob Kent's infantry in its assault of San Juan Hill, both of which were part of the San Juan Heights.

See also Las Guásimas, Battle of; O'Neill, William Owen "Buckey"; Roosevelt, Theodore; San Juan Hill, charge up; Wood, Leonard.

References and Further Readings

Cosmas, Graham. *An Army for Empire: The United States Army in the Spanish-American War.* College Station: Texas A&M University Press, 1998.

Herner, Charles. *The Arizona Rough Riders.* Tucson: University of Arizona Press, 1970.

Samuels, Peggy, and Harold Samuels. *Teddy Roosevelt at San Juan: The Making of a President.* College Station: Texas A&M University Press, 1997.

Walker, Dale L. *The Boys of '98: Theodore Roosevelt and the Rough Riders.* New York: Forge Books, 1998.

Westermeier, Clifford P. *Who Rush to Glory.* Caldwell, ID: Caxton Printers, 1958.

"Round Robin" Letter (3 August 1898)

The "Round Robin" letter was signed by nine general officers, plus Col. Theodore Roosevelt, and sent to Gen. William R. Shafter, commander of the U.S. Fifth Corps in Cuba. The letter, which was penned after the capitulation of Santiago and the onset of the fever season in Cuba, declared that tropical diseases were destroying the Fifth Corps and urged that the corps be withdrawn from Cuba before the entire command was stricken. The letter further reinforced General Shafter's own urging to the War Department in Washington. Somehow, the contents of the letter fell into the hands of the press, probably through the efforts of Theodore Roosevelt.

When the story appeared in print, the public was understandably outraged at the War Department for allowing the troops to be exposed to such conditions. However, since President McKinley and the War Department had already begun preparations to return the Fifth Corps to the United States, the letter did little more than embarrass the president and attract public attention.

See also Diseases; Roosevelt, Theodore; Santiago, Campaign and Siege of; Shafter, William Rufus.

References and Further Readings

Brown, Charles H. *The Correspondents' War: Journalists in the Spanish-American War.* New York: Charles Scribner's Sons, 1967.

Heatley, Jeff. *Bully! Colonel Theodore Roosevelt and the Rough Riders at Camp Wikoff, Montauk Point, NY.* Harrisburg, PA: Stackpole Books, 1998.

Rowan, Andrew Summers (1857–1943)

Born in what is now West Virginia, Andrew Summers Rowan graduated from West Point in 1881. In 1892, he was assigned to the new Military Information Division (MID), the forerunner of Army Intelligence. Early in 1898, Lt. Col. Arthur L. Wagner, head of the MID, believing that war with Spain was imminent, dispatched Lieutenant Rowan, his aide, on a secret mission to Cuba to assess the strengths of both the Spanish Army and the Cuban Revolutionary Army. Having studied Cuba and familiarized himself with the island, Rowan was a good choice for the assignment.

With the help of Cuban rebels, he entered Cuba secretly. After rendezvousing with Gen. Calixto García, Rowan completed his survey and returned to the United States with three Cubans. The intelligence he provided helped greatly in planning the invasion of Cuba by General William Shafter's Fifth Corps in June 1898. Rowan's adventure was later immortalized in Elbert Hubbard's stirring but factually inaccurate account "Message to Garcia." Rowan subsequently was awarded the Distinguished Service Cross.

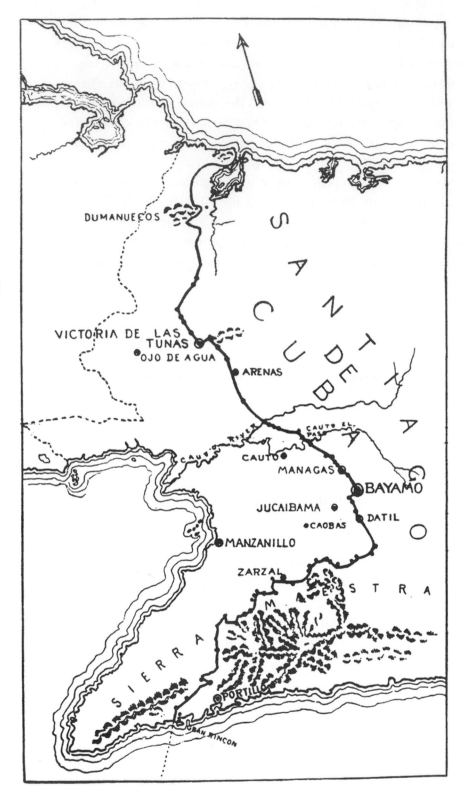

Lt. Andrew S. Rowan's route across Cuba while carrying the celebrated "Message to Garcia."
Source: *"Lieutenant-Colonel Rowan's Exploit: The American Delegate's Visit to Garcia,"*
Harper's Weekly *43 (July 2, 1898): 643.*

Lt. Andrew Summers Rowan. His covert mission to Cuban general Calixto García to gather intelligence prior to the outbreak of the Spanish-American War was immortalized in Elbert Hubbard's account Message to Garcia.

See also Cuban Revolution; García Íñiguez, Calixto; Santiago, Campaign and Siege of.

References and Further Readings

Chadwick, Rear Adm. French Ensor. *Relations of the United States and Spain: The Spanish American War.* 2 vols. New York: Charles Scribner's Sons, 1911 (reprinted in 1968).

Hubbard, Elbert. *Message to Garcia.* East Aurora, NY: n.p., 1899.

Rowan, Andrew S. "My Ride across Cuba." *McClure's Magazine,* August 1898.

Trask, David F. *The War with Spain in 1898.* Lincoln: University of Nebraska Press, 1996.

Sagasta, Práxedes Mateo (1827–1903)

Práxedes Mateo Sagasta was editor of a progressive journal and a member of the Spanish Cortes (legislature). When Antonio Cánovas del Castillo was assassinated in August 1897, Sagasta, who had been the leader of the Liberal Party and head of the government before Castillo's rise to power, was called by Queen Regent María Cristina to serve in that capacity once again. Sagasta was the leader of the Spanish government during the crucial period leading up to and throughout the Spanish-Cuban-American War.

Sagasta sought to avoid war with the United States. He believed the Cuban rebellion should be quashed but at the same time sought a peaceful resolution. For example, he replaced the notorious Governor-General Valeriano "Butcher" Weyler with Ramón Blanco, hoping that the latter's softer touch might demonstrate the sincerity of Spain's intention toward Cuba. It was, if anything, too little too late, as U.S. public opinion was already firmly set against Spain. Sagasta also hoped to cultivate help from the European community in mediating a settlement that would avoid hostilities with the United States.

Once war was officially declared, Sagasta approved Adm. Pascual Cervera's sortie to the Caribbean. In the wake of the huge U.S. victory over the Spanish fleet in the Battle of Santiago on 3 July 1898, Sagasta became convinced that Spain stood no chance of winning the war and worked toward negotiations with the United States to bring about an end to the conflict.

As head of the government, Sagasta was severely criticized for the Treaty of Paris, which resulted in Spain's loss of the Philippine Archipelago, along with Puerto Rico and the island of Guam.

See also Cervera y Topete, Pascual; Cuban Revolution; Spain; Weyler y Nicolau, Valeriano "Butcher."

References and Further Readings

Leech, Margaret. *In the Days of McKinley.* New York: Harper & Brothers, 1959.

Musicant, Ivan. *Empire by Default: The Spanish-American War and the Dawn of the American Century.* New York: Henry Holt and Company, 1998.

Samar Campaigns (Philippines)

Located in the eastern part of the Visayan group in the Philippines, the island of Samar is large, covering some 5,200 square miles. The interior is rugged and varied, ranging from swamps to large mountains. The campaign to secure Samar during the Philippine-American War, from 1899 to 1902, was costly. Like people on the other islands of the Visayan group, Samarenos spurned Emilio Aguinaldo's Filipino republican overtures, choosing to follow Vicente Lukban, who organized a powerful revolutionary force that often worked in conjunction with brigands. Interestingly, Lukban was himself a Tagalog. Ordinarily, because they were hereditary enemies, most other ethnic groups refused to submit to Tagalog rule, but Lukban's influence was such that he developed a strong following despite his ethnic background and harsh methods of dealing with any who betrayed the revolution.

In addition to its directive to pacify Samar (just as it was to do elsewhere in the archipelago), the U.S. Army was ordered to open the important hemp ports. Rope made from Philippine hemp was among the world's best, but the supply of hemp was limited because of the blockade imposed by the U.S. Navy. To avoid economic problems resulting from the shortage, President William McKinley ordered the hemp ports opened.

Early campaigns in the northern part of Samar, conducted by Maj. Henry T. Allen of the Forty-third Infantry, seemed to suggest that the inhabitants were ready to welcome Americans. By the spring of 1899, however, it became clear that this impression was erroneous. Outposts were attacked repeatedly, and in March, fierce fights took place on Catarman, Mataguino, and Paranas, during which guerrillas wielding lethal bolo knives killed and wounded 20 U.S. soldiers; the bolomen suffered some 200 casualties. On 15 April, the army garrison at Catubig—31 strong—lost half its number when attacked by 600 guerrillas.

By May 1900, the army's strategy on Samar (as well as elsewhere in the Visayas) had become one of holding the important positions while winning the war against Aguinaldo's republican Tagalogs in

Luzon. On Samar, the Forty-third Infantry was replaced by the Twenty-ninth, with orders to hold the hemp ports of Catbalogan and Calbayog on the west coast. Accordingly, between July 1900 and May 1901, the army undertook little offensive action, which worked to Lukban's advantage by allowing him time to organize and recruit.

When formal resistance ended on Leyte, a large island in the eastern Philippines, Lukban's guerrillas threatened to undermine that situation because of Leyte's importance to them as a source of supplies. Beginning in June 1901, Brig. Gen. Robert P. Hughes, commanding the Military Department of the Visayas—to whose jurisdiction Samar had only recently been returned—ordered the establishment of garrisons at key coastal ports on Samar's south and west coasts in an effort to shut off the flow of supplies from Leyte to Lukban's guerrillas on Samar. Navy gunboats also patrolled the surrounding waters, and joint —army-navy units conducted amphibious operations wherein detachments of troops landed at various spots to probe inland for guerrilla camps. These probes left a swath of destruction: Crops and houses were burned, and the heavy hand of war lay across the island. Between the navy's blockade and the army's efforts on land, guerrillas and nonguerrillas alike suffered. Then, on 13 August, a company of the First Infantry under Capt. Henry Jackson wounded Lukban in a surprise attack on the guerrilla leader's camp.

Notwithstanding these successes, army patrols often were on the receiving end of surprise attacks launched by wild, bolo-waving guerrillas, whose fanaticism made them particularly dangerous.

By far the most notorious episode of the Philippine-American War occurred on the island of Samar. On 28 September 1901, Company C of the Ninth Infantry, 74 men under the command of Capt. Thomas Connell and stationed in the village of Balangiga on the southern coast of Samar, were suddenly attacked by a combined force of guerrillas and villagers. Forty-eight men of the company were killed before the survivors managed to escape.

The unexpected attack, which quickly came to be known as the Balangiga Massacre, provoked more controversy than any other incident in the Philippine-American War, largely because of the harsh retaliatory measures that followed. Because the attack seemed unprovoked—though careful research reveals that this may not have been the case—and was carried out at the hands of supposedly friendly villagers, the incident infuriated the army, as well as Americans back home. In response, the military commander in the Philippines, Maj. Gen. Adna R. Chaffee, appointed Brig. Gen. Jacob

Smith to take command of the newly formed Sixth Separate Brigade, with orders to take appropriate retaliatory measures. Smith, an officer of questionable reputation at best, was an unwise choice. Exactly what Chaffee said to Smith over and above the written orders is unknown. Smith claimed he was told to "make the interior of Samar a howling wilderness" (Linn, p. 313), but that assertion is highly questionable. In any event, that is exactly what Smith proceeded to do. Smith's new brigade, including a U.S. Marine battalion under the command of Maj. Littleton Waller, ruthlessly stormed across the island, killing and applying the torch.

Eventually, the Balangiga Massacre resulted in a court of inquiry and several courts-martial. The incident and its aftermath received widespread coverage in the press and tainted the many commendable achievements of the U.S. military in the Philippines.

On 18 February 1902, Lukban was captured, and in April, most of his followers surrendered. Thus ended the organized resistance on Samar.

See also Balangiga Massacre; Chaffee, Adna Romanza; Marine Corps, U.S.; Smith, Jacob Hurd.

References and Further Readings

Beede, Benjamin R., ed. *The War of 1898 and U.S. Interventions, 1898–1934.* New York: Garland Publishing, 1994.

Gates, John Morgan. *Schoolbooks and Krags: The United States Army in the Philippines, 1898–1902.* Contributions in Military History no. 3. Westport, CT: Greenwood Press, 1973.

Linn, Brian McAllister. *The Philippine War, 1899–1902.* Lawrence: University Press of Kansas, 2000.

Sampson, William Thomas (1840–1902)

Born in Palmyra, New York, William Thomas Sampson graduated first in his class from the U.S. Naval Academy in 1861. One of the brightest young naval stars of his day, Sampson began his career as an instructor. Although he saw only limited action during the Civil War, he nearly lost his life while serving on the monitor *Patapsco*, which struck a mine in Charleston harbor while operating as part of the South Atlantic Blockading Squadron. Sampson was one of the few survivors of that incident.

After the Civil War, Sampson served in the European Squadron and was promoted to lieutenant commander. During the three decades between the end of the Civil War and the outbreak of the Spanish-American War, Sampson further enhanced his reputation as an outstanding officer and a man of considerable intellect, serving as superintendent of the Naval Academy and the Naval Observatory, as well as chief of the Bureau of Ordnance. In 1897, Sampson was given command of the new battleship *Iowa*.

After the *Maine* was destroyed in Havana harbor on 15 February 1898, President William McKinley named Sampson to head a naval board to investigate the cause of the disaster. In March, he was promoted to rear admiral and named to command the North Atlantic Squadron, replacing Rear Adm. Montgomery Sicard, who had taken ill. Sampson's promotion may have planted the seed of his later troubles with Commodore Winfield Scott Schley, who, along with a number of other officers, was senior to Sampson.

With the outbreak of war with Spain, Sampson's assignment was twofold: to blockade Cuba and to destroy the Spanish fleet under Adm. Pascual Cervera, whose exact whereabouts were not immediately known. Some evidence indicates that Sampson was not in the best of health at the time—a fact he apparently managed to conceal from all but those closest to him. One historian has suggested that Sampson had what we now know as Alzheimer's disease (see Dawson, p. 49).

In any case, after establishing the blockade, Sampson, with a small task force under his personal command, bombarded San Juan, Puerto Rico, then returned to blockade duty. After learning that Admiral Cervera's fleet had entered Santiago harbor, Sampson, having in the meantime been reinforced by Commodore Schley's Flying Squadron, positioned his fleet so as to block the entrance to Santiago harbor. With the Spanish fleet now effectively neutralized, Sampson was in a position to support the landing of Gen. William R. Shafter's U.S. Fifth Corps at Daiquirí and Siboney.

Unfortunately, interservice relations between the War Department and the Navy Department were poor at best. General Shafter believed the navy should enter the harbor and destroy the Spanish

Adm. William T. Sampson commanded the U.S. fleet in Cuban waters during the Spanish-American War.

fleet, but Sampson argued that the ground forces should first capture the forts whose guns dominated the harbor entrance and posed a serious threat to the navy's ships. The bickering and lack of cooperation between Sampson and Shafter was illustrative of the lack of rapport between the two departments.

Early on the morning of 3 July 1898, Sampson, now flying his flag aboard the new armored cruiser *New York* (under the command of Capt. French Ensor Chadwick), headed east for a conference with General Shafter. As luck would have it, Admiral Cervera chose that moment to attempt a breakout. In Sampson's absence, Schley, in command of the fleet, attacked the Spanish ships as they emerged from the sanctuary of Santiago harbor.

Learning of the battle by means of smoke and signal flags, Sampson turned around and headed back at flank speed. But even the *New York,* the fastest ship in the fleet, could not make it back in time to contribute to the near total destruction of the Spanish Squadron. Officially, Sampson was credited with a great naval victory, but it was Commodore Schley who received the plaudits in the press. This led to controversy and ill feelings between the two officers.

After the war, Sampson served for a time as a Cuban commissioner. All the while, his health had continued to deteriorate, leading to his death in 1902.

See also Chadwick, French Ensor; *Maine,* Inquiries into the Sinking of; Santiago de Cuba, Naval Battle of; Schley, Winfield Scott.

References and Further Readings

Chadwick, Rear Adm. French Ensor. *Relations of the United States and Spain: The Spanish American War.* 2 vols. New York: Charles Scribner's Sons, 1911 (reprinted in 1968).

Dawson, Joseph T., III. "William T. Sampson and Santiago: Blockade, Victory, and Controversy." In James C. Bradford, ed., *Crucible of Empire: The Spanish-American War and Its Aftermath,* pp. 47–68. Annapolis, MD: Naval Institute Press, 1993.

Sampson, Rear Adm. William T. "The Atlantic Fleet in the Spanish War." *Century Magazine,* April 1899.

Schley, Rear Adm. Winfield Scott. "Admiral Schley's Own Story." *Cosmopolitan Magazine,* December 1911.

Trask, David F. *The War with Spain in 1898.* Lincoln: University of Nebraska Press, 1996.

Sampson-Schley Controversy

In the aftermath of the U.S. naval victory at Santiago de Cuba on 3 July 1898, Adm. William T. Sampson, commander of the North Atlantic fleet, received official credit for the victory, even though he exercised little tactical control over the battle, having left the area early that morning to consult with Fifth Corps commander Gen. William R. Shafter at Siboney, 7 miles down the coast. In his absence, tactical command devolved to Commodore Winfield Scott Schley, who led the Flying Squadron. After learning that the Spanish fleet was attempting to sortie, Admiral Sampson, aboard the fast battleship *New York,* hurried back to the scene, arriving during the final phase of the fight.

As a result of the great U.S. victory, Schley was commended and promoted to rear admiral. However, accounts in the press began to suggest that Schley ought to have received full credit. Apparently unhappy with this development, Sampson, in comments to Secretary of the Navy John D. Long, was critical of Schley's failure to respond promptly to his (Sampson's) orders to investigate whether the Spanish fleet was at Santiago as earlier reported.

Not surprisingly, a feud began brewing, with each man having his own coterie of supporters. Outwardly, both officers were cordial toward each other, but privately, each was distressed. Schley was greatly embarrassed, and there is some reason to suspect that Sampson may have been suffering from Alzheimer's disease, which might possibly explain his behavior.

In his memoirs published in 1901, Capt. Robley Evans, who had commanded the *Iowa* during the battle, was sharply critical of Schley. In view of this criticism, Schley felt compelled to request a court of inquiry to examine his conduct during the war. Subsequently, a court was convened, with Adm. George Dewey as president. Testimony was taken from a number of individuals over forty days. After lengthy deliberation, the court found that Schley's conduct during the naval battle of Santiago was commendable. But the court was also critical of his failure to act promptly on Admiral Sampson's directive to blockade Santiago. Dissenting from the board, Admiral Dewey issued his opinion that Schley deserved full credit for the naval victory at Santiago.

Believing that the court's verdict was unfair, Schley appealed. After considering the matter, President Theodore Roosevelt toned down the findings, but Schley remained convinced that he had been wronged. Shortly after the president's finding, Admiral Sampson died, but the controversy did not end there. Secretary of the Navy John Long's history of the navy, which was published a year later, supported Sampson. The following year, Schley's memoirs continued his own defense. Even after Schley's death in 1909, bitter feelings continued to polarize the navy's upper echelons.

See also Dewey, George; Sampson, William Thomas; Santiago de Cuba, Naval Battle of; Schley, Winfield Scott.

References and Further Readings

Evans, Robley D. *A Sailor's Log.* New York: D. Appleton & Company, 1901.

Langley, Harold D. "Winfield S. Schley and Santiago." In James C. Bradford, ed. *Crucible of Empire: The Spanish-American War and Its Aftermath,* pp. 69–101. Annapolis, MD: Naval Institute Press, 1993.

Long, John D. *The New American Navy.* New York: Outlook, 1903.

Schley, Winfield Scott. *Forty-five Years under the Flag.* New York: n.p., 1904.

———. "Admiral Schley's Own Story." *Cosmopolitan Magazine,* December 1911.

San Juan Hill, Charge up (1 July 1898)

The famous charge up San Juan Hill during the Spanish-American War has become an enduring American legend, with Teddy Roosevelt leading the Rough Riders to immortality. Actually, Roosevelt's famous charge was up Kettle Hill—and made on foot, rather than on horseback—and it was followed by a second assault on the adjacent San Juan Hill.

After defeating the Spanish in the Battle of Las Guísimas, Gen. William R. Shafter devised a strategy for taking Santiago that involved first seizing the high ground east of the city known as San Juan Heights, which included the prominent points of San Juan Hill and Kettle Hill. Shafter's plan called for Gen. Jacob Ford Kent's division to attack San Juan Hill, while the dismounted cavalry—including the Rough Riders, now commanded by Col. Theodore Roosevelt—assaulted nearby Kettle Hill. It was also expected that Gen. Henry Lawton's division would complete its subjugation of El Caney in about two hours, allowing him to participate in the general attack on the San Juan Heights. As it turned out, Lawton found himself embroiled in a daylong fight and was unable to add his support to the general attack.

To defend Santiago, the Spanish commander, Gen. Arsenio Linares, established a defensive line, the strongest section of which was along San Juan Heights, where some 500 troops, supported by two pieces of artillery, were divided between two high points, Kettle Hill and San Juan Hill. The former, located some 400 yards northeast of San Juan Hill, was the location of a sugar-refining operation, which included two large iron kettles that gave rise to the hill's name.

San Juan Hill, 1898.

Both the cavalry and General Kent's infantry were delayed nearly two hours getting into position, so the forward movement did not get under way until noon. Then, the Seventy-first New York Volunteers panicked under fire and had to be replaced by other units. This setback further delayed the attack, which finally got started about 1 P.M.

In the advance on San Juan Hill, General Kent's First Brigade, under Brig. Gen. Hamilton Hawkins, moving up the slope through high grass, at first made good progress. Unwittingly, the Spanish had established their line along the top of the hill rather than just below, where they would have had a better angle of fire on the advancing Americans. However, Hawkins's troops soon found the going tough enough. Fortunately, some support was provided by Lt. John Parker's battery of Gatling guns, which raked the Spanish positions.

To the right of the infantry, General Sumner's dismounted cavalry advanced up Kettle Hill, with the Ninth Cavalry in the lead, followed by the First Cavalry. On his personal mount, Little Texas, rode Col. Theodore Roosevelt, sporting a blue polka-dot havelock. It was his finest hour. Shouting encouragement and brandishing a revolver salvaged from the sunken *Maine,* Roosevelt led the Rough Riders up that slope and into history.

En route, the men had to work their way around or over barbed wire and palmetto poles stuck in the ground. As the troopers advanced, their ranks became intermingled. Near the top, Roosevelt dismounted and charged the remainder of the distance on foot. The afternoon heat was brutal, and the fire from the Spanish defenders was telling, but the troopers steadily fought their way to the crest only to discover that the defenders had evacuated just before their arrival. It is not clear whether Roosevelt was first to reach the top; he thought he was, but if not, he was surely among the first.

From the newly won position on Kettle Hill, Roosevelt, observing that Kent's troops were struggling to reach the top of San Juan Hill, received permission from General Sumner to support that movement. He called on his men to follow him. At first, in the confusion and exhaustion following their assault up Kettle Hill, the men failed to respond to Roosevelt's call. Angry and embarrassed at their failure to respond immediately and no doubt riding an emotional high, Roosevelt again exhorted his men to follow and not to show cowardice. Stung, the men collected themselves and followed their colonel to support the capture of San Juan Hill. Roosevelt later regretted his accusation and commended the Rough Riders for the courage they showed on that day.

Historically, though referring to the Rough Riders' charge on San Juan Hill is not wrong, the famous charge for which they have become immortalized was up Kettle Hill. In either case, the assault was made on foot; it was not a mounted charge as is so often depicted.

See also Kent, Jacob Ford; Roosevelt, Theodore; San Juan Hill, Charge up; Santiago, Campaign and Siege of.

References and Further Readings

Roosevelt, Theodore. *The Rough Riders.* New York: Charles Scribner's Sons, 1925.

Samuels, Peggy, and Harold Samuels. *Teddy Roosevelt at San Juan: The Making of a President.* College Station: Texas A&M University Press, 1997.

Trask, David F. *The War with Spain in 1898.* Lincoln: University of Nebraska Press, 1996.

Walker, Dale L. *The Boys of '98: Theodore Roosevelt and the Rough Riders.* New York: Forge Books, 1998.

Santiago, Campaign and Siege of (22 June–17 July 1898)

When Adm. Pascual Cervera's Spanish fleet slipped into the harbor of Santiago de Cuba on 19 May 1898, the U.S. war strategy shifted from capturing Havana to capturing Santiago. By 1 June, Adm. William T. Sampson's North Atlantic fleet had effectively blocked the entrance to Santiago harbor, thereby neutralizing the threat posed by the Spanish fleet, at least temporarily. It followed that the capture of Santiago would place Cervera's fleet in harm's way and, it was hoped, compel Spain to surrender.

U.S. trenches before the Battle of Santiago, 1898.

Between 22 and 26 June, the U.S. Fifth Corps, commanded by Maj. Gen. William R. Shafter, landed at Daiquirí and Siboney on the southeastern coast of Cuba. Some 17,000 troops were put ashore, albeit under awkward and confused conditions. Fortunately, the Spanish offered no real resistance.

Shafter's assignment was to capture Santiago and in so doing to aid the U.S. Navy in destroying Admiral Cervera's squadron. Shafter had two options: He could march from Daiquirí to seize the fort at El Morro, guarding the entrance to Santiago harbor, or he could drive inland from Siboney directly to Santiago and capture the high ground overlooking Santiago, known as San Juan Heights. The advance was to be supported by Gen. Calixto García's Cuban revolutionary forces.

Interservice disagreement and squabbling clouded the issue from the beginning, both in Cuba between Shafter and Sampson and in Washington, DC, where the secretary of war and the secretary of the navy were frequently in dispute. Admiral Sampson believed Shafter's objective should be El Morro, the capture of which would allow the navy to clear the mines that had been laid in the harbor's entrance. Shafter, by contrast, thought the navy simply ought to enter the harbor and attack the Spanish fleet.

Moreover, reports indicated that the Spanish had established a strong defensive position at El Morro, which gave Shafter pause. Accordingly, he elected to move inland on Santiago from Siboney.

This option would also promise a more complete victory by greatly enhancing the army's role in the war—the army would not be relegated to a subordinate role. There is evidence as well that President William McKinley believed a strong showing by Shafter's Fifth Corps would strengthen the U.S. position against Spain.

In any case, the forward movement commenced on 24 June, with elements of Gen. Joseph Wheeler's cavalry division driving back the Spanish defenders at Las Guásimas. This was an unplanned but hard-fought action that resulted in 68 U.S. casualties.

Supply problems prevented the forward movement of all but the army's most essential needs—rations and basic medical supplies. These problems forced the Fifth Corps to confront the Spanish without artillery support.

On 1 July 1898, as part of an overall effort to attack San Juan Heights, Gen. Henry Lawton's division was to attack El Caney. After securing that point, which Lawton thought would take approximately two hours, his troops were to unite with those of Gen. Joseph Wheeler and Gen. Jacob Kent to assault the heights. As events unfolded, however, it took nearly the whole day to capture El Caney, so Lawton was unable to cooperate in the overall attack.

Meanwhile, the troops of Gen. Jacob Kent and Gen. Samuel Sumner (Wheeler was ill and General Sumner was in temporary command of the division) encountered stiff resistance from the Spanish defenders, who were well concealed and hard to spot because of the smokeless powder used in their rifle cartridges.

On the right flank, facing Kettle Hill (so called because of the large iron kettles there that were used to refine sugar), the Rough Riders, now under the command of Col. Theodore Roosevelt (Col. Leonard Wood had temporarily taken General Sumner's place as brigade commander), in company with the Ninth and Tenth (black) Cavalry Regiments, drove forward up the slope. With Roosevelt riding on his personal horse, Little Texas, the dismounted cavalrymen fought their way to the crest of Kettle Hill.

From there, Roosevelt, noting that General Kent's troops were still struggling to reach the top of San Juan Hill, received permission from General Sumner to lead his regiment across the ground that separated Kettle and San Juan Hills. Thus, Roosevelt's cavalrymen launched their second charge of the afternoon. Supported by three Gatling guns, which the battery commander, Lt. John K. Parker, and his men had managed to wrestle up to the battle zone, Roosevelt's troopers and Kent's infantry secured the hill. By day's end, the Fifth

Gen. Nelson Miles, Gen. William Shafter, and Gen. Joseph Wheeler returning from a conference with Gen. José Toral on the surrender of Santiago.

Corps was in command of San Juan Heights. The campaign thus far had cost a total of 1,300 U.S. casualties.

With the capture of San Juan Heights, what had been the campaign of Santiago became the siege of Santiago. On 22 June, some 3,700 men under the command of Col. Federico Escario left Manzanillo for Santiago, 160 miles distant. Throughout the march, Cuban guerrillas harassed the force constantly. Although the column finally reached Santiago on the night of 2 July, its arrival did little more than add to the burden on the city's food supply, which by now had reached a critical level, as the city was effectively cut off from supplies or reinforcements.

Shafter perceived that Santiago was still much too strong for him to storm. Further, he feared that reinforcements were on the way. In a communiqué to Washington, he requested authorization to withdraw to a more secure position. Withdrawal was not on the minds of those in Washington, however, and Shafter was promptly directed to hold the heights. Reinforcements were en route. Indeed, the leaders in Washington moved quickly. More troops were ordered to Cuba, along with General of the Army Nelson Miles, with instructions to do whatever he judged necessary to hold San Juan Heights.

On the one hand, U.S. authorities, especially Shafter, might have been less concerned had they known of the desperate situation inside

Twenty-third Kansas Volunteers in Santiago, Cuba, embarking for home, 1899.

Santiago, where the wounded commander, Gen. Arsenio Linares, had been replaced by Gen. José Toral and the city's inhabitants had been reduced to a starvation diet. On the other hand, Shafter's Fifth Corps was suffering an alarming increase in casualties due to fevers brought on by the onset of the tropical disease season.

Meanwhile, on 3 July, the picture was dramatically altered when Admiral Cervera's squadron, attempting to break out of Santiago harbor, was destroyed by the U.S. fleet. With the defeat of the Spanish fleet, the military value of Santiago suddenly became questionable. Accordingly, on 3 July, Shafter advised General Toral to surrender or the city would be shelled. Toral declined, but negotiations nevertheless continued. Toral then proposed surrendering the city, providing the garrison was allowed to retain its arms and march unopposed to Holguín. Shafter was disposed to accept those terms, but President McKinley insisted on unconditional surrender.

On 10 and 11 July, the two sides engaged in a final battle, with the Spanish sustaining 50 casualties, compared to 4 for Shafter's army. Two days later, on 13 July, Shafter and Miles (who had finally arrived) met again with Toral, offering to ship all Spanish troops back to Spain at U.S. expense if Toral agreed to surrender unconditionally. Recognizing that he had little choice, Toral agreed, but he needed the permission of Governor-General Ramón Blanco in Havana. Blanco eventually conceded, and on 17 July, Toral surrendered the city of Santiago, together with Guantánamo and a number of smaller posts that fell under the authority of the Santiago commander.

See also Linares y Pomba, Arsenio; McKinley, William, Jr.; Miles, Nelson Appleton; Roosevelt, Theodore; Shafter, William Rufus.

References and Further Readings

Cosmas, Graham. *An Army for Empire: The United States Army in the Spanish-American War.* College Station: Texas A&M University Press, 1998.

Leech, Margaret. *In the Days of McKinley.* New York: Harper & Brothers, 1959.

Samuels, Peggy, and Harold Samuels. *Teddy Roosevelt at San Juan: The Making of a President.* College Station: Texas A&M University Press, 1997.

Trask, David F. *The War with Spain in 1898.* Lincoln: University of Nebraska Press, 1996.

Walker, Dale L. *The Boys of '98: Theodore Roosevelt and the Rough Riders.* New York: Forge Books, 1998.

Santiago de Cuba, Naval Battle of (3 July 1898)

The arrival of Adm. Pascual Cervera's Spanish Squadron at Santiago de Cuba on 19 May 1898 set the stage for one of Spain's key defeats in the Spanish-American War. Upon reaching Santiago, Cervera discovered that there was little coal with which to resupply his ships and what was available was of inferior quality. Between 19 and 26 May, Cervera might have slipped out of the harbor unopposed, as the U.S. fleet had not yet arrived to blockade the port, although Adm. William T. Sampson had directed Commodore Winfield Scott Schley to do just that with his squadron.

After a council of war with his captains, Cervera elected to remain in the harbor to perform necessary maintenance on his ships. That move would prove to be his squadron's undoing. The decision was not unanimous, and by early June, the opportunity to slip out of Santiago uncontested had passed, as Admiral Sampson had by that time completed his blockade of the harbor entrance.

During the next few weeks, Sampson ordered the *Vesuvius* to bombard Spanish shore batteries every night, using its experimental dynamite guns to lob 500-pound shells into the harbor. The shells, made of nitrocellulose (guncotton), exploded with a thunderous roar but did little damage except to have an unsettling effect on the ships'

AT NIGHT.

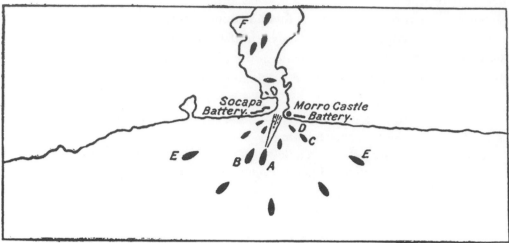

A *Battleship with searchlight.*
B *Supporting battleship ready to open fire*
in case of appearance of enemy.
C *Three small cruisers as pickets.*

D *Three steam-launch pickets.*
E *Blockade outer line.*
F *Spanish ships.*

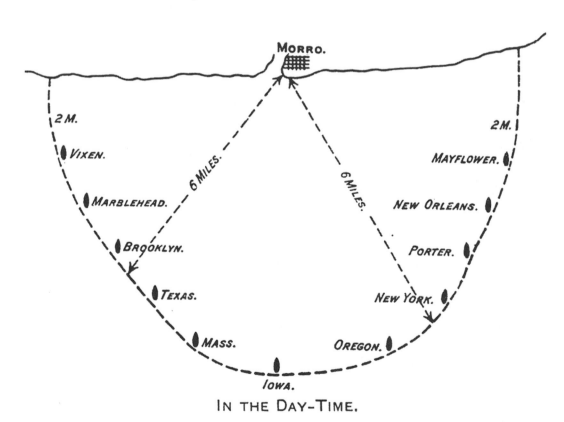

IN THE DAY-TIME.

The U.S. naval blockade of Santiago, Cuba, 1898.
Source: *Severo Gomez Nunez, "The Spanish-American War: Blockades and Coast Defense," in
U.S. Navy, Office of Naval Intelligence,* Notes on the Spanish-American War *(Washington, DC:
Government Printing Office, 1900), p. 77.*

356

crews. Also, Lt. Richmond P. Hobson and a small, handpicked crew had attempted unsuccessfully to scuttle the collier *Merrimac* in the harbor entrance to prevent the Spanish ships from leaving. As a result, Sampson concluded that it was wiser to await Cervera's eventual breakout, which seemed certain, rather than risk losing any of his ships by trying to force an entry.

Sampson had his own North Atlantic Squadron, together with that of Commodore Schley, stationed some 6 miles from the harbor entrance, in a rough V-shaped formation. Along one leg were Schley's ships, the *Vixen*, the *Brooklyn* (Schley's flagship), the *Texas*, and the *Iowa*. Along the other leg were the *Gloucester*, the *New York*, the *New Orleans*, the *Indiana*, and the *Oregon*, with the *Iowa* near the apex of the "V."

On the morning of Sunday, 3 July 1898, the sky was overcast early but cleared as the sun rose higher. About 8 A.M., the battleship *Massachusetts* pulled out of line and headed for Guantánamo to take on coal. At the same time, Admiral Sampson, aboard his flagship *New York*, left for a strategy meeting with General Shafter several miles down the coast at Siboney.

With General Shafter's investment of Santiago, Admiral Cervera's squadron clearly had to make a break. Capt. Gen. Ramón Blanco, who had replaced Valeriano Weyler as governor of Cuba, directed Cervera to sortie as soon as possible. At a council of war with Cervera and his captains, the consensus was that they had little choice but to sortie on Sunday morning, hoping to catch the U.S. ships in the midst of religious services. Cervera's plan called for his lead vessels to ram any U.S. ships close enough to interfere with the movement, then head west for Cienfuegos. Accordingly, at 9 A.M., the Spanish Squadron got under way, led by Cervera's flagship, *María Teresa*, followed by the *Cristóbal Colón*, *Almirante Oquendo*, and *Vizcaya*, plus a pair of torpedo boats, the *Furor* and *Plutón*.

At about 9:30 A.M., the waiting U.S. ships finally spotted Spanish vessels emerging from the harbor. The *Oregon* fired its 6-pound alarm gun, the signal "250" was raised, and the U.S. ships prepared to engage.

As the Spanish ships emerged, the *María Teresa* opened fire, which was returned by the *Brooklyn*. Save for the little armed yacht *Vixen*, the *Brooklyn* was closest in line to the oncoming Spanish ships, and so it became Cervera's immediate objective. Aboard the *Brooklyn*, Schley could see the growing peril. To avoid exposing his flagship to broadside fire from the oncoming Spanish ships, he maneuvered out of harm's way by executing a 360-degree loop away from the Spanish fleet before coming back around to pursue. Schley's reasoning was that the maneuver would avoid broadside fire and also give the other U.S. ships an opportunity to close the gap. However, in the confusion of the maneuver, the *Brooklyn* nearly collided with the *Texas*, which was coming on strong. Fortunately, a collision was avoided, and the *Brooklyn* soon was back in pursuit of the fleeing Spanish Squadron, now steaming for all its worth along the Cuban coastline.

Behind the *Brooklyn*, commanded by Capt. Francis Cook, were the *Oregon*, under Capt. Charles Clark, the *Texas*, under Capt. John Philip, and the *Iowa*, captained by Robley D. "Fighting Bob" Evans. Evans had it in mind to ram one of the two leading Spanish ships, which were thundering forth salvos at their pursuers—albeit with subpar accuracy. U.S. gunfire, by contrast, was wreaking much damage on Cervera's ships.

Cervera's squadron did possess one advantage: The Spanish ships were faster. Indeed, with the capability of making 21 knots, they were the fastest ships in the world and could outrun the U.S. vessels. The *New York* and the *Brooklyn* could manage 20 knots, and the others could make somewhat less. However, the *New York* was away with Sampson, leaving only the *Brooklyn* to stay close.

Meanwhile, some 7 miles to the east, Admiral Sampson, aboard the *New York*, learned of Cervera's sortie. Lookouts observed smoke and spotted the signal "250." Wasting no time, Sampson ordered the *New York* to put about and head for the action.

Behind the Spanish capital ships came the torpedo boats *Furor* and *Plutón*. Fast and capable of sinking nearly anything afloat with one of their torpedoes, they moved in to attack the U.S. ships. At just about that time, the armed yacht *Gloucester* steamed into the breech. (In more peaceful times, the *Gloucester* had been John Jacob Astor's private yacht *Corsair*, which Astor sold to the navy in support of the war effort.) The *Gloucester*'s skipper, interestingly enough, was Lt. Cmdr. Richard Wainright, who had been executive officer on the *Maine* when it blew up in Havana harbor.

The Spanish torpedo boats fired their small batteries at the *Gloucester* but failed to score a hit. Although not heavily armed, the *Gloucester* returned the fire but without notable success. Fortunately for Wainright, the *Gloucester* was supported by the big guns of the *Iowa* and the *Indiana*, which blasted away at the Spanish torpedo boats as they sped by in pursuit of bigger game. The little boats tried to stay as close to the shore as water depth would allow, but the guns of the U.S. ships finally tore them apart.

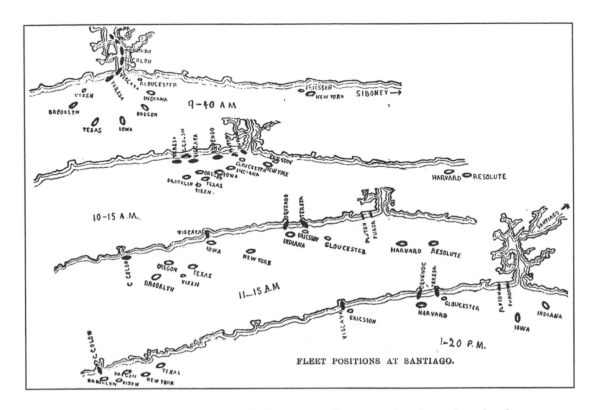

The naval battle of Santiago, Cuba, 1898: Four stages from morning through early afternoon.
Source: *Henry F. Keenan,* The Conflict with Spain: A History of the War *(Philadelphia: P. W. Ziegler and Co., 1898), p. 204.*

By this time, the *Brooklyn* had completed its maneuver and was back in pursuit, running parallel with the *Teresa,* followed by the *Vizcaya,* the *Cristóbol Colón,* and the *Oquendo.* Coming on fast, though, was the hard-driving *Oregon*—still reveling in its record-setting voyage around Cape Horn—then the old *Texas.* The U.S. ships laid it on as heavily as they were able, and the Spanish returned fire as best they could. Fortunately for Schley's ships, the Spanish gunners continued to fire high while the aim of the U.S. gunners was better.

The Spanish had additional problems with which to contend. The *María Teresa*'s secondary batteries could not be brought into action because, it seems, their shells did not fit and the primers malfunctioned. Then, the captain was killed, and Admiral Cervera was compelled to take personal command of the ship. Fires started by hits from the U.S. guns were getting out of control, and Cervera, realizing the futility of further resistance, headed the stricken vessel toward shore, where it was beached some 6 miles from the harbor entrance.

While the *Teresa* was being pounded, the *Vizcaya, Colón,* and *Oquendo* were doing their best to escape, relying on speed to outdistance the U.S. ships. But even their superior speed could not get them out of range of the big U.S. guns before fearful damage had been inflicted on them. The Spanish replied with counter-battery fire, but it was intermittent and mostly inaccurate. An hour after emerging from Santiago harbor, the battered *Oquendo* ran aground, devastated by hits from the U.S. guns.

Meanwhile, Admiral Sampson was steadily closing the gap, as the *New York* surged forward beneath a hot, blue tropical sky, passing through the debris left from the battle's opening round. Only two Spanish ships (the *Vizcaya* and *Cristóbal Colón*) were still afloat and trying to escape, with the *Brooklyn, Oregon,* and *Texas* in hot pursuit. Although both sides were firing furiously, the *Brooklyn*'s guns were inflicting especially heavy punishment. The *Vizcaya*, about to try and ram Schley's flagship, was hit by a shell that exploded one of its torpedoes, tearing a gaping chunk out of the prow. The *Vizcaya*'s wounds were mortal. Its courageous and gallant commander, Capt. Juan Eulate, though severely wounded, retained command and directed his dying ship to shore, following the fate of the *Teresa*.

Alone now, the *Cristóbol Colón* plunged ahead but the crew misjudged its course. The ship came too close to shore and was forced to make a short detour—enough for the *Brooklyn* and *Oregon* to draw closer, their boilers working overtime. Suddenly, the *Colón*'s speed began to fall off because of the inferior coal loaded at Santiago. This turn of events enabled the *Oregon* to hit the Spanish ship with a 13-inch shell. At about 12:30 P.M., *Colón* struck its colors, and an hour later, it, too, was on the beach.

The naval battle of Santiago was over. Like Adm. George Dewey's battle at Manila Bay, this U.S. victory was lopsided—heady wine, indeed, and a Fourth of July gift for the nation. Incredibly, the U.S. Navy suffered only 1 battle-related death. Spanish losses amounted to nearly 500 killed and wounded and some 1,800 captured.

Officially, Admiral Sampson, as overall commander, was credited with a great victory, but the popular hero of the day was Commodore Schley. Accounts of the battle in the press snubbed Sampson and gave credit to Schley, resulting in a feud and hard feelings between the two officers that tarnished the careers of both men.

See also Cervera y Topete, Pascual; Evans, Robley Dunglison; *Oregon*; Sampson, William Thomas; Santiago, Campaign and Siege of; Schley, Winfield Scott.

References and Further Readings

Dierks, Jack Cameron. *A Leap to Arms: The Cuban Campaign of 1898*. Philadelphia: J. B. Lippincott, 1970.

Sampson, Rear Adm. William T. "The Atlantic Fleet in the Spanish War." *Century Magazine,* April 1899.

Schley, Rear Adm. Winfield Scott. "Admiral Schley's Own Story." *Cosmopolitan Magazine,* December 1911.

Sternlicht, Sanford. *McKinley's Bulldog: The Battleship* Oregon. Chicago: Nelson-Hall, 1977.

Trask, David F. *The War with Spain in 1898.* Lincoln: University of Nebraska Press, 1996.

Schley, Winfield Scott (1839–1909)

A controversial figure from the Spanish-American War period, Winfield Scott Schley was born in Maryland and was named for the great U.S. hero of the Mexican War, Gen. Winfield Scott.

Following graduation from the U.S. Naval Academy in 1860, Schley saw action in the Civil War, serving under Admiral David Farragut at Mobile Bay. Schley's post–Civil War career was largely uneventful, save for an incident at Valparaiso, Chile, in 1878, when two sailors from his ship, the *Baltimore,* were killed in a riot that fortunately did not have the long-range repercussions it might have had.

In February 1898, as war with Spain loomed ever closer on the horizon, Schley was promoted to commodore and given command of the Flying Squadron. With the official declaration of war in April, Schley's orders were to cover the U.S. East Coast but to be prepared to move to the Caribbean, as dictated by circumstances.

In May, Schley was ordered to move his squadron to the southeast coast of the United States, from where he could either join Adm. William T. Sampson's Cuban blockading force or confront the Spanish fleet under Adm. Pascual Cervera. As events continued to unfold, Schley was ordered to report to Sampson, where the Flying Squadron merged with the North Atlantic Squadron. The assignment meant that Schley was now subordinate to Sampson, who recently had been promoted to rear admiral and given command of the North Atlantic Squadron over Schley and sixteen other officers.

Although Sampson issued specific orders to Schley to participate in the blockade by covering Santiago and Cienfuegos, Schley was unable to take up station until the end of May, by which time Admiral Cervera had slipped into Santiago harbor undetected. When it was learned that the Spanish fleet was in Santiago, Sampson established a blockade around the harbor entrance to prevent Cervera's escape.

On the morning of 3 July 1898, Admiral Sampson left the blockade for a meeting with Maj. Gen. William R. Shafter down the coast at Siboney. When Cervera chose this moment to attempt a breakout,

command of the U.S. fleet devolved to Schley, who immediately gave the order to attack. In the furious action that followed, the Spanish fleet was destroyed.

Meanwhile, upon learning that Admiral Cervera was attempting to escape, Sampson immediately turned around and headed back but was unable to reach the scene in time to participate in the action. As a result of the great U.S. victory, Sampson—being in overall command—received official congratulations. In the press, though, Schley was the one who garnered the plaudits. The situation created hard feelings between the two men, which never healed and dogged both Sampson and Schley through the rest of their lives.

See also Cervera y Topete, Pascual; Sampson, William Thomas; Santiago de Cuba, Naval Battle of; Sampson-Schley Controversy.

References and Further Readings

Chadwick, Rear Adm. French Ensor. *Relations of the United States and Spain: The Spanish American War.* 2 vols. New York: Charles Scribner's Sons, 1911 (reprinted in 1968).

Graham, George Edward. *Schley and Santiago: An Historical Account of the Blockade and Final Destruction of the Spanish Fleet under the Command of Admiral Pasquale Cervera, July 3, 1898.* Chicago: W. B. Conkey Company, 1902.

Langley, Harold D. "Winfield S. Schley and Santiago." In James C. Bradford, ed. *Crucible of Empire: The Spanish-American War and Its Aftermath,* pp. 69–101. Annapolis, MD: Naval Institute Press, 1993.

Schley, Rear Adm. Winfield Scott. "Admiral Schley's Own Story." *Cosmopolitan Magazine,* December 1911.

Adm. Winfield Scott Schley. Officially, Adm. William T. Sampson was given credit for the great U.S. naval victory at Santiago de Cuba, but it was Schley who received the public plaudits.

Schofield, John McAllister (1831–1906)

Born in New York, John McAllister Schofield graduated from West Point in 1853. Following a distinguished Civil War career, he served as secretary of war in President Andrew Johnson's cabinet. In 1888, he was named commanding general of the army, a post he held until

1895, when he was succeeded by Gen. Nelson A. Miles. In the years immediately preceding the Spanish-American War, Schofield argued strongly for U.S. intervention to aid Cuban suffering.

After the outbreak of the war, President William McKinley frequently took counsel with the now officially retired Schofield, rather than with Secretary of War Russell Alger or General of the Army Miles. Because of their continual bickering, the president lacked confidence in those men. Schofield was largely responsible for persuading President McKinley to increase the size of the regular army. Eventually, however, he may have come to view his counsel to the president to be more important than it really was, and McKinley gradually turned elsewhere for military advice—increasingly to Adj. Gen. Henry Corbin.

See also Alger, Russell Alexander; Corbin, Henry Clark; McKinley, William, Jr.; Miles, Nelson Appleton; War Department, U.S.
References and Further Readings
Leech, Margaret. *In the Days of McKinley.* New York: Harper & Brothers, 1959.
Schofield, John M. *Forty-six Years in the Army.* New York: Century, 1897.

Schwan, Theodore (1841–1926)

Born in Germany, Theodore Schwan emigrated to the United States in 1857. He enlisted in the Union army during the Civil War and served with distinction. He was promoted to captain and awarded the Medal of Honor. In May 1898, Schwan was appointed brigadier general of volunteers. Assigned to the Puerto Rican Expedition under Gen. Nelson Miles, Schwan's column, 1,400 strong, landed at Ponce on 30 July with orders to operate as the westernmost column in the advance on San Juan. On 10 August, Schwan's troops fought the Spanish at Hormigueros and on 12 August fought them again at Los Marias, where Schwan learned that the Protocol of Peace had been signed two days earlier, officially ending the Puerto Rican Campaign.

Afterward, Schwan served in the Philippines. He was promoted to major general in 1916.

See also Miles, Nelson Appleton; Puerto Rican Campaign.
References and Further Readings
Cosmas, Graham. *An Army for Empire: The United States Army in the Spanish-American War.* College Station: Texas A&M University Press, 1998.
Hermann, Karl S. *A Recent Campaign in Puerto Rico.* Boston: E. H. Bacon & Company, 1907.
Wilson, James Harrison. *Under the Old Flag: Recollections of Military Operations in the War for the Union, the Spanish War, the Boxer Rebellion, etc.* 2 vols. New York: D. Appleton & Company, 1912.

Scovel, Henry (Harry) Sylvester (1869–1905)

Best known as a journalist during the Spanish-American War, Henry (Harry) Sylvester Scovel was born in Pennsylvania. He was educated as an engineer but turned to journalism and in 1895 was in Cuba providing stories of the Cuban War of Independence for the *New York Herald.* The Spanish, evidently tired of Scovel's snooping, arrested him. He soon escaped and returned to the United States, where he joined Joseph Pulitzer's *New York World* and began a series of stories that argued for Cuban independence and U.S. support thereof.

Returning to Cuba, Scovel lived for a time with the rebels until Spanish authorities captured him again. Thanks to the efforts of his paper and the U.S. government, however, he soon was released. After reporting on the Greco-Turkish War in the Mediterranean, Scovel returned to the United States when the battleship *Maine* was destroyed and subsequently covered the Santiago Campaign.

With the possible exception of Richard Harding Davis, Harry Scovel probably was the best-known U.S. journalist of the Spanish-American War. The most celebrated incident of his career was his attempt to punch Gen. William R. Shafter in the nose when the latter refused to include him in the official victory photo following the Spanish surrender at Santiago.

Scovel remained in Cuba after the war. He died in 1905 of complications arising from liver surgery.

See also Cuban Revolution; Davis, Richard Harding; Journalism; Shafter, William Rufus.

References and Further Readings

Brown, Charles H. *The Correspondents' War: Journalists in the Spanish-American War.* New York: Charles Scribner's Sons, 1967.
Milton, Joyce. *The Yellow Kids: Foreign Correspondents in the Heyday of Yellow Journalism.* New York: Harper & Row, 1989.

Shafter, William Rufus (1835–1906)

Born in Kalamazoo, Michigan, William Rufus Shafter served as a volunteer officer in the Civil War, including stints at the battles of Fair Oaks and Nashville. Remaining in the army after the war, he served for a time on the Staked Plains of west Texas, where he earned the sobriquet "Pecos Bill" while commanding the Twenty-fourth (black) Infantry. By 1897, he was a brigadier general, commanding the Department of California. At the time of the Spanish-American War, Shafter was promoted to major general and given command of the Fifth Corps—the Cuban Expeditionary Force. Despite his lengthy service, Shafter never had commanded anything larger than a regi-

Conference between Gen. Nelson Miles (right), *Gen. William Shafter* (center), *and Gen. Joseph Wheeler* (left) *during the siege of Santiago, 1898.*

ment, although by 1898, few of the army's senior officers had experience commanding large bodies of troops in the field.

At age 63 in 1898, Shafter was a large man whose weight had ballooned to 300 pounds. He was clearly out of shape and in poor health, suffering from gout. In retrospect, Shafter would seem to have been a poor choice for the Cuban command, though he was the first pick of General of the Army Nelson Miles and Adj. Gen. Henry Corbin.

In early June 1898, after some indecision by the War Department due in part to the movement of the Spanish fleet, Shafter was ordered to assemble 10,000 men at Tampa, Florida, and prepare to invade Cuba. Originally, the objective was Havana, but upon learning that Adm. Pascual Cervera's fleet had reached Santiago harbor, the focal point of the campaign became Santiago.

From the outset in Tampa, Shafter's ineptness became evident. In his defense, like so many regular army officers of that day, he had no experience managing large bodies of troops. But aside from that, he lacked the energy and organizational skills needed in such a challenging situation. Fortunately for the Fifth Corps, Shafter had an able staff that made up, at least in part, for his shortcomings.

Departing from Tampa on 14 June 1898, Shafter began landing his Fifth Corps at Daiquirí and Siboney on 22 June. With orders to capture Santiago, he proposed to move on that city as quickly as possible, with the hope of reaching his objective before the fever season began. Moving inland, Shafter planned to defeat the Spanish at El Caney, then assault San Juan Heights, the high ground outside Santiago.

Following the great U.S. naval victory over Admiral Cervera's fleet on 3 July 1898, Shafter invested Santiago. After a series of negotiations with the Spanish commander, Gen. José Toral, the city was surrendered to Shafter on 17 July.

Ill with gout and suffering from the enervating tropical heat, Shafter was barely able to function as commander during the Santiago Campaign and was forced to follow the action from the rear, issuing orders through a deputy. Because of Shafter's poor health, a number of his officers believed him unfit for command. Indeed, that the Fifth Corps was victorious in Cuba was attributable less to Shafter's presence than to the ability of some of his senior commanders and the courage of the U.S. troops. Finally, Shafter could not—or perhaps simply chose not to—develop a harmonious rapport with his naval counterpart, Adm. William T. Sampson. Fortunately for the United States, the weakness of the Spanish position offset the absence of a strong army-navy relationship.

See also Army, U.S.; Camps, Staging Areas, and Embarkation Points, U.S. Army; Diseases; Santiago, Campaign and Siege of.

References and Further Readings

Carlson, Paul H. *Pecos Bill: A Military Biography of William R. Shafter.* College Station: Texas A&M University Press, 1989.

Cosmas, Graham. *An Army for Empire: The United States Army in the Spanish-American War.* College Station: Texas A&M University Press, 1998.

Walker, Dale L. *The Boys of '98: Theodore Roosevelt and the Rough Riders.* New York: Forge Books, 1998.

Sherman, John (1823–1900)

The younger brother of the great Union general William Tecumseh Sherman, John Sherman was born in Lancaster, Ohio. He studied law before entering politics in 1854. His public service spanned nearly half a century, of which more than three decades were spent as a U.S. senator from Ohio. During his prime, Sherman was one of the most powerful men in Washington. In 1868, his daughter Mary married a young army officer named Nelson Miles, who would be general of the army during the Spanish-American War.

In 1897, President William McKinley named Sherman to be his secretary of state. The appointment was probably a political move on McKinley's part so he could name his friend Marcus Hanna to fill Sherman's vacant senatorial seat.

During his career, Sherman went on record as favoring Cuban independence. As secretary of state, he attempted to persuade McKinley to avoid war with Spain. At that stage, however, Sherman seemed to be little more than a figurehead in the Department of State. Perhaps his age (he was then 74) had begun to dull his faculties. In any case, McKinley turned increasingly for counsel to Judge William R. Day, the assistant secretary of state. It seems likely that McKinley hoped Sherman would retire, which in fact he did on 25 April 1898, two days after the declaration of war with Spain.

See also Cuban Revolution; Hanna, Marcus Alonzo; McKinley, William, Jr.

References and Further Readings

Burton, Theodore E. *John Sherman*. Boston: Houghton Mifflin, 1906.

Leech, Margaret. *In the Days of McKinley*. New York: Harper & Brothers, 1959.

Signal "250"

Signal "250" was a U.S. Navy sign designed to alert ships of the North Atlantic Squadron to the attempted departure of the Spanish fleet from the harbor of Santiago de Cuba. Three flags were used to create the signal: One was a yellow flag with a blue ball in the center, the second was half yellow and half red, and the third was a swallow-tailed pennant with a blue cross. The flags symbolized the numbers 2, 5, and 0—hence 250.

See also Santiago de Cuba, Naval Battle of.

References and Further Readings

Chadwick, Rear Adm. French Ensor. *Relations of the United States and Spain: The Spanish American War*. 2 vols. New York: Charles Scribner's Sons, 1911 (reprinted in 1968).

Feuer, A. B. *The Spanish-American War at Sea*. Westport, CT: Greenwood Press, 1995.

Trask, David F. *The War with Spain in 1898*. Lincoln: University of Nebraska Press, 1996.

Sigsbee, Charles Dwight (1845–1923)

Born in Albany, New York, Charles Dwight Sigsbee graduated from the U.S. Naval Academy in 1863 and served with distinction under Adm. David Farragut at Mobile Bay during the Civil War. Following the Civil War, Sigsbee saw a variety of duty, including deep-sea exploration in the Gulf of Mexico. He was the U.S Navy's chief hydrographer from 1893 to 1897. Sigsbee also taught at the Naval Academy and saw service with both the European and Asiatic Squadrons, in addition to service during the Spanish-American War.

Following his promotion to the rank of captain in March 1897, he was assigned to command of the battleship *Maine*, a position he held when the vessel blew up in Havana harbor on the night of 15 February 1898. Sigsbee and most of the officers survived the blast because the explosion occurred in the forward sections of the ship.

Although Sigsbee had a reputation as a capable and courageous officer, he seems not to have been a particularly vigilant ship commander. He apparently was indifferent to routine safety checks and inspections that might have avoided the kind of disaster that befell the *Maine*—if, of course, one is disposed to believe the explosion was internal. Although two examining boards declared that the ship was destroyed by an external explosion (a mine), a third investigation concluded that the blast had been caused by internal combustion in a coal bunker adjacent to one of the ammunition magazines.

It is worth noting that in the report he filed in the immediate aftermath of the *Maine*'s destruction, Sigsbee, recognizing the danger of hasty conclusions, urged a calm and careful assessment of the situation before reaching any conclusions. The *Maine* disaster seemingly had no ill effect on Sigsbee's career. He later commanded the cruiser *St. Paul* during the war with Spain, sinking a Spanish destroyer off Puerto Rico. He retired as rear admiral in 1907.

See also *Maine*; *Maine*, Inquiries into the Sinking of; Naval Strategy, U.S.
References and Further Readings
Blow, Michael. *A Ship to Remember: The* Maine *and the Spanish-American War*. New York: William Morrow, 1992.

Capt. Charles Sigsbee, who commanded the battleship Maine *at the time of its destruction in Havana harbor on 15 February 1898.*

Samuels, Peggy, and Harold Samuels. *Remembering the* Maine. Washington, DC: Smithsonian Institution Press, 1995.

Sigsbee, Charles D. *The* Maine: *An Account of Her Destruction in Havana Harbor.* New York: Century, 1899.

Sims, William Sowden (1858–1936)

Born in Canada to an American father, William Sowden Sims graduated from the U.S. Naval Academy in 1880. He was an important though largely unrecognized figure of the Spanish-American War period. Sims, who worked for the relatively new Office of Naval Intelligence (ONI), was assigned as naval attaché in Paris, where he coordinated a widely diverse group of spies who provided the ONI information on Spanish activities. Of particular use was information regarding the movements of Adm. Manuel Cámara's fleet to the Philippines.

See also Cámara y Libermoore, Manuel de la; Naval Strategy, Spanish; Naval Stratevy, U.S.

References and Further Readings

O'Toole, G. J. A. *The Spanish War: An American Epic, 1898.* New York: W. W. Norton, 1984.

Trask, David F. *The War with Spain in 1898.* Lincoln: University of Nebraska Press, 1996.

Smith, Jacob Hurd (1840–1918)

Born in Kentucky, Jacob Hurd Smith served in the Civil War. He remained in the army after the war, serving on the western frontier. During the Spanish-American War, Smith served in Cuba with the Fifth Corps.

Nicknamed "Hell-Roaring Jake" because of his unusually loud voice, Smith apparently was involved in questionable financial dealings involving federal bounty money for blacks. His later career included other instances of misconduct, which nearly resulted in his dismissal from the service, but he was saved by a presidential reprieve.

Upon recovering from a wound received at El Caney during the Spanish-American War, he was reassigned to the Philippines, where he was placed in command of the Twelfth U.S. Infantry.

In 1901, Smith was given command of the newly formed Sixth Separate Brigade, with orders to pacify the islands of Samar and Leyte. In the stunning aftermath of the notorious Balangiga Massacre at Samar on 28 September 1901, Smith reportedly ordered his troops to take no prisoners—to kill and burn and turn Samar into a "howling wilderness" (Linn, p. 313).

In 1902, after the full extent of his orders had been brought to light, Smith was court-martialed. President Theodore Roosevelt later reduced his sentence and directed that Smith not be dismissed but instead be placed on the retired list. At the time, many in the U.S. Army remained supportive of Smith, arguing that he had been a scapegoat and that his actions were in response to the brutal, uncivilized type of guerrilla warfare then being waged in parts of the Philippines. Although both sides certainly were guilty of atrocities during the Philippine-American War and retaliation to an act of atrocity is understandable, to a point, Smith's measures seemed to have gone far beyond what might be regarded as an understandable response.

See also Atrocities; Balangiga Massacre; Chaffee, Adna Romanza.

References and Further Readings

Beede, Benjamin R., ed. *The War of 1898 and U.S. Interventions, 1898–1934.* New York: Garland Publishing, 1994.

Fritz, David L. "Before the 'Howling Wilderness': The Military Career of Jacob Hurd Smith, 1861–1902." *Military Affairs,* 39, December 1979.

Linn, Brian McAllister. *The Philippine War, 1899–1902.* Lawrence: University Press of Kansas, 2000.

Socapa Point (Cuba)

A point of land 174 feet high, Socapa Point, Cuba, is located on the west side of the entrance leading into Santiago harbor and approximately 400 yards across the water from Morro Battery. During the Spanish-American War, Socapa featured two batteries: upper and lower. The former consisted of three 8-inch muzzle-loading howitzers and a pair of 16.3-inch Hontoria guns, which had been removed from the *Reina Mercedes.*

The lower battery mounted one 57-millimeter piece, four 37-millimeter Hotchkiss guns, and one machine gun. The purpose of the lower battery was to defend the mines that had been laid across the channel entrance.

See also Cervera y Topete, Pascual; Naval Blockade of Cuba; Santiago de Cuba, Naval Battle of.

References and Further Readings

Chadwick, Rear Adm. French Ensor. *Relations of the United States and Spain: The Spanish American War.* 2 vols. New York: Charles Scribner's Sons, 1911 (reprinted in 1968).

Trask, David F. *The War with Spain in 1898.* Lincoln: University of Nebraska Press, 1996.

Spain

Once the most powerful empire in the world, Spain was the first European nation to establish a permanent presence in North America. By the late nineteenth century, however, the once vast Spanish empire had been reduced to Cuba, Puerto Rico, the Philippines, and a few Pacific islands. Twice during the nineteenth century, Spain had undergone civil war, and the nation was wracked by political dissension among those who favored the traditional monarchy with a strong Catholic Church and those Progressives who argued for a liberal government. Standing in opposition to both were the Marxists and anarchists.

The Progressives argued that Spain could not expect to move forward into the twentieth century as a strong nation as long as it clung to the kind of extreme religious conservatism once characterized by the notorious Inquisition. Conservatives, by contrast, believed this had always been and would continue to be the source of Spain's power and greatness.

As a result of the Carlist upheavals, Queen Isabella abdicated her throne in 1870 in favor of her son, Alfonso XII. Following the death of his first wife, Alfonso married María Cristina of Austria in 1879. He died in 1885 before the birth of his son, Alfonso XIII. María Cristina, acting as queen regent, ruled Spain for her young son and was the ruling monarch at the time of the Spanish-American War.

The Cuban Revolution that began in 1895 intensified Spain's internal turmoil, and as the revolt continued, the issue of Cuba became a festering sore, reflected in the fluid political scene. In 1897, Práxedes Sagasta stepped down as prime minister in favor of the Conservative Antonio Cánovas del Castillo. With Castillo's assassination in October, Sagasta, at the queen regent's behest, returned as prime minister.

Although Spain's power had waned considerably since the halcyon days of the sixteenth and seventeenth centuries, it remained a proud, if at times haughty, nation with a strong core of support among the Spanish people for their fading empire.

See also María Cristina, Queen Regent of Spain; Sagasta, Práxedes Mateo.

References and Further Readings

Chadwick, Rear Adm. French Ensor. *Relations of the United States and Spain: The Spanish American War.* 2 vols. New York: Charles Scribner's Sons, 1911 (reprinted in 1968).

Musicant, Ivan. *Empire by Default: The Spanish-American War and the Dawn of the American Century.* New York: Henry Holt and Company, 1998.

Trask, David F. *The War with Spain in 1898.* Lincoln: University of Nebraska Press, 1996.

Spanish-American War, International Reaction to

On 9 December 1896, Sen. James Cameron of Pennsylvania introduced a resolution to recognize Cuban belligerency—that is, to recognize the official status of the revolutionary government. Although the resolution did not pass, several major powers that were friendly to Spain, including France, Germany, Japan, and Russia, were prepared to seek diplomatic intervention in an effort to avoid war between Spain and the United States.

European concern was based on the fear that a U.S. victory might affect the balance of power. Indeed, one Russian paper clearly stated that Europe had nothing to gain by strengthening U.S. power and influence in the Western Hemisphere. There was fear, too, that if Spain was defeated, its monarchy would collapse, which in turn might affect other European monarchies.

In April 1898, before the declaration of war, European powers in Madrid urged Spain to accept U.S. conditions for Cuba, in order to avoid war. But the mood of the Spanish people was disposed toward war, as was the mood in the United States, and the ruling party in Spain refused to consider Cuban independence.

See also Cuba; Spain; Spanish-American War, U.S. Public Reaction to.

References and Further Readings

Leech, Margaret. *In the Days of McKinley.* New York: Harper & Brothers, 1959.

Musicant, Ivan. *Empire by Default: The Spanish-American War and the Dawn of the American Century.* New York: Henry Holt and Company, 1998.

Spanish-American War, U.S. Public Reaction to

The Cuban War of Independence, which began in 1895, provided a fertile field for U.S. newspapers that exploited the saleability of sensational stories. Led by Joseph Pulitzer's *New York World* and William Randolph Hearst's *New York Journal,* the U.S. press focused on the plight of the Cuban people, who were described as living under the heel of Spanish tyranny. Stories of atrocities, injustices, and suffering, which were often exaggerated, sowed the seeds of anger and indignation among a great many U.S. citizens.

When the battleship *Maine* blew up in Havana harbor on the night of 15 February 1898, the U.S. public was outraged. Later, when a naval court of inquiry concluded that the cause was an external explosion set off by a party or parties unknown, many, if not most, Americans believed that Spain was guilty. As a result, public opinion was strongly in favor of going to war with Spain, not just to avenge the *Maine* but also to redress the wrongs inflicted on the Cuban people. The destruction of the *Maine* unified an angry public opinion that clearly supported a war with Spain.

See also Hearst, William Randolph; Journalism; *Maine*; *Maine*, Inquiries into the Sinking of; Pulitzer, Joseph.

References and Further Readings

Beede, Benjamin R., ed. *The War of 1898 and U.S. Interventions, 1898–1934*. New York: Garland Publishing, 1994.

May, Ernest R. *American Imperialism: A Speculative Essay*. Chicago: Imprint Publications, 1991.

Wilkerson, Marcus M. *Public Opinion and the Spanish-American War: A Study in War Propaganda*. New York: Russell and Russell, 1967.

Wisan, Joseph Ezra. *The Cuban Crisis as Reflected in the New York Press (1895–1898)*. New York: Columbia University Press, 1934.

"Splendid Little War"

See **Hay, John**

Sternberg, George Miller (1838–1915)

A pioneer in the field of bacteriology and epidemiology, George Miller Sternberg was born in Ostego County, New York. As surgeon general of the U.S. Army during the Spanish-American War, he continued a research program to find causes and cures for tropical fevers.

After graduating from the College of Physicians and Surgeons in 1860, he served as an assistant surgeon in the Civil War, during which time he contracted typhus. After recovering, he spent the remainder of the war in the Washington, DC, area. His post–Civil War service gave him an opportunity to study the current treatment for yellow fever, which led eventually to articles published in the *New Orleans Medical and Surgical Journal*. These articles were largely responsible for establishing him as an authority on yellow fever.

After studying with the Yellow Fever Commission in Cuba, Sternberg was named surgeon general of the U.S. Army, a post he held for nine years. During his tenure as the army's top medical officer, he was responsible for creating the Army Medical School, the Army Nurse Corps, and the Army Dental Corps. During the Spanish-American War, Sternberg, continuing his research to find causes and cures for tropical fevers, established the Yellow Fever Board, which included one of his protégés, Walter Reed. Had Sternberg's directives regarding sanitation practices in army camps been followed, the health problems in those camps would have been greatly reduced.

Sternberg retired from the army in 1902.

See also Camps, Staging Areas, and Embarkation Points, U.S. Army; Diseases; Medical Department, U.S. Army; Reed, Walter.

References and Further Readings

Cosmas, Graham. *An Army for Empire: The United States Army in the Spanish-American War.* College Station: Texas A&M University Press, 1998.

Gibson, John M. *Soldier in White: The Life of General George Miller Sternberg.* Durham, NC: Duke University Press, 1958.

Storey, Moorfield (1845–1929)

Born in Roxbury, Massachusetts, Moorfield Storey graduated from Harvard and practiced law in Boston. A political activist and Anti-Imperialist, Storey lobbied most vigorously against U.S. annexation of any Spanish territory. He also was active in the fight for black rights and civil service reform. He authored a number of books and articles on the various issues he supported, including works opposing annexation of the Philippines.

See also Anti-Imperialist League; Philippine Islands, Acquisition of, by the United States.

References and Further Readings

Gould, Lewis L. *The Spanish-American War and President McKinley.* Lawrence: University of Kansas Press, 1982.

Hixon, William B. *Moorfield Storey and the Abolitionist Tradition.* New York: Oxford University Press, 1972.

Storey, Moorfield, and Marcial P. Lichauco. *The Conquest of the Philippines by the United States, 1898–1925.* New York: G. P. Putnam's Sons, 1926.

Subig (Subic) Bay (Philippines)

Subig (or Subic) Bay is a narrow harbor on the island of Luzon, 50 miles west of Manila. In preparing to defend the Philippines, Adm. Patricio Montojo at first concentrated his naval squadron on Subig Bay. Upon discovering that no defensive preparations had been made at Subig, Montojo conducted his defense on Manila Bay instead, where he was subsequently defeated by Adm. George Dewey in the 1 May 1898 Battle of Manila Bay.

See also Dewey, George; Manila Bay, Battle of; Montojo y Pasarón, Patricio.

References and Further Readings

Musicant, Ivan. *Empire by Default: The Spanish-American War and the Dawn of the American Century.* New York: Henry Holt and Company, 1998.

O'Toole, G. J. A. *The Spanish War: An American Epic, 1898.* New York: W. W. Norton, 1984.

Trask, David F. *The War with Spain in 1898.* Lincoln: University of Nebraska Press, 1996.

Sumner, Samuel Storrow (1842–1937)

The son of an army officer, Samuel Storrow Sumner was born in Pennsylvania. He served as a cavalryman during the Civil War, rising through the ranks to major of volunteers. Later, he served on the frontier during the western Indian wars. At the time of the Spanish-American War, he was appointed brigadier general of volunteers and placed in command of the Second Brigade of the U.S. Volunteer Cavalry Division, which included the Rough Riders.

During the advance on Santiago, when Gen. Joseph Wheeler, commanding the Cavalry Division, was taken ill with fever, Sumner took temporary command of the division. Through the subsequent hard fighting for the high ground known as San Juan Heights (which encompassed San Juan and Kettle Hills), Sumner served with great distinction and received an award for bravery.

After the Cuban Campaign, Sumner was sent to China during the Boxer Rebellion, before being transferred to the Philippines, where he served from 1901 to 1902. There, he achieved solid results during the later campaigns on Luzon, despite a lack of cooperation from his superior, Gen. Adna R. Chaffee.

See also Boxer Rebellion; Chaffee, Adna Romanza; Luzon Campaigns; Philippine-American War, U.S. Public Reaction to; San Juan Hill, Charge up; Santiago, Campaign and Siege of.

References and Further Readings

Feuer, A. B. *The Santiago Campaign of 1898.* Westport, CT: Praeger Publishers, 1993.

Linn, Brian McAllister. *The Philippine War, 1899–1902.* Lawrence: University Press of Kansas, 2000.

Samuels, Peggy, and Harold Samuels. *Teddy Roosevelt at San Juan: The Making of a President.* College Station: Texas A&M University Press, 1997.

Taft, William Howard (1857–1930)

Born in Cincinnati, Ohio, William Howard Taft graduated from Yale and Cincinnati Law School. After practicing law in Ohio, he served as a member of the Ohio Superior Court from 1887 to 1890, then as U.S. solicitor general from 1890 to 1892 and U.S. circuit court judge from 1892 to 1900. In 1900, President William McKinley appointed him to serve as president of the Second Philippine Commission to examine the problems and the growing issues of disagreement between the United States and Filipino Nationalists.

Taft was not welcomed by the army's senior commanders in the Philippines, who resented his and the commission's interference in governing the archipelago. He disagreed with the army's approach to the guerrilla problem, arguing that guerrillas should receive harsh treatment and that, in some cases, the suspension of civil liberties was justified. The conflict might well have been predicted: civil versus military authority.

By 1901, the United States was wearying of the war in the Philippines. President Theodore Roosevelt's Republican Party sought to make it clear that the situation in the Philippines was under control, that the guerrillas were being dealt with, and that the Filipino people were not yet ready for self-government. Taft successfully communicated that feeling and, in 1901, was named the first civil governor of the Philippine Islands.

Taft later went on to serve as secretary of war, provisional governor of Cuba, and the twenty-seventh president of the United States. Weighing over 300 pounds, he may have been the largest man to ever inhabit the White House.

See also McKinley, William, Jr.; Philippine Commission.

References and Further Readings
Beede, Benjamin R., ed. *The War of 1898 and U.S. Interventions, 1898–1934.* New York: Garland Publishing, 1994.

Linn, Brian McAllister. *The Philippine War, 1899–1902.* Lawrence: University Press of Kansas, 2000.

Tagalogs (Philippines)

The Tagalogs were one of five major linguistic groups found on the large island of Luzon in the Philippine Archipelago. A powerful and influential group, the Tagalogs produced most of the Filipino revolutionary leadership; Emilio Aguinaldo, for example, was a Tagalog. Because of their large numbers and high percentage of revolutionary commanders, many U.S. military leaders incorrectly came to believe that during the Philippine-American War the Tagalogs were the main force behind the resistance to U.S. authority. In fact, others were equally strong in their opposition, depending on the particular island province in question.

See also Aguinaldo y Famy, Emilio; Katipunan.

References and Further Readings
Gates, John Morgan. *Schoolbooks and Krags: The United States Army in the Philippines, 1898–1902.* Contributions in Military History no. 3. Westport, CT: Greenwood Press, 1973.
Linn, Brian McAllister. *The U.S. Army and Counterinsurgency in the Philippine War, 1899–1902.* Chapel Hill: University of North Carolina Press, 1989.
———. *The Philippine War, 1899–1902.* Lawrence: University Press of Kansas, 2000.
Wolff, Leon. *Little Brown Brother: America's Forgotten Bid for Empire Which Cost 250,000 Lives.* New York: Kraus Reprint, 1970.

Tampa (Florida)

See **Camps, Staging Areas, and Embarkation Points, U.S. Army**

Taylor, Henry Clay (1845–1904)

Henry Clay Taylor was born in Washington, DC, and entered the U.S. Navy in 1860. Following three largely uneventful decades of service, he was made president of the Naval War College from 1893 to 1896. During his tenure at the college, he proposed a new strategy for a possible war with Spain, which included a movement against the Philippines.

During the war with Spain, he commanded the battleship *Indiana,* which participated in the bombardment of San Juan, Puerto Rico, in May 1898. Later, Taylor commanded the naval convoy that carried the Fifth Corps to Cuba. Under Taylor's command, the *Indiana* played a prominent role in the great naval battle of Santiago on 3 July 1898.

An author and intellectual, Taylor was instrumental in creating the Navy's General Board, which provided counsel to the secretary of the navy on naval matters. Promoted to rear admiral, he died in 1904.

See also Cuban Expeditionary Force, U.S.; Santiago de Cuba, Naval Battle of.

References and Further Readings

Hagan, Kenneth J. *This People's Navy: The Making of American Sea Power.* New York: Free Press, 1991.

Musicant, Ivan. *Empire by Default: The Spanish-American War and the Dawn of the American Century.* New York: Henry Holt and Company, 1998.

Trask, David F. *The War with Spain in 1898.* Lincoln: University of Nebraska Press, 1996.

Technology

By 1898, technological advances had significantly changed the way war was conducted, particularly in the fields of communication and weaponry. In the Executive Mansion, for example, President William McKinley created a "war room" in which 25 telegraph lines and 15 telephone lines were installed. This network enabled the president to monitor developments in the field and issue directives faster than had ever been possible.

Since 1858, Europe and North America had been able to exchange telegraphic messages using an underwater cable that spanned the Atlantic Ocean. The Spanish-American War was the first conflict in which the U.S. government could direct operations at sea. For example, a cable could be sent to Key West, Florida, then relayed to a fleet commander by a small, fast messenger vessel. In 1898, submarine cable had not yet been laid across the vast Pacific. Consequently, communications to that part of the world took a more circuitous route, but in the North Atlantic and Caribbean, the system was quite effective.

The Spanish-American War was also the first war that could be filmed using motion picture cameras. Several filmmakers, including Edison, Vitagraph, and Biograph, produced footage on various aspects of the war.

Electricity was used on most modern naval vessels, and the fighting ships had witnessed the introduction of heavy side and deck armor. Propulsion systems had also been refined and improved. The new armored cruisers *New York* and *Brooklyn* could make 20 knots, and the battleship *Iowa* could do 17 knots.

An experimental naval weapon of the period was the dynamite gun, which fired a 500-pound projectile of nitrocellulose, called *gun-cotton,* using pneumatic force to send the projectile on its way. Three such weapons were mounted on the *Vesuvius.*

Another notable technological advance was smokeless powder in rifle cartridges. Spanish infantrymen, armed with Mauser rifles that used smokeless powder cartridges, were tremendously effective against U.S. troops, who were unable to locate their opponents. By contrast, many U.S. volunteers were armed with the old Springfield rifles whose bullets, propelled by black powder, released clouds of smoke when fired, making it easy to locate the positions of those firing.

See also Communications; Weapons.

References and Further Readings

Dierks, Jack Cameron. *A Leap to Arms: The Cuban Campaign of 1898.* Philadelphia: J. B. Lippincott, 1970.

Leech, Margaret. *In the Days of McKinley.* New York: Harper & Brothers, 1959.

Standage, Tom. *The Victorian Internet.* New York: Walker & Company, 1998.

Trask, David F. *The War with Spain in 1898.* Lincoln: University of Nebraska Press, 1996.

Teddy's Terrors

See **Rough Riders**

Teller Amendment

See **Teller, Henry Moore**

Teller, Henry Moore (1830–1914)

Born in Alleghany County, New York, Henry Moore Teller, a teacher, lawyer, and politician, moved to Colorado Territory in 1859 and began practicing law. In 1876, he became Colorado's first U.S. senator. He was named secretary of the interior in 1882, a post he held for three years before returning to the Senate in 1885, where he was to remain for twenty-four years, a fervent supporter of the Cuban independence movement.

In April 1898, Teller introduced an amendment that was to carry his name, probably the most important accomplishment of his political career. The Teller Amendment proposed that the United States recognize Cuban independence. However, as a statement to the international community, the amendment made it clear that the United States had no intention of annexing Cuba and that the U.S. presence in Cuba would end once the Cuban Republic was firmly established. The Teller Amendment was received in Congress with great enthusiasm.

A very small faction in the United States was partial to Cuban annexation. However, the majority of the nation had serious misgivings about, if not outright disdain for, the idea of eventually opening the door to statehood to a population that was largely Roman Catholic and heavily black. The Teller Amendment provided an opportunity to sidestep that issue and, at the same time, ride to Cuba's aid and promote its independence.

> **See also** Cuban Revolution; McKinley, William, Jr.
> **References and Further Readings**
> Leech, Margaret. *In the Days of McKinley.* New York: Harper & Brothers, 1959.

Ten Years' War (1868–1878)

From 1868 to 1878, disgruntled Cuban nationals waged a largely uncoordinated uprising against the Spanish that came to be known as the Ten Years' War. As a result of increasing dissatisfaction among Cuban Nationalists because of Spain's refusal to introduce political and economic reform, a revolutionary movement under the leadership of Carlos Manuel de Céspedes began to take shape in the late 1860s. The movement grew and attracted many followers, among whom were future luminaries of the Cuban independence movement that immediately preceded the Spanish-American War: Máximo Gómez, José Martí, and Antonio Maceo.

Despite its early success, the movement lacked internal solidarity and, as a result, began to fall apart. Céspedes, who had fallen out of favor with some of his followers, was killed by Spanish troops in 1874. In the subsequent four years, Spain crushed the moribund revolution. The 1878 Treaty of Zanjón officially terminated the Ten Years' War.

> **See also** Cuban Revolution; Gómez Báez, Máximo; Martí y Peréz, José.
> **References and Further Readings**
> Foner, Philip S. *The Spanish-Cuban-American War.* 2 vols. New York: Monthly Review Press, 1972.
> Thomas, Hugh. *Cuba: The Pursuit of Freedom.* New York: Harper & Row, 1971.

Tinio, Manuel (1877–1924)

Born in Nueva Ecija Province in central Luzon, Manuel Tinio was one of the foremost figures in the Philippine independence movement, fighting first against the Spanish and later against the Americans. As a youth, Tinio joined the Katipunan, and after the Pact of Biyak-na-Bató was signed, he accompanied Emilio Aguinaldo into exile in Hong Kong.

Following the U.S. declaration of war against Spain and the subsequent Battle of Mobile Bay, Aguinaldo and his entourage, including Tinio, returned to the Philippines. Together with his brothers, Tinio led the fight to liberate his home province from Spanish rule.

At the outbreak of the Philippine-American War, Tinio, though barely 22, was appointed a general and placed in command of the republican forces in the Ilocano provinces. Here, his natural military skills were complemented by his ability to persuade the local populace not to support the Americans.

Although lacking the men and matériel to contain the U.S. forces, he inflicted heavy casualties on the Americans at San Jacinto before his troops were driven back by the heavy and accurate rifle fire of the U.S. soldiers.

Realizing that he could not compete with U.S. forces on a conventional level, Tinio, following Aguinaldo's directive, waged desperate but futile guerrilla warfare. In March 1901, Aguinaldo was captured and signed an oath of allegiance to the United States, urging his followers to do the same. Tinio followed Aguinaldo's wishes and thereafter proved an active supporter of the new government established by the United States.

See also Aguinaldo y Famy, Emilio.

References and Further Readings

Beede, Benjamin R., ed. *The War of 1898 and U.S. Interventions, 1898–1934.* New York: Garland Publishing, 1994.

Linn, Brian McAllister. *The U.S. Army and Counterinsurgency in the Philippine War, 1899–1902.* Chapel Hill: University of North Carolina Press, 1989.

———. *The Philippine War, 1899–1902.* Lawrence: University Press of Kansas, 2000.

Toral y Vázquez, José (1834–1904)

Initially in charge of a Spanish brigade at Santiago, Gen. José Toral took command of the Fourth Corps when Gen. Arsenio Linares was wounded on 1 July 1898. As commander of the city's defenses, Toral received Gen. William R. Shafter's demand for surrender, which he rejected despite Shafter's warning that the city would be shelled. Negotiations continued nonetheless. Toral agreed to surrender providing that the garrison was allowed to retain its arms and march unopposed to Holguín. Shafter was disposed to accept those terms, but President McKinley insisted on unconditional surrender.

On 10 and 11 July, Toral waged one last fruitless fight for the city. Following the fight, Shafter proposed that the United States agree to return all Spanish prisoners to Spain at U.S. expense providing that Toral surrendered unconditionally. By now, it had become clear to Toral that there was no hope of relief, so he accepted Shafter's proposal. In this decision, he was supported by his superior in Havana, and on 17 July 1898, Toral surrendered the city of Santiago, along with a number of outlying posts.

Upon his return to Spain, Toral was severely criticized and court-martialed. However, after a strong defense by Julián Suárez Inclán, he was acquitted. Notwithstanding the acquittal, Toral never fully recovered from the stigma of his surrender and finally died in a mental institution in 1904.

See also Linares y Pomba, Arsenio; Santiago, Campaign and Siege of.

References and Further Readings

Cosmas, Graham. *An Army for Empire: The United States Army in the Spanish-American War.* College Station: Texas A&M University Press, 1998.

Inclán, Julián Suárez. *Defensa del General Toral ante el Consejo Supremo de Guerra y Marina reunido y Constituido en Sala de Justicia.* Madrid: n.p., 1899.

Musicant, Ivan. *Empire by Default: The Spanish-American War and the Dawn of the American Century.* New York: Henry Holt and Company, 1998.

Trask, David F. *The War with Spain in 1898.* Lincoln: University of Nebraska Press, 1996.

Treaty of Paris (10 December 1898)

On 1 October 1898, following the end of the Spanish-American War, commissioners from both countries convened in Paris with the mutual goal of arriving at a peace agreement that was acceptable to all parties. After nearly three months of negotiating, the commission came to an agreement on 10 December 1898.

As victor in the brief war, the United States bargained from a position of great strength, as was evident from the terms of the treaty. Although there were a number of provisions in the agreement, the heart of the treaty stipulated that Spain relinquish its sovereign rights to Cuba. Further, Spain agreed to cede Puerto Rico, the island of Guam, and the entire Philippine Archipelago to the United States. As compensation, the United States agreed to pay Spain $20 million for the Philippines and to guarantee Spain commercial trading rights in the Philippines for a period of ten years. The United States also agreed to return all Spanish prisoners to Spain at U.S. expense.

The treaty was ratified by the U.S. Senate on 6 February 1899. In Spain, however, the agreement was not well received and finally required the signature of the queen regent, María Cristina, to break the deadlock in the legislature, allowing the treaty to be ratified on 19 March.

See also McKinley, William, Jr.; Peace Commission; Reid, Whitelaw.
References and Further Readings
Leech, Margaret. *In the Days of McKinley.* New York: Harper & Brothers, 1959.
Morgan, H. Wayne, ed. *Making Peace with Spain: The Diary of Whitelaw Reid—September–December, 1898.* Austin: University of Texas Press, 1965.
Musicant, Ivan. *Empire by Default: The Spanish-American War and the Dawn of the American Century.* New York: Henry Holt and Company, 1998.

Trocha

The *trocha* was a fortified line that was first used by the Spanish during the Ten Years' War (1868–1878). The purpose was to confine the Cuban rebels to one part of the island, thereby limiting the range of their movement and their effectiveness.

The eastern *trocha* used in the Ten Years' War cut Cuba in half at its narrowest point. As designed, it was 50 miles long and some 200 yards wide, flanked by a row of trees on each side. Blockhouses were built every half mile, with smaller fortified outposts and heavy stands of barbed wire in between the blockhouses. At key points, where it seemed likely that an attack would occur, bombs were set in place with trip-wire attachments to set them off.

Gen. Arsenio Martínez de Campos, who was sent to Cuba in 1895 to deal with the new revolution, used the *trocha* to combat the *insurrectos.* The *trocha* was also used in conjunction with the notorious *reconcentrado* policy introduced by Governor-General Valeriano "Butcher" Weyler, who replaced Campos. Weyler's strategy was to isolate the rebels from the nonrebels through his *reconcentrado* policy and to restrict the rebels' freedom of movement by using the *trocha.*

Although the *trochas* did contain rebel movements up to a point, the system was thought to be of questionable value, particularly when weighed against the groundswell of sympathy for the Cuban people who were forced to live under the harsh conditions imposed by Spanish rule.

See also Cuban Revolution; Martínez de Campos, Arsenio; *Reconcentrado* System; Weyler y Nicolau, Valeriano "Butcher."

References and Further Readings

Foner, Philip S. *The Spanish-Cuban-American War.* 2 vols. New York: Monthly Review Press, 1972.

Musicant, Ivan. *Empire by Default: The Spanish-American War and the Dawn of the American Century.* New York: Henry Holt and Company, 1998.

Uniforms

In 1898, the U.S. Army was ill prepared to fight a war, especially one in the Tropics. Essentially, the army was issuing the same all-wool blue uniform that it had used for decades. A fatigue uniform made of canvas material had been issued in limited quantities in the 1880s, but it was hardly more appropriate than the woolen one for service in warm or hot climates.

At the outbreak of the Spanish-American War, General of the Army Nelson Miles recommended that the army purchase uniforms made of cotton khaki, which the British had used successfully in hot-weather regions. Initially, U.S. manufacturers lacked the equipment necessary to weave and dye this kind of material, so the quartermaster general improvised by reducing the weight of wool in the old blue uniforms. Some regiments did receive the new uniforms, but they were little better than the old-style ones. As a consequence, many U.S. soldiers in Cuba not only had to march and fight in brutally hot weather but also had to do so wearing uniforms made of material that was better suited to cold climes.

By the end of the Cuban Campaign, new khaki uniforms began rolling off the production lines, but it was not until the last stages of the Philippine-American War that troops had appropriate uniforms in which to fight.

By contrast, the Spanish Army, with years of experience in tropical climates, outfitted its soldiers in a striped, light-cotton uniform known as *rayadillo,* which was far more appropriate for fighting in regions such as Cuba and the Philippines.

See also Army, Spanish; Army, U.S.

References and Further Readings
Cosmas, Graham. *An Army for Empire: The United States Army in the Spanish-American War.* College Station: Texas A&M University Press, 1998.
Field, Ron. *Spanish-American War: 1898.* London: Brasseys, 1998.

Vatican Role in Spanish-American War

See **Papal Mediation**

Vesuvius

See **Weapons**

Villaverde, Domingo

See **Hellings, Martin Luther**

Virginius Affair (31 October 1873)

Although it occurred twenty-five years before the Spanish-American War, the *Virginius* affair is important in the context of the war for two reasons. First, it had an impact on the future of U.S. naval development, and second, it played a part in establishing an anti-Spanish attitude in the minds of many U.S. citizens.

In October 1873, the *Virginius,* an 1864-vintage side-wheel steamer that had once served as a Confederate blockade runner, was overtaken in Caribbean waters by a Spanish ship, the *Tornado.* The *Virginius* was ferrying arms, ammunition, and volunteers to aid the Cuban rebels in the Ten Years' War. Although the *Virginius* was of U.S. registry (though not a navy vessel), it was taken to Cuba, where its captain and 53 officers and men were summarily executed by a firing squad.

The incident created an international stir and might well have provoked a war with Spain had it not been for the deplorable condition of the U.S. Navy, which was in no shape to face any opponent. As a consequence, the United States had no alternative but to negotiate a settlement that eventually resulted in Spain paying an indemnity.

The *Virginius* affair served as a reminder to the United States that its navy needed to be updated. Washington took heed. By 1898, it was a far different fleet that virtually destroyed the Spanish Navy. The incident also left a lasting sense of anger and humiliation within many Americans that carried forward to 1898.

See also Filibuster; Navy, U.S.; Ten Years' War.

References and Further Readings

Bradford, Richard H. *The* Virginius *Affair*. Boulder: Colorado Associated University Press, 1980.

Musicant, Ivan. *Empire by Default: The Spanish-American War and the Dawn of the American Century*. New York: Henry Holt and Company, 1998.

Visayan Campaigns (Philippines)

Ethnic diversity posed a far greater impediment to U.S. victory in the Philippine-American War than many senior U.S. military officials recognized at the outset. Initially, the primary focus of the war effort was Luzon, largest of the islands in the Philippine Archipelago and home of the Tagalogs, the largest of the archipelago's ethnic groups. The Filipino Nationalist movement was composed mainly of Tagalogs, and the de facto leader of the Republicans, Emilio Aguinaldo, was himself a Tagalog. Consequently, U.S. military leaders became wedded to the notion that in order to win the war, it was only necessary to defeat Aguinaldo and his Tagalogs. Given this premise, it followed that there would be little or no opposition elsewhere in the archipelago.

As the war evolved, it became increasingly clear to many (though not all) officers that this assessment of the situation was far from realistic. Nowhere in the archipelago was this fact better illustrated than in the Visayas, a cluster of islands in the central Philippines, of which the principal islands in the group are Cebu, Samar, Negros, Leyte, Panay, and Bohol. The inhabitants of these islands, though generally in favor of Philippine independence, refused to follow Aguinaldo and his largely Tagalog government, preferring their individual islands' political systems and leaders.

On Panay, leader Martin Delgado formed the Federal State of the Visayas, refusing to accept Aguinaldo's authority. With the outbreak of hostilities between Filipino and U.S. forces, Brig. Gen. Marcus Miller landed his troops from gunboats and seized Iloilo City on 11 February 1899. Resistance was stiff, though mostly in the form of sniper fire. With the city torched, each side pointed a finger at the other. Nevertheless, a smoldering Iloilo City was in American hands by dark. The U.S. Army and U.S. Navy argued as to who should get credit for the capture, since the latter felt it was their gunboat activity that secured the victory. This dispute was indicative of the rivalry that often characterized army-navy relations during the Spanish-American and Philippine-American Wars.

Although Miller occupied and controlled Iloilo City, his position was somewhat tenuous. He had insufficient troops to control the entire island and was therefore more or less confined to the city. Patrols were subjected to random attacks by snipers, and banditry flourished.

On 5 May 1899, Miller was replaced by Brig. Gen. Robert P. Hughes, a distinguished soldier who soon discovered that Visayans were no more willing to accept U.S. rule than they were to acquiesce to Aguinaldo's directives. Like his predecessor, Hughes lacked the troops to do more than confine his operations to Iloilo City.

Across the water, the island of Negros appeared more promising. A profitable island because of its many rich sugar plantations, Negros was roughly composed of two parts: Negros Occidental on the west and Negros Oriental on the east. On 1 March, Brig. Gen. James Smith had been named military governor of the new subdistrict of Negros. An able and savvy commander, Smith worked diligently to develop a strong rapport with the inhabitants, following President McKinley's policy of benevolent assimilation.

On Negros, just as on Panay, a political faction created the Federal Republic of Negros Oriental. General Smith's efforts paid dividends, which included the creation of a local constabulary to maintain law and order. Yet despite his efforts and the presence of a local police force, he still lacked sufficient man power to control the outlaw bands that flourished on the island. One such group was composed of former policemen led by a fanatic named Luis Ginete. Still another group that ravaged and terrorized Negros Occidental was the Babylanes, a militant political sect.

On 19 July 1899, Capt. Bernard Byrne, leading two companies of the Sixth Infantry, attacked the Babylane village of Bobong near La Carlota, after a herculean march through mud and up steep mountain slopes in drenching rain. When the attack faltered in the face of a sudden charge by Filipino bolomen, Bryne ordered a small detachment of his own exhausted command to charge. The stratagem caught the Filipinos off guard and resulted in a Babylane retreat with heavy casualties. Six weeks later, Byrne destroyed another Babylane camp, continuing a string of army successes that lasted into the fall.

Led by Arcadio Maxilom, the inhabitants of the island of Cebu, like those of other islands, both rejected Aguinaldo's demands and resisted the Americans. On 21 February 1899, the U.S. Navy took control of Cebu City, although again there was some question as to whether the army or navy had taken control. As occurred elsewhere in the Visayas, the U.S. Army simply lacked the strength to control the brigands and revolutionary guerrillas.

In August 1899, a column of the Nineteenth and Twenty-third Infantry Regiments and the First Tennessee moved to seek and destroy the headquarters of revolutionary leader Arcadio Maxilom. After a torturous march in stifling heat, the column exchanged fire with the rebels but failed to accomplish its main mission.

On the island of Leyte, Gen. Ambrosio Moxica commanded a potent revolutionary force. Opposing him was Col. Arthur Murray, who had only five companies of the Forty-third Infantry. Detachments sent into the interior were continually harassed by Moxica's troops. Between February and June 1901, there were 125 engagements on Leyte.

In April 1901, Murray received reinforcements and launched a punitive strike against Moxica. During the next several weeks, the revolutionary forces at Ormoc (26 April) and Hilongas (6 May) experienced severe losses. Further reinforced that summer of 1901, Murray finally occupied towns that he had earlier lacked the strength to take. And like General Smith on Negros, Murray developed a rapport with the natives and local leaders, attempting to demonstrate why it was to their benefit to work with the Americans.

Although Murray tried hard to implement social reforms, he did get tough when revolutionaries and bandits attacked. During the spring of 1901, punitive columns moved against Moxica and again inflicted heavy losses, destroying stocks of supplies and capturing many prisoners. Moxica himself surrendered after his main camp was attacked on 9 April. Moxica's surrender officially ended organized resistance on Leyte.

The Visayan Campaigns were conducted as backdoor operations, with the bulk of the army's strength concentrated in Luzon. It was a strange kind of soldiering that ranged from implementing social reforms among the native people to tough, hard-nosed campaigning against brigands and revolutionary groups.

(*Note:* Although the island of Samar is part of the Visayan group, the campaigns thereon are discussed in a separate entry.)

See also Aguinaldo y Famy, Emilio; Luzon Campaigns; Samar Campaigns.

References and Further Readings

Gates, John Morgan. *Schoolbooks and Krags: The United States Army in the Philippines, 1898–1902.* Contributions in Military History no. 3. Westport, CT: Greenwood Press, 1973.

Linn, Brian McAllister. *The Philippine War, 1899–1902.* Lawrence: University Press of Kansas, 2000.

Volunteers (U.S.) in Cuban Revolt

See **Filibuster**

von Bülow, Prince Bernhard (1849–1929)

The son of Bernhard Ernst von Bülow, Prince Bernhard von Bülow was born in Holstein, Prussia. A statesman and diplomat, he served as German foreign minister from 1897 to 1900. During that time, he negotiated with Spain for the purchase of the Pacific islands, including the strategically important Carolines. Prince von Bülow also convinced Kaiser Wilhelm that Germany had to remain neutral in the conflict between Spain and the United States, notwithstanding the kaiser's strong objections to what he regarded as America's aggressive posture.

See also Spanish-American War, International Reaction to; Treaty of Paris.

References and Further Readings

Morgan, H. Wayne, ed. *Making Peace with Spain: The Diary of Whitelaw Reid—September–December, 1898.* Austin: University of Texas Press, 1965.

O'Toole, G. J. A. *The Spanish War: An American Epic, 1898.* New York: W. W. Norton, 1984.

Trask, David F. *The War with Spain in 1898.* Lincoln: University of Nebraska Press, 1996.

Wade, James Franklin (1843–1921)

Born in Ohio, James Franklin Wade was appointed a lieutenant of volunteers in the Union army during the Civil War, rising to brigadier general by war's end. At the time of the Spanish-American War, Wade was in charge of an assembly area at Tampa, Florida. He was then assigned to command of the Third Corps at Camp Thomas, Chickamauga, Georgia, and was later responsible for coordinating the movement of volunteer troops from Camp Thomas to Cuba. After the war, he was given the job of overseeing the evacuation of Spanish forces from Cuba and Puerto Rico. He then saw duty in the Philippines from 1901 to 1904 and retired in 1907.

> **See also** Army, U.S.; Camps, Staging Areas, and Embarkation Points, U.S. Army.
> **References and Further Readings**
> Cosmas, Graham. *An Army for Empire: The United States Army in the Spanish-American War.* College Station: Texas A&M University Press, 1998.
> Wilson, James Harrison. *Under the Old Flag: Recollections of Military Operations in the War for the Union, the Spanish War, the Boxer Rebellion, etc.* 2 vols. New York: D. Appleton & Company, 1912.

Wagner, Arthur Lockwood (1853–1905)

Born in Illinois, Arthur Lockwood Wagner graduated from West Point in 1875 and served on the western frontier. Despite a poor academic showing while at West Point (he graduated near the bottom of his class), Wagner blossomed into a prolific writer. By 1898, he had earned a reputation as an intellectual and one of the army's foremost authorities on tactics and military doctrine. He was integral in planning the U.S. naval movement during the Spanish-American War.

In the spring of 1898, as war with Spain drew closer, Wagner and navy captain Albert Barker prepared a war plan that called for landing 50,000 troops near Havana while the U.S. Navy neutralized the threat posed by the Spanish Navy. Their recommendation contained the proviso that the invasion not take place until after the rainy months, when the tropical fever season posed a serious threat to land operations. However, President McKinley's desire to force a settlement with Spain as early as possible, coupled with the news that Adm. Pascual Cervera's fleet had slipped into Santiago harbor, caused the United States to revise its strategy.

When the Fifth Corps, under the command of Maj. Gen. William R. Shafter, sailed to Santiago in June, Wagner accompanied the expedition, despite the fact that his health was not good; indeed, he had been declared unfit for field service by the surgeon general. But Wagner was determined not to be left behind and managed to secure an assignment from General of the Army Nelson Miles, under whom he had served on the frontier. Miles authorized Wagner to create the Bureau of Military Intelligence to evaluate information from the field. General Shafter, however, claimed he knew nothing of this arrangement and appointed Gen. William Ludlow to essentially fill the role for which Wagner had been appointed.

Disappointed, Wagner nevertheless remained in the field but came down with malaria after the Battle of El Caney. After recovering, he accompanied General Miles on the Puerto Rican Expedition.

See also Ludlow, William; Miles, Nelson Appleton; Military Intelligence, U.S.; Santiago, Campaign and Siege of; Shafter, William Rufus.

References and Further Readings

Brereton, T. R. "First Lessons in Modern War: Arthur Wagner, the 1898 Santiago Campaign and U.S. Army Lesson-Learning." *Journal of Military History,* vol. 64, no. 1, January 2000.

Cosmas, Graham. *An Army for Empire: The United States Army in the Spanish-American War.* College Station: Texas A&M University Press, 1998.

Wainright, Richard (1849–1926)

Richard Wainright was the son of a distinguished naval officer who had commanded Adm. David Glasgow Farragut's flagship on the Mississippi River during the Civil War. Wainright, who was to prove a fine naval officer himself, graduated from the U.S. Naval Academy at Annapolis in 1868. From 1896 to 1897, he was chief of the Office of Naval Intelligence. In 1898, he was executive officer aboard the *Maine* when it was destroyed in Havana harbor. As executive officer, he oversaw the recovery of bodies and later testified at the court of inquiry investigating the incident.

Following the declaration of war with Spain, Wainright was

placed in command of the *Gloucester*, which had once been financier J. P. Morgan's personal yacht. Acquired by the navy, the yacht was converted into a ship of war. During the naval battle of Santiago, both Wainright and the *Gloucester* acquitted themselves with distinction. Later, Wainright participated in the Puerto Rican Campaign, capturing the port of Guánica, for which he received a commendation for gallantry.

Promoted to commander in 1899, he then served two years as superintendent of the Naval Academy. He was promoted to rear admiral in 1902 and retired in 1911.

See also *Maine*; *Maine*, Inquiries into the Sinking of; Military Intelligence, U.S.; Santiago de Cuba, Naval Battle of.

References and Further Readings

Chadwick, Rear Adm. French Ensor. *Relations of the United States and Spain: The Spanish American War.* 2 vols. New York: Charles Scribner's Sons, 1911 (reprinted in 1968).

Feuer, A. B. *The Spanish-American War at Sea.* Westport, CT: Greenwood Press, 1995.

Trask, David F. *The War with Spain in 1898.* Lincoln: University of Nebraska Press, 1996.

War Department Investigating Commission

On 8 September 1898, in response to heavy criticism of the War Department for its prosecution of the recently ended war with Spain, Secretary of War Russell Alger requested an investigation to clear the air. Of particular concern was the alarming number of soldiers stationed in Cuba who were suffering from tropical fevers, notably yellow fever.

President William McKinley approved the request and eventually appointed Gen. Grenville Dodge of Iowa as head of the commission to investigate these charges. Dodge had served under Gen. William Tecumseh Sherman in the Civil War and later established a reputation as a railroad builder. Altogether, the commission consisted of nine members, including Dodge. Six were former soldiers.

The Dodge Commission, as it came to be known, was seen by some (such as former General of the Army John Schofield) as a political maneuver by McKinley to escape being contaminated by War Department bungling. The commissioners spent most of the fall of 1898 questioning Secretary of War Alger, along with a number of the army's senior officers. They also visited the sites of several former camps and traveled to a number of cities to take testimony from former soldiers and others who might be in a position to illuminate the issues at hand. Public reaction to the commission's work was positive enough that the Republicans retained control of Congress after that fall's election.

Of all those interviewed by the commission, none proved more controversial than General of the Army Nelson Miles, who brought charges against the War Department and Secretary Alger (with whom he had quarreled continuously) for ignoring his recommendations—particularly with regard to campaigning in Cuba during the rain and fever season—and otherwise undermining his efforts to bring the war to a speedy conclusion.

However, it was the so-called beef scandal that really drew public attention. Miles charged that the army's issuance of both canned and refrigerated beef had been hazardous to the health of soldiers in the field and stated that many had become ill because of the beef they consumed. The charges seemed justified by testimony affirming the beef's horrible taste.

Miles's accusation brought forth a violent response from Commissary General Charles P. Eagan, who called Miles a liar. As a result of his action, Eagan was subsequently reduced in rank for insubordination and court-martialed.

After examining all of the evidence and listening to hours of testimony, the Dodge Commission ruled that Miles's allegations were without foundation: Ingestion of the beef, despite its terrible taste, was not injurious to health. The commission also acknowledged, however, that the Commissary Department seriously erred in distributing the beef without first subjecting it to proper testing procedures.

In February 1899, the Dodge Commission issued a lengthy report stating that although there was no evidence of wrongdoing in the War Department, there was a breakdown in the system of administration and supply. The report recommended a reorganization of the Medical and Commissary Departments.

See also Alger, Russell Alexander; Beef Scandal; Camps, Staging Areas, and Embarkation Points, U.S. Army; Diseases; Dodge, Grenville Mellen; Eagan, Charles Patrick; McKinley, William, Jr.; Miles, Nelson Appleton.
References and Further Readings
Cosmas, Graham. *An Army for Empire: The United States Army in the Spanish-American War.* College Station: Texas A&M University Press, 1998.

War Department, U.S.

Originally created in 1789, the War Department controlled all activities of the U.S. Army in peace and war; its counterpart was the Navy

Department. Each was under a civilian head (secretary) who served as a member of the presidential cabinet.

In the years between the Civil War and Spanish-American War, the War Department became a sleepy little sinecure for political appointees. In the hierarchy of the department, the secretary of war executed his orders through the general of the army and a group of bureau chiefs. The general of the army was responsible for all field or line units of the army, namely, infantry, cavalry, and artillery. The ten bureau chiefs each held sway in their own domain. Their bureaus were: Adjutant General, Judge Advocate General, Inspector General, Quartermaster General, Subsistence (Commissary), Medical Department, Corps of Engineers, Ordnance, Signal Corps, and Paymaster.

When William McKinley was elected president in 1896, he appointed Russell A. Alger as secretary of war. Alger, a Michigan politician and businessman and Civil War veteran, was a good example of a political appointee rewarded for faithful service to the party in power. Alger, who was comfortable with the status quo, would probably have gone unnoticed by history had it not been for the tumult of the Spanish-American War.

The army's commanding general, Nelson A. Miles, by contrast, was a veteran of the Civil War and Indian wars and one of the country's most distinguished soldiers. He was also vain to a fault and contentious. It was unfortunate for the nation and the army that Miles and Alger, the two most powerful men in the army, squabbled continuously before and during the Spanish-American War. As a consequence, President McKinley lost patience or faith or both with Miles and Alger and turned increasingly to Adj. Gen. Henry Corbin for military counsel.

When the army was small, as it was in the decades after the Civil War, the War Department's bureau system worked tolerably well. But when war with Spain was declared, the system failed. Its weakness lay in an inability to coordinate the functions of each bureau so as to meet the army's high-volume needs in a fast, efficient manner. Although the bureaus strove to correct their own inadequacies, the Spanish-American War, with its full-scale mobilization, illuminated the need for change.

When Alger resigned under heavy criticism for what was perceived as War Department bungling, which came to be synonomous with the term *Algerism*, he was replaced by Elihu Root, who opened the door to army reform.

In 1947, the name of the War Department was officially changed to the Department of Defense.

See also Alger, Russell Alexander; Army, U.S.; McKinley, William, Jr.; Miles, Nelson Appleton.
References and Further Readings

Cosmas, Graham. *An Army for Empire: The United States Army in the Spanish-American War.* College Station: Texas A&M University Press, 1998.

Musicant, Ivan. *Empire by Default: The Spanish-American War and the Dawn of the American Century.* New York: Henry Holt and Company, 1998.

Trask, David F. *The War with Spain in 1898.* Lincoln: University of Nebraska Press, 1996.

Weigley, Russell F. *History of the United States Army.* New York: Macmillan Publishing, 1967.

War, Spanish-American, U.S. Financing of

The U.S. economy had not been healthy for most of the 1890s, but a slow upturn was in progress as the century drew to a close. In March 1898, when war with Spain seemed increasingly likely, Congress, at the urging of President William McKinley, passed what was known as the Fifty Million Dollar Bill to help finance the war. The direct cost of the war, however, was five to six times that amount ($250 to $300 million), a sum nearly equal to the federal government's total annual revenue.

In order to generate sufficient funds to carry on the war, Congress also passed the War Revenue Bill, which was signed by President McKinley in June 1898. The bill enabled the government to reinstate some old taxes and increase certain excise taxes. Fundamentally, it provided for tax increases on beer and tobacco and set a new license tax on bankers and stockbrokers, as well as an amusement tax on places of entertainment. These new taxes generated an estimated $150 million per year. Congress also authorized the government to borrow needed funds through short-term treasury notes and longer-term bonds.

The war was a model of financing, so much so that by 1900, the budget showed its first surplus in some time and the government was able to pay off a part of the national debt.

See also Fifty Million Dollar Bill; McKinley, William, Jr.
References and Further Readings

Beede, Benjamin R., ed. *The War of 1898 and U.S. Interventions, 1898–1934.* New York: Garland Publishing, 1994.

Leech, Margaret. *In the Days of McKinley.* New York: Harper & Brothers, 1959.

Watkins, Kathleen Blake (1866–?)

Born in Ireland as Catherine Ferguson Willis, "Kit" Blake (as she came to be known professionally) turned to newspaper work after a failed marriage. By the time of the Spanish-American War, she was an established reporter for the *Toronto Daily Mail.*

While the Fifth Corps was assembling in Tampa, Florida, preparatory to its invasion of Cuba, Blake and Anna Benjamin, another newswoman, reported on the army's condition and overall readiness for war. Despite considerable resistance from army officers and male reporters, both women wrote informative stories on army life in Tampa, including articles on rations, camp conditions, and the soldiers' behavior. In addition, their stories sometimes described the activities of the Cuban rebels, providing details often absent from the stories of their male counterparts.

Blake was refused permission to accompany the expedition to Cuba (as was Benjamin), most likely because she was a woman and because she violated the censorship rules imposed by the Fifth Corps commander, Gen. William Shafter. Nevertheless, she was resourceful and managed to reach Cuba on her own, though not until late July, by which time the fighting had ended. She was, however, able to report on conditions as she found them, particularly on how tropical diseases were decimating the ranks of the Fifth Corps.

See also Benjamin, Anna Northend; Journalism; Santiago, Campaign and Siege of.

References and Further Readings

Brown, Charles H. *The Correspondents' War: Journalists in the Spanish-American War.* New York: Charles Scribner's Sons, 1967.

Freeman, Barbara M. "An Impertinent Fly: Kathleen Blake Watkins Covers the Spanish-American War." *Journalism History,* winter 1988.

Watson, John C. (1842–1923)

Born in Kentucky, John Watson graduated from the U.S. Naval Academy in 1861 and saw action while serving under Adm. David Glasgow Farragut in the Civil War. During the Spanish-American War, he participated in the Cuban blockade and was given command of the Eastern Squadron in June 1898. Watson's mission was to threaten the Iberian Peninsula, thereby compelling the Spanish to recall Adm. Manuel Cámara's squadron from its mission to reinforce the Philippines.

In March 1899, Watson was promoted to rear admiral and succeeded Adm. George Dewey as commander of the Asiatic Squadron in the Philippines.

See also Cámara y Libermoore, Manuel de la; Dewey, George;
Eastern Squadron, U.S. Navy; Naval Blockade of Cuba.

References and Further Readings

Chadwick, Rear Adm. French Ensor. *Relations of the United States
and Spain: The Spanish American War.* 2 vols. New York: Charles
Scribner's Sons, 1911 (reprinted in 1968).

Trask, David F. *The War with Spain in 1898.* Lincoln: University of
Nebraska Press, 1996.

Weapons

In the years following the end of the Civil War in 1865, technological advances in weapons, armament, and explosive projectiles resulted in a new breed of warfare. Improvements in infantry rifles, field artillery, and naval guns heralded the forthcoming conflicts of the twentieth century. The following is not intended to be a comprehensive survey of all weapons used in the Spanish-American War but rather a picture of the more important weapons of that period.

Ground Forces

Perhaps the single most important innovation of the Spanish-American War was smokeless powder. Prior to the advent of smokeless powder, weapons used black powder, which emitted a dense cloud of smoke when ignited, clearly revealing the location of the shooter. Smokeless powder produced no telltale smoke. Accordingly, once soldiers began firing from concealed positions using smokeless powder, the character of a battlefield changed dramatically.

Regular U.S. army troops (as opposed to the volunteers) were equipped with the Krag-Jörgensen rifle, a .30-caliber, bolt-action, magazine-fed weapon, adopted as the standard infantry shoulder arm in 1892. It remained the standard weapon until it was replaced by the 1903 Springfield rifle. However, due to a shortage of Krags, the volunteer units were armed with the 1873 Springfield from the Indian wars period, which fired a .45-caliber bullet propelled by black powder, as opposed to the Krag, which employed smokeless powder.

Spanish troops used a 7-millimeter Mauser of Turkish design, which the Spanish Army adopted as their standard infantry shoulder arm in 1893. Like the U.S. Krag, the Mauser used smokeless powder but was considered superior to the Krag because of its improved loading capabilities. Some Remington rolling-block rifles were also used by Spanish forces.

Cuban revolutionary forces used a variety of weapons, ranging from shotguns, 1873 Springfields, and .50-caliber Spencers, brought in by gunrunners, to captured Spanish Army weapons. Many insurgents were often armed with nothing more than a machete, deadly and fearsome in close encounters.

Like the Cubans, the Filipino Nationalist Army was equipped with whatever it could purchase—which did not amount to much—or steal from the enemy. Filipinos also employed the machete, and the fierce Moros from the southern part of the archipelago used spears, bolos, axes, and a wavy sword called a kris.

The U.S. infantry also benefited from the Gatling gun, in existence for some years but further refined by the time of the Spanish-American War. Invented by Richard Gatling, this weapon consisted of multiple barrels—anywhere from 6 to 10—arranged around a rotating cylinder that was turned by a handcrank, allowing the gun to fire up to 1,200 rounds of .30-caliber ammunition per minute. Some models used a motor-powered cylinder that fired up to 3,000 rounds per minute. During the fight for San Juan Hill, Lt John Parker's Gatling guns proved very effective.

By 1898, U.S. field artillery primarily used rifled breechloaders, ranging in caliber from 3.2-inch field pieces to large 7-inch howitzers and 3.6-inch mortars used as siege weapons. Spanish field pieces were of either 8- or 9-centimeter caliber. Cuban and Filipino revolutionary forces had little if any artillery, except that which had been captured or, in the case of the Cubans, brought in by filibusters. The Rough Riders were also equipped with a land version of the navy's experimental dynamite gun.

The main weakness of artillery from this era was its inability to employ indirect fire, that is, to fire at a target without seeing it. As a consequence, artillery batteries had to be on the front line with the infantry to observe a target before firing on it. The indirect firing technique was an innovation still to come.

Some U.S. coastal defense fortifications still employed old muzzle-loading cannons of Civil War vintage, as did the Spanish forts in both Cuba and the Philippines.

Naval Forces

By the time of the Spanish-American War, naval vessels had moved into the age of steel. Increasingly, ships of war were designed with belts of protective steel armor around their sides. Some were constructed with protected decks as well as gun turrets. The larger warships were armed with main batteries ranging from 6-inch to 13-inch rifled guns, along with a variety of smaller weapons.

As with field artillery, naval gunnery was unable to fire indirectly. A gunnery officer had to be able to see his target in order to have much hope of hitting it. Although the two major naval engagements of the war—Manila Bay and Santiago—were great victories for the U.S. Navy, neither navy compiled a good record of shooting accuracy, although the U.S. Navy's aim was superior to that of the Spanish.

The term *torpedo* was often used interchangeably with the term *underwater (submarine) mine,* although there was a difference between the two. More precisely, the torpedo was a self-powered explosive device developed by an Austrian named Luppis and a Scottish engineer named Whitehead. The torpedo, though used by both navies, was not very effective, being slow and erratic of movement.

Unquestionably, the most intriguing weapon of the Spanish-American War was the dynamite gun. Introduced in 1886, the dynamite gun propelled a shell of nitrocellulose, called *guncotton.* A close relative of dynamite, nitrocellulose was a far more powerful charge than black powder. Projectiles came in three sizes, with the largest being nearly 7 feet long and containing 500 pounds of guncotton.

Shells armed with guncotton were extremely sensitive and unstable. In the early 1880s, an army officer, Lt. Edmund Zalinsky, discovered the shells could be fired using pneumatic or compressed air. The deck of a navy ship was deemed ideal for testing this weapon, and accordingly, the *Vesuvius* was designed to accommodate three of these large pneumatic tubes. The effective range of a shell fired from a tube was 500 to 2,000 yards, depending on the size of shell used. The drawback was that the tubes themselves could not be aimed but had to be pointed toward the target by maneuvering the ship. Thus, the weapons were awkward to use, but the shells created fearful explosions when they landed. During the blockade of Adm. Pascual Cervera's fleet in Santiago harbor, Adm. William Sampson used the *Vesuvius* to bombard the harbor. Even if little real damage was done to the Spanish ships or defenses, the dynamite gun did unsettle the defenders.

See also Army, Filipino Nationalist; Army, Spanish; Army, U.S.; Cuban Revolutionary Army; Navy, Spanish; Navy, U.S.

References and Further Readings

Cosmas, Graham. *An Army for Empire: The United States Army in the Spanish-American War.* College Station: Texas A&M University Press, 1998.

Field, Ron. *Spanish-American War: 1898.* London: Brasseys, 1998.

Nofi, Albert A. *The Spanish-American War, 1898.* Conshohocken, PA: Combined Books, 1998.

Trask, David F. *The War with Spain in 1898.* Lincoln: University of Nebraska Press, 1996.

Weyler y Nicolau, Valeriano "Butcher" (1838–1930)

Born in Palma de Mallorca, Canary Islands, of a German father and a Spanish mother, Valeriano Weyler y Nicolau was a pivotal figure in the events leading up to the U.S. war with Spain.

The most prominent Spanish figure in Cuba in the months immediately preceding the war, Weyler was a graduate of the military college in Toledo, Spain. His early career in the Caribbean was distinguished, during operations in Santo Domingo (Dominican Republic) from 1863 to 1865 and in Cuba from 1868 to 1872. He saw action against the Carlist forces in Spain and was promoted to brigadier general and in 1876 to major general. He was also named marquis of Tenerife, serving in the Canary Islands and the Philippines, where he dealt successfully with a rebellion on the island of Mindanao.

An admirer of the Civil War Union general William Tecumseh Sherman, Weyler was sent back to Cuba in early 1896 to deal with a new rebellion that had begun the previous year. Dubbed "Butcher" by William Randolph Hearst, Weyler used a brutal concentration-camp approach to dealing with the rebels, which provoked outrage in the United States. As a result of horror stories published in the papers of Hearst and Joseph Pulitzer, sympathy for the Cuban people ran high, adding fuel to an increasing amount of war rhetoric. The reaction resulted in Weyler's recall to Spain in October 1897.

Following his return to Spain, he served as captain general of New Castile and served as minister of war for three terms. In 1910, he was appointed to the Supreme War Council and in that same year published his Cuban memoirs. Weyler died in 1930, an able commander who, unfortunately, will best be remembered for his ruthless tactics during the Cuban Revolution.

See also Cuban Revolution; Hearst, William Randolph; *Reconcentrado* System; Ten Years' War.

References and Further Readings

Musicant, Ivan. *Empire by Default: The Spanish-American War and the Dawn of the American Century.* New York: Henry Holt and Company, 1998.

O'Toole, G. J. A. *The Spanish War: An American Epic, 1898.* New York: W. W. Norton, 1984.

Trask, David F. *The War with Spain in 1898.* Lincoln: University of Nebraska Press, 1996.

Weyler y Nicolau, Valeriano. *Mi mando en Cuba: Historia militar y política de la última guerra separtista.* 5 vols. Madrid: Imprenta de Felipe González Rojas, 1910–1911.

Wheaton, Lloyd (1838–1918)

Born in Michigan, Lloyd Wheaton served with distinction during the Civil War, rising to the rank of colonel. He was awarded the Medal of Honor for his Civil War service and later served in the Spanish-American War.

Wheaton remained in the army after the Civil War and saw action in the Indian wars. In 1898, he was appointed brigadier general of volunteers and, after duty in Cuba, was sent to the Philippines in 1899. Wheaton played a key role in the campaigns against Emilio Aguinaldo's republican army during the Philippine-American War. In March 1899, while part of Gen. Arthur MacArthur's divison, Wheaton earned the general's praise for the conduct of his brigade in a fight at Guiguintó. However, by the following fall, Wheaton seemed to have temporarily misplaced his usual aggressive tendencies as a commander. As a result, he missed a prime opportunity to capture Aguinaldo and perhaps shorten the war.

In 1901, Wheaton was promoted to major general and given command of the Department of Northern Luzon. There, he employed harsh tactics to combat the guerrilla warfare that characterized the last two years of the Philippine-American War.

See also Aguinaldo y Famy, Emilio; Lawton, Henry Ware; Luzon Campaigns; MacArthur, Arthur; Philippine-American War, U.S. Public Reaction to.

References and Further Readings

Gates, John Morgan. *Schoolbooks and Krags: The United States Army in the Philippines, 1898–1902.* Contributions in Military History no. 3. Westport, CT: Greenwood Press, 1973.

Linn, Brian McAllister. *The U.S. Army and Counterinsurgency in the Philippine War, 1899–1902.* Chapel Hill: University of North Carolina Press, 1989.

———. *The Philippine War, 1899–1902.* Lawrence: University Press of Kansas, 2000.

Wolff, Leon. *Little Brown Brother: America's Forgotten Bid for Empire Which Cost 250,000 Lives.* New York: Kraus Reprint, 1970.

Wheeler, Joseph "Fighting Joe" (1836–1906)

Born in Georgia, Joseph Wheeler was one of the South's premier cavalry leaders during the Civil War, earning the sobriquet "Fighting Joe." At the time of the Spanish-American War, he was serving in the House of Representatives from Alabama, where he had moved after the Civil War.

In mobilizing the army for war with Spain, President William McKinley named Wheeler a major general of volunteers, believing that this appointment, along with that of Fitzhugh Lee (another ex-Confederate cavalry leader and former U.S. consul to Havana), would further help to heal old wounds between North and South.

During the Santiago Campaign, Wheeler commanded the dismounted cavalry division and was second in overall command to Gen. William R. Shafter. In the initial advance on Santiago, Wheeler took advantage of the wording in General Shafter's orders, which were directed to the senior commander present. That senior commander just happened to be Wheeler, although Shafter had expected it to be Gen. Henry Lawton. The diminutive and combative Wheeler initiated an attack on the Spanish position at Las Guásimas on 24 June 1898 and carried the day. During an emotional moment in the battle, Wheeler is reported to have declared that the U.S. troops "had the Yankees on the run," meaning of course to say "the Spanish." The action at Las Guásimas was the second clash between U.S. and Spanish forces on Cuban soil.

Prior to the advance on San Juan Heights, Wheeler was stricken with a tropical fever and forced to relinquish command of the division to Gen. Samuel Sumner. After recuperating at Montauk Point, New York, he served briefly in the Philippines, where his excitable, undisciplined ways did not sit well with his superior, Gen. Arthur MacArthur. In November 1899 during the fighting at Bamban, Wheeler disobeyed orders and sent his brigade charging across the river to score a notable victory,

Maj. Gen. Joseph "Fighting Joe" Wheeler, who commanded the cavalry division in Cuba during the Spanish-American War. He had been one of the Confederate army's most distinguished cavalry leaders during the Civil War.

though it could just as easily have been a disaster. As a result, MacArthur sent Wheeler and his command to the rear, where they would not pose a hazard to future operations.

Wheeler returned to the United States in 1900 and died in 1906.

See also Las Guásimas, Battle of; Luzon Campaigns; McKinley, William, Jr.; Roosevelt, Theodore; Santiago, Campaign and Siege of; Shafter, William Rufus.

References and Further Readings

Cosmas, Graham. *An Army for Empire: The United States Army in the Spanish-American War.* College Station: Texas A&M University Press, 1998.

Linn, Brian McAllister. *The Philippine War, 1899–1902.* Lawrence: University Press of Kansas, 2000.

Samuels, Peggy, and Harold Samuels. *Teddy Roosevelt at San Juan: The Making of a President.* College Station: Texas A&M University Press, 1997.

Trask, David F. *The War with Spain in 1898.* Lincoln: University of Nebraska Press, 1996.

Wikoff, Charles Augustus (?–1898)

Born in Pennsylvania, Charles Augustus Wikoff began his military service in the Civil War. During the Spanish-American War, he commanded the Twenty-second Infantry and was killed by enemy fire while preparing his troops to assault San Juan Hill. The military rest and recovery camp at Montauk Point, New York, was later named Camp Wikoff in his honor.

See also Diseases; Medical Department, U.S. Army; Santiago, Campaign and Siege of.

References and Further Readings

Cosmas, Graham. *An Army for Empire: The United States Army in the Spanish-American War.* College Station: Texas A&M University Press, 1998.

Heatley, Jeff. *Bully! Colonel Theodore Roosevelt and the Rough Riders at Camp Wikoff, Montauk Point, NY.* Harrisburg, PA: Stackpole Books, 1998.

Wilson, James Harrison (1837–1925)

Born in Illinois, James Harrison Wilson graduated from the U.S. Military Academy at West Point in 1860, sixth in his class. He was one of the Civil War's famous boy generals, having reached the rank of major general of volunteers by the war's end, when he was 28 years old.

After the war, he remained in the army only a short time before turning to various business pursuits. When war with Spain broke out, Wilson was named major general of volunteers and assigned to the command of the Sixth Corps at Camp Thomas, Chickamauga, Georgia. Much to his chagrin, the Sixth Corps was never actually created. However, Wilson later served under Gen. Nelson Miles in the Puerto Rican Campaign, commanding one of the four columns in the field. On 9 August, Wilson's force defeated the Spanish at Coamo and had another engagement at Asomonte Hills, where the campaign ended with news of the signing of the Protocol of Peace between Spain and the United States.

After the war, Wilson was appointed military governor of Matanzas Province, Cuba, and later served as second in command to Gen. Adna R. Chaffee on the China Relief Expedition during the Boxer Rebellion. One of America's most distinguished soldiers, Wilson was also a prolific writer. His autobiography, if somewhat self-serving, remains an excellent source of history for the Civil War and Spanish-American War periods.

See also Boxer Rebellion; Chaffee, Adna Romanza; Miles, Nelson Appleton; Puerto Rican Campaign.

References and Further Readings

Cosmas, Graham. *An Army for Empire: The United States Army in the Spanish-American War.* College Station: Texas A&M University Press, 1998.

Musicant, Ivan. *Empire by Default: The Spanish-American War and the Dawn of the American Century.* New York: Henry Holt and Company, 1998.

Trask, David F. *The War with Spain in 1898.* Lincoln: University of Nebraska Press, 1996.

Wilson, James Harrison. *Under the Old Flag: Recollections of Military Operations in the War for the Union, the Spanish War, the Boxer Rebellion, etc.* Vol. 2. New York: D. Appleton & Company, 1912.

Wood, Leonard (1860–1927)

Born in New Hampshire and the son of a physician, Leonard Wood graduated from Harvard in 1884 with a medical degree. In 1886, he was appointed to the U.S. Army as an assistant surgeon and served with distinction on the Arizona frontier during the Apache wars. In 1898, he was awarded the Medal of Honor for his Apache service. In 1895, Wood was appointed White House physician to President Grover Cleveland and continued in that capacity after William McKinley was elected president.

A close friend of Theodore Roosevelt, the two men shared the sames views on Cuba and U.S. involvement in that crisis. Indeed, their single-mindedness about Cuba was common knowledge around the White House. After the *Maine* blew up, President McKinley reportedly asked Wood whether he and Roosevelt had declared war as yet, to which Wood replied no, but they thought he (McKinley) ought to do so.

After the declaration of war with Spain, Wood and Roosevelt organized the First U.S. Volunteer Cavalry, later to be known as the Rough Riders. Roosevelt was first offered the colonelcy of the regiment but deferred to his friend Wood, probably more out of an awareness of his own lack of experience rather than out of any sense of humility or desire to see a friend given the top spot. In any case, Wood became the colonel and regimental commander, with Roosevelt serving as its lieutenant colonel and second in command.

During the Santiago Campaign, Wood commanded the Rough Riders in the action at Las Guásimas. Later, when Brig. Gen. S. B. Young fell ill, Wood moved up to brigade command, a position he held throughout the remainder of the campaign.

After the surrender of Santiago, Wood was promoted to brigadier general and appointed military governor of the city. In this capacity, he improved the deplorable conditions of Santiago by instituting better sanitary practices.

In December 1898, he was promoted to major general and later served in the Philippines against the Moros. In 1901, he was named army chief of staff. A contentious personality made Wood a difficult individual with whom to work.

See also Cuba, U.S. Military Occupation of; Roosevelt, Theodore; Rough Riders.

References and Further Readings

Cosmas, Graham. *An Army for Empire: The United States Army in the Spanish-American War.* College Station: Texas A&M University Press, 1998.

Leech, Margaret. *In the Days of McKinley.* New York: Harper & Brothers, 1959.

Samuels, Peggy, and Harold Samuels. *Teddy Roosevelt at San Juan: The Making of a President.* College Station: Texas A&M University Press, 1997.

Walker, Dale L. *The Boys of '98: Theodore Roosevelt and the Rough Riders.* New York: Forge Books, 1998.

Woodford, Stewart Lyndon (1835–1913)

Born in New York City, Stewart Lyndon Woodford studied law and graduated from Columbia. After service as a brigadier general of volunteers during the Civil War, he was elected congressman and lieutenant governor of New York and later served as U.S. attorney for the Southern District of New York. Just prior to the Spanish-American War, he served as U.S. minister to Spain.

A staunch Republican, Woodford was considered for the post of secretary of the navy but was rejected by President William McKinley. The president did, however, appoint him minister to Spain, despite the fact that he had no prior diplomatic experience. Woodford's mission was to make the Spanish government aware of the fact that the United States was rapidly losing patience with Spain's seeming inability to end the fighting in Cuba.

After the *Maine* disaster, Woodford sensed Spain's desire to sell Cuba and supported the idea. Subsequently, however, he found that neither the Spanish government nor the Spanish people were ready to give up Cuba.

With the outbreak of war, Woodford returned to the United States and resumed his law practice.

See also Cuban Revolution; McKinley, William, Jr.; Spain.

References and Further Readings

Leech, Margaret. *In the Days of McKinley.* New York: Harper & Brothers, 1959.

Musicant, Ivan. *Empire by Default: The Spanish-American War and the Dawn of the American Century.* New York: Henry Holt and Company, 1998.

Yellow Journalism

See **Journalism**

Young, Samuel Baldwin Marks (1840–1924)

Born in Pennsylvania, Samuel Baldwin Young began his military career in the Civil War, becoming a brigadier general of volunteers by 1865. After the war, he transferred to the regulars and by 1898 was a colonel of cavalry. When the Spanish-American War began, he was appointed a brigadier general of volunteers and given command of a cavalry brigade in Gen. Joseph Wheeler's division. Young's brigade, including the Rough Riders, was among the first elements of the Cuban Expeditionary Force to see action in the Battle at Las Guásimas on 24 June 1898. Young had promised Theodore Roosevelt that the Rough Riders would see action early, and he fulfilled that pledge.

Shortly after Las Guásimas, however, Young fell ill; he returned to the United States in August. After recovering, he was assigned to prepare a rest and recovery camp at Montauk Point, New York, for the returning Fifth Corps. The camp was later named Camp Wikoff in honor of Col. Charles Wikoff, who was killed in the fight for San Juan Hill.

In 1899, Young was sent to the Philippines, where he commanded a cavalry brigade during the fall campaign in central Luzon. Later, he was placed in command of Luzon's First District, where he was an advocate of strong civic-action programs. A fine cavalryman, Young was also an able administrator. In 1902, he served as president of the Army War College.

> **See also** Benevolent Assimilation; Camps, Staging Areas, and Embarkation Points, U.S. Army; Las Guásimas, Battle of; Luzon Campaigns; Roosevelt, Theodore; Rough Riders; Wikoff, Charles Augustus.

References and Further Readings

Linn, Brian McAllister. *The Philippine War, 1899–1902*. Lawrence: University Press of Kansas, 2000.

Samuels, Peggy, and Harold Samuels. *Teddy Roosevelt at San Juan: The Making of a President*. College Station: Texas A&M University Press, 1997.

Zanjón, Treaty (Pact) of

See **Ten Years' War**

Zapote Line, Philippines

See **Manila Bay, Battle of**

Zogbaum, Rufus Fairchild (1849–1925)

An outstanding illustrator of military subjects, Rufus Fairchild Zogbaum was born in Charleston, South Carolina. He studied art in Germany and France before returning to the United States to be an illustrator for *Harper's*. Like his contemporary Frederic Remington, Zogbaum soon specialized in the western frontier, the military, and the navy, particularly the latter.

In May 1898, Zogbaum was aboard the ill-fated *Gussie* under Capt. Joseph Dorst, which attempted to deliver guns and ammunition to Cuban revolutionaries. He also observed the Cuban blockade from the deck of Adm. William Sampson's flagship, the *New York*. Later, he was in Cuba with the Fifth Corps, recording his impressions of the war.

Although not as widely known as some of his contemporaries, such as Remington, Zogbaum was arguably the premier illustrator of military subjects of his period.

See also Artists and Illustrators; Dorst, Joseph Haddox; Remington, Frederic Sackrider; Sampson, William Thomas.

References and Further Readings

Harrington, Peter, and Frederic A. Sharf. *"A Splendid Little War": The Spanish-American War, 1898—The Artists' Perspective.* London: Greenhill Books, 1998.

Taft, Robert. *Artists and Illustrators of the Old West, 1850–1900.* New York: Charles Scribner's Sons, 1953.

Books

Abbot, Willis John. *Blue Jackets of '98: A History of the Spanish American War.* New York. Dodd, Mead, 1908.

Adams, Gerald M. *The Bells of Balangiga.* Cheyenne, WY: Lagumo Corp., 1998.

Agoncillo, Tedoro A. *Malolos: The Crisis of the Republic.* Quezon City: University of the Philippines Press, 1960.

Alberts, Don E. *Brandy Station to Manila Bay: A Biography of General Wesley Merritt.* Austin, TX: Presidial Press, 1980.

Alden, John D. *The American Steel Navy.* Annapolis, MD: Naval Institute Press, 1972.

Alejandrino, José M. *The Price of Freedom.* Manila: Reprint Solar Publishing, 1987.

Alfonso, Oscar M. *Theodore Roosevelt and the Philippines, 1897–1909.* Quezon City: University of the Philippines Press, 1970.

Alger, Russell A. *The Spanish-American War.* New York: Harper & Brothers, 1901.

Allen, Douglas. *Frederic Remington and the Spanish-American War.* New York: Crown Publishers, 1971.

Anderson, David D. *William Jennings Bryan.* Boston: Twayne Publishers, 1981.

Ashburn, Percy M. *A History of the Medical Department of the United States Army.* Boston: Houghton Mifflin, 1929.

Asprey, Robert B. *War in the Shadows: The Guerrilla in History.* Vol. 1. New York: Doubleday & Company, 1975.

Atkins, Edwin F. *Sixty Years in Cuba*. Cambridge: Harvard University Press, 1926.

Azoy, A. C. M. *Charge! The Story of the Battle of San Juan Hill*. New York: Longmans, Green, 1961.

Bacevich, A. J. *Diplomat in Khaki: Major General Frank Ross McCoy and American Foreign Policy, 1898–1949*. Lawrence: University Press of Kansas, 1989.

Bain, David Haward. *Sitting in Darkness: Americans in the Philippines*. Boston: Houghton Mifflin, 1984.

Baker, Arthur G. *The Colorado Volunteers by Private A. G. Baker, Co. H, 1st C.V.I.* N.p., [1899?].

Barrett, James Wyman. *Joseph Pulitzer and His World*. New York: Vanguard Press, 1941.

Barton, Clara. *The Red Cross in Peace and War*. Washington, DC: American Historical Press, 1910.

Bean, William B. *Walter A. Reed: A Biography*. Charlottesville: University Press of Virginia, 1982.

Beede, Benjamin R., ed. *The War of 1898 and U.S. Interventions, 1898–1934*. New York: Garland Publishing, 1994.

Beer, Thomas. *Stephen Crane*. New York: Alfred Knopf, 1923.

Beisner, Robert L. *Twelve against Empire: The Anti-Imperialists, 1898–1900*. New York: McGraw-Hill, 1968.

———. *From the Old Diplomacy to the New, 1865–1900*. 2nd ed. Arlington Heights, IL: Harlan Davidson, 1986.

Berner, Brad K. *The Spanish-American War: An Historical Dictionary*. Metuchen, NJ: Scarecrow Press, 1998.

Bertram, Marshall. *The Birth of Anglo-American Friendship*. New York: University Press of America, 1992.

Bigelow, John. *Reminiscences of the Santiago Campaign*. New York: Harper & Brothers, 1899.

Blount, James H. *The American Occupation of the Philippines, 1898–1912*. New York: G. P. Putnam's Sons, 1913.

Blow, Michael. *A Ship to Remember: The* Maine *and the Spanish-American War*. New York: William Morrow, 1992.

Bonsal, Stephen. *The Fight for Santiago: The Story of the Soldier in the Cuban Campaign, from Tampa to the Surrender*. New York: Doubleday, McClure & Company, 1899.

Borchers, Duane D. *1898: Efficiency of the Revenue Cutter Service during the Spanish-American War*. Annapolis: Maryland Silver Company, 1994.

Boyd, James P., ed. *Men and Issues of 1900*. Philadelphia: Ziegler, 1900.

Bradford, James C., ed. *Crucible of Empire: The Spanish-American War and Its Aftermath.* Annapolis, MD: Naval Institute Press, 1993.

———. *Admirals of the New Steel Navy.* Annapolis, MD: Naval Institute Press, 1996.

Bradford, Richard H. *The* Virginius *Affair.* Boulder: Colorado Associated University Press, 1980.

Braistead, William Reynolds. *The United States Navy in the Pacific, 1897–1909.* Austin: University of Texas Press, 1958.

Brands, H. W. *Bound to Empire: The United States and the Philippines.* New York: Oxford University Press, 1992.

———. *The Reckless Decade: America in the 1890s.* New York: St. Martin's Press, 1995.

———. *TR: The Last Romantic.* New York: Basic Books, 1997.

Bremner, John B. *Words on Words: A Dictionary for Writers and Others Who Care about Words.* New York: MJF Books, 1980.

Brown, Charles H. *The Correspondents' War: Journalists in the Spanish-American War.* New York: Charles Scribner's Sons, 1907.

Brown, W. C. *The Diary of a Captain: Extracts from the Diary of Captain W. C. Brown, Commanding Troop E, First U.S. Cavalry.* Reprinted from Santiago Souvenir Book. N.p, 1898.

Bruce, Anthony, and William Cogar. *An Encyclopedia of Naval History.* New York: Facts on File, 1998.

Buel, J. W., ed. *Behind the Guns with American Heroes.* New Haven, CT: Butler and Alger, 1899.

Burton, Theodore E. *John Sherman.* Boston: Houghton Mifflin, 1906.

Carlson, Paul H. *Pecos Bill: A Military Biography of William R. Shafter.* College Station: Texas A&M University Press, 1989.

Carr, Raymond, ed. *Spain: A History.* New York: Oxford University Press, 2000.

Cashin, Herschel V. *Under Fire with the Tenth U.S. Cavalry.* Niwot: University Press of Colorado, 1993.

Cerezo, Capt. Don Saturnino Martin. *Under the Red and Gold, Being Notes and Recollections of the Siege of Baler.* Translated and edited by F. L. Dodds, Major, U.S. Army. Kansas City, MO: Franklin Hudson Publishing, 1909.

Cervera y Topete, Pascual. *The Spanish-American War.* Washington, DC: U.S. Government Printing Office, 1899.

Chadwick, Rear Adm. French Ensor. *Relations of the United States and Spain: The Spanish American War.* 2 vols. New York: Charles Scribner's Sons, 1911 (reprinted in 1968).

Chidsey, Donald Barr. *The Spanish-American War: A Behind the Scenes Account of the War in Cuba.* New York: Crown Publishers, 1971.

Cisneros, Evangelina, and Karl Decker. *The Story of Evangelina Cisneros.* Richmond, VA: n.p., 1897.

Cloman, Lt. Col. Sydney. *Myself and a Few Moros.* Garden City, NY: Doubleday Page & Company, 1923.

Cohen, Stan. *Images of the Spanish-American War.* Missoula, MT: Pictorial Histories Publishing, 1998.

Coletta, Paolo E. *French Ensor Chadwick, Scholarly Warrior.* Lanham, MD: University Press of America, 1980.

———. *A Survey of U.S. Naval Affairs, 1865–1917.* Lanham, MD: University Press of America, 1987.

———, ed. *Threshold to American Imperialism: Essays on the Foreign Policies of William McKinley.* New York: Exposition Press, 1970.

Cooper, Jerry. *The Rise of the National Guard: The Evolution of the American Militia, 1865–1920.* Lincoln: University of Nebraska Press, 1997.

Corry, John A. *1898: Prelude to a Century.* New York: John A. Corry, 1998.

Cortada, James. *A Bibliographical Guide to Spanish Diplomatic History.* Westport, CT: Greenwood Press, 1977.

Cortissoz, Royal. *The Life of Whitelaw Reid.* New York: Charles Scribner's Sons, 1921.

Cosmas, Graham. *An Army for Empire: The United States Army in the Spanish-American War.* College Station: Texas A&M University Press, 1998.

Crawford, Michael J., Mark L. Hayes, and Michael D. Sessions. *The Spanish-American War: Historical Overview and Select Bibliography.* Naval History Bibliographies, no. 5. Washington, DC: Naval Historical Center, Department of the Navy, 1998.

Creelman, James. *On the Great Highway: The Wanderings and Adventures of a Special Correspondent.* Boston: Lothrop, 1901.

Croly, Herbert David. *Marcus Alonzo Hanna: His Life and Work.* New York: Macmillan and Company, 1912.

Crouch, Thomas W. *A Yankee Guerrillero: Frederick Funston and the Cuban Insurrection, 1896–1897.* Memphis, TN: Memphis State University Press, 1975.

———. *A Leader of Volunteers: Frederick Funston and the 20th Kansas in the Philippines, 1898–1899.* Lawrence, KS: Coronado Press, 1984.

Damiani, Brian P. *Advocates of Empire: William McKinley, the Senate, and American Expansion, 1898–1899.* New York: Garland, 1987.

Davis, Charles Belmont. *Adventures and Letters of Richard Harding Davis.* New York: n.p., 1917.

Davis, Linda H. *Badge of Courage: The Life of Stephen Crane.* Boston: Houghton Mifflin, 1998.

Davis, Richard Harding. *The Cuban and Porto Rican Campaigns.* New York: Charles Scribner's Sons, 1898.

Dawes, Charles G. *A Journal of the McKinley Years.* Chicago: Lakeside Press, 1950.

DeMontravel, Peter R. *A Hero to His Fighting Men: Nelson A. Miles, 1839–1925.* Kent, OH: Kent State University Press, 1998.

Dewey, George. *Autobiography of George Dewey, Admiral of the Navy.* Annapolis, MD: Naval Institute Press, 1987.

Dierks, Jack Cameron. *A Leap to Arms: The Cuban Campaign of 1898.* Philadelphia: J. B. Lippincott, 1970.

Dobson, John. *Reticent Expansionism: The Foreign Policy of William McKinley.* Pittsburgh, PA: Duquesne University Press, 1988.

Dunne, Finley Peter. *Mr. Dooley in Peace and War.* Boston: Small, Maynard & Company, 1898.

———. *Mr. Dooley's Opinions.* New York: Harper & Company, 1901.

Dyal, Donald H. *Historical Dictionary of the Spanish American War.* Westport, CT: Greenwood Press, 1996.

Eggert, Gerald G. *Richard Olney: Evolution of a Statesman.* University Park: Pennsylvania State University Press, 1974.

Evans, Robley D. *A Sailor's Log.* New York: D. Appleton & Company, 1901.

Falk, Edwin A. *Fighting Bob Evans.* New York: Jonathan Cape & Harrison Smith, 1931.

Faragher, John Mack. *Daniel Boone: The Life and Legend of an American Pioneer.* New York: Henry Holt and Company, 1992.

Faust, Karl Irving. *Campaigning in the Philippines.* San Francisco: Hicks-Judd, 1899.

Ferrara, Orestes. *The Last Spanish War: Revelations in Diplomacy.* Translated from the Spanish by William E. Shea. New York: Paisley Press, 1937.

Feuer, A. B. *The Santiago Campaign of 1898.* Westport, CT: Praeger Publishers, 1993.

———. *The Spanish-American War at Sea.* Westport, CT: Greenwood Press, 1995.

Field, Ron. *Spanish-American War: 1898.* London: Brasseys, 1998.

Fletcher, Marvin. *The Black Soldier and Officer in the United States Army, 1891–1917.* Columbia: University of Missouri Press, 1974.

Flint, Grover. *Marching with Gomez.* New York: n.p., 1898.

Foner, Philip S. *The Spanish-Cuban-American War.* 2 vols. New York: Monthly Review Press, 1972.

———. *Antonio Maceo: The Bronze Titan of Cuba's Struggle for Independence.* New York. Monthly Review Press, 1977.

Freidel, Frank. *The Splendid Little War.* Boston: Little, Brown, 1958.

Funston, Frederick. *Memories of Two Wars.* New York: Charles Scribner's Sons, 1911.

Garraty, John A. *Henry Cabot Lodge: A Biography.* New York: Alfred A. Knopf, 1953.

Gates, John Morgan. *Schoolbooks and Krags: The United States Army in the Philippines, 1898–1902.* Contributions in Military History no. 3. Westport, CT: Greenwood Press, 1973.

Gatewood, Willard B., Jr. *Smoked Yankees and the Struggle for Empire: Letters from Negro Soldiers, 1898–1902.* Urbana: University of Illinois Press, 1971.

———. *Black Americans and the White Man's Burden: 1898–1903.* Urbana: University of Illinois Press, 1975.

Gibson, John M. *Soldier in White: The Life of General George Miller Sternberg.* Durham, NC: Duke University Press, 1958.

Giddings, Howard. *Exploits of the Signal Corps in the War with Spain.* Kansas City, MO: n.p., 1900.

Goldstein, Donald M., and Katherine V. Dillon, with J. Michael Wenger and Robert J. Cressman. *The Spanish-American War: The Story and Photographs, Centennial Edition.* Washington, DC: Brasseys, 1998.

Goode, William A. M. *With Sampson through the War.* New York: Doubleday & McClure, 1899.

Gould, Lewis L. *The Spanish-American War and President McKinley.* Lawrence: University of Kansas Press, 1982.

Gowing, Peter G. *Mandate in Moroland: The American Government of Muslim Filipinos, 1899–1920.* Manila: University of the Philippines, 1977.

Graff, Henry F. *American Imperialism in the Philippine Insurrection.* Boston: Little, Brown, 1969.

Graham, George Edward. *Schley and Santiago: An Historical Account of the Blockade and Final Destruction of the Spanish Fleet under the Command of Admiral Pasquale Cervera, July 3, 1898.* Chicago: W. B. Conkey Company, 1902.

Gray, Richard B. *José Martí, Cuban Patriot.* Gainesville: University of Florida Press, 1962.

Griffin, Charles C. *Privateering from Baltimore during the Spanish-American Wars of Independence.* Baltimore: Maryland Historical Society, 1940.

Guam Visitor's Bureau. *Guam: Guam's Natural, Cultural and Historic Site Guidebook.* Tumon: Guam Visitor's Bureau, 1998.

Hagan, Kenneth J. *This People's Navy: The Making of American Sea Power.* New York: Free Press, 1991.

Halstead, Murat. *Full Official History of the War with Spain.* Chicago: Dominion Company, 1899.

Hard, Curtis V. *Banners in the Air: The Eighth Ohio Volunteers and the Spanish-American War.* Edited by Robert H. Ferrell. Kent, OH: Kent State University Press, 1988.

Harper, Frank, comp. and ed. *Just Outside Manila: Letters from Members of the First Colorado Regiment in the Spanish-American and Philippine-American Wars.* Monograph 7. Denver: Colorado Historical Society, 1991.

Harper's Pictorial History of the War. New York: Harper's, 1899.

Harrington, Peter, and Frederic A. Sharf. *"A Splendid Little War": The Spanish-American War, 1898—The Artists' Perspective.* London: Greenhill Books, 1998.

Hart, Edward H. *The Authentic Photographic Views of the United States Navy; and Scenes of the Ill-fated* Maine, *before and after the Explosion, Group Pictures of Army and Navy Officers; also Photos of the Leading Spanish Men-of-War.* Chicago: W. B. Conkey, 1898.

Healy, David. *US Expansionism: The Imperialist Urge in the 1890s.* Milwaukee: University of Wisconsin Press, 1970.

Heatley, Jeff. *Bully! Colonel Theodore Roosevelt and the Rough Riders at Camp Wikoff, Montauk Point, NY.* Harrisburg, PA: Stackpole Books, 1998.

Heitman, Francis B. *Historical Register and Dictionary of the United States Army, 1789–1903.* 2 vols. Urbana: University of Illinois Press, 1965.

Heller, Clarence E., and William A. Stofft. *America's First Battles, 1776–1965.* Lawrence: University Press of Kansas, 1986.

Hermann, Karl S. *A Recent Campaign in Puerto Rico.* Boston: E. H. Bacon & Company, 1907.

Herner, Charles. *The Arizona Rough Riders.* Tucson: University of Arizona Press, 1970.

———. *Cowboy Cavalry: A Photographic History of the Arizona Rough Riders.* Tucson: Arizona Historical Society, 2000.

———, ed. *"It Was the Grandest Sight I Ever Saw": Experiences of a Rough Rider as Recorded in the Letters of Lieutenant John Campbell Greenway.* Museum Monograph no. 11. Tucson: Arizona Historical Society, 2001.

Hirshon, Stanley P. *Grenville M. Dodge.* Bloomington: Indiana University Press, 1967.

Hixon, William B. *Moorfield Storey and the Abolitionist Tradition.* New York: Oxford University Press, 1972.

Hobson, Richmond Pearson. *The Sinking of the* Merrimac. New York: n.p., 1900.

Hoganson, Kristin L. *Fighting for American Manhood: How Gender Politics Provoked the Spanish-American and Philippine-American Wars.* New Haven, CT: Yale University Press, 1998.

Hooker, Terry D. *The Spanish-American War: The Cuban Land Campaign, Order of Battle.* Cottingham, England: El Dorado Books, 1995.

Hopkins, Joseph G. E., ed. *The Concise Dictionary of American Biography.* New York: Charles Scribner's Sons, 1964.

Hubbard, Elbert. *Message to Garcia.* East Aurora, NY: n.p., 1899.

Hurley, Vic. *Swish of the Kris: The Story of the Moros.* New York: E. P. Dutton, 1936.

———. *Jungle Patrol: The Story of the Philippine Constabulary.* New York: E. P. Dutton, 1938.

Hutton, Paul Andrew, ed. *Soldiers West: Biographies from the Military Frontier.* Lincoln: University of Nebraska Press, 1987.

Ingalls, John J. *America's War for Humanity: Related in Story and Picture Embracing a Complete History of Cuba's Struggle for Liberty.* New York: N. D. Thompson Publishing, 1898.

Jackson, Donald Dale. *The Aeronauts* (The Epic of Flight Series). Alexandria, VA: Time Life Books, 1980.

Jeffers, H. Paul. *Colonel Roosevelt: Theodore Roosevelt Goes to War, 1897–1898.* New York: John Wiley & Sons, 1996.

Jessup, Philip C. *Elihu Root.* 2 vols. New York: Dodd, Mead & Company, 1938.

Johnson, Virginia. *The Unregimented General: A Biography of Nelson A. Miles.* Boston: Houghton Mifflin, 1962.

Johnston, Lt. Edgar. *The Great American-Spanish War Scenes, with Official Photographs by United States Naval Photographer E. H. Hart.* Chicago: W. B. Conkey, 1898.

Jones, Harry Wilmer. *A Chaplain's Experience Ashore and Afloat: The Texas under Fire.* New York: A. G. Sherwood & Company, 1901.

Jones, J. R., ed. *The Story of Our Wonderful Victories, Told by Dewey, Schley, Wheeler, and Other Heroes.* Philadelphia: American Book and Bible Company, 1899.

Kalaw, Tedoro M. *The Philippine Revolution.* Manila: Vargas Filipiana Foundation, 1969.

———. *An Acceptable Holocaust: Life and Death of a Boy General.* Translated by M. A. Foronda. Manila: National Historical Commission, 1974.

Karnow, Stanley. *In Our Image: America's Empire in the Philippines.* New York: Random House, 1989.

Katcher, Philip. *The U.S. Army, 1890–1920.* London: Osprey Publishing, 1990.

Kennan, George. *Campaigning in Cuba.* Reprint. Port Washington, NY: Kennikat Press, 1971.

King, William N. *The Story of the Spanish-American War and the Revolt in the Philippines.* New York: P. F. Collier, 1898.

Kirk, John M. *José Martí: Mentor of the Cuban Nation.* Tampa: University Presses of Florida, 1983.

LaFeber, Walter. *The New Empire.* Ithaca, NY: Cornell University Press, 1963.

Landon, William H. *The U.S. Army's Deployment to the Spanish-American War and Our Future Strategic Outlook.* Carlisle Barracks, PA: U.S. Army War College, 1998.

Langellier, John P. *Uncle Sam's Little Wars: The Spanish-American War, Philippine Insurrection and Boxer Rebellion, 1898–1902.* London: Greenhill Books, 1999.

Larkin, John A. *The Pampagans: Colonial Society in a Philippine Province.* Berkeley: University of California Press, 1972.

Lee, Fitzhugh. *Cuba's Struggle against Spain, with the Causes for American Intervention and a Full Account of the Spanish-American War, Including Final Peace Negotiations.* New York: American Historical Press, 1899.

Leech, Margaret. *In the Days of McKinley.* New York: Harper & Brothers, 1959.

LeRoy, James. *Americans in the Philippines.* 2 vols. Boston: Houghton Mifflin, 1914.

Linderman, Gerald F. *The Mirror of War: American Society and the Spanish-American War.* Ann Arbor: University of Michigan Press, 1974.

Linn, Brian McAllister. *The U.S. Army and Counterinsurgency in the Philippine War, 1899–1902.* Chapel Hill: University of North Carolina Press, 1989.

———. *Guardians of Empire: The U.S. Army and the Pacific, 1902–1940.* Chapel Hill: University of North Carolina Press, 1997.

———. *The Philippine War, 1899–1902.* Lawrence: University Press of Kansas, 2000.

Lodge, Henry Cabot. *The War with Spain.* Reprint. New York: Arno Press, 1970.

Long, John D. *The New American Navy.* New York: Outlook, 1903.

———. *America of Yesterday as Reflected in the Journal of John Davis Long.* Boston: Atlantic Monthly Press, 1923.

Mahan, Alfred Thayer. *Influence of Sea Power upon History, 1670–1783.* Boston: Little, Brown, 1890.

———. *Lessons of the War with Spain.* Boston: Little, Brown, 1899.

March, Alden. *The History and Conquest of the Philippines and Our Other Island Possessions.* New York: Arno Press & *New York Times,* 1970.

Marks, George P., ed. and comp. *The Black Press Views American Imperialism (1898–1900).* New York: Arno Press, 1971.

Martin, William A. *Remember the Maine, or the Spanish-American War Revisited.* Columbia: Missouri Library Association Quarterly, 1968.

Mason, Gregory. *Remember the Maine.* New York: Henry Holt, 1939.

Mawson, Harry P. *Leslie's Official History of the Spanish-American War.* Washington, DC: Leslie's Weekly, 1899.

May, Ernest R. *Imperial Democracy: The Emergence of America as a Great Power.* New York: Harcourt, Brace & World, 1961.

———. *American Imperialism: A Speculative Essay.* Chicago: Imprint Publications, 1991.

May, Glenn A. *Battle for Batangas: A Philippine Province at War.* New Haven, CT: Yale University Press, 1991.

———. *Inventing a Hero: The Posthumous Re-Creation of Andres Bonifacio.* Madison: University of Wisconsin Center for Southeastern Asian Studies, 1996.

McCullough, David. *The Path between the Seas.* New York: Simon and Schuster, 1977.

McIntosh, Burr. *The Little I Saw of Cuba.* New York: F. T. Neely, 1899.

Miles, Nelson A. *Personal Recollections and Observations of General Nelson A. Miles.* 2 vols. Lincoln: University of Nebraska Press, 1992.

Miley, John D. *In Cuba with Shafter.* New York: Charles Scribner's Sons, 1899.

Miller, Nathan. *Theodore Roosevelt: A Life.* New York: William Morrow, 1992.

Miller, Richard H., ed. *American Imperialism in 1898.* New York: John Wiley & Sons, 1970.

Miller, Stuart C. *Benevolent Assimilation: The American Conquest of the Philippines, 1899–1903.* New Haven, CT: Yale University Press, 1983.

Millett, Allan R. *Semper Fidelis: The History of the United States Marine Corps.* New York: Macmillan Publishing, 1982.

Millis, Walter. *The Martial Spirit.* Chicago: Ivan R. Dee, 1989.

Milton, Joyce. *The Yellow Kids: Foreign Correspondents in the Heyday of Yellow Journalism.* New York: Harper & Row, 1989.

Morgan, H. Wayne. *America's Road to Empire: The War with Spain and Overseas Expansion.* New York: John Wiley & Sons, 1965.

———, ed. *Making Peace with Spain: The Diary of Whitelaw Reid—September–December, 1898.* Austin: University of Texas Press, 1965.

Morris, Edmund. *The Rise of Theodore Roosevelt.* New York: Coward, McCann & Geoghegan, 1979.

Moskin, J. Robert. *U.S. Marine Corps Story.* New York: McGraw-Hill, 1977.

Müller y Tejeiro, José. *Battles and Capitulation of Santiago de Cuba.* Washington, DC: U.S. Government Printing Office, 1899.

Musicant, Ivan. *U.S. Armored Cruisers.* Annapolis, MD: Naval Institute Press, 1985.

———. *Empire by Default: The Spanish-American War and the Dawn of the American Century.* New York: Henry Holt and Company, 1998.

Neale, R. G. *Great Britain and United States Expansion: 1898–1900.* East Lansing: Michigan State University Press, 1966.

Newhart, Max R. *American Battleships: A Pictorial History of BB-1 to BB-71, with Prototypes* Maine *and* Texas. Missoula, MT: Pictorial Histories Publishing, 1995.

Nichols, James L. *General Fitzhugh Lee: A Biography.* Lynchburg, VA: H. E. Howard, 1989.

Nofi, Albert A. *The Spanish-American War, 1898.* Conshohocken, PA: Combined Books, 1998.

O'Connor, Richard. *The Spirit Soldiers: A Historical Narrative of the Boxer Rebellion.* New York: G. P. Putnam, 1973.

Office of Naval Intelligence. *Comments on the Spanish-American War.* Washington, DC: U.S. Government Printing Office, 1898.

Offner, John L. *An Unwanted War: The Diplomacy of the United States and Spain over Cuba.* Chapel Hill: University of North Carolina Press, 1992.

Olson, James S., ed. *Historical Dictionary of the Spanish Empire, 1492–1975.* New York: Greenwood Press, 1992.

O'Toole, G. J. A. *The Spanish War: An American Epic, 1898.* New York: W. W. Norton, 1984.

Paine, Ralph Delahave. *Roads of Adventure.* Boston: Houghton Mifflin, 1922.

Palmer, Frederick. *With My Own Eyes: A Personal Study of Battle Years.* Indianapolis, IN: Bobbs-Merrill, 1932.

———. *Bliss, Peacemaker: The Life and Letters of Tasker Howard Bliss.* New York: Dodd, Mead, 1934.

Parker, John H. *History of the Gatling Gun Detachment, Fifth Army Corps at Santiago.* Kansas City, MO: Kimberly Publishing, 1898.

————. *Admirals Schley, Sampson and Cervera: A Review of the Naval Campaign of 1898, in Pursuit and Destruction of the Spanish Fleet Commanded by Rear Admiral Cervera.* New York: Neale Publishing, 1910.

Pérez, Louis A., Jr. *Cuba between Empires, 1878–1902.* Pittsburgh, PA: University of Pittsburgh Press, 1983.

————. *The War of 1898: The United States and Cuba in History and Historiography.* Chapel Hill: University of North Carolina Press, 1998.

Plumridge, John H. *Hospital Ships and Ambulance Trains.* N.p.: Seeley, Service & Company, 1975.

Pohanka, Brian C. *Nelson A. Miles: A Documentary Biography of His U.S. Military Career, 1861–1903.* Glendale, CA: Arthur H. Clark Company, 1985.

Pomeroy, William J. *American Neo-Colonialism: Its Emergence in the Philippines and Asia.* New York: International Publishers, 1970.

Post, Charles Johnson. *The Little War of Private Post.* Boston: Little, Brown, 1960.

Pratt, Julius W. *The Expansionists of 1898: The Acquisition of Hawaii and the Spanish Islands.* Baltimore, MD: Johns Hopkins University Press, 1936.

Pryor, Elizabeth Brown. *Clara Barton, Professional Angel.* Philadelphia: University of Pennsylvania Press, 1987.

Quesada, Alejandro M. de. *The Spanish-American War in Tampa Bay.* New York: Arcadia Press, 1999.

Quesada, Gonzalo de. *The War in Cuba: Being a Full Account of Her Great Struggle for Freedom.* Washington, DC: Liberty Publishing, 1896.

Rea, George Bronson. *Facts and Fakes about Cuba.* New York: George Monro's Sons, 1897.

Reuter, Bertha Ann. *Anglo-American Relations during the Spanish-American War.* New York: Macmillan Company, 1924.

Rickover, H. G. *How the Battleship* Maine *Was Destroyed.* Washington, DC: Department of the Navy, 1976.

Roby, Edward. *The Unfair Treatment of the Admiral and the Captains Who Destroyed the Naval Power of Spain in 1898.* Chicago: Barnard & Miller Print, 1901.

Roosevelt, Theodore. *The Rough Riders.* New York: Charles Scribner's Sons, 1925.

Root, Elihu. *The Military and Colonial Policy of the United States: Addresses and Reports.* Collected and edited by Robert Bacon and James Brown Scott. New York: AMS Press, 1970 (reprint).

Rosenberg, Morton M. *Indiana and the Coming of the Spanish-American War.* Muncie, IN: Ball State University Press, 1976.

Rosenfeld, Harvey. *Diary of a Dirty Little War: The Spanish-American War of 1898.* Westport, CT: Praeger Publishers, 2000.

Roth, Mitchel P. *Historical Dictionary of War Journalism.* Westport, CT: Greenwood Press, 1997.

Roth, Russell. *Muddy Glory: America's Indian Wars in the Philippines, 1899–1935.* West Hanover, MA: Christopher Publishing House, 1981.

Rowan, Andrew Summers. *How I Carried the Message to Garcia, by Colonel Andrew Summers Rowan.* San Francisco: W. D. Harney, 1922.

Russell, Charles E. *The Hero of the Filipinos: The Story of José Rizal.* New York: Century, 1923.

Russell, Henry B. *The Story of Two Wars.* Hartford, CT: Hartford Publishing Company, 1899.

Salamanca, Bonifacio C. *The Filipino Reaction to American Rule, 1901–1913.* Quezon City, Philippines: New Day Press, 1984.

Samuels, Peggy, and Harold Samuels. *Remembering the* Maine. Washington, DC: Smithsonian Institution Press, 1995.

———. *Teddy Roosevelt at San Juan: The Making of a President.* College Station: Texas A&M University Press, 1997.

Sargent, Herbert H. *The Campaign of Santiago de Cuba.* Chicago: A. C. McClurg and Company, 1907.

Sargent, Nathan. *Admiral Dewey and the Manila Campaign.* Washington, DC: Naval Historical Foundation, 1947.

Sauers, Richard. *Pennsylvania in the Spanish-American War.* Philadelphia: Pennsylvania Capitol Preservation Committee, 1998.

Sawyer, Claude E. *A Soldier's Letter: April 19, 1900, Lipa, Tatangas, Philippines.* Manila: DeLaSalle University Press, 1995.

Schley, Winfield Scott. *Forty-five Years under the Flag.* New York: n.p., 1904.

Schofield, John M. *Forty-six Years in the Army.* New York: Century, 1897.

Schott, Joseph L. *The Ordeal of Samar.* Indianapolis, IN: Bobbs-Merrill Company, 1964.

Scott, Edward Van Zile. *The Unwept: Black American Soldiers and the Spanish-American War.* Montgomery, AL: Black Belt Press, 1996.

Scott, Hugh Lenox. *Some Memories of a Soldier.* New York: Century Company, 1928.

Seager, Robert. *Alfred Thayer Mahan: The Man and His Letters.* Annapolis, MD: Naval Institute Press, 1977.

Seitz, Don C. *The James Gordon Bennetts.* Indianapolis, IN: Bobbs-Merrill Company, 1928.

Sexton, Capt. William Thaddeus. *Soldiers in the Sun: An Adventure in Imperialism.* Harrisburg, PA: Military Service Publishing Company, 1939 (reprinted by Books for Libraries Press, Freeport, NY, 1971).

Sigsbee, Charles D. *The* Maine: *An Account of Her Destruction in Havana Harbor.* New York: Century, 1899.

Slattery, Thomas. *The Spanish-American War: Its Impact on the Rock Island Arsenal.* Rock Island, IL: Rock Island Arsenal Museum, 1996.

Smith, Cornelius C., Jr. *Don't Settle for Second: Life and Times of Cornelius C. Smith.* San Rafael, CA: Presidio Press, 1977.

Smith, Horace. *A Captain Unafraid: The Strange Adventures of Dynamite Johnny O'Brien.* New York: Harper & Brothers, 1912.

Smith, Joseph. *The Spanish-American War: Conflict in the Caribbean and the Pacific, 1895–1902.* New York: Longman, 1994.

Smythe, Donald. *Guerrilla Warrior: The Early Life of John J. Pershing.* New York: Charles Scribner's Sons, 1973.

Spears, John. *Our Navy in the War with Spain.* New York: Charles Scribner's Sons, 1898.

Spector, Ronald. *Admiral of the New Empire: The Life and Career of George Dewey.* Greenville: University of South Carolina Press, 1988.

Stallman, F. R. *Stephen Crane: A Biography.* New York: George Braziller, 1968.

Standage, Tom. *The Victorian Internet.* New York: Walker & Company, 1998.

Steinbach, Robert H. *A Long March: The Lives of Frank and Alice Baldwin.* Austin: University of Texas Press, 1989.

Steinberg, David Joel. *The Philippines: A Singular and a Plural Place.* Boulder, CO: Westview Press, 1994.

Sternberg, George M. *Sanitary Lessons of the War.* Washington, DC: Byron S. Adams, 1912.

Sternlicht, Sanford. *McKinley's Bulldog: The Battleship* Oregon. Chicago: Nelson-Hall, 1977.

Storey, Moorfield, and Marcial P. Lichauco. *The Conquest of the Philippines by the United States, 1898–1925.* New York: G. P. Putnam's Sons, 1926.

Sues, Otto L. *Grigsby's Cowboys, Third United States Volunteer Cavalry, Spanish-American War.* Salem, SD: James E. Patten, 1900.

Swanberg, W. A. *Citizen Hearst: A Biography of William Randolph Hearst.* New York: Charles Scribner's Sons, 1961.

Taft, Robert. *Artists and Illustrators of the Old West, 1850–1900.* New York: Charles Scribner's Sons, 1953.

Tan, Samuel K. *The Filipino Armed Struggle, 1900–1972.* Manila: Filipina Foundation, 1977.

Tebbel, John. *America's Great Patriotic War with Spain: Mixed Motives, Lies, and Racism in Cuba and the Philippines.* Manchester Center, VT: Marshall Jones, 1996.

Thomas, Hugh. *Cuba: The Pursuit of Freedom*. New York: Harper & Row, 1971.

Titherington, Richard H. *A History of the Spanish-American War of 1898*. New York: D. Appleton & Company, 1900.

Tomlinson, Rodney G. *A Rocky Mountain Sailor in Teddy Roosevelt's Navy: The Letters of Petty Officer Charles Fowler from the Asiatic Station, 1905–1910*. Boulder, CO: Westview Press, 1998.

Tompkins, E. Berkeley. *Anti-Imperialism in the United States: The Great Debate, 1890–1920*. Philadelphia: University of Pennsylvania Press, 1970.

Trask, David F. *The War with Spain in 1898*. Lincoln: University of Nebraska Press, 1996.

Traxel, David. *1898: The Birth of the American Century*. New York: Alfred A. Knopf, 1998.

U.S. Coast Guard. *Coast Guard History*. Washington, DC: Department of Transportation, U.S. Coast Guard, 1982.

U.S. Revenue Cutter Service in the War with Spain, 1898. Washington, DC: U.S. Government Printing Office, 1899.

U.S. Warships in the Spanish-American War. New York: New York Life Insurance Company, n.d.

Vandiver, Frank E. *Black Jack: The Life and Times of John J. Pershing*. 2 vols. College Station: Texas A&M University Press, 1977.

Walker, Dale L. *Death Was the Black Horse: The Story of Rough Rider Buckey O'Neill*. Austin, TX: Madrona Press, 1975.

———. *The Boys of '98: Theodore Roosevelt and the Rough Riders*. New York: Forge Books, 1998.

Watterson, Henry. *History of the Spanish-American War, Embracing a Complete Review of Our Relations with Spain*. Hartford, CT: American Publishing, 1898.

Weems, John Edward. *The Fate of the* Maine. New York: Henry Holt and Company, 1958.

Weigley, Russell F. *History of the United States Army*. New York: Macmillan Publishing, 1967.

Weisburger, Bernard A., and the editors of Time Life Books. *The Life and History of the United States: Reaching for Empire*. Vol. 8, 1890–1990. Alexandria, VA: Time Life Books, 1964.

Welch, Richard E., Jr. *George Frisbie Hoar and the Half-Breed Republicans*. Cambridge: Harvard University Press, 1971.

———. *Response to Imperialism: The United States and the Philippine-American War, 1899–1902*. Chapel Hill: University of North Carolina Press, 1979.

———. *The Presidencies of Grover Cleveland.* Lawrence: University Press of Kansas, 1988.

Werstein, Irving. *Ninety-eight: The Story of the Spanish-American War and the Philippine Insurrection.* New York: Cooper Square, 1966.

Westermeier, Clifford P. *Who Rush to Glory.* Caldwell, ID: Caxton Printers, 1958.

Wheeler, Joseph. *The Santiago Campaign, 1898.* Port Washington, NY: Kennikat Press, 1971.

White, Col. John R. *Bullets and Bolos: Fifteen Years in the Philippine Islands.* New York: Century Company, 1928.

White, Trumbull. *Pictorial History of Our War with Spain.* Chicago: Imperial Publishing, 1898.

Widenor, William C. *Henry Cabot Lodge and the Search for an American Foreign Policy.* Berkeley: University of California Press, 1980.

Wilkerson, Marcus M. *Public Opinion and the Spanish-American War: A Study in War Propaganda.* New York: Russell and Russell, 1967.

Wilson, Herbert Wrigley. *The Downfall of Spain.* London: Low Marston and Company, 1900.

Wilson, James Harrison. *Under the Old Flag: Recollections of Military Operations in the War for the Union, the Spanish War, the Boxer Rebellion, etc.* 2 vols. New York: D. Appleton & Company, 1912.

Wisan, Joseph Ezra. *The Cuban Crisis as Reflected in the New York Press (1895–1898).* New York: Columbia University Press, 1934.

Wolff, Leon. *Little Brown Brother: America's Forgotten Bid for Empire Which Cost 250,000 Lives.* New York: Kraus Reprint, 1970.

Woolsey, Theodore Salisbury. *America's Foreign Policy: Essays and Address by Theodore Salisbury.* New York: Century Company, 1898.

Young, James Rankin. *History of Our War with Spain.* N.p., 1898.

———. *Reminiscences and Thrilling Stories of the War by Returned Heroes, Containing Vivid Accounts of Personal Experiences by Officers and Men.* Denver: Western Book Company, 1899.

Young, Kenneth Ray. *The General's General: The Life and Times of Arthur MacArthur.* Boulder, CO: Westview Press, 1994.

Zaide, Gregorio F. *The Philippine Revolution.* Manila: Modern Book Company, 1954.

Ziel, Ron. *Mattituck.* New York: Amereon House, 1997.

Articles

Adams, Brooks. "Reciprocity or the Alternative." *Atlantic Monthly,* August 1901.

Adams, Earl R. "First Man to Hear about the *Maine* Disaster." *Key West Citizen,* February 15, 1974.

Allen, Thomas B. "What Really Sank the *Maine*?" *Naval History,* vol. 12, no. 2, 1998.

"An Achievement and a Hope," Topics of the Time Editorial. *Century Magazine,* February 1898.

Andrews, Robert Hardy. "The Truth about Theodore Roosevelt and the Rough Riders." *Mankind,* vol. 1, no. 9, pp. 21–27, 41–52.

Angell, Roger. "The Greatest of the Boys: Like His Work, Stephen Crane's Life Reflects a Younger, More Adventurous America." *New Yorker,* September 7, 1998.

Archibald, James. "The Day of the Surrender of Santiago." *Scribner's Magazine,* 24, 1898.

Bailey, Thomas A. "Was the Presidential Election of 1000 a Mandate on Imperialism?" *Mississippi Valley Historical Review,* 24, January 1937.

———. "Dewey and the Germans at Manila Bay." *American Historical Review,* 45, October 1939.

Ballard, Larry A. "Camp Russell A. Alger, Virginia, 1898." *Northern Virginia Heritage,* 5, June 1983.

Barron, Marietta. "The Letters of a U.S. Soldier Reflect the Savagery of the Philippine Insurrection." *Military History,* vol. 17, no. 2, June 2000.

Beardsley, Rear Adm. C. A. "The Trial of the *Oregon.*" *Harper's New Monthly Magazine,* 98, 1899, pp. 699–707.

Benjamin, Anna Northend. "The Darker Side of War." *Leslie's Magazine,* August 4, 1898.

———. "A Woman's Visit to Santiago." *Leslie's Magazine,* August 25, 1898.

Bernadou, Lt. J. B. "The 'Winslow' at Cardenas (May 11, 1898)." *Century Magazine,* March 1899.

Bigelow, Poultney. "The Battle of Cabañas." *Harper's Weekly,* May 28, 1898.

———. "In Camp at Tampa." *Harper's Weekly,* June 4, 1898.

Bird, Roy. "Kansas Volunteers on the Line." *Military History,* vol. 15, no. 6, February 1999.

Birtle, Andrew J. "The U.S. Army's Pacification of Marinduque, Philippine Islands, April 1900–April 1901." *Journal of Military History,* vol. 61, no. 2, April 1997.

Blankenship, Janie. "Post No. 1 Preserves Founders' Memories: Philippine Veterans Come Home to Colorado." *VFW Magazine,* vol. 86, no. 6, February 1999.

Blow, Michael. "The Trochas." *MHQ: The Quarterly Journal of Military History,* vol. 10, no. 4, summer 1998.

Brennan, Matthew. "Notes on the Life of the Common Soldier in the Spanish-American War." *Journal of America's Military Past,* vol. 26, no. 3, winter 2000.

Brereton, T. R. "First Lessons in Modern War: Arthur Wagner, the 1898 Santiago Campaign and U.S. Army Lesson-Learning." *Journal of Military History,* vol. 64, no. 1, January 2000.

Burdett, Thomas F. "A New Evaluation of General Otis' Leadership in the Philippines." *Military Review,* 55, 1975.

Bybee, John. "Blind Tiger—The USS *Maine* in Havana Harbor." *Journal of America's Military Past,* vol. 24, no. 4, winter 1998.

"Catastrophe at Catubig." *VFW Magazine,* vol. 87, no. 8, April 2000.

Chapman, Gregory D. "Army Life at Camp Thomas, Georgia, during the Spanish-American War." *Georgia Historical Quarterly,* 70, winter 1970.

Cherpak, Evelyn M. "Cable Cutting at Cienfuegos." *Proceedings of the United States Naval Institute,* 113, February 1987.

Chettle, John H. "When War Called, Davis Answered." *Smithsonian,* vol. 31, no. 1, April 2000.

Christy, Howard Chandler. "An Artist at El Pozo." *Scribner's Magazine,* 24, 1898.

Cosmas, Graham A. "From Order to Chaos: The War Department, the National Guard, and Military Policy, 1898." *Military Affairs,* 29, summer 1965.

———. "Securing the Fruits of Victory: The U.S. Army Occupies Cuba, 1898–1899." *Military Affairs,* vol. 38, no. 3, October 1974.

———."San Juan Hill and El Caney, 1–2 July 1898." In Charles E. Heller and William A. Stofft, eds. *America's First Battles, 1775–1965.* Lawrence: University Press of Kansas, 1986.

Crane, Stephen. "Under Fire at Guantanamo." *McClure's Magazine,* February 1899.

Daugherty, Leo J., III. "Heroism of a Rare Kind: Sergeant Major John Henry Quick, USMC." *Leatherneck, Magazine of the Marines,* vol. 81, no. 2, February 1998.

Davis, Richard Harding. "The First Bombardment." *Scribner's,* July 1898.

———. "The Rocking Chair Period of the War." *Scribner's,* July 1898.

———. "The Landing of the Army." *Scribner's,* August 1898.

———. "The Battle of San Juan." *Scribner's,* October 1898.

———. "In the Rifle Pits." *Scribner's,* December 1898.

Dawson, Joseph T., III. "William T. Sampson and Santiago: Blockade, Victory, and Controversy." In James C. Bradford, ed. *Crucible of Empire: The Spanish-American War and Its Aftermath,* pp. 47–68. Annapolis, MD: Naval Institute Press, 1993.

Diederichs, Otto von. "A Statement of Events in Manila Bay, May–October, 1898." *Journal of the Royal United Service Institution,* November 1914.

Dyhouse, Tim. "Manila, 1899—A 'Bloody Lane.' " *VFW Magazine,* vol. 86, no. 6, February 1999.

Emerson, Edwin, Jr. "Life at Camp Wikoff." *Munsey's Magazine,* October 1898.

Eyre, James K. "Russia and the American Acquisition of the Philippines." *Mississippi Valley Historical Review,* March 1942.

Feuer, A. B. "Spanish Fleet Sacrificed at Santiago." *Military History,* vol. 15, no. 2, June 1998.

———."Journal of Infantry Captain Jacob Krebs." *Military History,* vol. 15, no. 6, February 1999.

———. "In 1899 the U.S. Army in the Philippines Was Supported by Utah Artillerymen aboard Spanish Gunboats." *Military History,* vol. 16, no. 5, December 1999.

———. "The U.S. Marines at Guantánamo Bay." *Military Heritage,* vol. 1, no. 3, December 1999.

Fiske, Lt. B. A., U.S.N. "Why We Won at Manila." *Century Magazine,* November 1898.

Fletcher, Marvin. "The Black Volunteers in the Spanish-American War." *Military Affairs,* vol. 38, no. 2, April 1974.

Freeman, Barbara M. "An Impertinent Fly: Kathleen Blake Watkins Covers the Spanish-American War." *Journalism History,* winter 1988.

Freidel, Frank B. "Dissent in the Spanish-American War and the Philippine Insurrection." In Samuel L. Morison, Frederick Merk, and Frank B. Freidel, eds. *Dissent in Three American Wars.* Cambridge: Harvard University Press, 1970.

Fritz, David L. "Before the 'Howling Wilderness': The Military Career of Jacob Hurd Smith, 1861–1902." *Military Affairs,* 39, December 1979.

Fry, Joseph A. "William McKinley and the Coming of the Spanish-American War: A Study of the Besmirching and Redemption of an Historical Image." *Diplomatic History,* 3, winter 1979.

Gable, John A. " 'Rough Rider' Roosevelt's Quest for the MOH." *VFW Magazine,* vol. 85, no. 10, June-July 1898.

Gagliasso, Dan. "Rough Riders, Moviemakers, and History: Hollywood Images of Theodore Roosevelt and the First U.S. Volunteer Cavalry." *Journal of Arizona History,* vol. 41, no. 3, autumn 2000.

Gosoroski, David M. "'Children of the Dragon's Blood,' Veterans of the Imperial Era." *VFW Magazine,* vol. 84, no. 11, August 1997.

———. "Memorial Preserves Memory of *Maine*'s Crew." *VFW Magazine,* vol. 85, no. 6, February 1998.

Greely, Adolphus Washington. "The Signal Corps in War Time." *Century Magazine,* 1903.

Greene, Maj. Gen. Francis V., U.S.V. "The Capture of Manila." *Century Magazine,* April 1899.

Greguras, Fred. "Spanish-American War Camps, 1898–99 Period." *Journal of America's Military Past,* vol. 26, no. 3, winter 2000.

Grenville, John A. S. "American Naval Preparations for War with Spain, 1896–1898." *Journal of American Studies,* April 1968.

Gulliver, Louis J. "Sampson and Shafter at Santiago." *Proceedings of the United States Naval Institute,* 65, June 1939.

Hanks, Carlos C. "Marines at Playa del Este." *Proceedings of the United States Naval Institute,* 58, July 1932.

———. "When a Cruiser Captured an Island." *Proceedings of the United States Naval Institute,* 58, July 1932.

Harrington, Fred H. "The Anti-Imperialist Movement in the United States, 1898–1900." *Mississippi Valley Historical Review,* 22, September 1935.

Harrington, Peter. "You Supply the Pictures, I'll Supply the War." *MHQ: Quarterly Journal of Military History,* vol. 10, no. 4, summer 1998.

Hatch, Frederick. "Edwin O. Loucks Described the Last Days of the Spanish-American War in Cuba." *Military History,* vol. 15, no. 3, August 1998.

Haydock, Michael D. "Sinking of USS *Maine* Brings War with Spain." *VFW Magazine,* vol. 85, no. 6, February 1998.

———. "Headlong over the Heights: Capturing San Juan Hill." *VFW Magazine,* vol. 85, no. 10, June-July 1998.

———. "Santiago de Cuba: Battle of Santiago Bay." *VFW Magazine,* vol. 85, no. 10, June-July 1998.

———. "Mock Battle for Manila." *VFW Magazine,* vol. 85, no. 11, August 1998.

———. "Picnic on Puerto Rico." *VFW Magazine,* vol. 85, no. 11, August 1998.

Hazeltine, Mayo. "What If Spain Should Declare War?" *Review of Reviews,* 13, 1896.

Heinl, Robert D., Jr. "How We Got Guantanamo." *American Heritage,* vol. 13, no. 2, February 1962.

Hemingway, Al. "Death to the Dons: Guantanamo Bay, 1898." *VFW Magazine,* vol. 10, no. 4, June-July 1998.

Hernández, Miguel J. "San Juan under Siege." *Military History,* vol. 15, no. 1, April 1998.

Hitt, Parker. "Amphibious Infantry: A Fleet on Lake Lanao." *Proceedings of the United States Naval Institute,* 64, 1938.

Hobson, Richmond Pearson. "The Sinking of the *Merrimac.*" *Century Magazine.* Four parts: Part 1, "The Scheme and Preparations," December 1898; Part 2, "The Run In," January 1899; Part 3, "The Imprisonment in Morro Castle," February 1899; Part 4, "Prison Life in Santiago and Observations of the Siege," March 1899.

Holbo, Paul S. "William McKinley and the Turpie-Foraker Amendment." *American Historical Review,* 72, July 1967.

———. "The Convergence of Moods and the Cuban Bond 'Conspiracy' of 1898." *Journal of American History,* 55, June 1968.

Keene, R. R. "Remember the *Maine.* To Hell with Spain!" *Leatherneck, Magazine of the Marines,* vol. 81, no. 4, April 1998, pp. 22–27.

———. "That Splendid Little War in the Pacific." *Leatherneck, Magazine of the Marines,* vol. 81, no. 4, July 1998, pp. 38–42.

———. "The Battle for Cuzco Well." *Leatherneck, Magazine of the Marines,* vol. 81, no. 9, September 1998.

———. "The Lure of Asiatic Service." *Leatherneck, Magazine of the Marines,* vol. 82, no. 10, October 1999.

Keller, Peter. "The Rescue of Admiral Cervera." *Harper's Magazine,* 98, April 1899.

Kelly, Edmond. "An American in Madrid during the War." *Century Magazine,* January 1899.

Kennon, John W. "USS *Vesuvius.*" *Proceedings of the United States Naval Institute,* 80, February 1954.

Keuchel, Edward F. "Chemicals and Meat: The Embalmed Beef Scandal of the Spanish-American War." *Bulletin of the History of Medicine,* 48, 1974.

Killblane, Richard E. "Assault on San Juan Hill." *Military History,* vol. 15, no. 2, June 1998.

Kolb, Richard K. " 'Bamboo Vets' Fought in Philippines." *VFW Magazine,* vol. 86, no. 6, February 1999.

———. "Jayhawker Regiment Shows Its Mettle in the Philippines." *VFW Magazine,* vol. 86, no. 8, April 1999.

———. "Young's Scouts Show Valor in Battle." *VFW Magazine,* vol. 86, no. 9, May 1999.

———. "Battle across the Zapote River." *VFW Magazine,* vol. 86, no. 10, June-July 1999.

———. "Marching through Hell in China." *VFW Magazine,* vol. 87, no. 9, May 2000.

Langellier, J. Phillip. "From Kersey Blue to Khaki Drill: The Field Uniform of the U.S. Army, 1898–1901." *Military Collector and Historian* (Journal of the Company of Military Historians), vol. 34, no. 4, winter 1982.

Langley, Harold D. "Winfield S. Schley and Santiago." In James C. Bradford, ed. *Crucible of Empire: The Spanish-American War and Its Aftermath,* pp. 69–101. Annapolis, MD: Naval Institute Press, 1993.

Lee, Arthur H. "The Regulars at El Caney." *Scribner's Magazine,* 24, 1898.

Legrand, John. "The Landing at Daiquiri." *Proceedings of the United States Naval Institute,* 26, March 1900.

Levstik, Frank R. "William T. Anderson: Army Officer, Doctor, Minister, and Writer." *Negro History Bulletin,* vol. 40, no. 1, 1977.

Lewis, Henry Harrison. "The Santiago Battlefield as It Is Today." *Munsey's Magazine,* March 1899.

Lindsay, David. "Postfix: War Fair." *Invention and Technology,* vol. 14, no. 2, fall 1998.

Linn, Brian M. "Guerrilla Fighter: Frederick Funston in the Philippines, 1900–1901." *Kansas History,* no. 10, 1987.

Livingston, Rebecca. "Genealogy Notes: Sailors, Soldiers, and Marines of the Spanish-American War—The Legacy of the U.S. *Maine.*" *Prologue,* vol. 30, no. 1, spring 1998.

"Loose, Disunited and Unrelated," Topics of the Time Editorial. *Century Magazine,* December 1898.

"Loss of USS *Maine* Continues in Debate." *Headquarters Heliogram, CAMP (Council on America's Military Past),* no. 268, May-June 1998.

Lukacs, John. "The Meaning of '98." *American Heritage,* May-June 1998.

Lynn, Robert A. "Call for Volunteers." *VFW Magazine,* vol. 85, no. 8, April 1998.

Mahon, John K. "The View from Washington through the Eyes of Adjutant General Henry C. Corbin." *Journal of America's Military Past,* vol. 26, no. 3, winter 2000.

Marshall, Edward. "A Wounded Correspondent's Recollections of Guasimas." *Scribner's Magazine,* 24, 1898.

"Massacre at Mabitac." *VFW Magazine,* vol. 88, no. 1, September 2000.

Maxim, Hiram Stevens. "New Engines of Warfare." *Munsey's Magazine,* October 1898.

May, Glenn A. "Why the United States Won the Philippine-American War, 1899–1902." *Pacific Historical Review,* 52, 1982.

McAndrews, Eugene V. "Theodore Roosevelt and the Medal of Honor." *Military Review,* vol. 47, no. 9, 1967.

McCawley, Charles L. "The Guantanamo Campaign of 1898." *Marine Corps Gazette,* September 1916.

McClernand, E. J. "The Santiago Campaign." *U.S. Infantry Journal,* vol. 21, no. 3, September 1922.

McCutcheon, John T. "The Surrender of Manila (August 13, 1898) as Seen from Admiral Dewey's Flagship." *Century Magazine,* April 1899.

Mead, Ernest E. "The Rescue of the *Winslow." Harper's Monthly,* 1898.

Melville, Rear Adm. George W., U.S.N. "The Destruction of the Battleship 'Maine.' " *North American Review,* vol. 193, no. 6, June 1911.

Meriwether, Walter Scott. "Remembering the *Maine." Proceedings of the United States Naval Institute,* 74, May 1948.

Miles, Nelson Appleton. "The War with Spain," parts 1, 2, and 3. *North American Review,* May, June, and July 1899

Nadel, Barbara A. "El Morro: Caribbean Citadel." *Journal of America's Military Past,* vol. 22, no. 74, spring 1996.

Neale, Robert G. "British-American Relations during the Spanish-American War: Some Problems." *Historical Studies: Australia and New Zealand,* 6, 1953.

Offley, C. N. "The *Oregon*'s Long Voyage." *The Great Republic,* 4, 1901.

Offner, John L. "President McKinley's Final Attempt to Avoid War with Spain." *Ohio History,* 94, summer-autumn 1985.

Palmer, Frederick. "White Man and Brown Man in the Philippines." *Scribner's Magazine,* 27, January-June 1900.

Parkinson, Russell J. "United States Signal Corps Balloons, 1871–1902." *Military Affairs,* winter 1960–1961.

Peake, Louis A. "Andrew Summers Rowan and the Message from Garcia." *West Virginia History,* 44, spring 1983.

Peuser, Richard W. "Documenting United States Naval Activities during the Spanish-American War." *Prologue,* vol. 30, no. 1, spring 1998.

"Philippines War: A Combat Chronology, 1899–1902." Editorial. *VFW Magazine,* vol. 86, no. 6, February 1999.

Plante, Trevor K. "New Glory to Its Already Gallant Record: The First Marine Battalion in the Spanish-American War." *Prologue,* vol. 30, no. 1, spring 1998.

Portusach, F. "History of the Capture of Guam by the United States Man-of-War *Charleston* and Its Transports." *Proceedings of the United States Naval Institute*, 43, April 1917, pp. 707–718.

Quinn, D. Michael. "The Mormon Church and the Spanish-American War: An End to Selective Pacifism." *Pacific Historical Review*, vol. 43, no. 3, August 1974.

Rickenbach, Richard V. "Filibustering with the *Dauntless*." *Florida Historical Quarterly*, 28, April 1950.

Ridgely, Randolph. "The Coast Guard Cutter *McCulloch* at Manila." *Proceedings of the United States Naval Institute*, no. 55, 1929.

Rippy, J. Fred. "The European Powers and the Spanish-American War." *James Sprunt Historical Studies*, vol. 19, no. 2, 1927.

Riske, Milt. "A History of Hospital Ships." *Annual Reports of the Surgeon-General, USN, 1866–1929*. U.S. Navy Department, 1904.

Rowan, Andrew S. "My Ride across Cuba." *McClure's Magazine*, August 1898.

Sampson, Rear Adm. William T. "The Atlantic Fleet in the Spanish War." *Century Magazine*, April 1899.

Sanford, Wayne L. "Battle of Bud Daju: 6 March 1906." *Indiana Military History Journal*, no. 7, May 1982.

Saum, Lewis O. "The Western Volunteer and the 'New Empire.' " *Pacific Northwest Quarterly*, 57, 1966.

Schley, Rear Adm. Winfield Scott. "Admiral Schley's Own Story." *Cosmopolitan Magazine*, December 1911.

Seaman, Louis Livingston. "The United States Army Ration in the Tropics." Open letter. *Century Magazine*, February 1899.

Shaffer, Ralph E. "The Race of the *Oregon*." *Oregon Historical Quarterly*, 76, September 1975.

Shafter, Maj. Gen. William R., U.S.V. "The Land Fight at Santiago." *Great Republic*, vol. 4.

———. "The Capture of Santiago de Cuba." *Century Magazine*, February 1899.

Shippee, Lester B. "Germany and the Spanish-American War." *American Historical Review*, 30, July 1925.

Shulimson, Jack. "Marines in the Spanish-American War." In James C. Bradford, ed. *Crucible of Empire: The Spanish-American War and Its Aftermath*, pp. 127–157. Annapolis, MD: Naval Institute Press, 1993.

Sigsbee, Capt. Charles Dwight, U.S.N. "Personal Narrative of the *Maine*." *Century Magazine*. Three parts: Part 1, "Our Reception at Manila,"

November 1898; Part 2, "The Explosion," December 1898; Part 3, "The Wrecking and the Inquiry," January 1899.

———. "My Story of the *Maine*." Two parts. *Cosmopolitan Magazine*, July and August 1912.

Smith, Ephraim K. "William McKinley's Enduring Legacy." In James C. Bradford, ed. *Crucible of Empire: The Spanish-American War and Its Aftermath*, pp. 205–250. Annapolis, MD: Naval Institute Press, 1993.

Smythe, Donald. "Pershing and the Mount Bagsak Campaign of 1913." *Philippine Studies*, no. 12, 1964.

———. "John J. Pershing in the Spanish-American War." *Military Affairs*, no. 30, spring 1966.

"Spanish-American War: A Combat Chronology." *VFW Magazine*, vol. 86, no. 1, September 1998.

Spears, John R. "Torpedo-Boats in the War with Spain." *The Great Republic*, vol. 4.

Spector, Ronald H. "Who Planned the Attack on Manila Bay?" *Mid-America*, 53, April 1971.

———. "The Battle of Santiago." *American History Illustrated*, vol. 9, no. 4, July 1974.

Stokessbury, James L. "Manila Bay—Battle or Execution." *American History Illustrated*, vol. 14, no. 5, August 1979.

Taylor, John M. "Matchless Race of the *Oregon*." *MHQ: Quarterly Journal of Military History*, spring 2001.

Titherington, Richard H. "Our War with Spain." Five parts. *Munsey's Magazine*, October 1898–March 1899.

Trask, David. "American Intelligence during the Spanish-American War." In James C. Bradford, ed. *Crucible of Empire: The Spanish-American War and Its Aftermath*, pp. 23–46. Annapolis, MD: Naval Institute Press, 1993.

Turbak, Gary. "Agony at Camp Wikoff." *VFW Magazine*, vol. 86, no. 1, September 1998.

Van Pelt, Charles B. "Fiasco at San Juan." *American History Illustrated*, vol. 3, no. 11, 1968.

"VFW and the Philippines War: A 100-Year Connection." Editorial. *VFW Magazine*, vol. 86, no. 6, February 1999.

Walker, L. W. "Guam's Seizure by the United States in 1898." *Pacific Historical Review*, 14, March 1945.

Weber, Heidi Amelia-Anne. "The Medical Department in the Spanish-American War." *Journal of America's Military Past*, vol. 26, no. 3, winter 2000.

Welch, Richard E., Jr. "American Atrocities in the Philippines: The Indictment and the Response." *Pacific Historical Review,* vol. 43, no. 2, May 1974.

Wexler, Alice. "Pain and Prejudice in the Santiago Campaign of 1898." *Journal of Inter-American Studies and World Affairs,* 18, February 1976.

Winslow, Cameron McRae. "Cable-cutting at Cienfuegos." *Century Magazine,* March 1899.

Yockelson, Mitchell. " 'I Am Entitled to the Medal of Honor and I Want It': Theodore Roosevelt and His Quest for Glory." *Prologue,* vol. 30, no. 1, spring 1998.

Dissertations, Manuscripts, and Government Documents

Adjutant General's Office, Illinois. *Papers of the Provisional Irish-American Regiment.* Springfield, IL: n.p., 1898–1899.

Adjutant General's Office, U.S. Army. *Correspondence Relating to the War with Spain: Including the Insurrection in the Philippine Islands and the China Relief Expedition, April 15, 1898 to July 30, 1902.* Washington, DC: Center for Military History, U.S. Army, 1993.

Coats, George Yarrington. "The Philippine Constabulary: 1901–1917." Ph.D. diss., Ohio State University, 1968.

Documents Pertaining to the Philippine Revolution. Edward E. Ayer Manuscript Collection. Chicago: Newberry Library, n.d.

Hunt, Geoffrey Roland. "The First Colorado Regiment in the Philippine Wars." Ph.D. diss., University of Colorado, 1997.

Johnson, John Reuben. "The First Nebraska Regiment in the Spanish-American and Philippine Wars." Master's thesis, University of Nebraska, 1927.

Schellings, William John. "The Role of Florida in the Spanish-American War." Ph.D. diss., University of Florida, 1958. Ann Arbor, MI: University Microfilms, 1972.

U.S. House Committee on War Claims. *Volunteer Officers and Soldiers in the Volunteer Service of the U.S. Who Served in the Philippine Islands beyond the Period of Their Enlistment, etc.: Hearings before the Committee on War Claims, Subcommittee no. 1 (War Claims),* 71st Cong., 3rd sess., 10 January 1931.

U.S. Senate Committee on the Philippines. *Affairs in the Philippine Islands: Hearings before the Committee on the Philippines.* 3 vols. Washington, DC: U.S. Government Printing Office, 1902.

Foreign-Language Titles

Amador y Carrandi, Ernesto. *La Guerra Hispano-Americana ante el derecho internacional* (The Spanish-American War before international law). Madrid: Imprenta de la Viuda de M. Minuesa de los Ríos, 1900.

Andres-Gallego, José. "Los grupos politicos del 98" (The political groups of '98). *Hispania*, 38, no. 138, January-April 1978.

Arderius, Francisco. *La escuadra española en Santiago de Cuba: Diario de un testigo por Francisco Arderius, ayudante de órdenes de D. Fernando Villaamil á bordo del Furor, con un prólogo de Jacinto Octavio Picón* (The Spanish squadron in Santiago de Cuba: The diary of a witness for Francisco Arderius, adjutant to D. Fernando Villaamil on board El Furor; with a prologue by Jacinto Octavio Picón). Barcelona: Casa Editorial Maucci, 1903.

Auñón y Villalón, Ramón. *Discursos pronunciados en el parlamento por el ministro de marina D. Ramón Auñón y Villalón durante la guerra con los Estados Unidos* (Speeches delivered in parliament by the secretary of the navy, D. Ramón Auñón y Villalón, during the war against the United States). Madrid: n.p., 1912.

Barón Fernandez, José. *La Guerra Hispano-Norteamericana de 1898* (The Spanish–North American War of 1898). N.p.: Ediciós do Castro, 1993.

Bécker, Jerónimo. *Historia de las relaciones exteriores de España durante el siglo XIX* (The history of Spanish foreign relations during the nineteenth century). Vol. 3. Madrid: J. Rates, 1926.

Bello, Antonio Martinez. *Ideas, economicas y sociales de Martí* (The economic and social ideas of Martí). Havana: n.p., 1940.

Bruti Liberati, Luigi. *La Santa Sede e le origini dell'impero americano: La guerra del 1898* (The Holy See and the rise of the American empire: The war of 1898). Milan: UNICOPLI, 1984.

Burguete, Ricardo. *La guerra! Filipinas (memorias de un herido) por Ricardo Burgette, del ejército español* (War! The Philippines [memoirs of a wounded soldier] by Ricardo Burgette, of the Spanish Army). Barcelona: Maucci, 1902.

Cervera y Topete, Pascual. *Guerra Hispano-Americana: Colección de documentos referents á la escuadra de operaciones de las Antillas* (The Spanish-American War: Collected documents pertaining to squadron operations in the Antilles). Madrid: El Ferrol, 1898.

Concas y Palau, Victor M. *Causa instruida por la destrucctió de la escuadra del Filipinas y entrega del arsenal de Cavite: Escrito y rectificación oral ante el consejo en defensa del comandante general apostadero y escuadra de Filipinas, Don Patricio Montojo y Pasarón* (A preliminary hearing in the case of the destruction of the squadron on board the Philippines and the surrender of the arsenal at Cavite: Brief and oral rectification presented before the council in defense of the station and squadron commanding general of the Philippines, Don Patricio Montojo y Pasarón). Madrid: Sucesores de Rivadeneyra, 1899.

Conde de Torre, Vélez. *Defensa del Excmo. Señor Don Enrique Sostoa y Ordóñez, ex-comandante general del arsenal de Cavite, ante el Consejo Superior de Guerra y Marina* (Defense proceedings at the court-martial of his Excellency Don Enrique Sostoa y Ordóñez, ex-commanding general of the arsenal at Cavite). Madrid: n.p., 1899.

Delgado, Sinesio. *España al terminar el siglo XIX: Apuntes de viaje por Sinesio Delgado, dibujos de Ramón Cilla, fotografías instantáneas, 1897–1900* (Spain at the end of the nineteenth century: Travel notes by Sinesio Delgado, drawings by Ramón Cilla, snapshots, 1897–1900). Madrid: Hijos de M. G. Hernández, 1900.

Gómez Núñez, Severo. *La Guerra Hispano-Americana* (The Spanish-American War). Madrid: Imprenta del Cuerpo de Artillería, 1899–1902.

González, Bernard J. M. *Proceso histórico del tratado de Paris de 10 diciembre de 1898, con algunas ideas de derecho internacional público* (The historic process of the Treaty of Paris on December 10, 1898, with some thoughts on public international law). Valencia: n.p., 1903.

Ibañez Marín, José. *Capitulación de Santiago de Cuba: Escrito leído ante el Consejo Supremo de Guerra y Marina en defensa del comandante military que fue del Cristo, D. Clemente Calva Peiro, y algunos appendices y notas* (The surrender of Santiago de Cuba: A brief read during the defense proceedings at the court-martial of the military commander of El Cristo, D. Clemente Calva Peiro; with appendixes and notes). Madrid: Est. Tipografía El Trabajo, 1899.

Inclán, Julián Suárez. *Defensa del General Toral ante el Consejo Supremo de Guerra y Marina reunido y Constituido en Sala de Justicia.* Madrid: n.p., 1899.

Jimenez-Grullón, Juan Isidro. *La filosofía de Jose Martí* (The philosophy of Jose Martí). N.p.: Universidad Central de Las Villas, 1960.

Kalaw, Tedoro M. *Gregorio H. del Pilar: El heroe de Tirad* (Gregorio H. del Pilar: The hero of Tirad). Manila: Bureau of Printing, 1930.

Mañach, Jorge. *El pensamiento politico y social de Martí* (The political and social thinking of Martí). Havana: n.p., 1941.

Martín Cerezo, Saturnino. *El sitio de Baler (notas y recuerdos).* Guadalajara: n.p., 1904. Translated by F. L. Dodds as *Under the Red and Gold: Being Notes and Recollections of the Siege of Baler.* Kansas City, MO: Franklin Hudson Publishing, 1909.

Misrecuerdos, 1880–1901 (Recollections, 1880–1901). Madrid: Compania Ibero-Americana de Publicaciones, 1930.

Montero Ríos, Don Eugenio. *El Tratado de Paris* (The Treaty of Paris). Madrid: Valesco, 1947.

Montojo, Patricio. "El desastre de Cavite, sus causas y sus efectos" (The cause and effect of the disaster at Cavite). *La España Moderna,* 1909.

Müller y Tejeiro, José. *Combates y capitulacion de Santiago de Cuba* (Battles and capitulation of Santiago de Cuba). War Notes no. 1. Washington, DC: Office of Naval Intelligence, 1899.

Pabón y Suárez de Urbina, Jesús. *El 98, acontecimiento internacional* (The international event of 1898). Madrid: Ministerio de Asuntos Exteriores, 1952.

Partido Revolucionario Cubano. *Correspondencia diplomática de la delegación cubana en Nueva York durante la Guerra de Independencia de 1895 á 1898* (The diplomatic correspondence of the Cuban delegation in New York during the War of Independence from 1895 to 1898). 5 vols. Havana: Los Talleres del Archivo Nacional, 1943–1946.

Reyna, Emilio Rizal. *Espiritu de libertad* (The spirit of liberty). Havana: n.p., 1958.

Rivero Méndez, Ángel. *Cronica de la Guerra Hispano Americana en Puerto Rico* (A chronicle of the Spanish-American War in Puerto Rico). New York: Plus Ultra, 1973.

Robles Muñoz, Cristóbal. *1898 diplomacia y opinión, Cristóbal Robles Muñoz* (Diplomacy and opinion in 1898, Cristóbal Robles Muñoz). Madrid: Consejo Superior de Investigaciones Científicas, 1991.

———. "La lucha de los independentistas cubanos y las relaciones de España con Estados Unidos" (The struggle of Cuban independence fighters and the relations between Spain and the United States). *Hispania,* vol. 50, no. 174, January-April 1992.

Rodríguez González, Augustín Ramón. "Operaciones menores en Cuba, 1898" (Minor operations in Cuba, 1898). *Revista de Historia Naval,* vol. 3, no. 9, 1985.

Roig de Leuchsenring, Emilio. *La Guerra Hispano-Cubanoamericana fue ganada por el lugarteniente general del ejercito libertador, Calixto Garcia Iñíguez* (The Spanish-Cuban-American War was won by the lieutenant general of the liberating army, Calixto Garcia Iñiguez). Havana: n.p., 1955.

Salinas y Angulo, Ignacio. *Defensa del General Jáudenes* (The defense of General Jáudenes). Madrid: n.p., 1899.

Weyler y Nicolau, Valeriano. *Mi mando en Cuba: Historia militar y política de la última guerra separtista.* 5 vols. Madrid: Imprenta de Felipe González Rojas, 1910–1911.

Topical (Chronological) Title List of Spanish-American War Motion Pictures

The motion pictures listed here are in the American Memory Collection at the Library of Congress. Further details concerning the collection may be found at the library's web site: www.loc.gov.

Films of the Beginning of the War

Burial of the "Maine" Victims

War Correspondents

N.Y. Journal Dispatch Yacht "Buccaneer"

Wreck of the Battleship "Maine"

Morro Castle, Havana Harbor

U.S. Battleship "Indiana"

Secretary Long and Captain Sigsbee

"Vizcaya" under Full Headway

Films of Military Preparations
10th U.S. Infantry, 2nd Battalion Leaving Cars

U.S. Cavalry Supplies Unloading at Tampa, Florida

Colored Troops Disembarking

9th Infantry Boys' Morning Wash

Military Camp at Tampa, Taken from Train

Transport "Whitney" Leaving Dock

Cuban Refugees Waiting for Rations

Troop Ships for the Philippines

Blanket-Tossing a New Recruit

Soldiers Washing Dishes

Trained Cavalry Horses

Roosevelt's Rough Riders Embarking for Santiago

Cuban Volunteers Embarking

Roosevelt's Rough Riders

Actualities of the War in Cuba
U.S. Troops Landing at Daiquirí, Cuba

Packing Ammunition on Mules, Cuba

Major General Shafter

Pack Mules with Ammunition on the Santiago Trail, Cuba

Troops Making Military Road in Front of Santiago

Wounded Soldiers Embarking in Row Boats

Wreck of the "Vizcaya"

Reenactments of Events in Cuba
Shooting Captured Insurgents

Cuban Ambush

Raising Old Glory over Morro Castle

U.S. Infantry Supported by Rough Riders at El Caney

Skirmish of Rough Riders

Admiral Sampson Homecoming Parade
The Fleet Steaming up North River

Reviewing the "Texas" at Grant's Tomb

U.S. Battleship "Oregon"

Observation Train Following Parade

Close View of the "Brooklyn" Naval Parade

Other Homecomings
Parade of Marines, U.S. Cruiser, "Brooklyn"

Astor Battery on Parade

Evacuation Day, Cuba
General Lee's Procession, Havana

Troops at Evacuation of Havana

Camp Wikoff
71st Regiment, Camp Wyckoff [Wikoff]

General Wheeler and Secretary Alger

McKinley and Party

President Roosevelt and the Rough Riders

Sampson-Schley Controversy
Sampson-Schley Controversy

Sampson and Schley Controversy—Tea Party

Actualities of Events in the Philippines
25th Infantry

Aguinaldo's Navy

An Historic Feat

Reenactments of Events in the Philippines
U.S. Troops and Red Cross in the Trenches before Caloocan

Advance of Kansas Volunteers at Caloocan

Colonel Funstan [Funston] Swimming the Baglag River

Filipinos Retreat from Trenches

Capture of Trenches at Candaba

Return of the *Raleigh*
Morning Colors on U.S. Cruiser "Raleigh"

U.S. Cruiser "Raleigh"

Dewey Homecoming

Admiral Dewey Landing at Gibraltar

Admiral Dewey Receiving the Washington and New York Committees

Admiral Dewey Taking Leave of Washington Committee on the U.S. Cruiser "Olympia"

U.S. Cruiser "Olympia" Leading Naval Parade

Governor Roosevelt and Staff

Admiral Dewey Leading Land Parade

The Dewey Arch

The Dandy Fifth

Drama

Love and War

Morgan, John T. *See* Morgan-Cameron Resolution

Moros, xxiii, 29, 32, 34–35, 52–54, 76, 185–187, 263, **268–269**, 300, 303, 410

Morro battery, Cuba, 121, 370

Morro Castle, Cuba. *See* Morro Heights

Morro Heights, Cuba, **269–270**

"Mosquito Squadron," 25, 263, 277

Motion Picture Cameras. *See* Journalism

Moxica, Ambrosio, 392

Mumps, 118. *See also* Diseases

Murray, Arthur, 392

Muslims. *See* Moros

Mussolini, Benito, 78

Nagasaki, Japan, 116

Naquib, Amil (Moro chief), 52

Nashville, xxvii, 79–80, 272, 280 (photo)

Nashville, Battle of (Civil War), 364

National Guard, 18, 20, 170. *See also* Army, U.S.

Naval blockade of Cuba, 78, 183, 237, **271–273**, 272 (photo), 278, 345, 347, 401, 415

Naval History of the War of 1812, 330

Naval Intelligence, Office of (ONI), 261, 275, 369, 396

Naval militia, 263

Naval Observatory, U.S., 345

Naval strategy, Spain, 64, 72, **273–274**

Naval strategy, U.S., 22, 64, 183, **275–277**, 395–396

Naval vessels, auxiliary, U.S., 277

Naval War Board, 126, 276, **277–278**

Naval War College, U.S., 75, 183, 216, 261, 275–276, 279, 281, 378

Navy Department, U.S., 85, 199, 281, 329

Navy, Spanish, **278–279**

Navy, U.S., 173, 183, **279–282**

Nebraska Volunteers, 235

Negros, Island of, Philippines, 303, 390

Negros Occidental, 391

Negros Oriental, 391

Netherlands Antilles, 73

New Mexico Territory, 86, 172, 335

New Orleans, 136, 357

New Orleans, Louisiana, 60, 116, 259

New Orleans Medical and Surgical Journal, 373

New York, 74, 246, 282, 346, 357–360, 380, 415

New York Herald, 23, 39, 324, 364

New York Journal, xxvi, 40, 81, 96–97, 113, 122, 163–164, 178, 313, 322, 328, 372

New York Post, 40

New York Sun, 111

New York Tribune, 39, 111

New York World, 97, 162–164, 178, 321, 327, 364, 372

influences public opinion on Cuba, 162

Newport News, Virginia, 60, 63

Nineteenth Infantry, U.S., 247, 392

Ninth Cavalry, U.S., 37, 42, 101, 349

Ninth Infantry, U.S., 27, 171, 343

Nipe Bay, Cuba, **281–282**

Nitrocellulose (guncotton). *See* Weapons

Noriel, Mariano, 57

North Atlantic Fleet, U.S. Navy, 346

North Atlantic Squadron, U.S. Navy, 75, 136, 183, 271, **282–283**, 320, 345, 357, 361, 367

North Dakota, 330

Northern Patrol Squadron, U.S. Navy, 169, 282–283

Nourmahl, 22

Novaleta, Philippines, action at, 208

Nueva Ecija Province, Philippines, 382

Nuevitas, Cuba, **283**

O'Brien, "Dynamite" Johnny, 134, 283, **285–286**

O'Donnell y Abréu, Carlos, **286–287**

O'Donnell Memorandum. *See* O'Donnell, Carlos

Office of Naval Intelligence (ONI), 261

Ohio Supreme Court, 377

Ojeda, Emilio de, 298

Olney, Richard, 91, 194, 286, **287**

Olongapo, Philippines, 243

Olympia, The, 22, 116, 151, 226, 229, 233

O'Neill, William Owen "Buckey," **287–288**

ONI. *See* Naval Intelligence, Office of

Open Door Policy, China, **288–289**

Ordnance Department, U.S. Army, 19, 198

Oregon, xxvi, 82–83, 276, 280, 282, **289–291**, 290 (photo), 291 (map), 357–360

ABOUT THE AUTHOR

Retired from the book-publishing business, Jerry Keenan now devotes his time to research and writing. In addition to numerous articles and book reviews, his published works include *Encyclopedia of the American Indian Wars, 1492–1890; Wilson's Cavalry Corps; Union Campaigns in the Western Theatre, 1864–1865;* and *The Wagon Box Fight.* He is currently completing a full-length biography of Luther S. "Yellowstone" Kelly. He makes his home in Colorado.

R 973.8903 KEE
Keenan, Jerry.
Encyclopedia of the Spanish-
 American & Philippine-

For Reference

Not to be taken from this room